2.98

JUDGMENTS

BOOKS BY LEONARD W. LEVY

JUDGMENTS

ESSAYS ON AMERICAN CONSTITUTIONAL HISTORY

BY

LEONARD W. LEVY

CHICAGO

QUADRANGLE BOOKS

1972

Library of Congress Catalog Card Number: 70-182508
International Standard Book Number: 0-8129-0243-2
DESIGNED BY THE INKWELL STUDIO

To My Mother
Rae Levy
With Love and Gratitude

ACKNOWLEDGMENTS

I am grateful for permission to reprint the following essays:

"Making the Constitution," introduction to *Essays on the Making of the Constitution*, edited by Leonard W. Levy, copyright © 1969 by Oxford University Press, Inc.

"The Constitution and the Court," introduction to *American Constitutional Law: Historical Essays*, edited by Leonard W. Levy, Harper Torchbooks, copyright © 1969 by Harper and Row, Publishers.

"Judicial Review, History, and Democracy," introduction to *Judicial Review and the Supreme Court*, edited by Leonard W. Levy, Harper Torchbooks, copyright © 1967 by Harper and Row, Publishers.

"The Fourteenth Amendment and the Bill of Rights," introduction to Charles Fairman and Stanley Morrison, *The Fourteenth Amendment and the Bill of Rights: the Incorporation Theory*, edited by Leonard W. Levy, copyright © 1970 by Da Capo Press.

"America's 'Greatest Magistrate,'" originally titled "Lemuel Shaw: America's 'Greatest Magistrate,'" from *Villanova Law Review*, 7, No. 3 (1962), 389–406, copyright © 1962 by Villanova University.

"Judicial Biography," from the *New York Times Book Review*, January 11, 1970, pp. 1, 30–32, copyright © 1970 by The New York Times Company.

"Editing the Framer," from the *Mississippi Valley Historical Review*, XLIX, No. 3 (December 1962), 504–506, and the *Journal of American History*, LI, No. 2 (September 1964), 299–301.

"Liberty of the Press from Zenger to Jefferson," introduction to *Liberty of the Press from Zenger to Jefferson*, edited by Leonard W. Levy, copyright © 1966 by the Bobbs-Merrill Company, Inc.

"Freedom in Turmoil: the Sedition Act Era," from *Major Crises in American History*, Vol. I, edited by Leonard W. Levy and Merrill D. Peterson, copyright © 1962 by Harcourt, Brace, Jovanovich, Inc.

"No Establishment of Religion: the Original Understanding," a memorandum originally prepared in 1958 for the Fund For the Republic; previously unpublished.

"School Prayers and the Founding Fathers," from *Commentary* (September 1962), copyright assigned by the publisher to the author.

"'Exotic Fruit': the Right against Compulsory Self-Incrimination in Colonial New York," from *William and Mary Quarterly* (January 1963), copyright assigned by the publisher to the main author. Co-author: Lawrence H. Leder.

"The Right Against Self-Incrimination: History and Judicial History," from *Political Science Quarterly*, 85 (March 1969), 1–29. Copyright © by the Academy of Political Science.

"Sims' Case: the Fugitive Slave Law in Boston," from the *Journal of Negro History*, xxxv, No. 1 (January 1950), copyright © by the Association for the Study of Negro Life and History, Inc.

"Jim Crow Education: Origins of the 'Separate but Equal' Doctrine," introduction to book of the same name, edited by Leonard W. Levy and Douglas L. Jones, copyright © 1971 by Da Capo Press.

L. W. L.

La Verne, California
November 1971

CONTENTS

PART I

The Supreme Law and Its Expounders

PART II

The First Amendment Freedoms

PART III

And Other Civil Rights

JUDGMENTS

PART I

The Supreme Law and

Its Expounders

MAKING
THE CONSTITUTION

THE members of the Constitutional Convention of 1787 seemingly belied their reputations as tough-minded realists on the most crucial of all issues. They behaved, rather, like innocent idealists for whom politics is the art of the impossible, because they framed a constitutional blueprint for the kind of government which history and political theory had proved to be not only unprecedented but impossible. It was to be "one grand federal republic," rhapsodized a supporter, for which "the world was too young to furnish a parallel." That indeed was precisely what made the proposed Constitution so different and frightening, for, as the same writer acknowledged, "It is generally agreed, that a great extended nation can long continue under no single form of government, except a despotism. . . ."

Men did not then take for granted that a national government for all of the states could survive and preserve liberty. Opponents of the Constitution shared Patrick Henry's conviction that a continent-wide republican form of government "contradicts all the experience of the world." A fellow Virginian, Richard Henry Lee, argued that "a free elective government cannot be extended over large territories," a proposition that Elbridge Gerry of Massachusetts, a member of the Constitutional Convention who refused to sign its handiwork, converted into "an insuperable objection to the adoption of the new system." Robert Yates of New York, who walked out of the Convention in disgust, contended that liberty would be "swallowed up," because thirteen states were too big for a republican government. James Winthrop of Massachusetts invoked the opinion of past sages to prove that the idea of a large republic was a dangerous absurdity unless "made up of a confederacy of smaller states." George Clinton of New York explained that the immensity and complexity of the United States—it had so large a population and such dissimilar climates, economies, morals, politics, and peoples—proved the "intuitive truth" that a "consolidated republican form of government" could not possibly achieve any of the great objectives stated in the preamble to the Constitution. In sum, the minority members of the Pennsylvania ratifying convention epitomized the nearly universal view among anti-Federalists when they declared, "We dissent, first, because it is the opinion of the most celebrated writers on government, and confirmed by uniform experience, that a very extensive territory cannot be governed on the principles of freedom, otherwise than by a confederation of republics."

Although these proved to be the views of a minority, the dangers to which they referred were real enough, increasing the natural difficulties attending the American experiment with a national union. The federal system was a novelty; the centralization of powers in the national government was awesome; and the lack of a national bill of rights was intimidating. No other republic had, in fact, been so vast, and no nation had ever begun its political existence without first achieving a cultural nationalism. The extraordinary diversity of the United States was commonly regarded as a handicap; it was composed of too many governments, local traditions, religions, races, national stocks, and economic interests to be a good bet for survival. In the face of so many centrifugal forces, there was no king, no national church, no army, and few centripetal loyalties to provide unity. Unique political forms only seemed to compound the problem and make even more "impracticable" and "visionary," in Gerry's words, the national enterprise designed by the framers of the Constitution.

If, seemingly, their politics was the art of the impossible, the most influential artist among them was James Madison of Virginia. He argued persuasively that opponents of the Constitution had confused a republic with a direct democracy. The latter alone was limited by geographic distance and population so that the citizens might meet together and exercise the government in person; but in a republic the citizens governed through elected representatives, and if they could meet as needed in some central place, size and numbers did not matter. As for America's great diversity, it was the very safeguard of liberty, an insurance that no one class, or religion, or section, or interest, or faction could become too powerful, jeopardizing the liberty of others. Diversity constituted a natural system of checks and balances, making for an equilibrium of powers that insured liberty. Moreover, Madison explained, the Constitution contained an elaborate scheme of checks and balances contributing to the same end, and chief among these was the distribution of powers between the national government and the states. Had the Constitution concentrated all government authority in the national government, the worst fears of its misinterpreters who spoke of "consolidation" would be justified. But the government's jurisdiction extended only to specific, enumerated objects; its powers were expressly delegated, leaving all others to the states.

Madison's argument was calculated, of course, to allay the fears and misapprehensions of doubters in and out of the Convention. Within the Convention, differences among the delegates were sharp, and many compromises were required to obtain agreement. Yet the traditional view of the work of the Convention as a bundle of compromises great and small obscures the more significant fact that, on the fundamental matters of transcendent importance, there were no compromises because none were needed; that is, the Constitution, whether construed as an economic or a political document, reflected a consensus whose importance far exceeded the areas of compromise. The breathtaking speed with which the framers moved revealed that consensus.

The Convention, which formally organized itself on Friday, May 25, 1787, lasted almost four months, yet reached its most crucial decisions almost at the outset. The first order of business on the following Tuesday was the nationalistic Virginia Plan (May 29), and the first vote of the Convention, acting as a Committee of the Whole, was the adoption of a resolution "that a *national* Government ought to be established consisting of a *supreme* Legislative, Executive and Judiciary" (May 30). Thus the Convention immediately agreed on abandoning, rather than amending, the Articles of Confederation; on writing a new Constitution; on creating a national government that would be supreme; and on having it consist of three branches.

The radical character of this early decision may be best understood by comparing it with the Articles of Confederation. The Articles had established what in the usage of the time was called a "federal" government, meaning a league or confederacy of autonomous or nearly sovereign states whose central government was their subordinate agent and could act only through them and with their consent. Consequently, although the Congress of the Confederation was crippled by lacking the crucial powers of taxation and commerce, the Articles failed mainly because there was no way to force the states to fulfill their obligations or to obey the exercise of such powers as Congress did possess. "The great and radical vice in the construction of the existing Confederation," said Alexander Hamilton, "is the principle of legislation for states or governments, in their corporate capacities, and as contradistinguished from the individuals of which they consist." The Convention remedied that vital defect in the Articles, as George Mason was the first to point out (May 30), by abandoning the impossibility of coercing delinquent states and by agreeing on a government that "could directly operate on individuals." Thus the framers solved the critical problem

7

of sanctions by establishing a national government that was independent of the states. Madison, reporting to Jefferson, who was in Paris, said,

It was generally agreed that the objects of the Union could not be secured by any system founded on the principle of a confederation of Sovereign States. A *voluntary* observance of the federal law by all the members [the states] could never be hoped for. A *compulsive* one could evidently never be reduced to practice, and if it could, involved . . . the necessity of a military force both obnoxious and dangerous, and, in general, a scene resembling much more a civil war than the administration of a regular Government. Hence was embraced the alternative of a Government which instead of operating on the States should operate without their intervention on the individuals composing them. . . .

Thus the framers, including even men like Mason who would eventually oppose the Constitution on other grounds, quickly solved the critical problem of sanctions by establishing a government whose legislation directly bound all citizens of the nation and whose independent executive and judicial branches—both of which were nonexistent under the Articles—could enforce national law.

On the next day, May 31, the Committee of the Whole made several other crucial decisions, each with little or no debate and with general consensus. One, though largely a matter of structure, reflected the nationalist bias of the Convention; it was the decision to establish a bicameral system whose larger house was to be elected by the people rather than in a manner directed by the state legislatures, as under the Articles of Confederation. As Mason, no less, explained, "Under the existing Confederacy, Congress represents the States not the people of the States; their acts operate on the States, not on the individuals. The case will be changed in the new plan of Government. The people will be represented; they ought therefore to choose the Representatives."

Another decision of May 31 was to vest in the Congress, in addition to those powers already possessed, the sweeping and undefined power, recommended by the Virginia Plan, "to legislate in all cases to which the separate States are incompetent; or in which the harmony of the U.S. may be interrupted by the exercise of individual [state] legislation; to negative all laws passed by the several States contravening in the opinion of the National Legislature the articles of Union, or any treaties subsisting under the authority of the Union." Not a single state voted "nay" to the various parts of this exceptionally nationalist proposition. Nor did any state oppose the decision of the next day to create a national executive with similarly broad, undefined powers.

After deliberating for two weeks, the Committee of the Whole presented the Convention with its recommendations, essentially the adoption of the Virginia Plan. We today, being so familiar with our national government, can scarcely appreciate how radically divergent it seemed from the scheme of the Confederation. Not surprisingly, several of the delegates had second thoughts about the hasty decisions that had been made. Gerry soberingly reiterated "that it was necessary to consider what the people would approve." Scrapping the Articles contrary to instructions and failing to provide for state equality in the system of representation provoked a reconsideration along lines described by William Paterson of New Jersey as "federal" in contradistinction to "national." Yet the powers of the national government were less the cause of dissension than was a simple sense of injured state pride. That is, some delegates were alarmed not so much because of an excessive centralization of powers in the national government at the expense of the states, but, rather, at the excessive advantages given to the largest states at the expense of the others. Three states—Virginia, Massachusetts, and Pennsylvania—had 45 per cent of the white population in the country. Under the proposed scheme of proportional representation, the large states, it was feared, might dominate the others by controlling the national government. Yielding an equality of status under the Articles in return for a position of subordination in a novel scheme of government was a sure way of losing support among the more numerous smaller states.

On June 15, therefore, Paterson of New Jersey submitted for the Convention's consideration a substitute plan. It can be described as a states' rights plan only by comparison with the Virginia Plan rather than with the Articles of Confederation. Paterson's Plan is more rightly understood as a small states' plan rather than a states' rights one, for it too had a strong nationalist orientation. Contemplating a revision, rather than a scrapping, of the Articles, it retained the unicameral Congress with its equality of state representation, thus appeasing the small states. But the plan vested in Congress one of the two critical powers previously lacking: "to pass Acts for the regulation of trade and commerce," foreign and interstate. The other, the power of taxation, appeared only in a stunted form: Congress was to be authorized to levy duties on imports and to pass stamp tax acts (the tyranny of 1765). The plan called, additionally, for retention of the requisition system of raising a revenue, but sought to strengthen it by an unworkable provision that authorized Congress "to direct the collection thereof" in noncomplying states and for that purpose to "pass acts authorizing the same." Except for its failure to grant full tax powers, the Paterson Plan proposed the same powers for the national legislature as did the finished Constitution. The Plan also contained the germ of the national supremacy clause of the Constitution, Article VI, by providing that all acts of Congress and all United States treaties "shall be the supreme law of the respective States . . . and that the Judiciary of the several States shall be bound thereby in their decisions, any thing in the respective laws of the Individual States to the contrary notwithstanding." The clause also provided that the executive could muster the military of the states to compel state obedience to the supreme law.

Despite its nationalist features, the Paterson Plan failed to transform the government of the Union in the only way that would make it effective: empowering it to operate directly on individuals. "You see the consequence of pushing things too far," said John Dickinson of Delaware to Madison. "Some of the members from the small States wish for two branches in the General Legislature and are friends to a good National Government; but we would sooner submit to a foreign power than submit to be deprived of an equality of suffrage in both branches of the Legislature, and thereby be thrown under the domination of the large states."

Only a very few dissidents, like John Lansing of New York, were irreconcilably opposed to "a good National Government." He condemned the recommendations of the Committee of the Whole by saying, "The scheme is itself totally novel. There is no parallel to it to be found." But most of the dissidents were men like Dickinson and Paterson, "friends to a good National Government" if it preserved a wider scope for small state authority and influence.

When Paterson submitted his plan on June 15, the Convention agreed that, to give it "a fair deliberation," it should be referred to the Committee of the Whole and "that in order to place the two plans in due comparison, the other should be recommitted." After a candid and searching debate on the two plans, the Committee of the Whole was ready for a vote on the critical issue, whether to reaffirm the original recommendations based on the Virginia Plan "as preferable to those of Mr. Paterson." Seven of the eleven states present that day, June 19, voted affirmatively; Maryland was divided; and only three states—New York, New Jersey, and Delaware—voted negatively. Thus, only three weeks after their deliberations had begun the framers decisively agreed, for the second time, on a strong, independent national government that would operate directly on individuals without the involvement of the states.

But the objections of the small states had not yet been satisfied. On the next day, Connecticut, which had voted against the Paterson Plan, proposed the famous compromise: proportional representation in one house, "provided each State had an equal voice in the other." On that latter point the Convention nearly broke up, so intense was the conflict and deep the division. The irreconcilables in this instance were the leaders of the large-state nationalist faction, otherwise the most constructive and influential members of the Convention: Madison and James Wilson of Pennsylvania. After several weeks of debate and deadlock, on July 16 the Convention narrowly voted for the compromise. With ten states present, five supported the compromise, four opposed (including Virginia and Pennsylvania), and one, Massachusetts, was divided, thereby saving small-state prestige and saving the Convention from utter failure. Thereafter consensus on fundamentals was restored, with Connecticut, New Jersey, and Delaware becoming fervent supporters of Madison and Wilson. A week later, for example, there was a motion that each state should be represented by two senators "and to vote per capita," that is, as individuals. Luther Martin of Maryland protested that per capita voting conflicted with the very idea of "the States being represented," yet the motion carried, with no further debate, nine to one.

On many matters of structure, mechanics, and detail there were angry disagreements, but agreement prevailed on the essentials. The office of the presidency is a good illustration. That there should be a powerful chief executive provoked no great debate, but the Convention almost broke up, for the second time, on the method of electing him. Some matters of detail occasioned practically no disagreement and revealed the nationalist consensus. Mason, of all people, made the motion that one qualification of Congressmen should be "citizenship of the United States," and no one disagreed. Under the Articles of Confederation, there was only state citizenship; that there should be a concept of national citizenship seemed natural to men framing a constitution for a nation. Even more a revelation of the nationalist consensus was the fact that three of the most crucial provisions of the Constitution—the taxing power, the necessary-and-proper clause, and the supremacy clause—were casually and unanimously accepted without debate.

Until midway during its sessions, the Convention did not take the trouble to define with care the distribution of power between the national government and the states, although the very nature of the "federal" system, as we use that term, depended on that distribution. Consensus on fundamentals once again provides the explanation. There would be no difficulty in making that distribution, and the framers had taken out insurance; at the very outset, they had endorsed the provision of the Virginia Plan vesting broad, undefined powers in a national legislature that would act on individuals. Some byplay of July 17 is illuminating. Roger Sherman of Connecticut thought that the line drawn between the powers of Congress and those left to the states was so vague that national legislation might "interfere . . . in any matters of internal police which respect the Government of such States only, and wherein the general welfare of the United States is not concerned." His motion to protect the "internal police" of the states brought no debaters to his side and was

11

summarily defeated; only Maryland supported Connecticut. Immediately after, another small-state delegate, Gunning Bedford of Delaware, shocked even Edmund Randolph of Virginia, who had presented the Virginia Plan, by a motion to extend the powers of Congress by vesting authority "to legislate in all cases for the general interests of the Union." Randolph observed, "This is a formidable idea indeed. It involves the power of violating all the laws and constitutions of the States, of intermeddling with their police." Yet the motion passed.

On July 26 the Convention adjourned till August 6 to allow a Committee on Detail to frame a "constitution conformable to the Resolutions passed by the Convention." Generously construing its charge, the committee acted as a miniature convention and introduced a number of significant changes. One was the explicit enumeration of the powers of Congress to replace the vague, omnibus provisions adopted previously by the Convention. Although enumerated, those powers were liberally expressed and formidable in their array. The committee had carried into specifics the spirit and intent of the Convention. Significantly the first enumerated power was that of taxation and the second that of regulating commerce among the states and with foreign nations: the two principal powers that had been withheld from Congress by the Articles. The transformation of the Confederation into a national government was nowhere more apparent. When the Convention voted on the provision that Congress "shall have the power to lay and collect taxes, duties, imposts and excises," the states were unanimous and only one delegate, Gerry, was opposed. When the Convention next turned to the commerce power, there was no discussion and even Gerry voted affirmatively.

Notwithstanding its enumeration of the legislative powers, all of which the Convention accepted, the Committee on Detail added an omnibus clause that has served as an ever-expanding source of national authority: "And to make all laws that shall be necessary and proper for carrying into execution the foregoing powers." The Convention agreed to that clause without a single dissenting vote by any state or delegate. The history of the great supremacy clause, Article Six, shows a similar consensus. After the Convention had defeated the Paterson Plan, in which the clause originated, Luther Martin, of all people, moved that the acts and treaties of the United States should be the supreme law of the states. There was no dissenting voice. The Committee on Detail strengthened the clause in minor respects, and, when it came before the Convention, it was still further strengthened in a major way. John Rutledge of South Carolina moved to amend the clause by making it begin with the words, "This Constitution," so that the Constitution itself, as well as laws made in pursuance of it and treaties, became the "supreme law." If the Constitution was not only "Law" but "supreme" law, no state acts contrary to it could also be law. Without debate the Convention adopted the supremacy clause as amended by Rutledge, and not a single state or delegate voted nay. Finally, Article I, Section 10, imposing restrictions on the economic powers of the states with respect to paper money, ex post facto laws, bills of credits, and contracts, also reflected a consensus in the Convention. In sum, whether the Constitution is interpreted as basically a political or an economic document, consensus, rather than compromise, was the most significant feature of the Convention, outweighing in importance the various compromises that occupied most of the time of the delegates.

But why was there such a consensus? There have been many interpretations of the framing and ratification of the Constitution, and Charles Beard managed to endorse most of them, at one point or another in his career, as well as dominate any discussion of them. In *The Supreme Court and the Constitution* (1912), he wrote, "It is not merely patriotic pride that compels one to assert that never in the history of assemblies has there been a convention of men richer in political experience and in practical knowledge, or endowed with a profounder insight into the springs of human action and the intimate essence of government." This estimate, which brings to mind Jefferson's more succinct judgment of the Constitutional Convention as "an assembly of demigods," is not necessarily inconsistent with Beard's most famous book, *An Economic Interpretation of the Constitution* (1913), but the tone is altogether different. The *Economic Interpretation* is written in the same spirit that would describe the performance of a great violin virtuoso as the scraping of horsehair on dried cats' guts. Beard explained the consensus by construing the Constitution as a conservative economic document framed by an unrepresentative minority employing undemocratic means to protect personal property interests by establishing a central government responsive to their needs and able to thwart populistic majorities in the states. He viewed the Constitution as the work of personalty interests, that is, of personal property interests as opposed to realty interests, in short, as Beard put it, "capital as opposed to land." Minority business groups—manufacturers, merchants, shippers, speculators in land values, and, above all, public securities holders—manipulated the call for the Convention in the hope of obtaining what Beard called "the adoption of a revolutionary program." They dominated the Convention in whose outcome they had a direct, immediate, personal stake. They wrote what is essentially an economic document consisting of two basic parts. The first or positive part comprised four great powers to be vested in the new national government: war, taxation, commerce, and control of western lands. Thus the government could protect business against foreign competition

13

and against internal disruption on the part of desperate debtors such as the Shaysites, and with its ample revenues could pay the claims of public creditors. The second basic part of the Constitution was negative in character, comprising the restrictions on the economic powers of the states. The same groups that wrote the Constitution also dominated the state conventions that ratified it, their opposition deriving mainly from small farmers and debtors.

Another prong of the Beard thesis was that the Constitution was an undemocratic document, indeed that it was the work of a conspiratorial, reactionary group, operating in an undemocratic society and utilizing undemocratic methods for the purpose of hamstringing democratic majorities by an elaborate system of checks and balances. There was no popular vote on the calling of the convention, and property qualifications for voting and officeholding excluded both the propertyless masses and the small farmer, debtor interests from participating in the framing and ratification of the Constitution. The scrapping of the Articles and the submission of the Constitution for ratification by nine specially elected state conventions, contrary to the requirement in the Articles for unanimous approval by the state legislatures, were, said Beard, revolutionary acts which if performed by a Napoleon would be pronounced a coup d'état. About three-fourths of the adult men failed to vote on the Constitution; it was ratified by probably not more than one-sixth of the adult men, and in five states there is doubt whether a majority of those voting actually approved of ratification despite the action of their respective conventions.

Since the *Economic Interpretation*, historians have engaged in a prolonged debate, which probably defies settlement, on questions raised by Beard either directly or indirectly. Were the framers enlightened, disinterested statesmen seeking to rescue—indeed to create—a nation then dangerously drifting toward anarchy? Were they conspiratorial representatives of a rising financial and industrial capitalism? Were they the leaders of a Thermidorian reaction to the Articles of Confederation which embodied the democratic principles of the Declaration of Independence? Was the Constitution mainly an economic or a political document? If its chief significance was political, was it the product of a clash and compromise between large and small states, or between town and tidewater against farm and frontier, or between conflicting north-south sectionalisms? Or was the political conflict between men of nationalist principles and those devoted to states' rights, or between an aristocratic elite and the localist forces of democratic majoritarianism? In short was the Constitution an undemocratic document framed and ratified by an undemocratic minority for an undemocratic society? Or were the framers practical, though masterly, politicians keenly conscious of the need for popular approval if their work was to be accepted? Did they substantially and even necessarily play the great game of politics according to the prevailing rules when radically reconstructing the American governmental system? These are among the questions to which the historians must address themselves.

THE CONSTITUTION
AND THE COURT

AS beauty exists in the eye of the beholder, so American constitutional law exists in the eye of the Supreme Court. Justice
Frankfurter, as if in disagreement, once remarked that the "ultimate
touchstone of constitutionality is the Constitution itself, not what we
have said about it." [1] The ultimate, however, is nearly as far off as
the infinite. What counts is what the Supreme Court has said about
the Constitution—in about three hundred and eighty volumes thus
far.

The Constitution itself plays a mere secondary role in American constitutional law. When, for example, the Court had to
construe the First Amendment's injunction against establishments
of religion, Justice Jackson candidly observed that it was "idle to
pretend that this task is one for which we can find in the Constitution one word to help us as judges to decide where the secular
ends and the sectarian begins in education." [2] Justices who look to
the Constitution for more than a puzzling, if majestic, phrase might
just as well turn to the comic strips for all the guidance they will
find on how to decide most of the great cases that involve national
public policy, whether the question relates to legislative apportionment, racial segregation, the regulation of utility rates, subversive
activities, the curtailment of crop production, or the seizure of steel
mills. There is not a word in the Constitution about these or most
of the subjects of great import with which the Court must deal.
That fact, paradoxically, is a great strength of the Constitution, ac-
counting in part for its longevity and vitality.

The members of the Philadelphia Convention of 1787, notwithstanding their enormous respect for the great John Locke, ignored
his example. Locke was a dreadfully inept constitution maker. On
the theory that written statements of fundamental law must be im-
mutable, like the laws of the universe, in order to be eternal, Locke

16

framed for Carolina a constitution expressly providing that "every part thereof, shall be and remain the sacred and unalterable form and rule of government for Carolina forever." As insurance, he futilely added that "all manner of comments and expositions on any part of these fundamental constitutions, or on any part of the common or statute laws of Carolina, are absolutely prohibited." [3] By contrast, the framers of the United States Constitution recognized the inevitability of change and the need for plasticity. They therefore provided for an orderly amendment procedure. They also provided for a Supreme Court whose duties—"the judicial power shall extend to all cases . . . arising under this Constitution, the Laws of the United States, and Treaties"—required it to engage in "all manner of comments and expositions."

The framers also had a genius for studied imprecision or calculated ambiguity. Their Constitution, expressed in very generalized terms, resembled Martin Chuzzlewit's grandnephew who had no more than "the first idea and sketchy notion of a face." It thereby permitted, even encouraged, nay necessitated, continuous reinterpretation and adaptation. Men trained in the common law habitually avoid minute specifications which become obsolete with a change in the particular circumstances for which they were adopted; such men tend rather to formulate principles that are expansive and comprehensive in nature. The principles themselves, not their framers' understanding and application of them, are meant to endure.

In determining "whether a provision of the Constitution applies to a new subject matter," declared Justice Stone, "it is of little significance that it is one with which the framers were not familiar. For in setting up an enduring framework of government they undertook to carry out for the indefinite future and in all the vicissitudes of the changing affairs of men, those fundamental principles which the instrument itself discloses. Hence we read its words, not as we read legislative codes which are subject to continuous revision with the changing course of events, but as the revelation of the great purposes which were intended to be achieved by the Constitution as a continuing instrument of government." [4] Thus the commerce clause applies to telestar communication, racial discrimination in motels, stolen cars, stock exchange transactions, and the wages of window washers. The Constitution, designed by an eighteenth-century rural society, serves as well today as ever, perhaps better than ever, because an antiquarian historicism that would freeze its original meanings, even if discernible, has not guided its interpretation and was not intended to. As Justice Holmes once said, "The present has a right to govern itself, so far as it can. . . . Historical continuity with the past is not a duty, only a necessity." [5]

The document itself, with all amendments, clearly delineates the structure of American national government but only roughly maps the contours of power. We know unmistakably that there is to be a President whose term of office is four years; but what is "the executive power" with which he is vested? Chief Justice Marshall happily noted that the Constitution has none of the "prolixity of a legal code"; it has, rather, the virtue of muddy brevity, a mere seven thousand words, including amendments. Scarcely 2 per cent of the verbiage possesses any significance in constitutional law. Almost without exception, these are the purposefully ambiguous words, like general welfare, due process of law, unreasonable searches, commerce among the states, liberty, equal protection, obligation of contracts, establishment of religion, necessary and proper, and direct taxes. Other words of crucial importance in constitutional law are not even in the Constitution, including clear and present danger, fair trial, war power, public purpose, separate but equal, liberty of contract, separation of church and state, interstate commerce, fair return, and police power. They are judicial glosses. In large measure we have an unwritten constitution whose history is the history of judicial review. James Beck made the point by comparing the work of the Supreme Court to that of a "continuous constitutional convention" which adapts the original charter by reinterpretation, making its duties "political in the highest sense of the word, as well as judicial." [6]

The Constitution's power of survival derives also from the fact that it incorporates and symbolizes the political values of a free people. It creates a representative, responsible government empowered to serve the general welfare at the same time that it keeps the government bitted and bridled. "In framing a government which is to be administered by men over men," noted Madison in *Federalist* #51, "the great difficulty lies in this; you must first enable the government to control the governed; and in the next place oblige it to control itself." The Constitution deals with great powers, many of them undefined, but they are decentralized, separated and distributed, checked and balanced, limited and prohibited. At the same time, most notably through the Bill of Rights and the great Reconstruction amendments, the Constitution requires that the game shall be played freely and fairly, with the judiciary as the umpire. "The great ideals of liberty and equality," wrote Justice Cardozo, "are preserved against the assaults of opportunism, the expediency of the passing hour, the erosion of small encroachments, the scorn and derision of those who have no patience with general principles, by enshrining them in constitutions, and consecrating to the task of their protection a body of defenders." [7] Charles Evans Hughes's much quoted remark, that "the Constitution is what the judges say it is," expressed only half his thought; he added, much like Cardozo, "and the judiciary is the safeguard of our liberty and of our property under the Constitution." [8] The Lord Chancellor in *Iolanthe* might have epitomized our Constitution and Supreme Court when he humorously asserted,

> The Law is the embodiment
> Of everything that's excellent.
> It has no kind of fault or flaw,
> And I, my Lords, embody the Law.

Constitutional law is the product of the entire federal judiciary, not just of the Supreme Court. Indeed, the history of constitutional law would be as illuminating as the dark side of the moon without also considering the participation of the nonjudicial branches of the government. The President makes constitutional history when, by simple executive order, he authorizes the internment of 70,000 American citizens of Japanese descent; or sends troops to Little Rock or Oxford, Mississippi; or ends racial discrimination in the armed forces, or in private employment under government contract, or in federally assisted housing projects; or establishes a loyalty-security program among government employees. The Congress makes constitutional history more obviously and with far greater frequency via the legislative process. Nevertheless, constitutional law is peculiarly the product of the Supreme Court. The President, Congress, and administrative agencies help make constitutional history; they even help make constitutional law, but only in the first instance. The sovereign people may even amend the Constitution itself, but unless they abolish judicial review, the Supreme Court still has the last word, for it construes not only the validity of the exercise of power by the other branches of government; it construes also the meaning of the Constitution. The point is implicit in Justice Holmes's quotation from Bishop Hoadly to the effect that the final authority to interpret the law, rather than its maker, is the real sovereign.[9]

As de Tocqueville observed long ago, "Scarcely any question arises in the United States which does not become, sooner or later, a subject of judicial debate. . . ." [10] Frankfurter, echoing the thought a century later, declared that most of the problems of modern society, "whether of industry, agriculture, of finance, of racial interactions or the eternal conflict between liberty and authority, become in the United States sooner or later legal problems for ultimate solution by the Supreme Court." [11] Thus trivial disputes between private litigants may be argued in terms of fundamental principles of government by judges and lawyers, and matters of the highest policy go to the courts for judgment, though the case itself may be insignificant in terms of the interest of the immediate parties. For example, on the outcome of the claim of a Mr. Norman for $15.60 against the Baltimore and Ohio Railroad depended the financial policy of the United States, involving some one hundred billion dollars and a possible 60 per cent increase in the national debt in the midst of a depression.[12] The role of the government in the economy, the relation of the individual to the state and of the states to the nation, the system of justice, and the legal standards of equality are among the subjects of our constitutional law. Its study is ennobled by an alliance with history, with statecraft, with the evolution of popular institutions of government, and with human rights.

Nearly every significant decision of the Supreme Court deals with rights or with power, whether government power or private economic power. Constitutional government is, by definition, limited government, a system of regularized restraints upon power; there is therefore an inevitable and enduring tension between the exercise of powers allegedly vested and limitations allegedly breached. In some periods in the history of constitutional law the Supreme Court tends to emphasize the affirmative aspects of power, in other periods its limitations. In each of the five periods of the Court's history, certain characteristic doctrines and precedents prevail, only to be abandoned or distinguished in a later period; as some wag once said, a distinguished case is one which is no longer distinguished. The Court also seems always to have special interest to protect. In one period it might be the Union or the state police power; in another corporations or organized labor; in still another, radicals or the criminally accused.

The first or formative period is identified with the chief justiceship of John Marshall. When John Jay, one of his predecessors who had resigned from the Court to run for state office, declined reappointment as chief justice, he said that the Court was fatally lacking in power. Marshall took the job and no one thereafter could make the same complaint. During Marshall's long tenure of office, the Court asserted the power of judicial review, precariously over Congress and firmly over the states, establishing the supremacy of the Constitution and federal law. A partisan organ of the national government, the Court's nationalistic opinions conjured up the image of screaming eagles and Old Glory on the rise. Marshall also made the Court, in Max Lerner's phrase, "the strategic link between capitalism and constitutionalism." [13] His nationalism, which was both real and enduringly constructive in *McCulloch* v. *Maryland* and *Gibbons* v. *Ogden*, was more frequently a guise for the invalidation of state statutes that trenched on private property. Doctrines of vested rights, derived from extra-constitutional sources, found lodgement mainly in the contract clause.

Under Taney's chief justiceship, which was marred by the aberrational *Dred Scott* decision, the Court deviated only slightly from the course set by Marshall. Its vigorous exercise of judicial review and extension of its jurisdiction into unprecedented fields fortified the national judicial power. Less inclined to see state legislation as an assault upon the supremacy of the union, the Taney Court refused to let unused national powers serve as a rationale for the invalidation of state acts not in operative conflict with national acts. It behaved more like an impartial arbitrator between states and nation than like a strident champion of the latter. Despite some rhetoric about community rights and public welfare, property rights vested by contract were usually treated as if sacred, and corporate business was encouraged and protected. The trend, if not the tone, of decision was rather conservative.

In the third period of the Court's history, from the close of the Civil War to the 1890's, the state police power enjoyed its greatest triumphs, despite threatening judicial language which laid the groundwork for new doctrines of constitutional limitations. The contract clause, although revealed to have weaknesses, still served as the principal justification for the invalidation of much regulatory legislation. During this time the Court struck down or emasculated most of a comprehensive Congressional program for the protection of civil rights, making corporations rather than Negroes the chief beneficiary of the Fourteenth Amendment. Judicial interpretation eroded away the historic meanings of due process of law as a protection of the rights of the criminally accused, and engrafted a new economic substance to due process, making it a device for keeping man's relation to his Gold as private as possible.

From 1895 to 1936, the period of "judicial supremacy," the Court acted, in Justice Brandeis' phrase, as a "superlegislature" and the due process clause was the most formidable weapon in the armory of judicial review. Brooks Adams tartly observed that the historic purpose of the federal judiciary seemed to be to "dislocate any comprehensive body of legislation, whose effect would be to change the social status." [14] Doctrines of constitutional law were arrogantly, artlessly, and inconsistently manipulated against an array of statutory reforms that sought to protect consumers, trade unions, farmers, unorganized workers, women, and children from the exploitation and abuses of business enterprise. The high point of the Court's attempt to control public policy was reached during seventeen months of 1935–1936 in a massive and unprecedented judicial assault against a single Administration. No less than twelve acts of Congress, parts of a systematic program to combat economic and social disaster, were held unconstitutional. Public opinion, though opposed to "packing" the Court, was outraged and the Court made a timely, strategic retreat, belatedly validating Mr. Dooley's observation that it followed the election returns.

During the present period of the Court's history, the most constructive since that of Marshall, constitutional law has been modernized. Outworn and reprehensible precedents have fallen like cold clinkers through an open grate. Economic due process and doctrines constricting government powers have been junked, as has a propensity to void legislation which the judges personally dislike. Plenitude of power, both national and state, and a concept of cooperative federalism now characterize our highest public law. The authority of the government to control the economy is virtually undisputed; from New Deal to Great Society, the welfare state has been sustained. At the same time that the Court emancipated government, it vitalized the constitutional law of human rights. Cases involving free speech, the claims of the criminally accused, and equality for racial minorities now bulk largest on the Court's docket. The supreme tribunal has at last caught up with folklore: it has become the protector of civil liberties and civil rights, sometimes anticipating rather than following the election returns.

The Court is most likely, nowadays, to follow the scholarly commentators and the law reviews. Chief Justice Hughes called the journals the "fourth estate of the law." [15] Responsible, informed critics have often led the way during this period of modern constitutional law; the justices, who are sensitive readers, are also far more conscious of constitutional history and the mistakes of their predecessors. They rarely decide a case without first canvassing the journals to determine whether the issue has been discussed by some extramural authority from whom some wisdom may be gleaned. Students of constitutional law, no less than the justices themselves, must know constitutional history. Although the Court will no longer hold unconstitutional a statute fixing maximum hours for labor or prohibiting racial discrimination in public facilities, the early cases are indispensable to any understanding of current constitutional law. Modern judicial tolerance is an outgrowth of yesterday's judicial intolerance; judicial humility is the child of judicial arrogance.

NOTES

[1] *Graves* v. *N.Y.*, 306 U.S. 466, 491 (1939).

[2] *McCollum* v. *Board of Education*, 334 U.S. 203, 237-238 (1948).

[3] Fundamental Constitutions of Carolina, 1669, Sections 80 and 120, in Francis Newton Thorpe, ed., *The Federal and State Constitutions, Colonial Charters, and Other Organic Laws* (Washington, D.C., 1909), v, 2782 and 2786.

[4] *U.S.* v. *Classic*, 313 U.S. 299, 315-316 (1941).

[5] Oliver Wendell Holmes, *Collected Legal Papers* (New York, 1920), p. 139.

[6] James M. Beck, *The Constitution of the United States* (New York, 1922), p. 221. The phrase "continuous constitutional convention" has been used independently by other writers. E.g., Henry S. Commager, "Constitutional History and the Higher Law," in Conyers Read, ed., *The Constitution Reconsidered* (New York, 1938), p. 231; and Robert H. Jackson, *The Struggle for Judicial Supremacy* (New York, 1941), pp. x–xi.

[7] Benjamin N. Cardozo, *The Nature of the Judicial Process* (New Haven, 1921), pp. 92–93.

[8] Charles Evans Hughes, *Addresses and Papers* (New York, 1908), pp. 139–140.

[9] Hoadly said, "Whoever hath an absolute authority to interpret any written or spoken laws, it is he who is truly the lawgiver, to all intents and purposes, and not the person who first wrote or spoke them." Quoted in James B. Thayer, "The Origin and Scope of the American Doctrine of Constitutional Law," *Harvard Law Review*, VII (1893), 152.

[10] Alexis de Tocqueville, *Democracy in America*, Henry S. Commager, ed., trans. Henry Reeve (New York, 1947), p. 177.

[11] Felix Frankfurter, "The Supreme Court," in Sydney D. Bailey, ed., *Aspects of American Government* (London, 1950), p. 35.

[12] *Perry v. U.S.*, 294 U.S. 330 (1935). See the discussion in Jackson, *Struggle for Judicial Supremacy*, pp. 96–103.

[13] Lerner, "John Marshall and the Campaign of History," *Columbia Law Review*, XXXIX (1939), 403. The essay is reprinted in Leonard W. Levy, ed., *American Constitutional Law: Historical Essays* (New York, 1969).

[14] Brooks Adams, *The Theory of Social Revolutions* (New York, 1914), p. 218.

[15] Quoted by Chester A. Newland, "Legal Periodicals and the United States Supreme Court," *Midwest Journal of Political Science*, III (February 1959), 59.

JUDICIAL REVIEW, HISTORY, AND DEMOCRACY

Much of the literature on the Supreme Court reflects the principle of the gored ox. Attitudes toward the Court quite often depend on whether its decisions are agreeable. More reflective commentators, however, seek to transcend their own immediate policy preferences and confront the basic and most perplexing questions which speak to the legitimacy of judicial review, its function and character in cases of constitutional law, and its harmony with democratic principles of government.

The legitimacy of judicial review as measured by the original intent of the framers of the Constitution merits discrete investigation, but few are attracted to a sheerly antiquarian issue for its own sake. They rummage through the wisdom of the past for a lineage that will authenticate either some present vision of the role of the Supreme Court in a political democracy, or some theory of the function of judicial review and the nature of the judicial process. The question whether judicial review was originally intended, in other words, is usually a dowsing rod to guide the wellsprings of judgment on whether the Court should have the power which, in loose and sometimes mischievous phrases, has resulted in "judicial supremacy," or "judicial policy-making," or "judicial legislation." The scope of that power, the conditions for its exercise, and the criteria for judging its practice have also attracted considerable attention.

Kipling in his *Just So Stories* described how the alligator gave the elephant his trunk. Charles Beard in his *Supreme Court and the Constitution* (1912) told how the framers of the Constitution gave the high tribunal its power of judicial review even over acts of Congress. Children find the story about the elephant enchantingly believable. Scholars and jurists read Beard's tale and say, "just so." But history has not really settled whether judicial review was originally intended, because decisive evidence cannot be marshalled to prove what the framers had in mind. Nor is it possible to show that judicial review was a normal function of courts at the time of the Constitutional Convention. Indeed, the evidence goes the other way.

The problem of legitimacy begins, of course, with the fact that the framers neglected to specify that the Supreme Court was empowered to exercise judicial review. If they intended the Court to have the power, why did they not provide for it? Since 1787 when Richard Dobbs Spaight, one of the framers, angrily denounced judicial review as "usurpation," [1] the cry that judges have usurped the power has echoed down the corridors of time. In 1924 Professor Felix Frankfurter exasperatedly declared, "Lack of historical scholarship, combined with fierce prepossessions, can alone account for the persistence of this talk. One would suppose that, at least, after the publication of Beard, *The Supreme Court and the Constitution*, there would be an end to this empty controversy." [2] The charge of usurpation most certainly cannot be proved; it is without merit. The difficulty is that the legitimacy of judicial review in terms of the original intent cannot be proved either; it may forever remain obscure, a seductive issue to those who would lift the veil.

In Beard's self-congratulatory preface to a reissue of his book in 1938, he declared that he had "settled" the great controversy over the legitimacy of the Court's most awesome power. The book had been favorably cited many times by expert witnesses before the Senate Judiciary Committee's hearings on the Roosevelt court-packing plan, and the committee itself seemed to accept the book as authoritative. "The ghost of usurpation," Beard announced, "was fairly laid. Whatever controversies may arise in the future over the exercise of judicial power, it is not likely that the historic right of the Supreme Court to pass upon acts of Congress will again be seriously challenged." As Alan F. Westin wryly observed in his introduction to a 1962 reprint of the book, despite Beard's prophecy the "ghost of usurpation" continued to clank its chains through legislative chambers, historical meetings, and publishing houses. Since the first edition of 1912, said Westin, several dozen books and perhaps a hundred articles "have persisted in treating this as still a debatable proposition, and not all of the commentators can be dismissed as incompetents or outraged partisans deprived of reason." [3]

"Judicial review is a matter of inference," [4] wrote Edward S. Corwin, Beard's sharpest and most formidable critic, though never one to endorse the charge of usurpation. One might add that inferences and insights will lead to any conclusions required by presuppositions. Beard's thesis on judicial review, as a matter of fact, was a foil for the book that he published in the following year, *An Economic Interpretation of the Constitution*. Chapter four of the 1912 volume, on "The

Spirit of the Constitution," foreshadows the 1913 volume. In Beard's opinion, judicial review over Congress must have been intended because it was part of the system of checks and balances by which the Convention "safeguarded the interests of property against attacks by majorities. . . . This very system of checks and balances, which is undeniably the essential element of the Constitution, is built upon the doctrine that the popular branch of the government cannot be allowed full sway, and least of all in the enactment of laws touching the rights of property." He concluded that it was incumbent upon opponents of his thesis "to show that the American federal system was not designed primarily to commit the established rights of property to the guardianship of a judiciary removed from direct contact with the popular electorates." [5] Divination, or reading the minds of the framers from a very incomplete and extraordinarily ambiguous record, may be an intriguing pastime; but it lacks empirical warrant.

The record of Corwin's vacillations testifies to the confusing and inconclusive nature of the evidence. In an unsympathetic review of Beard's book, published in 1913, Corwin argued that of the twenty-five framers whom Beard claimed supported "some form" of judicial review over Congress, only eight did so in the Constitutional Convention. Although the idea was challenged by only four members, "yet popular discussion previous to the Convention had shown their point of view to have too formidable backing to admit of its being crassly overridden." [6] Corwin concluded that the question was an open one when the Convention adjourned. Within a year, however, he was substantially in Beard's corner. In a little book which produced no new evidence whatever, Corwin asserted that the Convention undoubtedly did intend judicial review over Congress: ". . . it cannot be reasonably doubted." His 1913 figure of eight rose in 1914 to seventeen.[7] By 1937, however, it had fallen to only "five or six," and in blunt language he declared, "The people who say the framers intended it are talking nonsense"—to which he hastily added, "and the people who say they did not intend it are talking nonsense." In the same vein he remarked, there is "great uncertainty." [8] A close textual and contextual examination of the evidence will not result in an improvement on these propositions. Beard, to put it charitably, saw what he wanted to see. The same may be said of the eccentric studies made by Louis B. Boudin [9] and William Winslow Crosskey [10] in 1932 and 1953, respectively. They destroy credibility in Beard's work, but lend little to their own. The value of their work on judicial review and the Constitutional Convention, like Corwin's final statement in 1938,[11] is that it inspires an unredeemed skepticism.

Even a skimpy review of the remarks of Madison and Hamilton will suggest how treacherous is any generalization about their commitment to judicial review. Here, for example, is a complete sentence from a speech by Madison on July 23, 1787, wrenched out of context to give the misleading impression that Madison supported judicial review over Congress: "A law violating a constitution established by the people themselves, would be considered by the Judges as null and void." [12] The full context of the statement shows that Madison was referring to the possibility that state judges would declare unconstitutional a state act in violation of the federal Constitution. Moreover, the state act to which he was referring was an act of secession. On August 27, 1787, when the Convention considered a proposal to extend the jurisdiction of the Supreme Court to cases arising under the Constitution, Madison expressed doubt about "going too far" and advocated that jurisdiction over such cases be "limited to cases of a Judiciary Nature. The right of expounding the Constitution in cases not of this nature ought not to be given to that Department." [13] In 1788, Madison said that neither the state nor federal constitutions provided a means of settlement for the case of a disagreement in expounding the law; the courts, usually the last to decide, might stamp a law with its final character by refusing to execute it: "This makes the Judiciary Department paramount in fact to the Legislature, which was never intended and can never be proper." [14] On June 8, 1789, however, when advocating a Bill of Rights in the First Congress, Madison declared: "If they are incorporated into the Constitution, independent tribunals of justice will consider themselves in a peculiar manner the guardians of these rights; they will be an impenetrable bulwark against every assumption of power in the Legislature or Executive; they will be naturally led to resist every encroachment upon rights expressly stipulated for in the Constitution by the declaration of rights." [15]

Yet, eight days later, in a debate on the President's removal power, after acknowledging the duty of the judiciary to expound the laws and Constitution, Madison declared: ". . . but I beg to know upon what principle it can be contended that any one department draws from the Constitution greater powers than another, in marking out the limits of the powers of the several departments." No provision had been made, he contended, "for a particular authority to determine the limits of the constitutional division of power between the branches of government." [16] Beard, incidentally, did not use either the first of the Madison quotations given above nor the one on the Bill of Rights which is the only one that would justify his assertion that Madison's belief "in judicial control over legislation is unquestionable." Madison "was in no little confusion," Beard added.[17]

Hamilton contributed greatly to the ratification, not to the framing, of the Constitution. His views on judicial review are significant, however, because his *Federalist* #78 is second only to Marshall's *Marbury* opinion as the classic utterance on the subject. Beard simply quotes at length from #78 to demonstrate Hamilton's commitment to judicial review over Congress. It is not irrelevant, though, to recall that Hamilton offered to the Convention a complete plan for a new constitution, no part of which remotely provided for any sort of judicial review.[18] In *Federalist* #33, where he discussed the necessary and proper clause, which anti-ratificationists regarded as vesting carte blanche powers in Congress, Hamilton asked who was to judge if Congress "should overpass the just bounds of its authority." Not once in his answer did he allude to the Supreme Court. Congress in the first instance and the people in the last would judge. How then is *Federalist* #78 to be explained? It was a response to Robert Yates's "Letters of Brutus," an anti-ratificationist series which sought to discredit the Constitution by magnifying the powers of the federal judiciary into an engine for consolidating national powers at the expense of the states.[19] *Federalist* #78, in other words, was an attempt to quiet the fears stimulated by Yates; turning the latter's argument against him, Hamilton tried to convince his readers that the Court's power was intended to hold Congress in check, thereby safeguarding the states against national aggrandizement. A few other advocates of the Constitution, like Oliver Ellsworth and John Marshall, sought in the same manner to allay popular apprehensions that Congress might exceed its power, especially in the absence of a Bill of Rights to protect the people.[20] Their remarks, like Hamilton's in #78, are evidence of shrewd political tactics, not of the framers' intention to vest judicial review in the Supreme Court over acts of Congress.

The legitimacy of judicial review does rest on history, but not on the words of the Constitution nor of the framers during the 1787–1789 period. It was an historical outgrowth of the constitutional theory of the era of the American Revolution. *Federalist* #78 and Marshall's *Marbury* opinion were, significantly, arguments from general principles. Andrew C. McLaughlin wrote that judicial review is "the last word, logically and historically speaking, in the attempt of a free people to establish and maintain a non-autocratic government. It is the culmination of the essentials of Revolutionary thinking, and, indeed, of the thinking of those who a hundred years and more before the Revolution called for a government of laws and not of men." [21] That judicial review was "the natural outgrowth of ideas that were common property when the Constitution was established" was also asserted by Corwin. "In short," he wrote, "we are driven to the conclusion that judicial review was rested by the framers of the Constitution upon certain general principles which in their estimation made specific provision for it unnecessary. . . ." [22]

Corwin and McLaughlin were thinking of the theory of limited or constitutional government according to which an act of government in excess of its powers, which are held in subordination to a supreme law, is void. The difficulty with this theory is that it does not account for the definitive power of the judiciary to interpret finally the supreme law, nor does it account for the binding effect of court decisions on equal and coordinate branches of the same government. Articles III and VI of the Constitution, together with the Judiciary Act of 1789, established or made inevitable judicial review by the Supreme Court over the acts of the states, the subordinate agencies within the federal system, but not over the President and Congress. On the other hand, if judicial review was a normal function of courts at the time of the national government under the Constitution, there was no need for specific provision. Beard, Corwin, McLaughlin, Charles Warren, and Charles Grove Haines head a list of distinguished historians who believed that judicial review was so well known and normal a function of courts that it was taken for granted by the framers.[23]

One difficulty with this view is that the evidence is so sparing. If judicial review was a normal function of courts at the time of the Constitutional Convention, we might expect to find a considerable number of precedents in which legislation was invalidated on ground of repugnance to some higher law, either natural law or the written provisions of some constitution. The entire colonial period is without a single precedent. Although Virginia county courts announced in 1776 that the Stamp Act was unconstitutional, there was no case before those courts; their statements were gratuitous dicta.[24] Although many real precedents might be expected after the establishment of thirteen state governments, each with its own judiciary, what is striking is that there were so few. In the various books and articles which have been written to exhume the precedents, there are mythical cases that bring to mind the entries in *Appleton's Cyclopaedia of American Biography* with its forty-seven lives of men who never existed. The most influential and exhaustive of all works on the precedents is *The American Doctrine of Judicial Supremacy* by Charles Grove Haines. "By 1775," he concluded, "the principle had taken such a firm hold upon the minds of lawyers and judges that decisions were rendered in rapid succession in which was maintained the authority of courts, as guardians of a fundamental law, to pass upon the acts of coordinate departments. This authority was steadily asserted after the colonies became states, and by an irresistible process was made one of the prime features of the new federal system established by the Constitution of 1787. The state cases in which the American doctrine was first announced, and which were accepted as precedents in its development and extension, have an important role in the legal history of the United States."[25]

It is something of a letdown to discover that Haines lists only

seven state precedents for the period 1776–1787, a number hardly
warranting the confident statement that judicial review was such a
widely practiced, normal function of American courts that no provision for it had to be made in the Constitution. But there is an additional problem concerning these seven precedents. Several of them
are spurious, while others fudge the facts somewhat, like William
James when he was a young instructor assisting a lecturer on the
physiology of the heart. The lecturer used a turtle's heart supporting
an "index straw" which projected an enlarged moving shadow across
a screen to show the heart beat. To James's consternation, the turtle's
heart failed to function, jeopardizing the demonstration. "There was
no time for deliberation," he recalled, "so with my forefinger under
a part of the straw that cast no shadow, I found myself impulsively
and automatically imitating the rhythmical movements which my
colleague had prophesied the heart would undergo. I kept the experiment from failing, . . . and established in the audience the true view
of the subject." [26] Haines also supplied a finger to demonstrate the
"true view of the subject," or, more likely, did not realize that someone else had done so.

What is interesting about several of the spurious precedents, as
distinguished from the mythical cases, is that the court decisions were
either deliberately or mistakenly misrepresented for the purpose of
discrediting the judges. The Constitution was framed at a time when
the Blackstonian concept of legislative supremacy was dominant. As
the judge himself said in *Rutgers* v. *Waddington*, one of the alleged
precedents, if the legislature "think fit *positively* to enact a law there
is no power which can control them . . . the judges are not at liberty,
although it appear to them to be *unreasonable*, to reject it: for this
were to set the *judicial* above the legislative, which would be subversive of all government." [27] There were cases in Haines's list in which
disappointed parties, in an effort to inflame opposition to the court,
alleged baselessly that it had voided an act. *Holmes* v. *Walton*, decided by the New Jersey Supreme Court in 1780, was such a case.
It is not likely that the framers could have taken the misrepresenta-
tion for the fact because David Brearley, one of the delegates to the
Constitutional Convention, had been chief justice of the court which
decided the case.[28]

In other instances state legislatures, sensitive to even imagined
slights on their sovereignty, condemned state courts in the mistaken
belief that they had invalidated an act. *Trevett* v. *Weeden*, which
was well known to the framers, was such a case. The outraged legislature of Rhode Island summoned the judges as if they were
suspected criminals and demanded their reasons for an unprecedented
holding against the constitutionality of a legislative act. The judges
flatly denied the charge.[29] In *Rutgers*, despite the court's endorse-

ment of legislative supremacy, the construction given to the act defeated the legislature's purpose. As a result there were mass meetings, the governor called a special session of the legislature, the legislature censured the court, and there were impeachment threats.[30] In the Virginia "precedent" of 1782, two judges declared themselves in favor of the power of judicial review, one took a contrary position, and the rest of the court took none at all; the statute was sustained by a vote of six to two.[31] The mythical cases aren't worthy of mention.

There are but two legitimate precedents, both reported in the Philadelphia press when the Convention was in session. In the "Ten Pound Case" in New Hampshire, the court courageously voided an unconstitutional act in the face of threats from the legislature. An abortive attempt to impeach the judges failed by a vote of 35 to 21.[32] Very much the same thing happened in North Carolina in the case of *Bayard* v. *Singleton,* the only other legitimate precedent. The court took jurisdiction of a case contrary to a statute directing dismissal. The legislature then summoned the judges to explain their audacious disregard of its supreme authority. A committee which included William R. Davie and Richard Dobbs Spaight, shortly to be delegates to the Constitutional Convention, found the judges guilty as charged, but recommended no disciplinary action. The court in unmistakable terms then held the disputed statute unconstitutional.[33]

Such are the pre-Convention precedents, few as they are. Taken as a group, the spurious as well as the legitimate, they scarcely show that judicial review was a normal function of courts. On the contrary, they show that it was nowhere established, indeed that it seemed novel, controversial, and an encroachment on legislative authority. Its exercise, even when imagined, was disputed and liable to provoke the legislature to retaliation. If the framers intended judicial review, would they have omitted a provision for it, allowing it to rest on so precarious a foundation? They might have, on the supposition that an explicit provision might not have aided the cause of ratification, but the thought lacks evidentiary basis. Louis B. Boudin, who did much of the spadework in exposing the fraudulent character of some of the precedents, and W. W. Crosskey who followed his lead, observed that the precedents tended to arise in certain types of cases—those in which the legislatures had interfered with the normal jurisdiction of the courts or the trial procedures by which they normally did business. Such cases, in Madison's phrase, were "of a Judiciary Nature," as was *Marbury* v. *Madison.* Judicial review emerged, in other words, mainly in cases relating to the province of the judicial department or trial by jury. The precedents tend not to show that the courts could pass on the constitutionality of the gen-

31

eral powers of the legislatures. As Corwin concluded, in his last word on the subject, "the case that could be made for judicial review in 1787 on either the ground of proved workability or of 'precedent' was a shadowy one at best." [34]

The idea of judicial review was, nevertheless, rapidly emerging, a fact which adds retrospective significance to the few precedents, even to the scattered judicial dicta and lawyers' arguments. Federalism hastened the emergence, supported by Section 25 of the Judiciary Act of 1789; the ratification controversy and the demand for a Bill of Rights also quickened the spread of the idea. Madison's remark about the Supreme Court as protector of the Bill of Rights, quoted above, echoed Jefferson, Sam Adams, John Hancock, Patrick Henry, Richard Henry Lee, and others.[35] No less important in contributing to a widespread acceptance of the idea of judicial review was the emergence of party politics. Charles Warren's study of the records of Congress during its first decade shows that the parties, with little consistency or adherence to principle, argued the constitutionality of bills they liked and the unconstitutionality of those they disliked, but Federalists and Republicans alike "were united in one sentiment at least, that under the Constitution it was the Judiciary which was finally to determine the validity of an Act of Congress." Nor did they endorse judicial review in cases of a departmental or judiciary nature only. Republicans, for example, wanted the Supreme Court to strike down as unconstitutional such legislation as the Bank Act, the Carriage Tax, and the Alien and Sedition Acts.[36] The Court considered favorably the constitutionality of several congressional acts during its first decade, and there were a number of circuit cases in which the justices voided state legislation.[37] As late as 1800, Justice Chase observed that while an act in direct opposition to the prohibitions of the Constitution was void, "yet it still remains a question where the power resides to declare it void." The "general opinion" of the bar, he added, supported judicial review over acts of Congress.[38] In short, the path to *Marbury* v. *Madison* was wide open and it was never shut off by the people of the country after the Supreme Court under Marshall decided Chase's question.

Long acquiescence by the people and their representatives has legitimated judicial review. It was "not imposed by self-anointed fiat on an unwilling people." [39] Despite periodic and sometimes intense attacks on the Court by Congress or the White House, judicial review has survived unscathed for over a century and a half. Even the brief and unique encounter with Congress's controlling power over the Court's appellate jurisdiction during Reconstruction was only a glancing blow.[40] Within a year or so, the Court handed down a series of unprecedented decisions holding unconstitutional Congressional statutes which made greenbacks legal tender, exceeded the commerce power, and taxed state instrumentalities.[41] Judicial review would never have flourished had the people been opposed to it. They have opposed only its exercise in particular cases, but not the power itself. They have the sovereign power to abolish it outright or hamstring it by constitutional amendment. The President and Congress could bring the Court to heel even by ordinary legislation. The Court's membership, size, funds, staff, rules of procedure, and enforcement agencies are subject to the control of the "political" branches. Judicial review, in fact, exists by the tacit consent of the governed.

Judicial Review and Democracy

Is judicial review democratic? Not to those whose thinking reflects the Hoadly syndrome, *genus Americanus.* Its principal symptom is a conviction that the judgment of the representative branches of the government should not be thwarted or superseded by that of Platonic guardians who are not responsible to the electoral battalions. Related symptoms are a chronic commitment to majority rule, a trusting faith that the majority will not infringe the rights of the minority, a belief that a people with a demonstrated capacity for self-government will correct their own errors if left alone, and a sure sense that political salvation may be earned but can never be imposed from above.

The Hoadly syndrome, which is deeply Jeffersonian in its American context, may be traced to a celebrated remark of Benjamin Hoadly, the Bishop of Bangor, who in 1717 observed, "Whoever hath an absolute authority to interpret any written or spoken laws, it is he who is truly the lawgiver, to all intents and purposes, and not the person who first wrote or spoke them." [42] As far as our constitutional literature is concerned, this statement was discovered by Oliver Wendell Holmes and handed down in a sort of an apostolic succession to some of our greatest jurists, including Louis D. Brandeis, Learned Hand, Felix Frankfurter, and Robert H. Jackson, and to a distinguished group of constitutional scholars ranging, in time, from James Bradley Thayer, whom Frankfurter described as "our great master of constitutional law," [43] to Henry Steele Commager, one of the great teachers of constitutional history. Commager's influential book, *Majority Rule and Minority Rights,* which questions the democratic character of judicial review, was appropriately dedicated to Justice Frankfurter who repaid the compliment by borrowing some of its arguments and citing it in judicial opinions.[44]

Jefferson was one of the foremost carriers of the Hoadly syndrome. From his time and example, perceptive if jaundiced critics have noted the grand irony that at the very apex of our vaunted system of a government of laws and not of men, we have to a considerable degree a government of men in whose hands the supreme law, as Jefferson said, is "merely a thing of wax . . . which they may twist and shape into any form they please." At the apex of the system, of course, is the Supreme Court, which Jefferson thought of as "an irresponsible body," "independent of the nation itself," not subject "to some practical impartial control," and therefore, in Commager's summation of Jefferson's opinion, "a threat to democracy." [45] The Jeffersonian position pits the Court against the people and depicts the justices as elitist sappers of self-government. Some of the great presidents have also remarked on the estrangement between the Court and the popular will. Lincoln, for example, in his First Inaugural, declared: ". . . the candid citizen must confess that if the policy of the Government upon vital questions affecting the whole people is to be irrevocably fixed by decisions of the Supreme Court, the instant they are made in ordinary litigation between parties in personal actions the people will have ceased to be their own rulers, having to that extent practically resigned their Government into the hands of that eminent tribunal." [46]

In *The Struggle for Judicial Supremacy*, published in the same year as his appointment to the Supreme Court, Robert H. Jackson argued that the distinctive characteristics of the Court "tend to make it anti-democratic." Jackson echoed Jefferson in claiming that the Court was "completely independent of popular will," yet of such "supremacy" that it "could deny important powers to both state and nation, or between Congress and the executive departments, and could largely control the economic and social policy of the country." [47] Felix Frankfurter, when a member of the Court, repeated the bold words that he had used before his appointment to describe the "stupendous powers" and wide personal discretion of the justices. He declared that "tremendous and delicate" problems affecting the whole nation were decided by the interpretation of broad and undefined clauses of the Constitution whose scope of application "is relatively unrestricted and the room for play of individual judgment as to policy correspondingly broad . . . constitutional interpretation compels the translation of policy into judgment. . . ." [48] In opinions from the bench Frankfurter described judicial review as "a limitation on popular government" and therefore "an undemocratic aspect" of our system. He called the powers of the Court "uncontrollable" and "inherently oligarchic," the Court itself "the non-democratic organ of our Government." [49]

Henry Steele Commager's statement is the most sustained and representative of this school of thought, and it has the additional merit of being sophisticated. Commager, that is, knew and considered opposing arguments; he was fully aware that the Constitution establishes a limited government with many checks on majoritarianism, and he had as passionate a regard for the Bill of Rights as any. His book was a moving and magisterial defense of majority rule, deeply Jeffersonian in spirit. His cause was democratic government and his concern the undemocratic nature of judicial review in both theory and practice. Those who disagree with his thesis garb judicial review in democratic raiment, because not trusting the majority to govern unchecked, they seek the protection of the Court against the people. Judicial review restricts the electoral process which is at the center of democratic theory and practice; and it frustrates the policy-making power of the representative institutions which are the product of the electoral process. As Commager remarked, when the Court holds unconstitutional an act of Congress, we are confronted by the fact that the one nonelective and nonremovable element in the government rejects the conclusions of the two elective and removable branches. Although the Court can be responsive to the people—even more responsive than their own representatives, as the desegregation and reapportionment decisions prove—it need not be; it is not responsive except when belatedly correcting its own mistakes under pressure.

The problem is not, in Commager's words, "that of blind or malicious majorities riding down constitutional guarantees, but of differing interpretations of the Constitution. The crucial question is not so much whether an act does or does not conform to the Constitution, but who shall judge regarding its conformity?" [50] Commager questioned whether judges are better qualified to decide constitutional issues than legislators or executives, given that legal erudition is not, for the most part, required for decision; indeed, discretion and, in Holmes's phrase, "considerations of policy and of social advantage" rather than legal logic, legal rules, and legal research determine the resolution of questions that involve the ambiguous clauses of the Constitution, the very clauses usually involved in those cases resulting in the invalidation of acts of Congress. Commager argued that the political branches are as competent and objective as judges for the purpose of deciding such questions. His study of the cases in which the Court held Congressional legislation unconstitutional resulted in a cluster of striking conclusions in support of his contention. He found that our constitutional system would be essentially as it is had there never been an instance of judicial review; that the Court's record in the field of personal liberties is practically barren; that it rarely voided an act of Congress in order to protect minorities and the underprivileged; that Congress has rarely threatened the integrity of the constitutional system or the guarantees of the Bill of Rights; that Congress, not the Court, has a far better record for realizing those guarantees; and that almost every instance of judicial nullification of Congressional legislation has been a mistaken one.

Holmes once said that the Union would not come to an end if the Court lost its power of judicial review over Congress. Commager put the point far more forcibly, arguing that judicial review has done considerably more harm than good, and he would prefer to have none of it. He stressed that the absence of a judicial check would by no means result in unbridled majority rule. Not only does the constitutional system provide for many checks and balances other than judicial review. Our political system furnishes its own checks and balances. It matches various classes, sections, interests, and other groups against each other at the ballot box and in the legislative halls, producing compromises and shifting majorities that yield to public opinion. Our majority system, Commager demonstrated, "is not a system of unlimited government either in theory, in law, or in practice." Would majorities thus limited respect constitutional limitations and the rights of minorities in the absence of judicial obstacles? The American experience, Commager said, justified Jefferson's belief that men need no "masters—not even judges. It justifies us, too, in believing that majority will does not imperil minority rights, either in theory or in operation." American majorities, state and national, he added, have been remarkably respectful of the Constitution, law-abiding, stable, and conservative, belying the jeremiads of Adams and Hamilton. Our history is proof: majorities have not crushed the rights of property or minorities; they have not set up dictatorships; they have not evinced hostility to education, the press, science, or the arts. Ours is a free society, a fact for which the American people, not the courts in the exercise of judicial review, deserve the credit.[51]

Commager acknowledged that majorities, especially in the states, have made many mistakes including serious impairment of civil liberties. "It is here, if anywhere, that judicial review has justified itself," he added, referring to state impairments. "But grant the desirability of the necessity of calling in the judiciary to protect civil liberties, and we concede that the majority is not to be trusted in what is perhaps the most important / field of its legislative activity."[52] This proposition, a concession to theoretical consistency, was the weakest point in Commager's argument, if he was implying that adherence to principle required opposition to judicial review over state action even in the field of civil liberties. What he implied is not clear. At an earlier stage of his argument he noted in passing a distinction between judicial review "as a check upon democracy," professedly his only concern, and judicial review "as a harmonizer of the federal system."[53] Yet he also noted that the two overlapped, and indeed they do. Checking a state or local majority for the purpose of harmonizing the federal system is no less a check on majority will than checking the same majority for the purpose of enforcing a First Amendment limitation. But judicial review may be less a check upon democracy in the one case than in the other. That is, majority infringement on the First Amendment may be more of a check on democracy than would a violation of the commerce clause, with the result that judicial review in protection of a First Amendment freedom, or any provision of the Bill of Rights, may be counter majoritarian, but not undemocratic.

Not even Jefferson, contrary to Commager's assertion, rejected judicial review "in toto." [54] "In the arguments in favor of a declaration of rights," wrote Jefferson to Madison, "you omit one which has great weight with me; the legal check which it puts into the hands of the judiciary." In the same letter of 1789 he warned of the "tyranny of the legislatures." Two years earlier, when commenting on the proposed Constitution, Jefferson told Madison that he liked the executive veto and would have liked it even more had the judiciary "been associated for that purpose, or invested separately with a similar power." [55] As Commager himself observed, Jefferson's First Annual Message to Congress "repudiated legislative omnipotence where personal liberties were concerned." [56] The Bill of Rights and other constitutional limitations do exist, and if self-imposed are not self-enforcing. The checks of democratic politics as well as the formal checks and balances of the Constitution itself surely do not have the same operation in the states as in the nation, not even in the large urban, industrialized states with their complex political economics and mixed populations.

Commager recognized as "persuasive" the argument derived from Justice Stone's famous *Carolene Products* footnote to the effect that any law restricting the democratic process or directed against discrete and insular minorities, whether religious or racial, may call for the most searching judicial scrutiny.[57] But Commager was also disinclined to conclude that judicial review, even in state cases, was either necessary or desirable. He advanced a number of arguments in behalf of his position, among them the ambiguity of relevant constitutional provisions, the unclear distinction between civil liberties cases and other cases, and the fact that legislation apparently violating civil liberties is often inspired by a sincere, if misguided, desire to protect them. The most persuasive of Commager's arguments, applying with equal force to judicial review over national or state action, is as follows.

Although majorities have made mistakes, the judiciary has been equally liable to error, and when it checked the majority it has sapped the capacity of the people to learn from experience and to correct their own mistakes. The real battles of liberalism, said Commager, following Frankfurter, are not won in the Supreme Court; they are won in the legislatures and in the arena of public opinion. The impatient, confronted by some legislative stupidity or injustice, may scream for immediate rectification by the judiciary, but the effect of resolving issues, especially those of personal liberty or minority rights, in the judicial arena is to lull the people into apathy concerning matters that are fundamentally their concern. Comforted by the notion, empirically unsupportable, that courts will take care of personal and minority rights, the people are effectively deprived of the inestimable benefit of vindicating self-government by taking sober second thought. As Thayer pointed out, in a passage quoted by Commager, the exercise of judicial review, "even when unavoidable is always attended with a serious evil, namely, that the correction of legislative mistakes comes from the outside, and the people thus lose the political experience, and the moral education and stimulus that come from fighting the question out in the ordinary way, and correcting their own errors. The tendency of a common and easy resort to this great function, now lamentably too common, is to dwarf the political capacity of the people, and to deaden its sense of moral responsibility." Relying on Frankfurter again, Commager added that "education in the abandonment of foolish legislation is itself a training in liberty." The people, concluded Commager, must be persuaded that any legislation which limits inquiry or stunts minority growth is "treason to democracy." [58]

In the quarter of a century that has passed since Commager's analysis of the incidence of judicial review over Congress, the character of American constitutional law has radically altered. Even before Commager wrote, Franklin Roosevelt had reconstructed the Court by placing it in the hands of its critics, men like Frankfurter, Black, and Jackson, who promptly remade constitutional law from the dissenting opinions of Holmes, Brandeis, and Stone. The great issues of the thirties were quickly settled, although the power of judicial review remained unaffected. The Court sustained economic and social legislation, both state and national, against claims drawn from a restricted interpretation of the commerce clause or from the due process of law clauses construed to protect substantive economic rights. Old style cases on government regulation of the economy were gradually phased out of the Court's docket to be replaced, with increasing frequency, by cases bearing on civil, political, and criminal rights. The incidence of judicial review over Congress, as measured by the number of acts voided, declined precipitously. The question is whether developments of the past twenty-five years have seriously undermined that part of Commager's analysis which is based on historical experience as distinguished from political theory.

The general trend of decision has been increasingly equalitarian and libertarian, although the Court was an unreliable champion of constitutional limitations when it was most needed during the McCarthy years. Under Chief Justice Vinson (1946–1953) the Court generally genuflected toward the Bill of Rights but submitted to *force majeure:* public opinion expressed legislatively. When the state, under the hydraulic pressures of the passing hour, took uncivil liberties with the individual, the Vinson Court did not hold aloft the torch of enduring libertarian principles to light the way for a people drunk to become again a people sober. The Court, rather, inclined to the view that constitutional limitations should not straitjacket majoritarian government in its Cold War battle against subversive activities. The Court deplored encroachments on liberty, but out of deference to *vox populi* did not nullify them; the vigilant state approached the threshold of the vigilante state. So also, during World War II, the Court lent its authority to the racist, relocation, and detention-camp policies of the government in relation to the seventy thousand American citizens of Japanese descent. If majorities cannot be trusted during time of acute crisis, neither can the Supreme Court whose history reveals it to be a sunshine defender of the Bill of Rights. As John P. Frank said, "The dominant lesson of our history in the relation of the judiciary to repressions is that courts love liberty most when it is under pressure least." [59]

Under Chief Justice Warren, however, the constitutional law of civil liberties has enjoyed a golden age in our history. Never before has the Court been so bold and vigilant in its protection of constitutional rights in so many fields. The various First Amendment freedoms, the diverse rights of the criminally accused, and equal justice under the law for racial minorities have flourished and prospered in the pages of the Court's opinions, with considerable fallout in the world beyond. As Commager wrote of an earlier series of opinions, which now seem by comparison to be only the proverbial camels' noses, "The record of those nullifications is gratifying to every one who cherishes the great Anglo-American tradition of personal liberties." [60] Overwhelmingly the Warren Court's record of judicial review is based on decisions bearing on state action. Nevertheless there has been a noticeable revival of judicial review over Congress in recent years, and in every case the Court has intervened on libertarian grounds.

Commager's list of cases, which ended with *Carter* v. *Carter Coal Company*, decided in 1936—the last case in which the Court invalidated a Congressional regulation of the economy—may be brought up to date as follows. In 1943 in *Toth* v. *United States*, the Court held that Congress violated due process of law by an act which established a presumption of guilt against any individual with a prior record of conviction for a crime of violence who was found in possession of firearms.[61] In 1946 the Court ruled that a rider to an appropriations act, which forbade the payment of compensation to three named individuals suspected of subversive activities, was a bill of attainder.[62] These were the only Congressional statutes held unconstitutional by the Court under Chief Justices Stone and Vinson. By June of 1965, the end of the 1964 term, the Warren Court had handed down rulings of unconstitutionality in eleven cases.

In 1955, in *United States ex rel. Toth* v. *Quarles,* the Court held that a provision of Congress's Uniform Code of Military Justice, which subjected a former serviceman to trial by court martial for a crime alleged to have been committed while in uniform, denied due process of law, that is, trial by jury after indictment by grand jury.[63] The same grounds were invoked in *Reid* v. *Covert,*[64] decided in 1957, and in three closely related cases of 1960, which were decided the same day.[65] In these cases the Court struck down provisions of the Uniform Code of Military Justice which subjected overseas civilians—employees and dependents of the armed forces—to trial by court martial in either capital or noncapital cases. *Toth, Reid,* and the three 1960 cases dealt with the power of Congress to make rules for the governance of the armed forces.

In the 1958 case of *Trop* v. *Dulles,* the Court held unconstitutional a provision of the Nationality Act of 1940 which automatically denationalized or divested of citizenship any citizen convicted by court martial for wartime desertion.[66] The grounds of decision are not clear, because none of the opinions in the case mustered a majority. It seems, however, that the infirmity of the act resulted from its despoliation of the inviolable birthright of citizenship and, additionally, it conflicted with the constitutional guarantee against cruel and unusual punishments by imposing statelessness on its victims. In 1963, in *Kennedy* v. *Mendoza-Martinez,* the Court invalidated provisions of the same statute and of the McCarran Immigration and Nationality Act of 1952 which automatically denationalized citizens who left the country in wartime to avoid military service. The majority ruled that Congress had imposed loss of citizenship as a punishment without affording the procedural safeguards of the Fifth and Sixth Amendments.[67] A year later, in *Schneider* v. *Rusk,* the Court held that another provision of the same act, subjecting naturalized citizens to denationalization for staying abroad three years in their country of former citizenship or birth, violated the Fifth Amendment's due process clause by denying equal protection. The Court reasoned that all citizens, naturalized as well as the native born, possessed equal rights; to deny the naturalized citizen the right enjoyed by native-born citizens to remain abroad indefinitely created an unconstitutional status of second-class citizenship.[68]

Aptheker v. *Secretary of State,* decided in 1964, sustained the right to travel abroad as part of the liberty guaranteed by the Fifth Amendment's due process clause. In this case the Court voided a provision of the Subversive Activities Control Act of 1950 which made it a felony for a member of a Communist organization to apply for or use a passport.[69] In a 1965 case, *United States* v. *Brown*, the Court found a bill of attainder in the provision of the Labor Management Reporting and Disclosure Act of 1959 which made it a crime for a member of the Communist Party to serve as an officer or employee of a labor union.[70] The decision in another 1965 case, *Lamont* v. *Postmaster General*, discredited the discreditable fact that in all our history the Court had never struck down an act of Congress on First Amendment grounds.[71] In the unprecedented *Lamont* case, freedom of speech and press furnished the basis for a ruling against the constitutionality of a 1962 statute requiring the Post Office Department to detain and destroy unsealed foreign mail classified as communist propaganda, unless the addressee indicated his desire to receive it by returning a reply card. Finally, in 1965, the Court unanimously held that the registration orders under the Subversive Activities Control Act, requiring registration of members of the Communist Party on forms compelling admission of membership, conflicted with the Fifth Amendment's self-incrimination clause.[72]

Taken as a group the cases are of greater symbolic than practical importance. None received much attention from the press or Congress; most were unnoticed. The cases which evoked great public interest and were of first-rank magnitude involved judicial review of state action, chiefly the racial discrimination [73] and legislative apportionment cases whose revolutionary effects on American life are not yet played out.[74] Similarly the state cases on censorship and freedom of the press,[75] on church-state relations and freedom of religion,[76] and on the great procedural rights of accused persons,[77] loom greater in the public mind and have a more far-reaching significance than the cases in which the Court invalidated Congressional legislation. If the question of judicial review's compatibility with democracy is restricted to review of Congressional legislation, the problem described by Commager persists to the present.

Nothing that has happened since 1943 has impaired whatever validity Commager's principled or theoretical argument possessed, and events have merely modified, but scarcely impaired, his argument based on history. A single generation's experience with judicial review over Congress does not wipe out the experience of a century and a half. Indeed the libertarian instances of judicial review hardly antedate the Warren Court. But the real point is not that the democratic character of judicial review swells in proportion to the frequency of decisions voiding Congressional legislation on Bill of Rights grounds. The point, rather, is that even in the state cases which stir civil rights champions to euphoric applause, the Court's judgment cannot escape from the influence of its members' policy preferences. When, therefore, that judgment has the effect of redirecting American policy in genuinely significant areas of experience, whether political, educational, or social, the questions put by the Thayers, the Frankfurters, and the Commagers cannot be downed by the enjoyment of augmented freedom or equality. Where *are* the battles of democracy best won? And if judicial review is undemocratic as a matter of principle, does it lose its spots in the furtherance of a democratic clause? As Frankfurter once remarked. "The Court is not saved from being oligarchic because it professes to act in the service of humane ends." [78] For all practical purposes the Court is, in Learned Hand's phrase, "a third chamber," one that is "unaccountable to anyone but itself. . . ." Each of us, Hand remarked, must choose for himself how far he would like to leave our collective fate "to the wayward vagaries of popular assemblies. . . . For myself it would be most irksome to be ruled by a bevy of Platonic Guardians, even if I knew how to choose them, which I assuredly do not." [79]

The argument that judicial review is undemocratic is by no means conclusive. As in the cases that come before the Supreme Court, there are two sides—at least two—to every question, and both are invariably reasonable, well-matched, and even compelling. It is a wonder sometimes that the judges can have a preference or reach judgment. The case for the democratic character of judicial review is certainly a compelling one—although not a convincing one. It is, interestingly, of comparatively recent vintage, raising the suspicion that the arguments have been concocted to rationalize a growing satisfaction with judicial review among liberal intellectuals and scholars. But if a defense of judicial review on the grounds that it is democratic corresponds in time with the Court's increasing defense of racial and criminal justice and its libertarian decisions in First Amendment cases, the contrary position espoused by Commager is no less suspected as a response to a long record of preponderantly reactionary decisions. In any event, the defense of judicial review has come mainly from those who have welcomed the trend of judicial decision in recent years and have rushed to the Court's protection against the charges, often irresponsible, that it has coddled Communists and criminals, outlawed God from the public schools, legislated morality and sociology in its desegregation decisions, and has intruded into the "political thicket" of legislative apportionment. It is probably no coincidence either that the argument harmonizing judical review and democracy seems to have originated during the McCarthy era, when majoritarian excesses invited thoughtful, if overwrought, libertarians to reconsider the benefits of judicial intervention.

Advocates of the democratic character of judicial review invariably make the argument, which nobody disputes, that democracy is not synonymous with pure or unchecked majoritarianism, unlimited government, or legislative sovereignty. Reminders of fundamental principles are constantly in order. Thus, the problem is that of "majority rule *versus* limited government . . . . it was in America that the principle of limited government was first institutionalized and that machinery for maintaining it was first fashioned." Among the basics of our system is the principle "that governments are limited, that there are things no government may do, rights no government may impair, powers no government may exercise . . . that as government was instituted to secure certain rights, its jurisdiction was strictly limited to the fields assigned to it, and that if it overstepped the bounds of its jurisdiction its acts were not law." That the limits of government might not be misunderstood, its authority was described in written constitutions with bills of rights and the checks and balances of the federal system, of the tripartite division of powers, of the bicameral legislatures, of frequent elections, of impeachment, and "atop all this there developed—I would not say there was established—the practice of judicial review." The words are Commager's, not those of one who rejects his argument, and the point is that judicial review does not gain in democratic character by admonitory reminders that it gravely oversimplifies to say—as nobody does—that the system is undemocratic if the majority is unrestrained. It was Commager too who stressed that the remedial channels of the democratic process must be kept open and unobstructed, that restrictions on the electorate or on the opinions available to it for consideration violate that process, and who used "democracy" to mean majority rule within self-imposed restraints which included adherence to process and freedom for minority rights.[80] Thus it neither joins nor advances the argument to treat the critics of judicial review as if they did not subscribe to civil liberties. The question at the core of the controversy is, who, according to democratic theory, is best suited to decide what Charles Black, one of judicial review's foremost advocates, calls issues of "constitutional policy." [81]

Black's splendid book, *The People and the Court*, is a counterpart to Commager's and is every bit as challenging. As Commager relied on Thayer before him and presented Justice Frankfurter as a model jurist, Black relied on Eugene V. Rostow's seminal article, "The Democratic Character of Judicial Review," [82] and by implication offered Justice Hugo Black as his model. Professors Rostow and Black make much of the point that the Supreme Court, however influential, has distinctly limited power. Critics of judicial review tend to use loaded phrases like "judicial supremacy" or "government by judiciary" which somehow give the impression that the Supreme Court is the master institution of our system, dominating presidents, Congress, and states. A power so awesome exercised by a nonelective body with life tenure would heighten the seeming incompatibility with democracy. Accordingly, Black argued that "judicial supremacy" is a mere hyperbole, although he acknowledged that the Court is "one of the policy-making organs of the nation" and must reach judgment, at least in part, on the basis of the policy views of its members. Its powers, nevertheless, are negative, said Black, asking for consideration of the things that the Court could not conceivably do. It can't, for example, make war, conduct diplomatic relations, tax, spend, or do anything warranting justification for calling it "supreme" in the sphere of policy-making. "The very most the Court ever has," said Black, himself engaging in hyperbole, "is a veto." The power to declare school prayers unconstitutional is, in fact, merely a veto; but what appears to be merely a veto may sometimes be far more. A decision against the constitutionality of racial segregation, for example, effectively requires integration, just as a decision against unequal legislative apportionment requires reapportionment, and the result in either case is as far reaching as almost any act passed by Congress and signed by the President. On the other hand, Black correctly observed that the Court merely has "the last word" in a chronological sense—it is the last to decide, compared to what has gone before, but its authority is merely a "moral authority" which "could never have the strength to prevail in the fact of resolute public repudiation" of a given decision or, for that matter, of its legitimacy to decide at all.[83]

Loren Beth, who completely concurs in the views of Rostow and Black, amplifies the point by noting that whether the Court's decision has any effect depends on others.[84] All enforcement powers reside in the very agencies, whether federal or state, executive or legislative, that the Court may be trying to check, and the last word really belongs with them. It may come in the form of delay, circumvention, or noncompliance. In 1809 Chief Justice Marshall's opinion in the *Olmstead* case met with armed resistance from the state of Pennsylvania; it took two thousand federal marshals and a sharp warning from President Madison to bring the state to heel.[85] In our own time Presidents Eisenhower and Kennedy had to call out federal troops to secure compliance with judicial orders in school desegregation cases. Eleven years after the *School Desegregation* cases of 1954, only 7.5 per cent of Negro school children had been admitted to white schools in the South, despite Presidential and Congressional support of the Court.[86] Without some such support, the Court is helpless, as in the *Merryman* case when Lincoln let the army flout Chief Justice Taney's writ of habeas corpus.[87] A unanimous decision by the Court in the *Beef Trust* case of 1905 had no practical effect until Congress passed the Packers and Stockyards Act of 1921.[88] As long ago as 1880 the Court ruled that the exclusion of Negroes from juries violated the

Constitution,[89] but there are still many counties in the South where Negroes have never served as jurors. Outlawed religious practices still persist in many school systems in the country,[90] and third-degree tactics undoubtedly exist in many police stations despite Court decisions. The Supreme Court cannot even effectively enforce its decisions against lower courts, state or federal, if they choose to misunderstand, evade, or modify rulings of the high tribunal.[91]

There are other, more familiar, limitations on the powers of the Court.[92] It cannot strike down an act at will, however unconstitutional; it must wait, passively, for a zealous litigant to raise a real case or controversy over which it has jurisdiction and the parties have standing. And its jurisdiction, though vast, is wholly revocable at the pleasure of Congress except in cases to which foreign diplomats or states are parties. The very power of judicial review might be eradicated by constitutional amendment. Charles Black so emphasized the limitations on the Court's power, capacity, and effectiveness, that one would think that it should not be called "the least dangerous branch" but the helpless or powerless branch.[93] Whether the Court is puissant or puny, however, seems unrelated to the question whether judicial review is democratic.

The same observation applies to Black's argument that the judges are especially suited to the task of deciding issues of "constitutional policy." He entered a demurrer rather than a repudiation to the charge that the Court "legislates" or makes policy. That task, according to critics of judicial review, should belong only to those accountable to the people through their elected officials who are as competent as the judges. Black was right to acknowledge that judicial review necessarily involves policy-making, but he defended the Court on insupportable grounds. The upshot of new insights, he wrote, "is not that judges *ought* to form their judgments in part on the basis of nontechnical factors. It is that they *must* do so, in the very nature of the case, and *always have done so*, consciously or unconsciously." [94] So far so good, and the same may be said of Black's reminder that a good deal of constitutional law comprises "sheer legal technicality" which everyone would want judges to decide. The trouble with Black's analysis derives from the kinds of issues he classified as "sheer legal technicality." How far, in the light of the free speech guarantee, the legislature should be permitted to limit free speech, he wrote, is a policy issue. But, he continued, unless we abandon the notion that the Constitution is law, the judges must also consider "the history surrounding the proposal and ratification of the Bill of Rights, the roots of the free speech concept in earlier times, the legal precedents that have gone before, the meaning and operation of the challenged statute—all the things, in short, which the trained lawyer, as such, is skilled in dealing with." These, he added, are "traditionally 'legal' factors bearing on decision" and are inseparable from the policy factors. "What did the Framers intend?" is, said Black, "a legal question, a question of the sort that lawyers deal with every day." [95] In his other example of a technical or legal question which he found judges best suited to decide, he put the case whether a certain mode of business organization is a restraint of trade.

Rarely has there been so parochial a judgment. The history of the Bill of Rights, the roots of the free speech concept, the intentions of the framers or of Congress are all matters which historians are best suited, by far, to decide. Lawyers, trained in the adversary process, which is inherently hostile to the disinterested pursuit of truth, are poorly qualified to decide such questions. As for the economic issue posed by Black, it could be better settled by a panel of economists from his own university than by a group of judges. The expertise of academicians is not, of course, at issue. The point is that the expertise of Congress and the President is comparatively as good as that of the Court to decide the kinds of "technical" or "policy" issues that are woven together in the constitutional issues which have resulted in the Court's invalidation of an act of Congress. Senator Hugo Black and Governor Earl Warren were not less qualified than Justice Black and Chief Justice Warren. That there are technical questions in constitutional cases beyond the competence of many congressmen, especially those who are nonlawyers, is beyond dispute. That these questions are crucial to decision is a matter of dispute, as is the "technicality" of the issues which Black regarded as technical or legal. Not even the "precedents that have gone before" require a lawyer's craft for understanding or use. In any event, as Edward S. Corwin declared, "alternative principles of construction and alternative lines of precedent constantly vest the Court with a freedom virtually legislative in scope in choosing the values which it shall promote through its reading of the Constitution." [96]

Black himself admitted that proof of the Court's special competence does not make judicial review democratic. His argument gained in relevance when contending that there is no conflict between government under law and government by the people, no conflict, that is, between democracy, whether in theory or practice, and the decision of policy questions by a body which is neither politically responsible nor responsive to public opinion except at its own choice. Zeroing in from two angles, Black declared first that judicial review has popular support and is therefore a democratic institution, and second, that democracy does not require policy to be decided by bodies ever sensitive to electoral sentiment.

He called judicial review "a people's institution, confirmed by the people through history" and denied any antithesis between it and popular impulse. "Living, vigorous judicial review . . . can be justified as something that fulfills popular desire." As the means of insuring that government will be held accountable for forbidden acts, judicial review has been legitimized by popular acquiescence, and therefore popular approval, over the course of American history, making it "the creation of the American people, as definitely as is any other institutions they have created. . . ." And, implied Black, the judicial review on which public judgment was rendered was the worst kind of all. "It was on judicial review as actually practiced, on the judicial review of *Marbury* v. *Madison*, of the *Civil Rights Cases* (1883), of dozens of cases holding Acts of Congress unconstitutional where reasonable doubt obviously existed." Democracy does not guarantee immunity to the people from the consequences of their own acts, nor is it undemocratic of them to make the decision, "revokable whenever they are willing to pay the price of revoking it," that they want the Court to exercise judicial review. Those who reason otherwise, "Thayer and the neo-Thayerians," are caught in the deepest contradiction.

They are all for the people, and for the "political process." But they are striving drastically to alter and weaken a judicial function which the people have, precisely through the political process, given the stamp of approval in the only way they could give approval to an institution in being—by leaving it alone and by providing procedural and jurisdictional facilities for its exercise as they saw it being exercised. The Thayerians are saying, in effect, "The people are foolish to have acquiesced in the courts' performance of this function. Let us save the people from themselves, by bringing about a professional and judicial understanding that this antipopular function shall be shorn of its strength." What a consequence of trust in the people! [97]

The entire line of reasoning is a curious one which reduces to the principle that what is, is democratic. Failure of the people to exercise their sovereign power to abolish or impair judicial review implies their approval; their approval provides democratic credentials. By such reasoning slavery until the Thirteenth Amendment was democratic; segregation until recently was democratic; the electoral college remains the democratic way of electing a president. Whether acquiescence and approval are the same constitutes another difficulty. The simple fact is that at no time in our history have the American people passed judgment, pro or con, on the merits of judicial review over Congress. Consent freely given, by referendum, by legislation, or by amendment is simply not the same as failure to abolish or impair.

Black argued also that policy-making by the Court is not undemocratic simply because the Court is appointed, holds life tenure, and is not responsible to the electorate in a political sense. This argument was suggested by Rostow in his brilliant article. He asserted that a democracy need not elect all the officials who exercise important authority "in the name of the voters," a statement which taken literally has little relevance because the Court does not act in the name of the voters. But the point, of course, is that a town meeting show-of-hands is not a democratic requirement for all major policy decisions. Rostow observes that the military can win or lose wars in the exercise of their discretion. But the military are responsible to an elected Commander-in-Chief, and it is not likely that Rostow would agree that in a democracy the power to decide whether war shall be waged belongs to the military. The Federal Reserve Board, as Rostow said, does have the lawful power to plunge the country into depression; and the innumerable administrative agencies and regulatory commissions, whose members are chosen in the same way as the members of the Court, although for periods of fixed tenure only, have "enormous power over matters of policy," in Black's words, "and are not subject to supervision by the political departments." The various agencies were established because of the desirability of entrusting decisions involving policy and technicality to experts who should be isolated from immediate responsibility to the electorate; and, suggested Black, this is normal democratic practice. As Rostow put the point, "The task of democracy is not to have the people vote directly on every issue, but to assure their ultimate responsibility for the acts of their representatives, elected or appointed." [98]

If Rostow's proposition is accurate, the people are responsible only because they can, at least in theory, express their wishes at the ballot box, or, in the case of decisions made by appointed officials, they can exercise control through the elected officials who oversee appointees. But is not Rostow's proposition inverted? It is not the people who are responsible for the acts of their representatives, but their representatives who are responsible to the people. The voters retain a check, directly on those whom they elect and through them indirectly on the members of the agencies. The powers and procedures of all federal agencies are established by Congress, which may also stipulate the grounds for removal of members from office and investigate the operations of the agencies. Their policies, as Alexander M. Bickel wrote, are primarily interstitial "and are reversible by legislative majorities." One may also add that the decisions of the agencies are subject to judicial review. How relevant then is the comparison of the function of the agencies to that of the Supreme Court? Its power of judicial review over Congress, the power in question, has not been vested by Congress, and the Court is not accountable to the political branches and through them to the people at the polls. In Justice Stone's celebrated dictum, the only check on the Court, for all practical purposes, is its own sense of self-restraint. The comparison made by Rostow and Black is valid only with respect to the Court's powers of statutory interpretation. As Bickel says, "In the latter aspect, judges are indeed something like administrative officials, for their decisions are also reversible by any legislative majority—and not infrequently they are reversed." [99] But the exercise of the power to hold a statute void on constitutional grounds is reversible only by constitutional amendment as in the instances of the Eleventh, Thirteenth, and Sixteenth Amendments.

Rostow's principal argument for the democratic character of judicial review depends on decisions which promote democracy. He rejected the argument advanced by Thayer, Frankfurter, and Commager to the effect that the exercise of judicial review tends to sap the political responsibility of the people and popular government. "This contention has been belied by the course of history." In any case, Rostow added, the problem in our time has changed, because there is little or no danger that the Court will again become a third chamber annulling a wide variety of regulatory legislation. But there is a danger to democracy, he contended, should the Court not arrest the slow erosion of civil liberties. Defense of the rights of Negroes or of political groups to assemble and make speeches benefits the nation. "I for one," wrote Rostow, "believe that the defense of civil rights by the courts is a force not only for democratic values but for social order." [100]

He insisted that "as a matter of experience" it was not true that a vigorous lead from the Court inhibited or weakened popular responsibility in the crucial areas of freedom and justice. The Court is a vital element in the making of policy, through precept as well as power. "The Supreme Court is, among other things, an educational body, and the Justices are inevitably teachers in a vital national seminar. The prestige of the Supreme Court as an institution is high . . . and the members of the Court speak with a powerful voice." By way of proof, Rostow offered "the immensely constructive influence" of the series of decisions bearing on the equal rights of Negroes. They "have not paralyzed or supplanted legislative and community action. They have precipitated it. They have not created bigotry. They have helped to fight it . . . and . . . have played a crucial role in leading public opinion and encouraging public action towards meeting the challenge and burden of the Negro problem as a constitutional—that is, as a moral—obligation." [101] Rostow was, of course, completely right in this most important of all examples that might be adduced. He is also right in his other example, the constructive influence of the Court in reforming state criminal procedures. Since Rostow wrote, additional decisions on Negro rights and criminal procedures have wrought even further changes that can only be described as "releasing and encouraging the dominantly democratic forces of American life." Moreover, in a series of decisions on legislative reapportionment beginning a decade after Rostow's article, the Court did as much to democratize the political process as had been accomplished by the Fifteenth and Nineteenth Amendments. One could not be further from the mark than to say that the effect has been, in Thayer's phrase, "to dwarf the political capacity of the people and to deaden its sense of moral responsibility."

On the other hand the difficulty with Rostow's analysis is that something like a black-mass version of it is equally valid and can command the preponderance of historical evidence. For example, one may say, paraphrasing Rostow in reverse, that it is true as a matter of experience that a vigorous lead from the Supreme Court inhibits or weakens popular responsibility in the areas of liberty, equality, and justice. The subject of Negro rights is indeed the best of illustrations. Bearing in mind that the Court is an institution of enormous prestige whose declaration of principles teaches and leads the nation in the making of public policy, one cannot doubt the pernicious, highly undemocratic influence of the series of decisions in which the Court crippled and voided most of the comprehensive program for protecting the civil rights of Negroes after the Civil War. These decisions paralyzed or supplanted legislative and community action, created bigotry, and played a crucial role in destroying public opinion that favored meeting the challenge of the Negro problem as a constitutional—that is, as a moral—obligation.

The process began when the Court cut the heart out of the principal clause of the Fourteenth Amendment, the privileges and immunities clause. In the *Slaughterhouse* case of 1873, the Court ruled that with few exceptions civil rights were not attributes of United States citizenship and therefore were not constitutionally protected by the privileges and immunities clause against state violation.[102] The principle of the *Slaughterhouse* case doomed federal civil rights legislation and heralded the triumph of white supremacy in American constitutional law. That principle bore first fruit in the *Cruikshank* case which grew out of the infamous Colfax Massacre. The ringleaders of a band of armed whites who slaughtered fifty-nine Negroes, having been acquitted by a local Louisiana jury on a charge of murder, were convicted in a federal court for having conspired to interfere with the free exercise of rights granted or secured by the Constitution or laws of the United States. The Supreme Court unanimously decided that the rights in question—to assemble (unless for the purpose of petitioning Congress), to bear arms, to life, to liberty, and to vote—were not federal rights and therefore depended upon the states for their protection. The Act of Congress was not voided, but its usefulness was drastically impaired and the convictions were reversed.[103] In another case of 1876, the Court struck down the section of the Civil Rights Act of 1870 by which Congress made it a federal crime for state or local election officials to refuse to receive or count the vote of persons qualified to vote under state law.[104] This decision permitted the white South to circumvent the Fifteenth Amendment by denying Negroes the right to vote on any ground other than race, that is, by poll taxes, literacy tests, understanding clauses, good character tests, and other devices which resulted in mass disfranchisement.

In 1880 the Court ruled that in the absence of official state action excluding Negroes from jury service on explicitly racial grounds, Negro defendants would have to prove deliberate discrimination and the proof would have to consist of more than the fact that there had never been Negroes on the jury lists of the country.[105] This rule made possible the systematic exclusion of Negroes from jury service in the South. In one case of 1883, a banner year for white supremacy, the Court sustained state miscegenation laws, thereby giving constitutional sanction to poisonous notions of racial purity.[106] In another case of the same year the Court reversed the convictions of a mob of twenty whites who captured four Negroes from the custody of a sheriff, beat them, and lynched one. The ruling was that the defendants had been convicted under an unconstitutional Act of Congress, the 1871 Anti-Lynching Act which made it a federal crime to conspire for the purpose of depriving anyone of the equal protection of the laws.[107] Finally, in 1883, the Court held unconstitutional the great Civil Rights Act of 1875 by which Congress had outlawed segregation or any form of racial discrimination in all public transportation facilities, hotels and inns, and theaters and other places of public amusement.[108] In 1878 the Court had held unconstitutional, as a burden on interstate commerce, a Louisiana law requiring carriers to provide equal facilities without regard to race.[109] Following this decision, nine Southern states passed laws requiring Jim Crow in local transportation facilities, and in 1896, in the notorious *Plessy* case, the Court upheld this legislation.[110] Thus Congress and the states could not prohibit racial segregation, but the states could compel it. These nineteenth-century decisions most certainly dammed up and discouraged the democratic values of American life, stunted the political and moral capacity of the people, and released and energized the most unworthy, even bigoted, forces. One might also analyze early decisions on state criminal procedures and come to similar conclusions, quite opposite to Rostow's.[111]

Later decisions, both in the field of state criminal procedures and Negro rights, in nature and effect were as Rostow described them, but they begin at about the time of the Hughes Court and gained in both breadth and impact only under the Warren Court. Meanwhile millions of Negroes suffered lives of humiliation for five or six or more decades under a Jim Crow, white supremacist Constitution, because the Court betrayed the intent of the Reconstruction Amendments, emasculating, in particular, the privileges and immunities clause of the Fourteenth Amendment, and rendered meaningless the enabling clauses in those amendments—"Congress shall have power to enforce, by appropriate legislation, the provisions of this article." And how many thousands of cases of miscarriages of justice have there been, for both Negro and white defendants in criminal cases, because the Court took half a century to begin reforming and civilizing state criminal procedures under the Fourteenth Amendment?

The historian must take the long view of the matter, recalling that the justices on circuit duty enforced the Sedition Act of 1798; that the Fugitive Slave Acts were sustained but the Missouri Compromise and Personal Liberty Laws were invalidated: that the Fourteenth Amendment was turned into a nightmare of injustice for all but corporations; that Congressional statutes to combat the evils of yellow-dog contracts, child labor, and subminimal wages were held unconstitutional; that an anti-trust act was converted into an anti-union act while great corporations were found to be engaged in merely reasonable restraints of trade; that Debs's conviction was sustained under the Espionage Act of 1917 by a unanimous Court in an opinion by Holmes and that President Harding, of all people, pardoned Debs; and so on, ad nauseam. Over the course of our history, in other words, judicial review has worked out badly, a judgment from which Charles Black sharply dissented.

Are Thayer and Commager therefore right and Rostow and Black wrong in their analyses? Not necessarily, perhaps not at all. There is a story about Lincoln cutting short the rantings of an extremist by declaring, "Mister, haven't you lived long enough to know that two men may honestly differ about a question and both be right?" Choosing between Thayer and Commager on the one side and Rostow and Black on the other, or between Justices Frankfurter and Black, is like choosing a truth only partly perceived, or, rather, only partly expressed. Rostow, for example, knew that certain Court decisions stimulated or condoned injustice, inequality, and repression: witness his trenchant discussion of "The Japanese-American Cases— A Disaster," [112] or, for that matter, his attack on the opinion of the Court in the *Dennis* case,[113] which constitutes the second half of his essay on "The Democratic Character of Judicial Review." Writing when civil liberties were "in a state of grave crisis," he sought to show that the opinion in the *Dennis* case drew strength from a premise which he thought unwarranted, "that the power of judicial review is somehow tainted, and of undemocratic character. . . ." [114] It is more likely, though, that that premise was merely an excuse for the Vinson Court to reach a desired result, sustaining the Smith Act against First Amendment objections. Judicial self-restraint and deference to the political branches, except, perhaps, in the hands of a truly gifted judge like Holmes or Frankfurter, tends to be little more than a pose for rationalizing preferred ends. The Thayer theory when put to practice has the almost inevitable effect of sustaining challenged legislation, as Charles Black has stressed. But the Black-Rostow position is no less strategic; whether calculated or not, its effect is to produce decisions of a libertarian character. Yet Black certainly made a strong and appealing case.[115]

When Rostow claimed that a "vigorous lead" from the Court did not inhibit or weaken popular responsibility in the area of civil liberties, he must have meant by "vigorous lead" a decision striking down governmental infringements. Despite the title and the thrust of the argument in his article, his position is really as guarded as was Commager's on the question of judicial review over state action. Rostow did not, for example, flatly say that judicial review has the effect of releasing and encouraging the democratic forces of American life; he said that it *could* have that effect and does "when wisely exercised." [116] Whether it has that effect or is wisely exercised is very much a matter of personal judgment, depending largely on whether one agrees with a given decision. Here is where the difficulty lies: we inevitably end up with a result-oriented, subjective jurisprudence of constitutional law, raising in turn the specter of Hand's Platonic Guardians who ought to have no place in a self-governing society.

The question whether judicial review is democratic is no "mirage," as Black declared it to be. Judicial review is a power, a means to an end. As a means it is not a neutral instrument, for it is essentially undemocratic on the theoretical grounds specified by Commager. It may be used to thwart, cripple, or dam up democratic forces as in the *Civil Rights* cases of 1883 or *Hammer* v. *Dagenhart;* [117] it may be used to rationalize corruption of the democratic process as in the *Debs,*[118] *Korematsu,*[119] or *Dennis* cases. But it may also be used to promote and kindle democratic ends on the authority of the Court, as in the *White Primary* [120] or the *School Desegregation* cases, and it may be used too to legitimate the authority of government action on behalf of democratic ends, as in recent decisions sustaining the public accommodations provisions of the Civil Rights Act of 1964.[121] Whether judicial review is democratic, then, depends largely on the results it achieves. But a result-oriented jurisprudence corrupts the judicial process, leaving far behind the idea of the rule of law enforced by judges as impersonal and objective as is humanly possible. In constitutional cases, the judge who first chooses what the outcome should be and then reasons backwards to supply a rationalization replete with rules and precedents has betrayed his calling; he has decided on the basis of prejudice or prejudgment, and has made constitutional law little more than the embodiment of his policy preferences, reflecting his subjective predilections. From the standpoint of result-oriented jurisprudence, what was wrong with the opinions of the Court in the *Civil Rights* cases, or *Plessy*, or *Lochner*,[122] or *Debs*, or *Carter Coal* [123] was not that the justices decided on the basis of predilection, or made policy, or engaged in an act of will, or legislated, or did any of the things that a realist might say was inevitable; what was wrong, rather, was that the Court's preferences were illiberal, or its policy undemocratic, or its legislation reactionary. Viewed this way, which is only a bit short of politically monstrous—and this is not Black's or Rostow's view of the matter—the Court is but a Third Chamber. As Justice Frankfurter remarked, "If the function of this Court is to be essentially no different from that of a legislature, if the considerations governing constitutional construction are to be substantially those that underlie legislation, then indeed judges should not have life tenure and they should be made directly responsible to the electorate." [124]

The results that Black and Rostow want from the Court are decisions sustaining civil liberties. Black argued convincingly that constitutional prohibitions, such as those of the Bill of Rights, must be construed "with extreme breadth," and be enforced, if necessary, by the exercise of the power to hold abridgments unconstitutional. On balance that argument has compelling merits that are not downed by the contentions of Thayer and Commager. Taking the long view again, an historian may confidently assert that there has never been a single case of judicial review in favor of the Bill of Rights hurtful in any way to the democratic process, popular responsibility, or the moral sense of the community. The cases proving that judicial review has stunted the growth of the people or had undemocratic effects are those in which the Court checked statutory efforts, federal and state, to defend minorities or the underprivileged, but never those in which the Court has defended against legislatures, minorities, or the underprivileged or the unpopular.

Commager's *Majority Rule and Minority Rights* was written, in part, to dispel the widespread misunderstanding of Frankfurter's opinions in the *Flag Salute* cases. Yet, from a pragmatic standpoint, few cases better serve the Black-Rostow position, because few decisions of the Court more clearly and directly had the effect of deadening the sense of moral responsibility of the American people than *Gobitis*. The issue in that case was whether a local school board could compel a flag-salute from Jehovah's Witnesses, to them an obnoxious act of blasphemy which violated their consciences and forced them to bear false witness to their religion. J. Skelly Wright, one of our finest federal judges, has written:

But without guidance from the Supreme Court, the people misread their responsibilities. From the standpoint of religious freedom and respect for human rights, the effect of that Supreme Court decision in the First Flag Salute case was disastrous. School board after school board adopted new requirements commanding the flag salute, on pain of expulsion or other penalties. And often the school boards would quote the very words of the Supreme Court opinion in justification of their action. In many cases the salute to the flag was used simply as a device to expel the unpopular Jehovah's Witnesses. The words of the Supreme Court, that the protection of freedom could best be left the responsibility of local authorities, were perverted and used as an excuse for what was in effect religious persecution by the local school boards. At the same time, and worse than the official action against the Jehovah's Witnesses, was the nation-wide wave of mob violence, attempts in the name of patriotism and support for the Supreme Court opinion.[125]

Within three years the Court reversed itself, striking down as unconstitutional the flag-salute requirement when imposed against religious conscience. The Court acted on behalf of the freedom of a very small, unpopular minority not to salute the flag during time of war, yet the opinion in the *Second Flag Salute* case was honored by the nation's school boards and persecution of the Witnesses petered out.

One may validly extend the Black-Rostow position by arguing, therefore, that the failure of the Court to strike down abridgments of the Bill of Rights as unconstitutional will have the very effect which Thayer and Commager feared from judicial review. Rostow has correctly said that while Learned Hand may have been right in observing that no court can save a society bent on ruin, American society is not bent on ruin. Ruin, however, might come in imperceptible stages by the gradual acceptance of one immoral solution after another with Supreme Court endorsement. The treatment of the Japanese-Americans during World War II, as Rostow said, became the "precedent for the proposal that concentration camps be established for citizens suspected of believing in revolutionary ideas." [126] As Justice Jackson, dissenting in the *Korematsu* case, said of the program to deport and detain citizens of Japanese descent, "a judicial construction of the due process clause that will sustain this order is a far more subtle blow to liberty than the promulgation of the order itself." A military command, an executive order, even an act of Congress has a temporal life; but, remarked Jackson, "once a judicial opinion rationalizes such an order to show that it conforms to the Constitution, or rather rationalizes the Constitution to show that the Constitution sanctions such an order, the Court for all time has validated the principle of racial discrimination in criminal procedure and of transplanting American citizens. The principle then lies about like a loaded weapon ready for the hand of any authority that can bring forward a plausible claim of an urgent need." [127]

The argument applies with equal force to any repressive statute which has come before the Court and has received its approval as constitutional. When the Court legitimizes a Smith Act or a Taft-Hartley Non-Communist Affidavit or a Subversive Activities Control Act, it gives constitutional sanction to much that is pernicious or repressive.[128] The Court may offer highly technical reasons for its decisions, but the public, which has little understanding and less patience with constitutional niceties, assumes that the Court has also given its seal of approval to the wisdom or policy of the legislation. Decisions that sustain legislation tend to end further debate; the remedial channels for public reconsideration may remain open, but those who have had their "day in court" no longer have the public's ear.

By contrast, when the Court holds a Congressional measure unconstitutional, public controversy is stimulated by fresh debate on the merits of the controverted legislation as well as on the merits of the Court's opinion. It enters into the people's "education in the abandonment of foolish legislation" by encouraging, rather than discouraging "the people's active and intelligent interest in these matters"—contrary to Commager's assertions.[129] Invalidation on constitutional grounds is not always conclusive. Although the political branches will not override the Court by ignoring its constitutional objections, legislation can often be redrawn to achieve substantially the same end by constitutional means. The NIRA was succeeded in part by the Guffey-Snyder Bituminous Coal Act, which was succeeded in turn by the Wagner Act. The Frazier-Lemke Farm Mortgage Moratorium Act, upon being invalidated, was also reenacted in a form that won Court approval, as was the Agricultural Adjustment Act. Had the Smith Act been invalidated it could have been rewritten to protect advocacy of violent overthrow that was doctrinal in character, aimed at the remote future, and devoid of incitement to specific criminal action. Nor is there any reason why Congressional enactments outlawing subversive activities cannot be rewritten to protect all the procedural rights of accused persons. In short, validation by the Court of legislation adversely affecting civil liberties ends debate without stimulating the democratic process; judicial review can promote the debate and the process.

To argue that experience will teach the people to correct their mistakes of policy by remedial legislation, without a lead from the Court, ignores the high probability that they cannot learn in time to prevent irremediable injustice or damage. Pardoning victims of the Sedition Act could not reestablish lost presses or restore time spent in prison, just as the American-Japanese Evacuation Claims Act of 1948, which provided reparations for property losses, could not restore broken homes or the time spent behind barbed wire enclosures. The American people often dislike Court decisions that protect obnoxious or despised members of society, but the people respect appeals to their conscience or idealism. Americans comply, even if complainingly, with decisions against the constitutionality of legislation that can be explained by the Court to violate the Bill of Rights or any part of the Constitution protecting some historic principle of liberty, justice, or equality. The people seem to regard the Court as their conscience. Its restraining power, as Cardozo noted, holds "the standard aloft and visible to those who must run the race and keep the faith." [130]

It should be abundantly evident by now that the question whether judicial review is democratic has no one-sided answer that is the truth, the whole truth, and nothing but. What makes the question important is its capacity to engage the searching thought of men of deep commitment to our constitutional democracy, whose reasoned judgments, however diverse, serve to educate us all. If there must be an answer, the most satisfying is the most equivocal or gingerly balanced, that of the mugwump caught in the classic stance with his mug on one side of the fence and his wump on the other. Alexander M. Bickel seems to have the best of both sides and thus the best of the argument. The path of wisdom in this instance is the pragmatic one. Bickel does not admit judicial review to the democratic pantheon, but keeps the door wide open. Acknowledging that nothing "can alter the essential reality that judicial review is a deviant institution in the American democracy," Bickel argues that while "full consistency" with democratic politics cannot be established, judicial review can achieve "some measure of consonance . . . a tolerable accommodation with the theory and practice of democracy." [131]

NOTES

[1] Spaight to Iredell, August 12, 1787, in G. J. McRee, *Life and Correspondence of James Iredell* (New York, 1858), II, 168.

[2] Frankfurter, "A Note on Advisory Opinions," *Harvard Law Review*, XXXVI (1924), 1003, note 4.

[3] Charles A. Beard, *The Supreme Court and the Constitution*, Spectrum edition (Englewood Cliffs, N.J., 1962), with an introduction by Alan F. Westin. Beard's introduction to the 1938 edition is at pp. 35–36; the quotation from Westin is at p. 2.

[4] *Reorganization of the Federal Judiciary.* Hearings before the Committee on the Judiciary, United States Senate, 75th Cong., 1st Session, on S. 1392, Part 2, March 17 to 20, 1937, p. 184.

[5] Beard, *Supreme Court and Constitution*, Spectrum edition, pp. 95, 96, and 117.

[6] Edward S. Corwin, book review in *American Political Science Review*, VII (May 1913), 330.

[7] Corwin, *The Doctrine of Judicial Review* (Princeton, 1914), p. 10.

[8] *Reorganization of the Federal Judiciary*, pp. 175, 176, 172.

[9] *Government by Judiciary* (New York, 1932), 2 vols.

[10] *Politics and the Constitution in the History of the United States* (Chicago, 1953), 2 vols.

[11] *Court over Constitution: A Study of Judicial Review as an Instrument of Popular Government* (Princeton, 1938).

[12] Max Farrand, ed., *The Records of the Federal Convention* (New Haven, 1911), II, 93. Beard neither quoted nor misused this statement. Among those who did were Farrand, *The Framing of the Constitution* (New Haven, 1913), pp. 156–157; Charles Warren, *The Making of the Constitution* (Boston, 1928), pp. 333–334; and Corwin, *Doctrine of Judicial Review*, p. 43. Corwin did not repeat the error in his *Court over Constitution*, p. 32.

[13] Farrand, ed., *Records of the Federal Convention*, II, 430. What Madison meant by "cases of a Judiciary Nature" is not clear, but he seems to have meant cases involving the special province or jurisdiction of the Supreme Court. *Marbury* v. *Madison*, which turned on the power of the Court to issue a writ of mandamus in a case of original jurisdiction, was a case of "a Judiciary Nature."

[14] "Remarks on Mr. Jefferson's Draft of a Constitution," October 1788, in Gaillard Hunt, ed., *The Writings of James Madison* (New York, 1900–10), 9 vols., V, 294.

[15] *The Debates and Proceedings of the Congress of the United States* [*Annals of Congress*], comp. by Joseph Gales (Washington, 1834), 1st Cong., 1st Session, I, 439.

[16] *Ibid.*, I, 399.

[17] Beard, *Supreme Court and Constitution*, p. 55.

[18] Five versions of Hamilton's speech of presentation and his "Plan of Government," all dated June 18, 1787, are in *The Papers of Alexander Hamilton*, Harold C. Syrett and Jacob E. Cooke, eds. (New York, 1962), IV, 178–211.

[19] The three "Letters of Brutus" on judicial review are reprinted in the Appendix to Corwin's *Court over Constitution*, pp. 231–262.

[20] Beard combed the state ratifying convention debates and found only five statements endorsing judicial review over Congress. In addition to those by Marshall and Ellsworth, he quoted Luther Martin and William Grayson, who opposed ratification, and Edmund Pendleton. In the newspaper and pamphlet literature he found only Hamilton's statement in *Federalist* #78. Beard, *Supreme Court and Constitution*, pp. 80–83.

[21] McLaughlin, *A Constitutional History of the United States*, p. 310.

[22] *Doctrine of Judicial Review*, pp. 2 and 17.

[23] In addition to Warren's *Making of the Constitution*, p. 332, see his *Congress, the Constitution, and the Supreme Court* (Boston, 1925), pp. 41–57, 64–74, and 91–93. Haines's *The American Doctrine of Judicial Supremacy* (New York, 1914) is discussed below.

[24] David John Mays, *Edmund Pendleton* (Cambridge, 1952), II, 169–172.

[25] Haines, *American Doctrine*, p. 73.

[26] James, *Memories and Studies*, quoted by Jerome Frank, *Fate and Freedom*, rev. ed. (Boston, 1953), p. 181.

[27] *Rutgers* v. *Waddington*, 1784, Mayor's Court of New York City, opinion by James Duane, Mayor and Chief Judge, reprinted in entirety by Julius Goebel, Jr., ed., *The Law Practice of Alexander Hamilton: Documents and Commentary* (New York, 1964), I, chap. 3; the quotation is at p. 415.

[28] See Boudin, *Government by Judiciary*, I, 536–555; Crosskey, *Politics and the Constitution*, II, 948–952; and Haines, *American Doctrine*, pp. 80–83.

[29] Crosskey, *Politics and the Constitution*, II, 965–968; Haines, *American Doctrine*, pp. 88–92; Boudin, *Government by Judiciary*, I, 58–62.

[30] Crosskey, *Politics and the Constitution*, II, 965–968; Boudin, *Government by Judiciary*, I, 58–62; Haines, *American Doctrine*, pp. 85–88.

[31] *Commonwealth v. Caton*, 4 Call's Virginia Reports 5 (1782), discussed in Mays, *Edmund Pendleton*, I, 196–201 and 387, note 65; Crosskey, *Politics and the Constitution*, II, 952–960; Haines, *American Doctrine*, pp. 83–85.

[32] Crosskey, *Politics and the Constitution*, II, 968–970.

[33] *Bayard v. Singleton*, 1 Martin (N.C.) 42 (1787), discussed in Haines, *American Doctrine*, pp. 92–94; Crosskey, *Politics and the Constitution*, II, 971–973; and Boudin, *Government by Judiciary*, I, 63–66.

[34] *Court over Constitution*, p. 25. Henry M. Hart, Jr., "Professor Crosskey and Judicial Review," *Harvard Law Review*, LXVII (June 1954), 1463, disputes Crosskey's contention that the precedents emerged in cases of legislative invasion of judicial prerogatives. His article, *ibid.*, pp. 1456–1486, is a running critique, generally sound but overstated, on the point that Crosskey's evidence is suspect. He believes that the Constitutional Convention "repeatedly and with complete consistency" showed its understanding that the Court should have the power of judicial review over Congress, thus indicating that his own use of the evidence is also suspect. On the matter of the precedents Hart counts *Trevett* v. *Weeden* among the "square holdings" in favor of judicial review, despite the denial by the judges in that case.

[35] See Warren, *Congress, Court, and Constitution*, pp. 91–93.

[36] *Ibid.*, pp. 97–127; the quotation is at p. 99.

[37] See Warren, *The Supreme Court in United States History* (Boston, 1923), I, 65–84, 145–149.

[38] *Cooper* v. *Telfair*, 4 Dallas 14, 16 (1800).

[39] Charles L. Black, *The People and the Court: Judicial Review in a Democracy* (New York, 1960), p. 178.

[40] Ex parte McCardle, 7 Wallace 700 (1869), discussed in Warren, *The Supreme Court*, III, 187–210.

[41] *Hepburn* v. *Griswold*, 8 Wallace 603 (1870); *De Witt* v. *U.S.*, 9 Wallace 41 (1870); and *Collector* v. *Day*, 11 Wallace 113 (1871).

[42] Quoted in James Bradley Thayer, "The Origin and Scope of the American Doctrine of Constitutional Law," *Harvard Law Review*, VII (October 1893), 152.

[43] Frankfurter, "A Note on Advisory Opinions," *Harvard Law Review*, XXXVII (1924), 1004.

[44] Commager's book was first published in New York in 1943 and was republished in 1961; see Frankfurter's opinion in *A.F. of L.* v. *American Sash and Door Co.*, 335 U.S. 538, 555 note 16 (1949).

[45] Quoted in Commager, *Majority Rule*, pp. 34, 38, and by Frankfurter, *A.F. of L.* v. *American Sash and Door Co.*, 335 U.S. 538, 555 (1949).

[46] Quoted in Robert H. Jackson, *The Struggle for Judicial Supremacy* (New York, 1941), pp. 31–32.

[47] *Ibid.*, pp. viii–ix, 195. See also Jackson's *The Supreme Court in the American System of Government* (Cambridge, 1958), p. 79.

[48] Frankfurter, "Supreme Court, United States," *Encyclopaedia of Social Sciences* (New York, 1934), XIV, 474, 479, 480; reprinted in slightly revised form in Sydney D. Bailey, *Aspects of American Government* (London, 1950), pp. 33, 43, 45.

[49] See *Minersville School District* v. *Gobitis*, 310 U.S. 586, 600 (1940); *West*

Virginia State Board of Education v. *Barnette*, 319 U.S. 624, 650, 666 (1943); and *A.F. of L.* v. *American Sash and Door Co.*, 335 U.S. 538, 555 (1949).

[50] *Majority Rule*, p. 41. This paragraph is drawn from pp. 40–56 which were reprinted in substantially the same form in Commager's article, "Judicial Review and Democracy," *Virginia Quarterly Review*, XIX (Summer 1943), 417–428.

[51] *Majority Rule*, pp. 59–63, 80–83. The quotations are at pp. 60 and 82.

[52] *Ibid.*, pp. 66, 67.

[53] *Ibid.*, p. 27.

[54] *Ibid.*

[55] Jefferson to Madison, March 15, 1789, in *The Papers of Thomas Jefferson*, Julian P. Boyd, ed. (Princeton, 1959), XIV, 659, 661; Jefferson to Madison, December 20, 1787, in *ibid.*, XII, 440.

[56] *Majority Rule*, p. 16.

[57] *U.S.* v. *Carolene Products Co.*, 304 U.S. 144, 152 note 4 (1938).

[58] *Majority Rule*, pp. 71–77, quoting Frankfurter, "Can the Supreme Court Guarantee Toleration?," *Law and Politics, Occasional Papers of Felix Frankfurter*, Archibald MacLeish and E. F. Pritchard, Jr., eds. (New York, 1939); Frankfurter in *Minersville School District* v. *Gobitis*, 310 U.S. 586, 600 (1940); and James Bradley Thayer, *John Marshall* (Boston, 1901), p. 105.

[59] Frank, "Review and Basic Liberties," in Edmond Cahn, ed., *Supreme Court and Supreme Law* (Bloomington, Ind., 1954), p. 114. Frank's study, *ibid.*, pp. 109–139, made a decade after Commager's, bore out the latter's findings on the value of judicial review over Congress. Studying all cases of invalidation, Frank concluded that one test showed "not a single case of real consequence in which, in 160 years, judicial review has buttressed liberty." "If the test of the value of judicial review to the preservation of basic liberties were to be rested on consideration of actual invalidations, the balance is against judicial review." "At best, I repeat, judicial review is, so far as civil liberty is concerned, a near failure." ". . . the actual overt exercise of judicial review of acts of Congress has been of almost negligible good to civil liberties, and has probably harmed those liberties more than it has helped them." *Ibid.*, pp. 111, 112, 129, and 131. The best study of the Supreme Court for the period from 1937 to the present is Alfred H. Kelly and Winfred A. Harbison, *The American Constitution: Its Origins and Development*, 3rd ed. (New York, 1963), pp. 755–986.

[60] *Majority Rule*, p. 66.

[61] 319 U.S. 463 (1943).

[62] *U.S.* v. *Lovett, Watson, and Dodd*, 328 U.S. 303 (1946).

[63] 350 U.S. 11 (1955).

[64] 354 U.S. 1 (1957).

[65] *Kinsella* v. *U.S.*, 301 U.S. 234 (1960); *Grisham* v. *Hagan*, 301 U.S. 278 (1960); and, *McElroy* v. *U.S.*, 301 U.S. 281 (1960).

[66] 356 U.S. 86 (1958).

[67] 372 U.S. 144 (1963).

[68] 377 U.S. 163 (1964).

[69] 378 U.S. 500 (1964).

[70] 85 S. Ct. 1707 (1965).

[71] 85 S. Ct. 1493 (1965). But in *Aptheker* v. *Secretary of State*, decided a year earlier, there is a fuzzy passage implying that one ground of decision was that the act of Congress infringed the freedom of association protected by the First Amendment, 378 U.S. 500, 507.

[72] *Albertson* v. *Subversive Activities Control Board*, 86 S. Ct. 194 (1965).

[73] *Brown* v. *Board of Education*, 354 U.S. 234 (1954); *Cooper* v. *Aaron*, 358 U.S. 1 (1958); *Burton* v. *Wilmington Parking Authority*, 365 U.S. 715 (1961); *Peterson* v. *City of Greenville*, 373 U.S. 244 (1963); *Watson* v. *Memphis*, 373 U.S. 526 (1963); *Goss* v. *Board of Education*, 373 U.S. 683 (1963); *Griffin* v. *County School Board*, 377 U.S. 218 (1964); *Robinson* v. *Florida*, 378 U.S. 153 (1964); *Bell* v. *Maryland*, 378 U.S. 226 (1964); *McLaughlin* v. *Florida*, 379 U.S. 184 (1965); *Hamm* v. *City of Rock Hill*, 85 S. Ct. 384 (1965); *Bradley* v. *School Board of Richmond*, 86 S. Ct. 224 (1965); *S. Car.* v. *Katzenbach*, 86 S. Ct. 803 (1966); *Brown* v. *La.*, 86 S. Ct. 719 (1966); *Harper* v. *Va. State Board of Elections*, 86 S. Ct. 1079 (1966).

[74] *Baker* v. *Carr*, 369 U.S. 186 (1962); *Gray* v. *Sanders*, 372 U.S. 379 (1963); *Westbury* v. *Sanders*, 376 U.S. 1 (1964); *Reynolds* v. *Sims and other Reapportionment Cases*, 377 U.S. 533, 633, 656, 678, 695, 713 (1964).

[75] *Burstyn* v. *Wilson*, 343 U.S. 495 (1952); *Butler* v. *Michigan*, 352 U.S. 380 (1957); *Kingsley Pictures Corp.* v. *Regents*, 360 U.S. 684 (1959); *Smith* v. *California*, 361 U.S. 147 (1959); *Bantam Books, Inc.* v. *Sullivan*, 372 U.S. 58 (1963); *New York Times Co.* v. *Sullivan*, 376 U.S. 254 (1964); *Jacobellis* v. *Ohio*, 378 U.S. 184 (1964); *A Quantity of Books* v. *Kansas*, 378 U.S. 205 (1964); *Freedman* v. *Maryland*, 85 S. Ct. 734 (1965); The *Fanny Hill* Case, 86 S. Ct. 975 (1966), cf. *Ginzburg* v. *U.S.*, 86 S. Ct. 969 (1966); *DeGregory* v. *N.H.*, 86 S. Ct. 1148 (1966); *Elfbrandt* v. *Russell*, 86 S. Ct. 1238 (1966).

[76] *Engle* v. *Vitale*, 370 U.S. 421 (1962); *School District of Abington* v. *Schempp*, 374 U.S. 203 (1963); *Sherbert* v. *Viner*, 374 U.S. 398 (1963); *U.S.* v. *Seeger*, 380 U.S. 163 (1965).

[77] *Mapp* v. *Ohio*, 367 U.S. 643 (1961); *Gideon* v. *Wainwright*, 372 U.S. 335 (1963); *Stoner* v. *California*, 376 U.S. 483 (1964); *Malloy* v. *Hogan*, 378 U.S. 1 (1964); *Murphy* v. *Waterfront Commission of N.Y.*, 378 U.S. 52 (1964); *Escobedo* v. *Illinois*, 378 U.S. 478 (1964); *Stanford* v. *Texas*, 379 U.S. 476 (1965); *Pointer* v. *Texas*, 85 S. Ct. 1065 (1965); *Harris* v. *U.S.*, 86 S. Ct. 352 (1965).

[78] *A.F. of L.* v. *American Sash and Door Co.*, 335 U.S. 538, 555–556 (1949).

[79] Learned Hand, *The Bill of Rights* (Cambridge, 1958), pp. 42, 55, 68–69, and 73.

[80] *Majority Rule*, pp. 3, 4, 5, 8, 16, 60, 67, 74, 77, 82–83.

[81] *The People and the Court*, p. 172.

[82] *Harvard Law Review*, LXVI (December 1952), pp. 193–224.

[83] *The People and the Court*, pp. 167–168, 209.

[84] Beth, *Politics, the Constitution, and the Supreme Court* (Evanston, Ill., 1962), p. 82.

[85] Warren, *Supreme Court in United States History*, I, 374–383.

[86] *Time Magazine*, October 15, 1965, p. 67.

[87] Ex parte Merryman, 17 Federal Cases 145 (1861), #9487, discussed in David M. Silver, *Lincoln's Supreme Court* (Urbana, Ill., 1957), pp. 28–36.

[88] *Swift and Co.* v. *U.S.*, 196 U.S. 375 (1905).

[89] *Strauder* v. *West Va.*, 100 U.S. 303 (1880).

[90] A survey of 16,000 high school principals early in 1965 revealed that about one-fourth of the nation's high schools were "continuing to hold precisely the kind of classroom religious observance the court found unconstitutional." *Boston Sunday Globe*, October 17, 1965, A-39. See *Engle* v. *Vitale*, 370 U.S. 421 (1962) and *School District* v. *Schempp*, 374 U.S. 203 (1963).

[91] See Walter F. Murphy, "Lower Court Checks on Supreme Court Power," *American Political Science Review*, LIII (December 1959), 1017–1031.

[92] See John P. Roche, "Judicial Self-Restraint," *American Political Science Review*, XLIX (September 1955), 762–772; Jackson, *Supreme Court*, pp. 9–13, 23–26.

[93] *The People and the Court*, pp. 168–169, 184–187, 209. For the phrase, "the least dangerous branch," see note 99 below.

[94] *Ibid.*, p. 165.

[95] *Ibid.*, pp. 173–174.

[96] Corwin, *The Twilight of the Supreme Court* (New Haven, 1934), p. 117.

[97] *The People and the Court*, pp. 117, 178, 209–211.

[98] *Ibid.*, p. 180; Rostow, "The Democratic Character of Judicial Review," *Harvard Law Review*, LXVI, 197.

[99] Bickel, *The Least Dangerous Branch: the Supreme Court at the Bar of Politics* (Indianapolis, 1962), p. 20.

[100] Rostow, "Democratic Character of Judicial Review," pp. 201, 207.

[101] *Ibid.*, p. 208.

[102] *Slaughterhouse Case*, 16 Wallace 36 (1873).

[103] *U.S. v. Cruikshank*, 92 U.S. 542 (1876).

[104] *U.S. v. Reece*, 92 U.S. 214 (1876).

[105] *Virginia v. Rives*, 100 U.S. 313 (1880).

[106] *Pace v. Alabama*, 106 U.S. 583 (1883).

[107] *U.S. v. Harris*, 106 U.S. 629 (1883).

[108] *Civil Rights Cases*, 109 U.S. 3 (1883).

[109] *Hall v. DeCuir*, 95 U.S. 485 (1878).

[110] *Plessy v. Ferguson*, 163 U.S. 537 (1896).

[111] See Stanley Morrison, "Does the Fourteenth Amendment Incorporate the Bill of Rights? The Judicial Interpretation," *Stanford Law Review*, II (December 1949), 140–173 and cases there cited.

[112] *Yale Law Journal*, LIV (1945), 489, reprinted in Rostow's *The Sovereign Prerogative: the Supreme Court and the Quest for Law* (New Haven, 1962), pp. 193–266.

[113] *Dennis v. U.S.*, 341 U.S. 494 (1951).

[114] "Democratic Character of Judicial Review," p. 223.

[115] *The People and the Court*, chap. 4.

[116] "Democratic Character of Judicial Review," p. 210.

[117] 247 U.S. 251 (1918).

[118] *Debs v. U.S.*, 249 U.S. 211 (1919).

[119] *Korematsu v. U.S.*, 323 U.S. 214 (1944).

[120] *Smith v. Allwright*, 321 U.S. 649 (1944).

[121] *Heart of Atlanta Motel, Inc. v. U.S.*, 379 U.S. 241 (1965); *Katzenbach v. McClung*, 379 U.S. 294 (1965).

[122] *Lochner v. N.Y.*, 198 U.S. 45 (1905).

[123] *Carter v. Carter Coal Co.*, 298 U.S. 238 (1936).

[124] *West Virginia State Board of Education v. Barnette*, 319 U.S. 624, 653 (1943).

[125] J. Skelly Wright, "The Role of the Courts: Conscience of a Sovereign People," *The Reporter Magazine*, XXIX (September 26, 1963), 28. See also the outstanding study by David R. Manwaring, *Render unto Caesar: The Flag-Salute Controversy* (Chicago, 1962).

[126] "Democratic Character of Judicial Review," p. 207. Rostow referred to Title II, the "Emergency Detention" provisions of the Internal Security Act of 1950, which authorizes the President to proclaim the existence of an "Internal Security Emergency" and to order the arrest and detention of all persons "as to whom there is reasonable ground to believe . . . probably will engage in,

or probably will conspire with others to engage in, acts of espionage or of sabotage." 64 *Stat.* 987 (1950), Secs. 102–103. In the event that Title II becomes operative, the Government has six World War II camps in a state of readiness to serve as prisons, *New York Times,* December 27, 1955.

[127] *Korematsu* v. *U.S.,* 323 U.S. 214 (1944).

[128] *American Communications Assoc.* v. *Douds,* 339 U.S. 94 (1950); *Dennis* v. *U.S.,* 341 U.S. 494 (1951); and *Communist Party* v. *Subversive Activities Control Board,* 367 U.S. 1 (1961).

[129] *Majority Rule,* p. 75.

[130] Benjamin N. Cardozo, *The Nature of the Judicial Process* (New Haven, 1921), p. 93.

[131] Bickel, *Least Dangerous Branch,* pp. 27–28; see also pp. 235–239.

THE FOURTEENTH
AMENDMENT AND
THE BILL OF RIGHTS

O N July 1, 1949, Antonio Rochin was in bed with his common-law wife when three deputy sheriffs of Los Angeles County unlawfully broke into his home and forced open the door of his bedroom. The officers were acting on a tip that Rochin was pushing dope. Before they could seize some capsules that were on his nightstand, Rochin swallowed them in an effort to get rid of the evidence. The officers pummeled him in the stomach and jumped on him, hoping that he would throw up the capsules. Force failing, they handcuffed him and rushed him to a hospital where, against his violent protests, a physician, acting on the officers' instructions, pumped an emetic solution through a tube into Rochin's stomach. In the vomited matter were two capsules containing morphine. With that evidence the state convicted Rochin. Losing his appeals in the California courts, Rochin tried the court of last resort.

In 1952 the Supreme Court unanimously reversed the conviction,[1] but the justices divided significantly on the grounds of decision. The majority took the position that the state had violated Rochin's Fourteenth Amendment right to due process of law. Due process, said Justice Frankfurter, however "indefinite and vague," outlawed "conduct that shocks the conscience." This case showed conduct "too close to the rack and the screw." The states in their prosecutions must not, at the risk of violating due process, offend the "sense of justice" or of "fair play." Due process enjoined a respect for the "decencies of civilized conduct."

In separate opinions, Justice Black and Douglas concurred in the judgment but stridently repudiated Frankfurter's reasoning as highly subjective. His "nebulous" standards of due process, they believed, vested the Court with unlimited discretion to roam at large, drawing upon undefinable notions of justice or decency or fairness. With such standards, judges might play on the "accordion" qualities of due process, expanding or constricting personal liberties at will. The only true and safe course lay in obedience to the specific guarantees of the Bill of Rights, thus making the rule turn on the Constitution rather than on the "idiosyncrasies of the judges who sit here." The judgment of the Court in this case should have been based, said Black, on the clear command of the Fifth Amendment that no person in a criminal case should be compelled to be a witness against himself. Forcibly taking evidence from Rochin by stomach pump compelled him to incriminate himself as if he had been coerced to confess his guilt. Black would have decided the case, he declared, on the grounds explained in his dissenting opinion in *Adamson* v. *California*,[2] decided in 1947.

The division in the *Rochin* case was, in fact, a dramatic reflection of a quarrel that had erupted in the *Adamson* case. The principal issue in *Adamson* was whether the self-incrimination clause of the Fifth Amendment applied in state as well as federal proceedings. Speaking for the majority, Justice Reed tersely ruled that it did not. In an elaborate historical exposition of the legislative history of the Fourteenth Amendment, Black, dissenting, concluded that one of the chief objects of its first section, "separately, and as a whole . . . was to make the Bill of Rights applicable to the states." That section stipulates: "No state shall make or enforce any law which shall abridge the privileges or immunities of citizens of the United States; nor shall any State deprive any person of life, liberty, or property, without due process of law; nor deny to any person within its jurisdiction the equal protection of the laws."

Frankfurter, in a separate opinion concurring with the majority, addressed himself to Black's dissenting opinion. He denied that the Fourteenth Amendment was a shorthand summary of the first eight amendments (the Bill of Rights) and that the due process clause "incorporated" those eight amendments as restrictions upon state powers —that clause he construed as he did later in the *Rochin* case. In a remarkably anti-historical passage intended to dismiss as irrelevant Black's legislative history, Frankfurter claimed that the original meaning of the amendment was not to be found in the remarks of its proponents, because what was submitted for adoption was their proposal, not their remarks. More effectively, Frankfurter suggested that if the Fourteenth Amendment incorporated the Bill of Rights, the many states that lacked indictment by grand jury in felony cases or trial by jury in civil cases involving less than twenty dollars would have to revise their procedures. If, on the other hand, Black intended merely a "selective incorporation" of the Bill of Rights into the Fourteenth Amendment, he had provided no formula other than "a merely subjective test" for determining which rights were in and which were out.

The due process clause of the Fourteenth Amendment, Frankfurter noted, having been copied from the identical clause of the Fifth Amendment, could not mean one thing in the latter and another in the former amendment. Indeed, the Fifth Amendment itself included a variety of guarantees in federal proceedings in addition to due process of law, among them indictment by grand jury, freedom from compulsory self-incrimination, and the ban on double jeopardy. If the due process clause incorporated the first eight amendments of which it was a part, it incorporated the other clauses of the Fifth Amendment as well. In that event, either those clauses and the rest of the amendments were redundant, or the due process clause, if signifying all the rest, was meaningless or superfluous. But the framers of the Bill of Rights, Frankfurter concluded, had used neither redundant nor meaningless language. The due process clause, far from spaciously summarizing the other provisions of the Bill of Rights, referred to "those canons of decency and fairness which express the notions of justice of English-speaking peoples even toward those charged with the most heinous offenses." Due process had its own "historic meaning," said Frankfurter, though he did not specify the meaning or the canons of fairness.

Contrary to Frankfurter, the history of due process shows that it did mean trial by jury and many of the other traditional rights of accused persons that were specified separately in the Bill of Rights. Its framers were in many respects careless, even haphazard, draftsmen. They enumerated particular rights associated with due process and then added the due process clause itself, probably as a rhetorical flourish, a reinforced guarantee, and a genuflection toward traditional usage going back to medieval reenactments of Magna Carta. Frankfurter attributed to the framers a far greater precision than they exercised. He finally contented himself with the thought that the standards of justice were not "prescriptions in a pharmacopeia," nor were they based upon the "idiosyncrasies of a merely personal judgment."

Black, joined by Douglas, returned the accusation of subjectivity. The prescriptions in his pharmacopeia consisted of the specific guarantees of the Bill of Rights which the Fourteenth Amendment, he insisted, made applicable to the states. His reading of history supplied him with an arsenal of evidence in support of his fixed position, and he supplemented his historical exposition with a thirty-one-page appendix consisting mainly of extracts from the debates of the Congress that framed the Fourteenth Amendment.

Justices Murphy and Rutledge, who also dissented, expressed their agreement that the Bill of Rights should be carried over intact into the Fourteenth Amendment. But Murphy and Rutledge would have gone even further. They observed that some state action might fall so short of conforming to fundamental standards of procedure as to require constitutional condemnation on due process grounds "despite the absence of a specific provision in the Bill of Rights."

Whether the Bill of Rights applied to the states, restricting their powers as it did those of the national government, was a question that could arise only because of the existence of the Fourteenth Amendment. Before its ratification in 1868, there was nothing in the Constitution of the United States that could prevent a state from imprisoning religious heretics or political dissenters, or from abolishing trial by jury, or from torturing a suspect to force his confession of guilt. Although the original Constitution contained some libertarian guarantees—a tight definition of treason, a provision for jury trial in criminal cases and for the writ of habeas corpus, and a ban on ex post facto laws and bills of attainder—the failure to include a comprehensive catalog of rights (more properly, of restraints on the national government) almost resulted in rejection by the states of the Philadelphia Convention's handiwork. Massachusetts, the sixth state to ratify, recommended amendments to the Constitution, and every state convention thereafter followed the same course, obligating the First Congress to frame and submit to the states amendments which in due course became the Bill of Rights. Those amendments were clearly intended to appease popular fears by restricting the powers of the new national government. They were not intended to apply to the states.

Madison, who framed the amendments, had included one providing that "no State shall violate the equal rights of conscience, of the freedom of the press, or the trial by jury in criminal cases." He argued that this provision was "of equal, if not greater importance" than the prohibitions on state power imposed in Article I, Section 10. Although the House passed his amendment after adding a free speech clause, the Senate, yielding to the argument that there were already too many prohibitions on state powers, defeated it. History, therefore, was on the side of the Supreme Court when in 1833 Chief Justice Marshall, speaking for a unanimous bench, held that "the fifth amendment must be understood as restraining the power of the general government, not as applicable to the States." [3] He added, with equal validity, that the other amendments composing the Bill of Rights were equally inapplicable to the states. Thus, there was a double standard in the United States. The first eight amendments enjoined the national government to respect enumerated procedures and to refrain from enacting certain laws, but left the states free to do as they wished in relation to the same matters. State constitutions and common-law practices, rather than the United States Constitution, were the sources of any restraints on the states. The point of Black's argument in the *Adamson* case was that the first section of the

67

Fourteenth Amendment transformed that situation by embracing the Bill of Rights, thereby nationalizing its operation: what the United States could not do, the individual states could not do. This revolution in the federal system had been achieved "separately, and as a whole" by the three prohibitory clauses—privileges and immunities, due process, and equal protection—of the first section.

In 1949, two years after the *Adamson* case, Charles Fairman, then Professor of Law at Stanford University, published a lengthy article, "Does the Fourteenth Amendment Incorporate the Bill of Rights? The Original Understanding." [4] Fairman reviewed the same history that Black had traversed and came to the conclusion that the record "overwhelmingly" refuted Black's incorporation thesis. In addressing himself to the immediate background of the amendment, Fairman did not only analyze the congressional debates; he also explored the newspapers, the 1866 campaign speeches of significant members of Congress, the gubernatorial messages calling for state consideration of the proposed amendment, and the records of state ratifying legislatures. The evidence dictated his finding that Congress and the country, in framing and ratifying the amendment, did not understand that Section One incorporated the first eight amendments, that in fact they had no clear understanding of the meaning of the amendment's trilogy, taken separately or together. What was clear was only that Negroes were to have the same civil rights as white men and that the states could not deny the rights, undefined and unenumerated, of United States citizenship.

In a companion article, "Does the Fourteenth Amendment Incorporate the Bill of Rights? The Judicial Interpretation," [5] a colleague of Fairman's, Professor Stanley Morrison of Stanford, examined judicial interpretations of the Fourteenth Amendment and corroborated Fairman's findings. Black's position, Morrison concluded, was "fatally weak" and unable to withstand critical examination. The dissent in *Adamson* by seeking to read the Bill of Rights into the Fourteenth Amendment amounted "simply to an effort to put into the Constitution what the framers failed to put there."

In scholarly language, Fairman and Morrison condemned Black and his fellow dissenters for writing law-office history, a mere function of ex parte advocacy. I would go further: Black did not merely misread history, nor wishfully attribute to it a factual content that it did not possess; he mangled and manipulated it by artfully selecting facts from one side only, by generalizing from grossly inadequate "proof," by ignoring confusion and even contradictions in the minds of some of his key historical protagonists, and by assuming that silence on the part of their opponents signified acquiescence. In this way he invoked the fatherhood of "the framers" in support of his position.

68

The difficulty with Morrison's article is that in the Supreme Court opinions that he examined, from the *Slaughterhouse* cases in 1873,[6] the first to reach the Court on a Fourteenth Amendment question, to the many antecedents of *Adamson*, the justices who repudiated the incorporation theory (all but the first John Marshall Harlan) were no better historians than Black. Indeed, to his credit, Black had examined the records, however much his predilections colored his interpretation. The others, by contrast, occasionally invoked the name of history to support their findings but rarely bothered to examine the historical evidence. When they did, as in *Twining* v. *New Jersey*,[7] decided in 1908, they were invariably wrong. Morrison proved, to be sure, that the Supreme Court had never accepted the incorporation theory advanced by Black in *Adamson*, but he did not prove that the several rejections of that theory had had a scintilla of historical support.

In fact, the judicial record accurately described by Morrison constitutes a melancholy litany of judicial errors, beginning with the *Slaughterhouse* cases, which produced one of the most tragically wrong opinions ever given by the Court. Justice Miller, speaking for the majority, could have reached his decision, properly sustaining the statute, without emasculating the privileges and immunities clause. He reasoned instead that the clause offered protection against state impairment of the privileges and immunities of United States citizenship only, not those of state citizenship, and that those of state citizenship included "nearly every civil right for the establishment and protection of which organized government is instituted," embracing the whole Bill of Rights and other "fundamental" rights. One need not endorse Justice Field's dissenting opinion to agree with his anguished cry that the majority's construction of the privileges and immunities clause had rendered it "a vain and idle enactment, which accomplished nothing, and most unnecessarily excited Congress and the people on its passage." The privileges and immunities clause is central to the issue of incorporation because to the extent that any of the framers of the amendment suggested that it incorporated the Bill of Rights—and a few did—they relied principally on that clause; Black's reading of history was not an invention on his part.

The difficulty with Charles Fairman's article, despite its superb scholarship and exacting standards of proof, is that its compass is limited to the immediate background of the Fourteenth Amendment. Fairman focused only on the period after December of 1865. Moreover, to the extent possible, he adhered rigorously to the literal meaning of the words used and understandably construed them in a lawyer's terms. He therefore missed the history that was behind those words and that suffused them with a content that can be appreciated only by understanding them and the language of the amendment as expressions of the constitutional ideology of the abolitionists. Because Frankfurter curtly dismissed the notion that the clauses of Section One were a "shorthand summary of the first eight Amendments" and because Fairman used an excessively narrow and legalistic lens, neither had the full story. A generation gap, historically speaking, stood between them and much of the evidence. As early as the 1830's, abolitionist theorists like Theodore Weld, James Birney, Joshua Giddings, William W. Ellsworth, Calvin Goddard, and others, were employing due process, privileges and immunities, and equality to signify virtually all fundamental rights. Though they used those crucial concepts in a promiscuous way, as if they overlapped and were interchangeable in meaning, they used them in ways that lend credibility to the incorporation theory. By the 1840's and 1850's the abolitionist constitutional argument was popularized in countless speeches, resolves, legal briefs, letters, editorials, sermons, pamphlets, and books. From press, pulpit, and platform, the phrases that found their way into the Fourteenth Amendment's trilogy were invoked to support not only the abolition of slavery and equal civil rights for Negroes, but also freedom of speech, press, conscience, petition, and assembly, as well as the procedural rights of the criminally accused and such rights of property as making contracts and enjoying the fruits of one's labor. The clauses of Section One were at the least a "shorthand summary of the first eight Amendments" for the abolitionist generation whose constitutional climacteric found expression in the Reconstruction Amendments.

A year after Fairman and Morrison published their convincing refutation of Black, based on data of the post-1865 period, Howard Jay Graham published his articles on "The Early Antislavery Backgrounds of the Fourteenth Amendment," [8] and a year later Jacobus tenBroek published his *Antislavery Origins of the Fourteenth Amendment*.[9] Graham and tenBroek proved that the meaning of Section One must be sought in the pre-1865 period as well as later, and that the evidence of 1866–1868 must be read in the light of a received tradition of abolitionist constitutional argument. Fairman's findings were basically negative. He did not disprove that the Fourteenth incorporated the Bill of Rights; he proved, rather, that there is very little evidence either that its framers intended that result or that the country understood that intention. Fairman himself criticized Black for relying too heavily on negative evidence, yet he followed Black's example by drawing conclusions from silence or the absence of proof positive. In short, the historical record is not only complex and confusing; it is inconclusive.

Though the palm must be awarded to Fairman as the better historian by far, the greater issue—*should* the Bill of Rights be incorporated?—remained unresolved after the Black-Fairman debate.

The controversy between them was strictly limited to the history of the original understanding. But even if history spoke with a loud, clear, and conclusive voice, it ought not to control judgment. Whatever the framers of the Fourteenth intended, there is no reason to believe that they possessed the best insights or ultimate wisdom as to the meaning of their words for subsequent generations. What passed for wisdom in their time may very well have passed out of date. Words do not have fixed meanings. As Justice Holmes once remarked, a word is "the skin of living thought and may vary greatly in color and content according to the circumstances and time in which it is used." Questions of constitutional law involve matters of public policy which should not be decided merely because of the original meanings of words in the Constitution. They must be read as revelations of the general purposes which were to be achieved, or as expressions of imperishable principles that are expansive and comprehensive in character. Those principles and purposes, rather than their framers' original understanding of them, are what was intended to endure. The Constitution serves as well today as in earlier centuries because an antiquarian historicism that would freeze its original meaning, even when discernible, has not generally guided its interpretation—nor was it intended to. Holmes sagely remarked that "the present has a right to govern itself, so far as it can. . . . Historical continuity with the past is not a duty, only a necessity." We cannot avoid the influence of history, but we are not constitutionally obligated to repeat it. That the framers of the Fourteenth gave constitutional embodiment to the principles of due process, equal protection, and privileges and immunities is sufficient. With history and judicial precedents as guides, and no more than that, the task of the Court is one of statecraft: to reinterpret and adapt the old to changing conditions. Not the past but the noblest ideals of a democratic society should prevail in construing the Constitution.

The Court has, in fact, proved itself to be most adept in reading into the Constitution values and policy preferences that meet its approval, and its freedom to do so is virtually legislative in scope. As has been remarked so often, the Court sits as a continuous constitutional convention; its duties are political in the highest sense as well as judicial. The history of its treatment of the due process clause is as good an example of this as any and is directly relevant to the whole incorporation theory.

In 1884, in *Hurtado v. California,*[10] the issue before the Court was whether the Fourteenth Amendment's guarantee of due process of law required the state to provide indictment by grand jury to a defendant in a capital case. With Justice Harlan alone dissenting, the Court held that due process signified no fixed set of procedures; a reasonable substitute for grand jury proceedings would satisfy the due process clause as long as the principles of liberty and justice were preserved. To define due process exclusively in terms of ancient procedures, remarked Justice Matthews for the majority, "would be to deny every quality of the law but its age, and to render it incapable of progress or improvement. It would be to stamp upon our jurisprudence the unchangeableness atttributed to the laws of the Medes and Persians."

The *Hurtado* case initiated a long line of decisions in which the Court steadily eroded the traditional procedures that had been associated with due process of law. At about the same time, the Court began to invest a new content in the words "liberty" and "property" of the Fourteenth Amendment's due process clause. Walton Hamilton summarized the matter with trenchant wit when he wrote that liberty and property "came to be a single word with a constant shift of accent to the right." So-called substantive due process gave the Court a weapon to preserve vested rights from reform-minded majorities seeking to regulate railroad and utility rates, fix maximum hours of labor and minimum wages, and protect labor in other ways. By 1915 the old procedural concept of due process as fair play—"liberty and justice"—had been so withered by judicial interpretation that Justice Holmes was forced to declare, in his dissenting opinion in *Frank* v. *Mangum*,[11] that "mob law does not become due process of law by securing the assent of a terrorized jury." In *Coppage* v. *Kansas*,[12] decided the same year, Holmes again dissenting, the Court held unconstitutional as a violation of due process a state act that sought to ban "yellow-dog" contracts by which workers were prevented from joining unions. Speaking through Justice Pitney, who also wrote the opinion in *Frank* v. *Mangum*, the Court majority ruled that "the right of personal liberty and the right to private property—partaking of the nature of each—is the right to make contracts for the acquisition of property." Outlawing yellow-dog contracts infringed that right, thereby violating due process of law. The Court, in other words, had incorporated within the due process clause a variety of doctrines that secured property, particularly corporate property, against public regulation by legislation or administrative commissions. The principal doctrine that was incorporated within the word "liberty" was "liberty of contract," while "property" came to mean, among other things, the right to employ non-union labor and to a "fair return" or profit. In one case [13] the Court ruled that a "fair return" would be "7½% or even 8%," and thus held that the publicly fixed rate that permitted a profit of 6.26 per cent was not only "unfair" but "confiscatory," and therefore a denial of due process of law. Incorporation did not extend, however, to any of the provisions of the Bill of Rights save for the clause in the Fifth Amendment barring the seizure of property except for public use and at a just compensation.

After the traditional procedural meanings of due process were narrowed by *Hurtado*, counsel for accused individuals argued that even if the *concept* of due process did not mean indictment by grand jury, or freedom from cruel and unusual punishments, or trial by a twelve-man jury, or freedom of the press, or the right to be free from compulsory self-incrimination, the provisions in the first eight amendments that required observance in federal proceedings applied in the same way to state proceedings; that is, that these provisions were incorporated within the Fourteenth Amendment, either by the privileges and immunities clause or by the due process clause. In a series of cases between 1892 and 1908, however, all such arguments were rejected by the Court. In effect the 1833 rule of *Barron* v. *Baltimore* still operated, despite the adoption of the Fourteenth Amendment in 1868, and the holding of the *Slaughterhouse* cases kept the privileges and immunities clause a fossilized curiosity.

Judicial behavior is sometimes inexplicable. As late as 1922 the Court reasserted that the Constitution "imposes upon the states no obligation to confer upon those within their jurisdiction . . . the right of free speech." [14] Yet, three years later, Justice Sanford, speaking for a majority of the Court in the case of *Gitlow* v. *New York*,[15] observed in a remarkable *obiter dictum* that "for present purposes we may and do assume that freedom of speech and of the press, which are protected by the First Amendment from abridgment by Congress, are among the fundamental personal rights and liberties protected by the due process clause of the Fourteenth Amendment from impairment by the States." Thus, casually and without reasoned judgment, and despite the precedents to the contrary, the Court began a process of incorporating selected provisions of the Bill of Rights into the due process clause. The word "liberty" of that clause was about to undergo another radical transformation. Substantive due process with a libertarian content belatedly made its debut without the slightest nod in the direction of history.

In 1931, in *Near* v. *Minnesota*,[16] the Court made its first decision holding directly that the free-press clause of the First Amendment was incorporated within the Fourteenth's due process clause. Selective incorporation continued when in 1932, in *Powell* v. *Alabama*,[17] the right to be represented by counsel, a provision of the Sixth Amendment, was incorporated, or nationalized, in capital cases. *Hamilton* v. *University of California*,[18] decided in 1934, added, perhaps by dictum, the free exercise of religion clause of the First Amendment.[19] In 1937, in *De Jonge* v. *Oregon*,[20] the Court incorporated the free-assembly clause of the First Amendment. In each of these cases the justices reasoned that the right at issue was one of those "fundamental principles of liberty and justice which lie at the base of all our civil and political institutions" and must therefore be embraced by the due process clause of the Fourteenth Amendment.

The evolution of selective incorporation of the Bill of Rights came to a halt shortly after the *De Jonge* case. In *Palko* v. *Connecticut*,[21] the Court, in an opinion by Justice Cardozo, refused to incorporate the double jeopardy clause of the Fifth Amendment. Cardozo sought to provide a "rationalizing principle" to explain the selective incorporation process. He repudiated the notion that the due process clause embraced the entire Bill of Rights. The rights there guaranteed were of two classes, he found. Some were of such a nature that liberty and justice could not exist if they were sacrificed. These had been brought "within the Fourteenth Amendment by a process of absorption" because they were "of the very essence of a scheme of ordered liberty." They were, in short, "fundamental." The other classes of rights had "value and importance," but a "fair and enlightened system of justice" would be possible without them. Thus, freedom of speech was "the indispensable condition" of nearly every other form of freedom. But jury trials, indictments, and immunity from self-incrimination or from double jeopardy "might be lost, and justice still be done." Due process of law was itself fundamental. Therefore, certain rights protected by the first eight amendments against national abridgment might also be safeguarded against state action, because to deny them would be to deny due process of law. The concept of due process might safeguard them, though they were not absorbed within the "liberty" of the due process clause.

The coerced confessions cases illustrate the distinction made in *Palko*. In 1936 the Court ruled that a confession of guilt which had been forced from a suspect by brutal police beatings could not be accepted in evidence against him at his trial.[22] Torture, said the Court, is not due process of law. Four years later the Court recognized that coercion can be psychological as well as physical. The defendant in this case[23] had confessed after having been interrogated by relay teams of police for six days and nights.

Had the crimes in these cases been violations of federal law, had the officers been federal agents, and had the trials been held in federal courts, the convictions would have been reversed on the ground that coerced confessions violated the Fifth Amendment's protection against testimonial compulsion. But the cases having arisen from state prosecutions, the Court decided them on the theory that coerced confessions violated due process of law, rather than on the grounds that the liberty guaranteed by the due process clause incorporated the Fifth Amendment's protection against state abridgment. In the celebrated *Adamson* case, the court explicitly held that the self-incrimination clause of the Fifth did not apply to the states. In the dramatic *Rochin* case, the majority, in line with *Adamson*, found that forcing incriminating evidence from a person by means of stomach pump was equivalent to testimonial compulsion and therefore a denial of due process of law—but not because the Fourteenth incorporated the Fifth.

A year later, in *Brown* v. *Allen*,[24] the case was that of an illiterate Negro sentenced to death in North Carolina on the basis of a confession that he made after having been held on suspicion for five days without being charged of crime and for eighteen days thereafter without being brought before a magistrate for a preliminary hearing. (He also had not been permitted to have a lawyer until the day of his trial.) In the absence of proof showing the defendant's confession to be involuntary, a sharply divided Court ruled that its acceptance as evidence did not deny due process. A few years later in *Breithaupt* v. *Abram*,[25] the Court, again over bitter dissenting opinions, held that the police had not denied due process when they had had a compliant physician take a blood sample from an unconscious truck-driver to determine whether he had been drunk at the time of an accident in which three people died when his truck hit their car. Obviously, conduct that shocked the conscience or offended the sense of justice, thereby violating due process, varied from case to case and with the sensitivities of each of the justices. Black and Douglas, believing that the Fourteenth incorporated the Fifth, would have found the police conduct in the *Brown* and *Breithaupt* cases to be violations of the immunity against compulsory self-incrimination. So matters stood during the 1950's in coerced confession cases.

In the quarter century after *Palko* in 1937, the process of selective incorporation came to a halt—with one exception. In 1947, in *Everson* v. *Board of Education*,[26] the Court held that the liberty safeguarded by the Fourteenth's due process clause included the First Amendment's ban against establishments of religion. But in 1961 the dam against further incorporation burst wide open. In *Mapp* v. *Ohio*,[27] the guarantee of the Fourth Amendment against unreasonable search and seizure was absorbed into the Fourteenth, making the fruits of an illegal search as excludable as evidence in a state trial as they would be in a federal one. A year later, in *Robinson* v. *California*,[28] the Court incorporated the Eighth Amendment's ban against cruel and unusual punishments. In 1963 the Court added to the list of incorporated rights representation by counsel in all felony cases; the states were obligated to provide counsel to defendants too poor to hire their own. That was the rule of *Gideon* v. *Wainwright*.[29] In 1964, the controversial precedents in the *Twining* and *Adamson* cases were overruled when the Court incorporated the self-incrimination clause of the Fifth Amendment in *Malloy* v. *Hogan*[30] and *Murphy* v. *Waterfront Commissioners*.[31] In 1965, *Pointer* v. *Texas*[32] incorporated the Sixth Amendment's clause on the right of an accused to confront the witnesses against him. In the same year, the process of selective incorporation reached an apogee in *Griswold* v. *Connecticut*[33] when the Court voided the state's ban on the use of contraceptive devices. Justice Douglas, in the principal opinion, found in the specific guarantees of the Bill of Rights "penumbras, formed by emanations from those guarantees that help give them life and substance." The First, Third, Fourth, and Fifth Amendments, he declared, "created zones of privacy" and so, astonishingly, did the Ninth Amendment: "The enumeration in the Constitution, of certain rights, shall not be construed to deny or disparage others retained by the people." Thus, the position suggested by Murphy and Rutledge in their *Adamson* dissent became the law of the land. Not only did the Fourteenth incorporate, although selectively, specific guarantees of the first eight amendments; other rights not specified— in *Griswold*, the private right to employ contraceptive devices— might also be incorporated.

Simultaneously the Court expanded the scope of the rights incorporated from the Fifth and Sixth Amendments. The *Escobedo* case of 1965[34] followed in 1967 by the even more sensational *Miranda* case,[35] gave sweeping protection to the right to counsel and the freedom from compulsory self-incrimination. In the 1967 case of *Klopfer* v. *North Carolina*,[36] the Court also incorporated the right to a speedy trial, and in *Washington* v. *Texas*,[37] decided the same year, the right of an accused to compulsory process in securing witnesses in his behalf. In 1968, *Duncan* v. *Louisiana*[38] added the Sixth Amendment's trial by jury to the incorporated rights, and in the following year, *Benton* v. *Maryland*[39] overruled *Palko* by incorporating the ban against double jeopardy. Thus, by the gradual process of selective incorporation, most of the provisions of the Bill of Rights—indeed, all of the essential ones except the right against excessive bail—have found their way into the Fourteenth Amendment's due process clause.

Justice Black's dissenting position in *Adamson* has in effect prevailed, though the Court has never accepted his argument on behalf of total incorporation. In the *Duncan* case in 1968, riding the crest of the incorporation movement, Black, again in a concurring opinion joined by Douglas, reiterated his total incorporation theory. He also reopened the issue of the original understanding of the framers of the Fourteenth Amendment and belatedly replied to Professor Fairman's attack on his use of historical evidence in *Adamson*. Unconvinced by Fairman's article, Black claimed that "it has completely failed to refute the inferences and arguments that I suggested in my *Adamson* dissent. Professor Fairman's 'History' relies very heavily on what was *not* said in the state legislatures that passed on the Fourteenth Amendment. Instead of replying on this kind of negative pregnant, my legislative experience has convinced me that it is far wiser to rely on what *was* said, and most importantly, by the men who actually sponsored the Amendment in the Congress." Though Black grossly oversimplified Fairman's argument and evidence, he had a worthwhile point. Regrettably, however, to use Morrison's phrase, Black's own history "will not stand critical examination."

There are several good reasons. First, Black offers very little evidence indeed that the sponsors of the amendment did in fact intend to incorporate the Bill of Rights. Second, he offers no evidence that if they so intended, they meant to do so by the clauses of the First Section "separately, and as a whole." The fact is that Congressman Bingham, who was extremely confused and contradictory in his presentation, agreed in the end with Senator Howard that the privileges and immunities clause alone achieved the incorporation. Third, there is no reason to believe that Bingham and Howard expressed the views of the majority of Congress. Finally, a constitutional amendment, unlike a legislative enactment, represents the views not only of Congress, but also of the legislatures of three-fourths of the states, and on this point, too, Fairman's evidence is conclusive.

In *Duncan*, Justice Harlan, dissenting with Justice Stewart, accepted Fairman's article as overwhelming proof that the total incorporation theory is historically unsupportable. Harlan's opinion was not, however, based on historical evidence. Employing the Cardozo-Frankfurter standards of due process, he reached the conclusion that trial by jury, even in serious criminal cases, was not a fundamental right, because it was not indispensable to a fair resolution of guilt or innocence. Whatever one may think of Harlan's opinion, he provided reasoned explanations rather than resting on the authority of history or precedents.

Black, by contrast, operated in a different judicial universe. He was, paradoxically, the powerful judicial activist clinging to the belief that he was the impersonal spokesman of the Constitution. In his own mind, he represented the polar distance from subjectivity or, to use his favorite epithetical synonym, from natural-law judgment. He exercised neither will nor discretion, but merely responded to the clarity of words on parchment as illuminated by historical imperatives. With the comforting assurance that the intentions of the framers dictated his construction of the Fourteenth Amendment, he was the true apostle of judicial self-restraint.

In our judicial history, the powerful activists have tended to be justices in whom the judicial temperament flickers most weakly, whose deepest convictions cannot be bridled, and who believe unshakably not only that they are right, but that they have a mission to impose their convictions on the nation. Intellectual rectitude, skepticism, and a capacity for self-doubt are not among their strong points. And they have a nearly limitless ability to intoxicate themselves with fictions, chief among them that truth, history, and the Constitution are on their side, governing their opinions, which do little more than declare what the law is, rather than make it. In fact they have slight respect for history, hardly ever permitting it to stand in their way should it prove encumbering or contrary to their wishes; but they rarely need to ignore it because they have an infinite faculty for construing it to mean what they wish even if it means the opposite. History for the activist is a protean instrument, useful for legitimating a predetermined result. It always seems to teach the desired lesson, lending the appearance of objectivity to an opinion that reasons from unquestioned premises to foregone conclusions.

Many of our "greatest" judges—that is, the most influential ones— have been activists of this genre, foremost among them John Marshall. Stephen Field and the first John Marshall Harlan, whom Black most resembles, are other examples. Fortunately for those who share their intense convictions about the overpowering importance of the Bill of Rights to the maintenance of a democratic society and the equal need to construe the Reconstruction Amendments with the widest latitude as a means of defending equality and justice for all, Harlan and Black have been St. Georges in judicial armor. Though Black has failed to win a majority for total incorporation, he has almost reached that result on a piecemeal basis. In so doing he has vindicated the position expressed in so many dissenting opinions by the first Harlan. Incorporation on so widespread a scale will stand as Black's monument. Ironically, however, history, which he believes to be one of his strongest allies, has met in his hands the same fate as the dragon in St. George's.

NOTES

[1] *Rochin* v. *California*, 342 U.S. 165.
[2] 332 U.S. 165.
[3] *Barron* v. *Baltimore* (7 Peters 243).
[4] *Stanford Law Review*, 11 (December 1949), 5.
[5] *Ibid.*, p. 140.
[6] 16 Wall. 36.
[7] 211 U.S. 78.
[8] Reprinted in his book, *Everyman's Constitution* (Madison, Wis., 1968).
[9] (Berkeley, 1951); rev. ed., *Equal Under Law* (New York, 1965).
[10] 110 U.S. 516.
[11] 237 U.S. 309.
[12] 236 U.S. 1.

[13] *United Railways* v. *West,* 280 U.S. 234 (1934).
[14] *Prudential Insurance* v. *Cheek,* 259 U.S. 530.
[15] 268 U.S. 652 (1925).
[16] 283 U.S. 697.
[17] 287 U.S. 45.
[18] 293 U.S. 245.
[19] *Cantwell* v. *Connecticut* in 1940 (310 U.S. 296) confirmed the dictum of the Hamilton case.
[20] 299 U.S. 353.
[21] 302 U.S. 319 (1937).
[22] *Brown* v. *Mississippi,* 297 U.S. 278.
[23] *Chambers* v. *Florida,* 309 U.S. 227.
[24] 344 U.S. 443 (1953).
[25] 352 U.S. 432 (1957).
[26] 330 U.S. 1.
[27] 367 U.S. 643.
[28] 370 U.S. 660.
[29] 372 U.S. 335.
[30] 378 U.S. 1.
[31] 378 U.S. 52.
[32] 380 U.S. 400.
[33] 381 U.S. 479.
[34] 378 U.S. 478.
[35] 384 U.S. 436.
[36] 386 U.S. 213.
[37] 384 U.S. 14.
[38] 391 U.S. 145.
[39] 395 U.S. 784.

AMERICA'S
"GREATEST MAGIST·RATE"

LEMUEL Shaw served as Chief Justice of Massachusetts from 1830 to 1860, during an age which he said was remarkable for its "prodigious activity and energy in every department of life." [1] America was being transformed by the rise of railroads, steam power, the factory system, and the corporate form of business. A more complex society, urban and industrial, was superseding the older rural, agrarian one. Only a pace behind the astonishing rate of economic change came the democratization of politics and of society, while the federal system lumbered toward its greatest crisis. During this time Shaw delivered what is probably a record number of opinions for a single judge: over 2,200, enough to fill about twenty volumes if separately collected.

At the time of his appointment to the bench, American law was still in its formative period. Whole areas of law were largely uncultivated, many unknown, and few if any settled. Although Shaw was not writing on a completely clean slate, the strategy of time and place surely presented an unrivaled opportunity for a judge of strength and vision to mold the law. His domain was the whole field of jurisprudence excepting only admiralty. No other state judge through his opinions alone had so great an influence on the course of American law.

One of the major themes of his life work was the perpetuation of what Oscar and Mary Handlin have called "the commonwealth idea" [2]—essentially a quasi-mercantilist concept of the state within a democratic framework. In Europe where the state was not responsible to the people and was the product of remote historical forces, mercantilism served the ruling classes who controlled the state. In America men put the social-contract theory into practice and actually made their government. The people were the state; the state was their "Common Wealth." They identified themselves with it and felt that they should share, as of right, in the advantages that it could bring to them as a community. The state was their means of promoting the general interest.

The Commonwealth idea precluded the laissez-faire state whose function was simply to keep peace and order, and then, like a little child, not be heard. The people of Massachusetts expected their Commonwealth to participate actively in their economic affairs. Where risk-capital feared to tread or needed franchises, powers of incorporation, or the boost of special powers such as eminent domain, the duty of the state was to subsidize, grant, and supervise the whole process in the interests of the general welfare. But regulation was not restricted to those special interests which had been promoted by government aid. Banks, insurance companies, liquor dealers, food vendors, and others were all subjected to varying degrees of control, though the public trough had not been open to them. The beneficent hand of the state reached out to touch every part of the economy.

The Commonwealth idea profoundly influenced the development of law in Massachusetts. It was largely responsible for the direction taken by the law of eminent domain, for the development of the police power, and for the general precedence given by the courts to public rights over merely private ones. As employed by Shaw, the Commonwealth idea gave rise to legal doctrines of the public interest by which the power of the state to govern the economy was judicially sustained.

The idea "that some privately owned corporations are more public in character than others," as Edwin Merrick Dodd noted, "had already begun to emerge in judicial decisions before 1830." [3] The grant of powers of eminent domain to early turnpike and canal companies had been upheld because these were public highways, although privately owned. The mill acts, which originated as a means of promoting water-powered gristmills, had also been sustained in early decisions on the ground that a public purpose was served. While the earlier judges regretted the extension of the old gristmill acts to new manufacturing corporations, Shaw, by contrast, warmly accepted these acts because he believed that industrialization would bring prosperity and progress to the Commonwealth. Accordingly he declared that "a great mill-power for manufacturing purposes" was, like a railroad, a species of public works in which the public had a great interest. He even placed "steam manufactories" in the same class as water-powered mills, as devoted to a public use, although steam-powered factories were never granted powers of eminent domain.[4]

The Commonwealth idea underlay those remarkably prophetic opinions of Shaw's that established the basis of the emerging law of public utilities. The old common law of common calling had considered only millers, carriers, and innkeepers as "public employ-ments"; it "knew no such persons as the common road-maker or the common water-supplier." [5] The "common road-maker," that is, the turnpike, bridge, and canal companies, were added to the list of public employments or public works while Shaw was still at the bar. But it was Shaw who settled the legal character of power companies,[6] turnpikes,[7] railroads,[8] and water suppliers [9] as public utilities, pri-vately owned but subject to regulation for the public benefit. He would have included even manufacturers and banks. The Common-wealth idea left no doubt as to whether the state would master or be mastered by its creatures, the corporations, or whether the wel-fare of the economy was a matter of public or private concern.

The police power may be regarded as the legal expression of the Commonwealth idea, for it signifies the supremacy of public over private rights. To call the police power a Massachusetts doctrine would be an exaggeration, though not a great one. But it is certainly no coincidence that in Massachusetts, with its Commonwealth tradi-tion, the police power was first defined and carried to great extremes from the standpoint of vested interests. Shaw's foremost contribution in the field of public law was to the development of the police-power concept.

The power of the legislature "to trench somewhat largely on the profitable use of individual property," for the sake of the common good, as Shaw expressed the police power in *Commonwealth* v. *Alger*,[10] was consistently confirmed over thirty years of his opinions. Three decades later, when judges were acting on the supposition that the Fourteenth Amendment incorporated Herbert Spencer's *Social Statics*, the ideas expressed in Shaw's opinions seemed the very epit-ome of revolutionary socialism. Shaw's name was revered, but the implications of his police-power opinions were politely evaded. In the period between Shaw and the school of Holmes and Brandeis, American law threatened to become the graveyard of general-welfare or public-interest doctrines, and doctrines of vested rights dominated.

The trend toward legal Spencerianism was so pronounced by the end of the nineteenth century that legal historians concentrated on a search for the origins of doctrines of vested rights, almost as if con-trary doctrines had never existed. When touching the pre-Civil War period, it is conventional to quote de Tocqueville on the conservatism of the American bench and bar, to present American law almost exclusively in terms of Marshall, Story, and Kent, and to emphasize that the rights of property claimed the very warmest affections of the American judiciary. If, however, the work of the state courts were better known, this view of our legal history might be altered. But Gibson and Ruffin and Blackford are little more than distin-guished names, their work forgotten. Shaw's superb exposition of the police power is respectfully remembered, but it is usually treated as exceptional, or mistreated as an attempt to confine the police power to the common-law maxim of *sic utere tuo ut alienum non laedas*.[11]

Shaw taught that "all property . . . is derived directly or indirectly from the government, and held subject to those general regulations, which are necessary to the common good and general welfare."[12] Dean Pound, in discussing the "extreme individualist view" of the common law concerning the rights of riparian property owners, says the common law asked simply, "was the defendant acting on his own land and committing no nuisance?"[13] But Shaw believed that the common law of nuisances, which was founded on the *sic utere* maxim, inadequately protected the public, because it was restricted to the abatement of existing nuisances. He believed that the general welfare required the anticipation and prevention of prospective wrongs from the use of private property. Accordingly he held that the legislature might interfere with the use of property before its owner became amenable to the common law. So a man could not even remove stones from his own beach if prohibited by the legislature, nor erect a wharf on his property beyond boundary lines fixed by it. Even if his use of his property would be "harmless" or "indifferent," the necessity of restraints was to be judged "by those to whom all legislative power is intrusted by the sovereign authority." Similarly the "reasonableness" of such restraints was a matter of "expediency" to be determined by the legislature, not the court. The simple expedient of having a precise statutory rule for the obedience of all was sufficient reason for a finding of constitutionality.[14]

Thus Shaw, using the Commonwealth idea, established a broad base for the police power. He carried the law's conception of the public good and the power of government to protect it a long way from the straitjacketing ideas of Kent and Story. Their position may be summed up in Blackstone's language that "the public good is in nothing more essentially interested than the protection of every individual's private rights."[15]

A few other decisions of the Shaw Court on the police power will illustrate that the Chief Justice's *Alger* opinion was more than rhetoric. The authority of the legislature to shape private banking practices in the public interest was unequivocally sustained in two sweeping opinions. In one, Shaw said that a statute intended to prevent banks from "becoming dangerous to the public" was attacked as unconstitutional on the authority of Marshall, Story, and Kent. The statute allegedly operated retroactively against the bank in question; constituted a legislative assumption of judicial power because it required the Supreme Judicial Court to issue a preliminary injunction against banks on the findings of a government commission; and violated the federal contract clause by providing for a perpetual

83

injunction against the further doing of business, in effect a revocation of the charter. Rufus Choate probably never argued a stronger case. But Shaw sustained the statute and the injunction, peppering his opinion with references to the paramountcy of "the great interests of the community," the duty of the government to "provide security for its citizens," and the legitimacy of interferences with "the liberty of action, and even with the right of property, of such institutions." [16] In a second bank case of the same year, 1839, the Court refused "to raise banks above the control of the legislature." The holding was that a charter could be dissolved at the authority of the legislature, under the reserved police power, without a judicial proceeding. [17]

It has been said that from the standpoint of the doctrine of vested rights the most reprehensible legislation ever enacted was the prohibition on the sale of liquor. Such legislation wiped out the value of existing stocks and subjected violators to criminal sanctions, their property to public destruction. Similarly, buildings used for purposes of prostitution or gambling might, on the authority of the legislature, be torn down. The question presented by such statutes was whether the police power could justify uncompensated destruction of private property which had not been appropriated for a public use. The power of the Commonwealth over the health and morals of the public provided Shaw with the basis for sustaining legislation divesting vested rights. [18] On half a dozen occasions, the New York Wynehammer doctrine of substantive due process of law was repudiated in such cases. [19]

Regulation of railroads was another subject for the exercise of the police power, according to the Shaw Court. The same principles that justified grants of eminent domain to railroads, or to canals, bridges, turnpikes, power companies, and water suppliers, also provided the basis for sustaining controls over their rates, profits, and services. Railroads, said Shaw, were a "public work, established by public authority, intended for the public use and benefit. . . ." [20] The power to charge rates was "in every respect a public grant, a franchise . . . subject to certain regulations, within the power of government, if it should become excessive." [21]

These dicta by Shaw became holdings at the first moment the railroads challenged the "reasonableness" of the rates and services fixed by government railroad commissions. "Reasonableness" was held to be a matter for determination by the legislature or the commission to which it delegated its powers. Those powers, in turn, were broadly construed. The Court would not interfere with the regulatory process if the railroads had the benefit of notice, hearing, and other fair procedures. [22] Due process of law to the Shaw Court meant according to legal forms, not according to legislation which the Court approved or disapproved as a matter of policy.

The Shaw Court's latitudinarian attitude toward the police power was influenced by the strong tradition of judicial self-restraint among Massachusetts judges, an outgrowth of the Commonwealth idea. Shaw carried on the tradition of the Massachusetts judiciary. During the thirty years that Shaw presided, there were only ten cases, one unreported, in which the Supreme Judicial Court voided legislative enactments.

Four of these cases in no way related to the police power. One involved a special legislative resolution confirming a private sale that had divested property rights of third persons without compensation.[23] The second concerned an act by which Charlestown was annexed to Boston without providing the citizens of Charlestown with representative districts and an opportunity to vote.[24] The third, an unreported case decided by Shaw sitting alone, involved the "personal liberty act," by which the state sought to evade Congress' Fugitive Slave Law.[25] Here Shaw felt bound by the national Constitution and by a decision of the Supreme Court of the United States. In the fourth case he invalidated a state act which dispensed with the ancient requirement of grand jury proceedings in cases of high crimes.[26] In each of these four, the decisions are above any but trifling criticism.

Of the six cases bearing on the police power, three involved legislation egregiously violating procedural guarantees that are part of our civil liberties.[27] The statutes in question had validly prohibited the sale of liquor. But they invalidly stripped accused persons of virtually every safeguard of criminal justice, from the right to be free from unreasonable searches and seizures to the rights that cluster around the concept of fair trial. Shaw's decisions against these statutes, like his decisions insuring the maintenance of grand jury proceedings and the right to vote, were manifestations of judicial review in its best sense. There were also dicta by Shaw on the point that the legislature cannot restrain the use of property by ex post facto laws, by bills of attainder, or by discriminatory classifications. Thus the limitations placed upon the police power by the Shaw Court were indispensable to the protection of civil liberties.

The only exception to this generalization consists of the limitation derived from the contract clause of the United States Constitution. But there were only three cases during the long period of Shaw's chief justiceship in which this clause was the basis for the invalidation of statutes. In each of the three, the statutes were of limited operation and the decisions made no sacrifice of the public interest. The legislature in one case attempted to regulate in the absence of a reserved power to alter or amend public contracts; the Court left a way open for the legislature's purpose to be achieved under common law.[28] In the other two cases, regulatory powers had been reserved but were exercised in particularly faithless and arbitrary ways; in one case to increase substantially the obligations of a corporation for a second time, in effect doubling a liability which had been paid off; in the other case to repeal an explicit permission for a corporation to increase its capitalization in return for certain services rendered.[29] The legislature in all three cases had passed a high threshold of judicial tolerance for governmental interference with the sanctity of contracts. The decisions were hardly exceptional, considering the facts of the cases and their dates—they were decided between 1854 and 1860, after scores of similar decisions by Federalist, Whig, and Jacksonian jurists alike, in state and federal jurisdictions.

The striking fact is that there were so few such decisions by the Shaw Court in thirty years. Handsome opportunities were provided again and again by litigants claiming impairment of their charters of incorporation by a meddlesome legislature. But the Court's decisions were characterized by judicial self-restraint rather than an eagerness to erect a bulwark around chartered rights. The three cases in which statutes were voided for conflict with the contract clause were unusual for the Shaw Court.

Generally the attitude of the Court was typified by Shaw's remark that "immunities and privileges (vested by charter) do not exempt corporations from the operations of those made for the general regulation. . . ."[30] He habitually construed public grants in favor of the community and against private interests. When chartered powers were exercised in the public interest, he usually interpreted them broadly; but when they competed with the right of the community to protect itself or conserve its resources, he interpreted chartered powers narrowly. He did not permit the public control over matters of health, morals, or safety, nor the power of eminent domain, to be alienated by the contract clause.

In the face of such a record it is misleading to picture state courts assiduously searching for doctrines of vested rights to stymie the police power. Certainly no such doctrines appeared in the pre-Civil War decisions of the Supreme Judicial Court of Massachusetts, except for the one doctrine derived by John Marshall from the contract clause and so sparingly used by Shaw. The sources from which vested-rights doctrines were derived by others—the higher law, natural rights, the social compact, and other sources of implied, inherent limitations on majoritarian assemblies—these were invoked by Shaw when he was checking impairments or personal liberties or traditional procedures of criminal justice.

If this picture does not fit the stereotype of conservative Whig jurists, the stereotype may need revision. On the great issue which has historically divided liberals from conservatives in politics—government controls over property and corporations—Shaw supported the government. Even when the Commonwealth idea was being eroded away by those who welcomed the give-away state but not the regulatory state, Shaw was still endorsing a concept of the police power that kept private interests under government surveillance and restraint. He would not permit the Commonwealth idea to become just a rationale for legislative subventions and grants of chartered powers, with business as the only beneficiary. To Shaw, government aid implied government control, because the aid to business was merely incidental to the promotion of the public welfare. No general regulatory statute was invalidated while he was Chief Justice. His conservatism tended to crop out in common-law cases where the public interest had not been defined or suggested by statute. In such cases the law was as putty in his hands, shaped to meet the press of business needs. Nothing illustrates this better than the personal injury cases and the variety of novel cases to which railroad corporations were parties. The roar of the first locomotive in Massachusetts signaled the advent of a capitalist revolution in the common law, in the sense that Shaw made railroads the beneficiaries of legal doctrine.[31] To be sure, he believed that he was genuinely serving the general interest on the calculation that what was good for business was good for the Commonwealth.

It was when he had a free hand, in the absence of government action, that the character of his conservatism displayed itself: he construed the law so that corporate industrial interests prevailed over lesser, private ones. An individual farmer, shipper, passenger, worker, or pedestrian, when pitted against a corporation which in Shaw's mind personified industrial expansion and public prosperity, risked a rough sort of justice, whether the issue involved tort or contract.[32] Shaw strictly insisted that individuals look to themselves, not to the law, for protection of life and limb, for his beloved common law was incorrigibly individualistic. The hero of the common law was the property-owning, liberty-loving, self-reliant reasonable man. He was also the hero of American society, celebrated by Jefferson as the freehold farmer, by Hamilton as the town-merchant, by Jackson as the frontiersman. Between the American image of the common man and the common-law's ideal Everyman, there was a remarkable likeness. It harshly and uncompromisingly treated men as free-willed, self-reliant, risk-and-responsibility taking individuals. Its spirit was, let every man beware and care for himself. That spirit, together with Shaw's belief that the rapid growth of manufacturing and transportation heralded the coming of the good society, tended to minimize the legal liabilities of business.

This was especially striking in cases of industrial accident and personal injury cases generally. For example, when an accident occurred despite all precautions, Shaw held railroads liable for damage to freight but not for injuries to passengers. They, he reasoned, took the risk of accidents that might occur regardless of due care. His opinions went a long way to accentuate the inhumanity of the common law in the area of torts, and simultaneously, to spur capitalist enterprise. Here was the one great area of law in which he failed to protect the public interest. He might have done so without stymieing rapid industrialization, because the cost of accidents, if imposed on business, would have been ultimately shifted to the public by a hike in prices and rates.

The rigorous individualism of the common law was especially noticeable in the emergent doctrine of contributory negligence, of which Shaw was a leading exponent.[33] That doctrine required a degree of care and skill which no one but the mythical "prudent" or "reasonable man" of the common law could match. A misstep, however slight, from the ideal standard of conduct, placed upon the injured party the whole burden of his loss, even though the railroad was also at fault and perhaps more so. Comparative rather than contributory negligence would have been a fairer test, or perhaps some rule by which damages could be apportioned.

Probably the furthermost limit of the common law's individualism in accident cases was expressed in the rule that a right to action is personal and dies with the injured party. This contributed to the related rule that the wrongful death of a human being was no ground for an action of damages.[34] But for the intervention of the legislature, the common law would have left the relatives of victims of fatal accident without a legal remedy to obtain compensation. Shaw would also have made it more profitable for a railroad to kill a man outright than to scratch him, for if he lived he could sue.[35]

The fellow-servant rule was the most far-reaching consequence of individualism in the law as Shaw expounded it.[36] The rule was that a worker who was injured, through no fault of his own, by the negligence of a fellow employee, could not maintain a claim of damages against his employer. Shaw formulated this rule at a strategic moment for employers, because as industrialization expanded at an incredible pace, factory and railroad accidents multiplied frighteningly. Since the fellow-servant rule threw the whole loss from accidents upon innocent workers, capitalism was relieved of an enormous sum that would otherwise have been due as damages. The encouragement of "infant industries" had no greater social cost.

The fellow-servant rule was unmistakably an expression of legal thinking predicated upon the conception that a free man is one who is free to work out his own destiny, to pursue the calling of his choice, and to care for himself. If he undertakes a dangerous occupation, he voluntarily assumes the risks to which he has exposed himself. He should know that the others with whom he will have to work may cause him harm by their negligence. He must bear his loss because his voluntary conduct has implied his consent to assume it and to relieve his employer of it. On the other hand, there can be no implication that the employer has contracted to indemnify the worker for the negligence of anyone but himself. The employer, like his employees, is responsible for his own conduct, but cannot be liable without fault.

On such considerations Shaw exempted the employer from liability to his employees, although he was liable to the rest of the world for the injurious acts which they committed in the course of their employment. It is interesting to note that Shaw felt obliged to read the employee's assumption of risk into his contract of employment. This legal fiction also reflected the individualism of a time when it was felt that free men could not be bound except by a contract of their own making.

The public policy which Shaw confidently expounded in support of his reading of the law similarly expressed the independent man: safety would be promoted if each worker guarded himself against his own carelessness and just as prudently watched his neighbor; to remove this responsibility by setting up the liability of the employer would allegedly tend to create individual laxity rather than prudence. So Shaw reasoned. It seems not to have occurred to him that fear of being maimed prompted men to safety anyway, or that contributory negligence barred recovery of damages, or that freeing the employer from liability did not induce him to employ only the most careful persons and to utilize accident-saving devices. Nor, for all his reliance upon the voluntary choice of mature men, did it occur to Shaw that a worker undertook a dangerous occupation and "consented" to its risks because his poverty deprived him of real choice. For that matter, none of these considerations prompted the legislature to supersede the common law with employers' liability and workmen's compensation acts until many decades later. Shaw did no violence to the spirit of his age by the fellow-servant rule, or by the rules he applied in other personal injury cases, particularly those involving wrongful death. In all such cases his enlightened views, so evidenced in police-power cases, were absent, probably because government action was equally absent. On the other hand his exposition of the rule of implied malice in cases of homicide [37] and of the criminal responsibility of the insane [38] accorded with the growing humanitarianism of the day as well as with doctrines of individualism.

Shaw's conservatism tended to manifest itself in cases involving notable social issues of his time. For example, he handed down the leading opinion on the constitutionality of the Fugitive Slave Act of 1850; [39] he originated the "separate but equal" doctrine which became the legal linchpin of racial segregation in the public schools throughout the nation; [40] and in the celebrated Abner Kneeland case [41] he sustained a conviction for blasphemy that grossly abridged freedom of conscience and expression; still another opinion was a bulwark of the establishment of religion which was maintained in Massachusetts until 1833.[42]

But it would be misleading as well as minimally informing to conclude an analysis of Shaw's work by calling him a conservative, for the word reveals little about Shaw if it is also applied to Marshall, Kent, Story, Webster, and Choate.

When Story and Kent, steeped in the crusty lore of the *Year Books,* were wailing to each other that they were the last of an old race of judges and that Taney's *Charles River Bridge* decision [43] meant that the Constitution was gone,[44] Shaw was calmly noting that property was "fully subject to State regulation" in the interest of the "morals, health, internal commerce, and general prosperity of the community. . . ." [45] In 1860 at the age of eighty, in an opinion which is a little gem in the literature of the common law, he gave fresh evidence of his extraordinary talent for keeping hoary principles viable by adapting them—as he put it—"to new institutions and conditions of society, new modes of commerce, new usages and practices, as the society in the advancement of civilization may require." [46]

Shaw's mind was open to many of the liberal currents of his time. Witness his support from the bench of the free, public education movement,[47] or his public-interest doctrines,[48] or his defense of trade-union activities,[49] or his freeing sojourner slaves. While Shaw was Chief Justice all slaves whom fate brought to Massachusetts were guaranteed liberty, except for runaways. Whether they were brought by their masters who were temporarily visiting the Commonwealth or were just passing through, or whether they were cast up by the sea, they were set free by Shaw's definition of the law. Bound by neither precedent nor statute, he made that law. The principle of comity, he ruled, could not extend to human beings as property: because slavery was so odious and founded upon brute force it could exist only when sanctioned by positive, local law. There being no such law in Massachusetts, Shaw freed even slave seamen in the service of the United States Navy if they reached a port within his jurisdiction.[50]

In the area of criminal law dealing with conspiracies, Shaw seems on first glance to have run counter to individualist doctrines. He held, in what is probably his best-known opinion,[51] that a combination of workers to establish and maintain a closed shop by the use of peaceable coercion is not an indictable conspiracy even if it tends to injure employers. Shaw also indicated that he saw nothing unlawful in a peaceable, concerted effort to raise wages.

But other judges had been persuaded by the ideology of individualism, or at least used its rhetoric, to find criminality in trade-union activity and even in unions per se. Combination, labor's most effective means of economic improvement, was the very basis of the ancient doctrine of criminal conspiracy and the denial of individual effort. The closed shop was regarded as a hateful form of monopoly on the part of labor, organized action to raise wages as coercion, and both regarded as injurious to the workers themselves, as well as to trade and the public at large. When so much store was placed on self-reliance, the only proper way in law and economics for employees to better themselves seemed to be by atomistic bargaining. Unions were thought to impede the natural operation of free competition by individuals on both sides of the labor market. Or so Shaw's contemporaries and earlier judges had believed.

Individualism, however, has many facets, and like maxims relating to liberty, the free market, or competition, can be conscripted into the service of more than one cause. If self-reliance was one attribute of individualism, the pursuit of self-interest was another. As de Tocqueville noted, where individualism and freedom prevail, men pursue their self-interest and express themselves by developing an astonishing proclivity for association. As soon as several Americans of like interest "have found one another out, they combine," observed de Tocqueville. Shaw too noted the "general tendency of society in our times, to combine men into bodies and associations having some object of deep interest common to themselves. . . ." [52] He understood that freedom meant combination.

When the question arose whether it was criminal for a combination of employees to refuse to work for one who employed nonunion labor, Shaw replied in the disarming language of individualism that men who are not bound by contract are "free to work for whom they please, or not to work, if they so prefer. In this state of things, we cannot perceive, that it is criminal for men to agree together to exercise their acknowledged rights, in such a manner as best to subserve their own interests." [53]

He acknowledged that the pursuit of their own interests might result in injury to third parties, but that did not in his opinion make their combination criminal in the absence of fraud, violence, or other illegal behavior. To Shaw's mind the pursuit of self-interest was a hard, competitive game in which atomistic individuals stood less chance of getting hurt by joining forces. He also seems to have considered bargaining between capital and labor as a form of competition whose benefits to society, like those from competition of any kind, outweighed the costs. Finally, he was fair enough to believe that labor was entitled to combine if business could, and wary enough to understand that if the conspiracy doctrine were not modified, it might boomerang against combinations of businessmen who competed too energetically. Thus Shaw drew different conclusions from premises which he shared with others concerning individualism, freedom, and competition. The result of his interpretation of the criminal law of conspiracies was that the newly emerging trade-union movement was left viable.

But the corporate movement was left viable too, a fact which helps reconcile the fellow-servant and trade-union decisions. To regard one as "anti-labor" and the other as "pro-labor" adds nothing to an understanding of two cases governed by different legal considerations; on the one hand tort and contract, on the other criminal conspiracy. The fellow-servant case belongs to a line of harsh personal injury decisions that were unrelated to labor as such. To be sure, labor was saddled with much of the cost of industrial accidents, but victims of other accidents hardly fared better. The fellow-servant decision also represented a departure of the maxim *respondeat superior* which might impose liability without fault; while the trade-union decision, intended in part to draw the fangs of labor's support of the codification movement, represented a departure from Hawkin's conspiracy doctrine which might impose criminality on business as well as labor.

Despite the conflicting impact of the two decisions on labor's fortunes and the fact that they are not comparable from a legal standpoint, they harmonize as a part of Shaw's thought. He regarded the worker as a free agent competing with his employer as to the terms of employment, at liberty to refuse work if his demands were not met. As the best judge of his own welfare, he might assume risks, combine in a closed shop, or make other choices. For Shaw, workers possessed the same freedom of action enjoyed by employers against labor and against business rivals.

Compared to such Whig peers as Webster, Story, and Choate, Shaw was quite liberal in many respects. Indeed his judicial record is remarkably like the record one might expect from a jurist of the Jacksonian persuasion. Marcus Morton, during ten years of service as Shaw's associate, found it necessary to dissent only once, in *Kneeland*'s case. No doubt the inherited legal tradition created an area of agreement among American jurists that was more influential in the decision-making process than party differences. Yet it is revealing that many of Shaw's opinions might conceivably have been written by a Gibson, but not by a Kent. It was not just the taught tradition of the common law which Shaw and Gibson shared; they shared also taught traditions of judicial self-restraint, of the positive state, and the "Commonwealth idea," a term that is meaningful in Pennsylvania's history as well as in Massachusetts'.[54]

But personality makes a difference in law as in politics. It oversimplifies to say, as Pound has, that the "chiefest factor in determining the course which legal development will take with respect to any new situation or new problem is the analogy or analogies that chance to be at hand. . . ." [55] There are usually conflicting and alternative analogies, rules, and precedents from among which judges may choose. The direction of choice is shaped by such personal factors as the judge's calculation of the community's needs, his theory of the function of government, his concept of the role of the court, inexpressible intuitions, unrecognized predilections, and perhaps doting biases. It is difficult to name a single major case decided by Shaw which might not have gone the other way had another been sitting in his place.

Shaw interpreted the received law as he understood it, and his understanding was colored by his own presuppositions, particularly in respect to those interests and values he thought the legal order should secure. Few other judges have been so earnestly and consciously concerned with the public policy implicit in the principle of a case.

Much of his greatness lay in this concern for principle and policy. "It is not enough," he observed, "to say, that the law is so established. . . . The rule may be a good rule. . . . But some better reason must be given for it than that, so it was enacted, or so it was decided." [56] He thought it necessary to search out the rule which governed a case; to ask "upon what principle is it founded?" and to deliver a disquisition on the subject, with copious illustrations for the guidance of the future. From the bench he was one of the nation's foremost teachers of law.

His opinions did not overlook the question *"cui bono?"* which, he believed, "applies perhaps with still greater force to the laws, than to any other subject." [57] That is why he fixed "enlightened public policy" at the root of all legal principles, along with "reason" and "natural justice." [58] He understood that American law was a functioning instrument of a free society, embodying its ideals, serving its interests. It is not surprising, then, that he tended to minimize precedent and place his decisions on broad grounds of social advantage. Justice Holmes, attributing Shaw's greatness to his "accurate appreciation of the requirements of the community," thought that "few have lived who were his equals in their understanding of the grounds of public policy to which all laws must be ultimately referred. It was this which made him . . . the greatest magistrate which this country has produced." [59] To be sure, he made errors of judgment and policy. Yet the wonder is that his errors were so few, considering the record number of opinions which he delivered, on so many novel questions, in so many fields of law.

Perhaps his chief contribution was his day-by-day domestication of the English common law. He made it plastic and practical, preserving its continuities with what was worthwhile in the past, yet accommodating it to the ideals and shifting imperatives of American life. The Massachusetts Bar made a similar evaluation of his work when honoring the "old Chief" upon his resignation. The Bar, speaking through a distinguished committee, declared:

It was the task of those who went before you, to show that the principles of the common and the commercial law were available to the wants of communities which were far more recent than the origin of those systems. It was for you to adapt those systems to still newer and greater exigencies; to extend them to the solution of questions, which it required a profound sagacity to foresee, and for which an intimate knowledge of the law often enabled you to provide, before they had even fully arisen for judgment. Thus it has been that in your hands the law has met the demands of a period of unexampled activity and enterprise; while over all its varied and conflicting interests you have held the strong, conservative sway of a judge, who moulds the rule for the present and the future out of the principles and precedents of the past. Thus too it has been, that every tribunal in the country has felt the weight of your judgments, and jurists at home and abroad look to you as one of the great expositors of the law.[60]

Time has not diminished the force of this observation. As Professor Chafee has noted, "Probably no other state judge has so deeply influenced the development of commercial and constitutional law throughout the nation. Almost all the principles laid down by him have proved sound. . . ."[61]

He was sound in more than his principles. Like John Quincy Adams, his fellow Bay-Statesman whom he resembled in so many ways, he made his name a synonym for integrity, impartiality, and independence. Towering above class and party, doing everything for justice and nothing for fear or favor, he was a model for the American judicial character. And none but an Adams could compare with Shaw in his overpowering sense of public service and devotion to the good of the whole community. His achievement as a jurist is to be sought in his constructive influence upon the law of our country and in the fact so perfectly summed up in a tribute to him on his death: life, liberty, and property were safe in his hands.

NOTES

[1] Lemuel Shaw, "Profession of the Law in the United States" (extract from an address delivered before the Suffolk Bar, May 1827), *American Jurist*, VII (1832), 56–65.

[2] Oscar and Mary Handlin, *Commonwealth. A Study of the Role of Gov-*

ernment in the American Economy: Massachusetts 1784–1861 (New York, 1947), p. 31.

3 Edwin M. Dodd, *American Business Corporations Until 1860* (Cambridge, Mass., 1954), p. 44.

4 See *Hazen* v. *Essex Co.*, 66 Mass. (12 Cush.) 475 (1853); *Palmer Co.* v. *Ferrill*, 34 Mass. (17 Pick.) 58 (1835).

5 Dodd, *American Business Corporations*, p. 161.

6 See *Gould* v. *Boston Duck Co.*, 79 Mass. (13 Gray) 442 (1859); *Hazen* v. *Essex Co.*, 66 Mass. (12 Cush.) 475 (1853); *Murdock* v. *Stickney*, 62 Mass. (8 Cush.) 113 (1851); *Chase* v. *Sutton Mfg. Co.*, 58 Mass. (4 Cush.) 152 (1849); *Cary* v. *Daniels*, 49 Mass. (8 Met.) 466 (1844); *French* v. *Braintree Mfg. Co.*, 40 Mass. (23 Pick.) 216 (1839); *Williams* v. *Nelson*, 40 Mass. (23 Pick.) 141 (1839); *Palmer Co.* v. *Ferrill*, 34 Mass. (17 Pick.) 58 (1835); *Fiske* v. *Framingham Mfg. Co.*, 29 Mass. (12 Pick.) 68 (1831).

7 *Commonwealth* v. *Wilkinson*, 33 Mass. (16 Pick.) 175 (1834).

8 *City of Roxbury* v. *Boston & Providence R.R.*, 60 Mass. (6 Cush.) 424 (1850); *Newbury Tpk. Corp.* v. *Eastern R.R.*, 40 Mass. (23 Pick.) 326 (1839); *Boston Water Power Co.* v. *Boston & Worcester R.R.*, 33 Mass. (16 Pick.) 512 (1835); *Wellington, Petitioners*, 33 Mass. (16 Pick.) 87 (1834).

9 *Lumbard* v. *Stearns*, 58 Mass. (4 Cush.) 60 (1849).

10 61 Mass. (7 Cush.) 53 (1851).

11 Edward S. Corwin, *The Twilight of the Supreme Court* (New Haven, 1934), p. 68; Ernst Freund, *The Police Power* (Chicago, 1904), p. 425, § 405. For an extended discussion of the police power decisions by Shaw, see Leonard W. Levy, *The Law of the Commonwealth and Chief Justice Shaw* (Cambridge, Mass., 1957), chap. 13.

12 *Commonwealth* v. *Alger*, 61 Mass. (7 Cush.) 53, 83–84 (1851).

13 Roscoe Pound, *The Spirit of the Common Law* (Boston, 1921), pp. 53–54.

14 Quotations are from Shaw's opinions in the *Alger* case and in *Commonwealth* v. *Tewksbury*, 52 Mass. (11 Met.) 55 (1846).

15 Quoted by Pound, *The Spirit of the Common Law*, p. 53.

16 *Commonwealth* v. *Farmers & Mechanics Bank*, 38 Mass. (21 Pick.) 542 (1839).

17 *Crease* v. *Babcock*, 40 Mass. (23 Pick.) 334 (1839).

18 *Commonwealth* v. *Howe*, 79 Mass. (13 Gray) 26 (1859); *Brown* v. *Perkins*, 70 Mass. (12 Gray) 89 (1858); *Fisher* v. *McGirr*, 67 Mass. (1 Gray) 1 (1854); *Commonwealth* v. *Blackington*, 41 Mass. (24 Pick.) 352 (1837). These are the leading cases among dozens.

19 E.g., *Commonwealth* v. *Howe*, 79 Mass. (13 Gray) 26 (1859); *Commonwealth* v. *Logan*, 78 Mass. (12 Gray) 136 (1859); *Commonwealth* v. *Murphy*, 76 Mass. (10 Gray) 1 (1857); *Calder* v. *Kurby*, 71 Mass. (5 Gray) 597 (1856); *Commonwealth* v. *Hitchings*, 71 Mass. (5 Gray) 482 (1855); *Commonwealth* v. *Clap*, 71 Mass. (5 Gray) 97 (1855). For the Wynehammer doctrine see *Wynehammer* v. *People*, 13 N.Y. 378 (1856); *People* v. *Toynbee*, 20 Barb. 168 (N.Y. 1855); *Wynehammer* v. *People*, 20 Barb. 567 (N.Y. 1855).

20 *Worcester* v. *Western R.R.*, 45 Mass. (4 Met.) 564, 566 (1842).

21 *B. & L. R.R.* v. *S. & L. R.R.*, 68 Mass. (2 Gray) 1, 29 (1854).

22 *B. & W. R.R.* v. *Western R.R.*, 80 Mass. (14 Gray) 253 (1859) and *L. & W. R.R.* v. *Fitchburg R.R.*, 80 Mass. (14 Gray) 266 (1859).

23 *Sohier* v. *Mass. Gen. Hosp.*, 57 Mass. (3 Cush.) 483 (1849).

24 *Warren* v. *Mayor and Aldermen of Charlestown*, 57 Mass. (3 Gray) 84 (1854).

25 *Commonwealth* v. *Coolidge, Law Reporter,* v (Mass. 1843), 482.

26 *Jones* v. *Robbins,* 74 Mass. (8 Gray) 329 (1857).

27 *Robinson* v. *Richardson,* 79 Mass. (13 Gray) 454 (1859); *Sullivan* v. *Adams,* 69 Mass. (3 Gray) 476 (1855); *Fisher* v. *McGirr,* 67 Mass. (1 Gray) 1 (1854).

28 *Commonwealth* v. *New Bedford Bridge,* 68 Mass. (2 Gray) 339 (1854).

29 *Central Bridge Corp.* v. *City of Lowell,* 81 Mass. (15 Gray) 106 (1860); *Commonwealth* v. *Essex Co.,* 79 Mass. (13 Gray) 239 (1859). For an extended discussion of judicial review and of constitutional limitations under Shaw see Levy, *Law of the Commonwealth,* chap. 14.

30 *Commonwealth* v. *Farmers & Mechanics Bank,* 38 Mass. (21 Pick.) 542 (1838).

31 See Levy, *Law of the Commonwealth,* chaps. 8–9, "The Formative Period of Railroad Law."

32 *Denny* v. *New York Central R.R.,* 79 Mass. (13 Gray) 481 (1859); *Shaw* v. *Boston & Worcester R.R.,* 74 Mass. (8 Gray) 45 (1857); *Lucas* v. *New Bedford & Taunton R.R.,* 72 Mass. (6 Gray) 64 (1856); *Nutting* v. *Conn. River R.R.,* 67 Mass. (1 Gray) 502 (1854); *Norway ⎯lains Co.* v. *Boston & Me. R.R.,* 67 Mass. (1 Gray) 263 (1854); *Brown* v. *Eastern R.R.,* 65 Mass. (11 Cush.) 97 (1853); *Lichtenheim* v. *Boston & Providence R.R.,* 65 Mass. (11 Cush.) 70 (1853); *Props. of Locks and Canals* v. *Nashua & Lowell R.R.,* 64 Mass. (10 Cush.) 385 (1852); *Hollenbeck* v. *Berkshire R.R.,* 63 Mass. (9 Cush.) 478 (1852); *Kearney* v. *Boston & Worcester R.R.,* 63 Mass. (9 Cush.) 108 (1851); *McElroy* v. *Nashua & Lowell R.R.,* 58 Mass. (4 Cush.) 400 (1849); *Cary* v. *Berkshire R.R.,* 55 Mass. (1 Cush.) 475 (1848); *Snow* v. *Eastern R.R.,* 53 Mass. (12 Met.) 44 (1846); *Lewis* v. *Western R.R.,* 52 Mass. (11 Met.) 509 (1846); *Draper* v. *Worcester & Norwich R.R.,* 52 Mass. (11 Met.) 505 (1846); *Worcester* v. *Western R.R.,* 45 Mass. (4 Met.) 564 (1842); *Thompson* v. *Boston & Providence R.R., Daily Evening Transcript* (Boston), January 6, 1837; *Gerry* v. *Boston & Providence R.R.,* ibid., December 29, 1836.

33 *Shaw* v. *B. & W. R.R.,* 74 Mass. (8 Gray) 45 (1857); *Brown* v. *Kendell,* 60 Mass. (6 Cush.) 292 (1850).

34 *Carey* v. *Berkshire R.R.,* 55 Mass. (1 Cush.) 475 (1848).

35 *Hollenbeck* v. *Berkshire R.R.,* 63 Mass. (9 Cush.) 478 (1852); *Kearney* v. *Boston & Worcester R.R.,* 63 Mass. (9 Cush.) 108 (1851).

36 *Farwell* v. *Boston & Worcester R.R.,* 45 Mass. (4 Met.) 49 (1842). See Levy, *Law of the Commonwealth,* chap. 10.

37 *Commonwealth* v. *Hawkins,* 72 Mass. (6 Gray) 463 (1855); *Commonwealth* v. *Webster,* 59 Mass. (3 Cush.) 295 (1850); *Commonwealth* v. *York,* 50 Mass. (9 Met.) 93 (1845). See Levy, *Law of the Commonwealth,* pp. 218–228.

38 *Commonwealth* v. *Rogers,* 48 Mass. (7 Met.) 500 (1844). See Levy, *Law of the Commonwealth,* pp. 207–218.

39 Sims' Case, 61 Mass. (7 Cush.) 285 (1851). See Levy, "Sims' Case: The Fugitive Slave Law in Boston in 1851," *Journal of Negro History,* xxxv (1950), 39–74, reprinted in this volume, and Levy, *Law of the Commonwealth,* chap. 6.

40 *Roberts* v. *City of Boston,* 59 Mass. (5 Cush.) 198 (1849). See Levy and Phillips, "The Roberts Case: Source of the 'Separate but Equal' Doctrine," *American Historical Review,* lvi (1951), 510–518, and Levy, *Law of the Commonwealth,* chap. 7.

41 *Commonwealth* v. *Kneeland,* 37 Mass. (20 Pick.) 206 (1838). See Levy, "Satan's Last Apostle in Massachusetts," *American Quarterly,* v (1953), 16–30, and Levy, *Law of the Commonwealth,* chap. 5.

[42] *Stebbins* v. *Jennings*, 27 Mass. (10 Pick.) 172 (1830). See Levy, *Law of the Commonwealth*, chap. 3.

[43] *Charles River Bridge* v. *Warren Bridge*, 36 U.S. (11 Pet.) 420 (1837).

[44] John Theodore Horton, *James Kent* (New York and London, 1939), pp. 293–295; Carl B. Swisher, *Roger B. Taney* (New York, 1936), pp. 377–379.

[45] *Commonwealth* v. *Kimball*, 41 Mass. (24 Pick.) 359, 363 (1837).

[46] *Commonwealth* v. *Temple*, 77 Mass. (14 Gray) 69, 74 (1859).

[47] Shaw, "A Charge Delivered to the Grand Jury for the County of Essex, May Term 1832" (1832), pp. 15–16.

[48] See notes 6–9 above.

[49] *Commonwealth* v. *Hunt*, 45 Mass. (4 Met.) 111 (1842).

[50] The leading case is *Commonwealth* v. *Aves*, 35 Mass. (18 Pick.) 193 (1936). See also "Betty's Case," *Law Reporter*, xx (1857), 455; *Commonwealth* v. *Fitzgerald*, *Law Reporter*, vii (1844), 379; *Commonwealth* v. *Porterfield*, *ibid.*, p. 256; *Commonwealth* v. *Ludlum*, *The Liberator* (Boston), August 31, 1841; *Anne* v. *Eames* (1836) in "Report of the Holden Slave Case," Holden Anti-Slavery Society pamphlet (1839); *Commonwealth* v. *Howard*, *American Jurist*, ix (1832), 490.

[51] *Commonwealth* v. *Hunt*, 45 Mass. (4 Met.) 111 (1842). See Levy, *Law of the Commonwealth*, chap. 11.

[52] Shaw, "Charge to the Grand Jury," pp. 7–8.

[53] *Commonwealth* v. *Hunt*, 45 Mass. (4 Met.) 111, 130 (1842).

[54] See generally Louis Hartz, *Economic Policy and Democratic Thought: Pennsylvania, 1776–1860* (Cambridge, Mass., 1948).

[55] Pound, *The Spirit of the Common Law*, p. 12.

[56] Shaw, "Profession of the Law in the United States" (Extract from an address delivered before the Suffolk Bar, May 1827), *American Jurist*, vii (1832), 56–65.

[57] *Ibid.*

[58] *Norway Plains Co.* v. *Boston & Me. R.R.*, 67 Mass. (1 Gray) 263, 267 (1854).

[59] Oliver Wendell Holmes, *The Common Law* (Boston, 1881), p. 106.

[60] Address on Chief Justice Shaw's resignation, September 10, 1860, Supplement, 81 Mass. 599, 603 (1860).

[61] Zechariah Chafee, Jr., "Lemuel Shaw," *Dictionary of American Biography.*

JUDICIAL BIOGRAPHY

PRESIDENT William Howard Taft at his last press conference revealed that his proudest achievement was selecting six of the nine members of the Supreme Court. In 1929 Taft as Chief Justice believed that President Hoover would appoint "extreme destroyers of the Constitution" to fill vacancies on the Court. "I am older and slower and less acute and more confused," he wrote. "However, as long as things continue as they are, and I am able to answer in my place, I must stay on the Court in order to prevent the Bolsheviki from getting control." By his standards Taft was right. Hoover appointed Charles Evans Hughes, who championed the civil rights of Negroes, Communists, and pacifists; Owen Roberts, who wrote the opinion of the Court sustaining the power of the states to fix prices; and Benjamin Cardozo, whose most enduring opinion upheld the constitutionality of the Social Security Acts.

Judges should, to the extent humanly possible, be aware of their own predilections and decide cases without yielding to their own sympathies or reading the Constitution in the light of their own policy preferences. Yet even the best of judges in whom the judicial temperament is most finely cultivated cannot escape the currents that have tugged at them throughout their lives and color their judgment. Personality, the beliefs that make the man, is all the difference. When Truman's cold warriors, Sherman Minton and Tom Clark, replaced Wiley Rutledge and Frank Murphy, the Court under Chief Justice Vinson yielded to the hydraulic pressures of the passing hour. The government took uncivil liberties with the individual, and the Vinson Court adopted the position that the Bill of Rights should

A review of Leon Friedman and Fred L. Israel, eds., *The Justices of the United States Supreme Court, 1789–1969. Their Lives and Major Opinions,* 4 vols., 3,373 pp. (New York, 1969).

not straitjacket majoritarian government in its battle against un-American activities. The vigilant state threatened to become the vigilante state. Then Earl Warren succeeded Vinson, William Brennan and Arthur Goldberg filled vacancies left by Minton and Felix Frankfurter, and the constitutional law of civil liberties enjoyed its golden age. Never before had the Court been so bold in its protection of human rights in so many fields. President Nixon's present search for conservative strict-constructionists is more than a candid attempt to alter the trend of decision; it is an acknowledgment that at the apex of our system of a government of laws and not of men, the men who interpret the laws, rather than the laws themselves, are the decisive factors. Warren, on his retirement, observed that the Court consisted of nine independent men "who have no one to be responsible to except their own consciences."

To understand the work of the Court requires an understanding of the men who compose it and a glimpse of their consciences. Although the black robe may transform an appointee, for nothing is so emancipating as life tenure and freedom from accountability to the electoral battalions, his values shape his judicial opinions. That Henry Billings Brown, the author of *Plessy* v. *Ferguson,* believed in the racial inferiority of Negroes is not irrelevant. The public knows that Hugo Black was briefly a member of the Ku Klux Klan, but few know the more revealing facts about his early life—that his first client was a Negro convict, that he was a civil-rights lawyer in Alabama, that as a prosecutor he exposed third-degree tactics by the police against Negro suspects, and that when he first ran for the Senate, the Klan opposed him while he proudly stood on a poor-man's platform: "I am not now, and never have been, a railroad, power company, or corporation lawyer." Pierce Butler was such a lawyer, and he hated government regulation of business. "Are we to go into a state of socialism," he asked a bankers' association, "or are you men, and men like you, prepared to get out, take off your coats, and root for good old-fashioned Anglo-Saxon individualism?" As a member of the board of regents of a state university, he specialized in securing the discharge of professors whose opinions he disliked. Such biographical details bear a relationship to the fact that as a member of the Court Butler voted against free speech for radicals and wrote the opinion in 1935 holding minimum-wage laws unconstitutional. There is satisfaction in learning that he failed his constitutional law course in college. Louis D. Brandeis' advocacy of labor's rights and Hughes's defense of the Socialist assemblymen of New York are well-known forecasts of the paths they would follow on the Court.

Over thirty years ago Henry Steele Commager remarked that we know "shockingly little" about our highest judges. We still know too little about too many of them. Two-thirds of the ninety-seven who have been members of the Court have not been the subjects of biographies, and not more than twenty have had their lives described in books that are scholarly, readable, and comprehensive. The Chief Justices have fared best; there are splendid biographies of more than half: Jay, Marshall, Taney, Waite, Fuller, Taft, Hughes, and Stone. There are also excellent lives of some Associate Justices, generally major figures such as Samuel Freeman Miller, Stephen Field, Oliver Wendell Holmes, and Brandeis. But the still shocking fact is the neglect of so many men, now in the coffin of historical oblivion, who wrote opinions that affected the lives of their own and even succeeding generations. Moreover, every man who has been a member of the Court is historically important, because the Court is both a collective and a continuous institution. The principle of majority rule based on "one man, one vote" has always prevailed within the Court. Justice Robert Jackson declared that he enjoyed writing dissenting and concurring opinions better than majority opinions, "because you can just go off and express your own view without regard to anyone else. When you're writing for the Court, you try to bring your view within the limits of the views of all those who are supporting you. That often times requires that you temper down your opinion to suit some one who isn't quite as convinced as you are, or who has somewhat different grounds." Jackson might have added that even the lone dissent is tempered by the precedents of the past, the argument of the majority, and the hope of winning future votes.

But the large point is that even the magisterial opinions of a John Marshall and other judicial giants required the support of and were shaped by their brethren, many of whom were little known in their own times and are forgotten today even by legal scholars. To ignore Bushrod Washington, Henry Baldwin, Robert Grier, Noah Swayne, William Woods, Rufus Peckham, Joseph McKenna, Mahlon Pitney, and Edward Sanford in favor of the headliners like Holmes is to forget that the Constitution established "one Supreme Court" which wields the judicial power of the United States. The Court is more like a team, every man playing a vital part, rather than as individual stars. And unlike the other branches of the government, whose membership fluctuates with periodic elections, the Court has a perpetual corporate life. Its membership changes, to be sure, but the overlapping that comes from longevity of service creates a partnership between past and present, magnifying the role of every Justice as a connecting link. If a Methuselah could have attended every session of the Court from Washington's time to the present, he would have seen that its 97 members have been joined together by the presence at any session of just one of seven men (only one of whom has had a full-length biography): William Cushing, Joseph Story, Samuel Nelson, Stephen Field, John Marshall Harlan, Willis Van

Devanter, and Hugo Black. The voices and votes of all 97, even of the dead who are represented by the precedents, produce the opinions of the Court, now approaching 400 thick volumes.

The importance of every Justice and the fact that so very many have not even been treated in a scholarly article makes this four-volume set a feast for aficionados of the Court's history, a monumental reference work, and a point of departure for judicial biographers. Regrettably the set is as disappointing as it is valuable. Its allocation of space is grotesquely misproportioned; it is needlessly padded; and the biographical sketches are so uneven that they range from wretched to superb, with far too much that is merely passable.

There is a sketch of the life and judicial career of each of the 97, including Chief Justice Warren Burger. Each biography has a bibliography, some necessarily brief, lamenting the absence of previous studies, others useful for their references to obscure articles, unpublished doctoral dissertations, manuscript sources, and writings by the Justice. In addition there is at least one representative opinion for each Justice, introduced by a helpful headnote. The opinions are reprinted in entirety, two columns of small print to the page, and they add up to half the bulk of the four volumes. While there is much to be said for including opinions that show "the jurist in action," the same purpose could have been served by wisely edited extracts or by larding the essays with generous quotations from each Justice's work. The high price of the set puts it beyond the purchasing reach of students and scholars, its most likely users; and, they, like lawyers and judges, who will also find much instruction in these volumes, have access to the cases in library sets of the reports of the Supreme Court. Who else is likely to read complete reprints of selected opinions?

Volume Four has numerous appendices, including an informative statistical essay that provides for the 97 elaborate data on their backgrounds. There are also tables showing acts of Congress held unconstitutional and Supreme Court decisions overruled by subsequent decisions. In their effort to be up-to-date the editors outsmarted themselves by adding a brief sketch on Clement F. Haynsworth, Jr., with a summation of his major opinions, expecting, of course, that the Senate would ratify his nomination. The summation shows that he was reversed by the Supreme Court in four important cases on racially segregated schools in which he supported tactics of delay or circumvention, and that he dissented from a decision of his own circuit court ordering the admission of Negro patients and doctors to an all-white hospital constructed with federal funds. These cases alone, apart from Judge Haynsworth's alleged improprieties, made his nomination by President Nixon scandalous.

The 97 essays represent the work of 38 contributors, including several journalists and political scientists, 13 historians, and 13 lawyers, most of whom are law-school teachers. A minority of the authors, however, wrote many of the sketches—too many. Eight historians did over half of them, although only two of the eight are constitutional specialists; not surprisingly the high quality of their work is not matched by the others. As a group the law professors have written the best essays. The editors failed to attract enough of the distinguished experts that one would expect to see in such a project, men who could have added to the dimension of depth, variety, and sophisticated analysis that is rare here, because too few of dubious qualifications were burdened with so much.

The editors are responsible for the misshapen features of the books. For no discernible reason the essays range from five to thirty-two pages without any relations between their length and their subjects' judicial tenure, influence, or ability. Thus Thomas Johnson, who served for five months, receives more space than Willis Van Devanter (1911–1937), a leading "conservative." Howell Jackson, who served inconspicuously for two years, is treated at greater length than John McLean (1829–1861), a dominant figure of his time. John Rutledge, who actually sat for only a month, gets more attention than James Wayne (1835–1867), a major Jacksonian nationalist, and as much attention as the preeminent Harlan Fiske Stone (1925–1941). Alfred Moore, who wrote one minor opinion in five years, receives as much space as Owen Roberts (1930–1945), the swingman during the constitutional crisis of the New Deal years and prolific dissenter after. James Byrnes, who sat for a little more than a year, gets the same attention as Brandeis (1916–1939) and more than John Marshall Harlan (1877–1911), whose imperishable dissents in segregation, antitrust, criminal-justice, and maximum-hours cases have been vindicated by time. L. Q. C. Lamar, who sat with slight distinction for five years, receives more attention than anyone yet mentioned in this paragraph, more even than John Marshall (1801–1835) and Joseph Story (1811–1845), whom anyone would have to include on an all-star court of the greatest Justices. The two longest essays in the four volumes are, incredibly, on the most recent appointees—Thurgood Marshall and Warren Burger. The latter's appointment and installation as Chief Justice is depicted in greater detail than the Supreme Court career of Stephen Field (1863–1897), one of the half-dozen seminal influences of our judicial history.

There is no necessary connection, of course, between the number of pages accorded to a Justice and the quality of the author's treatment. But Paul A. Freund's essay is exceptional. He has contributed the best brief essay on Holmes ever written, matching its subject in pith, grace, and sagacity. Still, seven pages on Holmes (1902–1932) and three times as many on William Moody, who sat only a little more than two terms, suggests a distortion that is beyond explanation. The same may be said about the space given to the representative opinions. The opinions of George Sutherland do not merit more space than those of Holmes, Taft, and Brandeis combined. Burger's (circuit) opinions take up even more pages than Sutherland's, Fortas's more than Hughes's or Field's.

The great majority of the 97 essays are quite uncritical and divide into two categories. The first and by far the most numerous is reportorial or descriptive, like an encyclopedia article, with little or no interpretation except to the extent that superficial labels like conservative or liberal may add to or obscure understanding. In this category of essays there is rarely an analysis, apart from mere summary, of the Justice's leading opinions or an evaluation of his work as a whole. Yet even the most mediocre of these essays, such as the seven by Fred Israel, one of the editors, may add to our knowledge: in the instance of a Justice who has never before been the subject of a scholarly sketch, something is better than nothing. Many of the essays in this category are, however, valuable examples of their kind, including those by Frank Gatell on John Catron, Stanley Kutler on Ward Hunt, Louis Filler on the first Harlan, Samuel Hendel on Hughes, Leonard Dinnerstein on J. R. Lamar, Richard Kirkendall on Tom Clark, Fred Graham on Abe Fortas, and, the best of these, C. Herman Pritchett on Stanley Reed. Gatell deserves special mention, because he wrote more essays than any other, descriptively covering the eleven Justices appointed between 1829 and 1846. Although he tends to be strong on biographical data and weak on the judicial, he explains little.

By contrast the second category of uncritical essays is more readable and provocative: the deeply admiring appreciation of a Justice who reached results that his biographer applauds. Case analysis is absent, but general interpretation may be strong and sustained, though invariably oversimplistic. The best of the genre are the essays of Stephen J. Friedman on William Brennan and Arthur Goldberg, and especially, John P. Frank on Hugo Black and William Douglas. Frank's admiration of these great Justices so overpowers his judgment that he acknowledges no intemperate advocacy, serious mistakes, or inconsistencies in their opinions, and he fails, in his depiction of them as champions of human rights, to mention that Black, with Douglas' support, wrote the most suppressive opinion in the history of the Court in the *Korematsu* case in 1944. Over 110,000 people—70,000 of them American citizens—were removed from their homes by the military and placed in "relocation centers," because they were of Japanese descent. Roberts, dissenting, spoke of "imprisonment in a concentration camp, solely because of . . . ancestry," and Murphy, also dissenting, declared that the evacuation program "falls into the

103

ugly abyss of racism." Frank does not mention that Black's eloquent activist opinions are the expressions of a mind intoxicated with absolutist beliefs and the conviction that he is merely responding to the clarity of words on parchment. Yet, as Judge Learned Hand sagely noted, on a question of constitutional law the words a judge must construe "are empty vessels into which he can pour nearly anything he will."

According to the publisher these volumes consist of "soul-searching, deep, probing analytical essays based on original research." About twenty merit that characterization or are first rate for equally valid reasons. They may be subtle in character portrayal, critical and precise in their evaluation of opinions, sensitive to the complexity of constitutional issues, respectful of the judicial temperament and the agonizing difficulty of judging, exceptionally erudite, lucid, or convincing in their explanations, or filled with fresh insights into the motivation, style, and values of their subjects. Among the masterful essays are those by Donald Morgan on William Johnson (though he exaggerates Johnson's independence of Marshall), Albert Blaustein and Roy Mersky on Bushrod Washington, Gerald T. Dunne on Smith Thompson and Brockholst Livingston, William Gillette's quintet, Robert McCloskey on Stephen Field, Arnold Paul's quartet, and Alpheus T. Mason on Taft and Stone. On Brandeis, however, Mason is surprisingly flat and inexplicably ignores his work after 1932.

The five best essays in the set, in addition to Freund's little gem on Holmes, are by Andrew Kaufman on Cardozo, Albert Sacks on Frankfurter, Anthony Lewis on Warren, Norman Dorsen on the present Harlan, and Jerold Israel on Potter Stewart. All five tend to overvalue the virtues of judicial self-restraint, which in the hands of a Vinson may be a pose or tactic for reaching desired results without sacrificing the appearance of an appropriate deference to the political branches of government. Lewis, in particular, though perceptive in his understanding of Warren, seems overharsh in his criticism. He judges Warren against perfectionist standards as if demanding that Warren's results and acknowledged statesmanship be combined with Frankfurter's craftsmanship, judicial temperament, and theory of the judicial process.

With Lewis's standards in mind one might be overcome by melancholy in reflecting on how very few, if any, of the 97 justices have been "great." What we want in our highest judges is intellectual rectitude and brilliance, a self-conscious awareness of one's biases and a determination to be as detached as human fallibility will allow, a confidence in majority rule tempered with a passion for personal freedom, equality, and fairness in procedure, a vision of national and moral greatness combined with a respect for the federal system, a superior technical proficiency modified by a sense of justice and philosophic breadth, ethical behavior beyond suspicion, and, if the gods will grant perfection, even a competence in history, economics, statecraft, and literary skills. Not even Holmes or Cardozo approached the ultimate, certainly not the overwhelming advocates like Marshall, nor even Brandeis, who sought to muzzle his passionate convictions. But judges achieve greatness by varying combinations of talents, and different times call for differing abilities and emphases. Most of our highest jurists have been mediocre to competent, but greatness in any field is rare. Given man's limitations, the extraordinary demands of the office, and the politics of appointment which are surely not calculated to bring the ablest men to our supreme tribunal, it is perhaps remarkable that the nineteenth century could have produced nine men as gifted as Marshall, Story, Johnson, Taney, Curtis, Field, Miller, Bradley, and Harlan. Even more remarkable is the reassuring fact that our Court has been improving in quality, for one of the greatest of the justices, Black, has been privileged to remember Holmes and to serve with Hughes, Stone, Brandeis, Cardozo, Frankfurter, Douglas, Jackson, and Warren. Each in his own way has kept the Court the keeper of the nation's conscience.

EDITING THE FRAMER

THIS new edition of the papers of Madison, published under the joint sponsorship of the University of Chicago and the University of Virginia, is being done in the grand manner by the most exacting standards of superlative scholarship. Julian P. Boyd's "unusually close" association with the project is gratefully acknowledged by the editors, who deserve the highest compliment: they are disciples who have become peers of the master.

The papers of Madison as here presented and usefully indexed include all extant speeches and writings *by* him or which "appear" to have been "in large degree the product of his mind." That seems to mean any document with which Madison was associated, such as petitions not composed but merely signed by him along with many others. Also included are all extant letters *to* him and other papers to him which received his "careful attention"—a "test" which (the editors say) will exclude form documents such as commissions or passports and routine dispatches received by Madison as Secretary of State or President. The present edition of Madison's papers, in other words, aims to be complete, whereas the four previous editions included only 1,020 or about one-sixth of his own compositions and merely an "insignificant fraction" of the fifteen thousand letters addressed to him. Every item in the present edition will be printed in full, faithfully duplicating the original down to the last comma, misspelling, or variation in wording. In addition, there are fantastically meticulous annotations explaining each document's historical

A review of *The Papers of James Madison.* Volume I, *16 March 1751–16 December 1779.* Volume II, *20 March 1780–23 February 1781.* Volume III, *3 March 1781–31 December 1781.* Edited by William T. Hutchinson and William M. E. Rachal (Chicago, 1962, 1963).

context and significance as well as identifying the persons, places, events, and literary allusions mentioned.

The first two volumes of the series, which will total "some twenty volumes," cover Madison through his thirtieth year, as a college student, member of his country's committee of safety, delegate to the Virginia Convention of 1776, member of the Governor's Council, and delegate to the Continental Congress. Madison appears here, in the words of a contemporary, as a "gloomy, stiff creature" of rather conventional opinions. Even when his youthful interests were belletristic, he found the British reviews "loose in their principals [and] encourage[r]s of free enquiry even such as destroys the most essential Truths, Enemies to serious religion" (I, 101). "I do not meddle in Politicks," he wrote at the close of 1773. But, the "diabolical Hell conceived principle of persecution," even more than tax disputes with Britain, soon lured him from "amusing Studies," and he became a sober young revolutionist lamenting the weaknesses of the Confederation, inflationary measures, military reverses, and the inadequacies of troop supply. The greatly libertarian and judicious spirit of later years had only begun to emerge. Religious liberty was his first serious concern, and although his ideas on separation of church and state were too advanced for 1776, he was instrumental in securing a guarantee of the "free exercise" of religion, rather than mere "toleration," in the Virginia Declaration of Rights (the subject of an excellent editorial essay). In 1780, when hearing of a plan to offer slaves as bounties, he asked: "would it not be as well to liberate and make soldiers at once of the blacks themselves as to make them instruments for enlisting white Soldiers? It would certainly be more consonant to the principles of liberty which ought never to be lost sight of in a contest for liberty" (II, 209). But when Tory sedition was concerned, Madison possessed a strong tinge of the vigilante spirit (I, 147, 161–162, 190–191) and even suspected Franklin's loyalty on the basis of mere rumor ("the bare suspicion of his guilt amounts very nearly to a proof of its reality" [I, 151]).

The review of a new edition of the papers of a major statesman tends to follow a ritualized formula—expression of gratitude for the editors' contribution to the American heritage and historiography, of praise for their scholarship and conscientious dedication to exacting tasks, and of appreciation for the importance of their subject's life. Since these volumes undoubtedly deserve and will receive the ritualized treatment elsewhere, and in abundance, I prefer to conclude on a note of dissent.

I object to the editorial imperialism and compulsiveness that characterize these volumes. The editors have the collecting proclivities of a pack rat and promiscuously include just about everything— except Madison's laundry tickets, which presumably could not be located; and they treat every item, even the most trivial, to lavish editorial annotations which frequently amount to pedantry. Who really cares whether Madison advertised for a lost horse (I, 310–311; the elaborate annotation is so absurd as to be comical) or that his landlady was involved in a lawsuit over her furniture (the annotation to which exceeds that given to Madison's long, brilliant essay on "Money," the one and only essay by him in these volumes)? Why waste half a page on a "Letter not found" from the Virginia Board of Trade to the Virginia delegates in Congress (Madison was a delegate and all missives to and from the delegation are included), when it is not even certain that the dispatch was ever sent (II, 9; see also II, 70, 95)? Why publish fifteen items, rather than one sample, from the Board of Admiralty papers of the Continental Congress (each with notes as lengthy as the documents), for the brief period of his membership on the board, when they have been published elsewhere and Madison admittedly wrote none and contributed little, if anything, to any; and why republish so very many Council of State papers when there is no evidence that Madison shared the composition of any? What is the importance of the two-line receipt (I, 48) or the two-line authorization of payment (II, 78), the former with twenty-eight lines of footnotes giving biographical sketches of the nonentities borrowing money and the latter with forty lines of footnotes, mostly identifying the state auditors? Why devote a five-page editorial headnote (admirably done) to the problem of the cession of western lands, when Madison merely made a perfunctory second (not published) to a motion (published) made by a colleague?

Given the number of pages per volume, they are overpriced compared to other "Papers" being published. They are padded with many barely relevant and often piddling documents laboriously glossed. The editors substitute an overabundance of industry for a sense of proportion. At the present pace, the promised twenty volumes will probably become many more than that, for Madison lived until 1836 (56 years yet to go), the volume of his correspondence and essays prodigiously increased, and the most important stretches of his public career lie ahead. Considering these volumes, much can be said for the old-fashioned "Selected Papers of," the use of a calendar of unimportant papers, and a more spartan employment of annotations; the prodigious talents of the editors should be reserved for the really significant documents. These two volumes deserve to be reviewed by a Frank Sullivan, whose "Garland of Ibids," a devastating parody of Van Wyck Brooks' use of footnotes, should be read by the editors.

Volume III makes a shambles of the old canard that Madison's father was overjoyed to learn that Captain William Murray shot Colonel Francis Taliaferro in the pants with a rampart musket near the forks of the Pomunkey. Boldly ignoring the canard as if it did not exist, the editors calmly set the record straight in unconnected, elaborate, and monumentally trifling footnotes. Madison père, it now appears, might have been overjoyed at something else (p. 13, note 11); William Murray, brother of Dan, was selling pork and tallow at the time to George Rogers Clark out in Illinois, far from the forks of the Pomunkey (also spelled Pamunkey) which is the junction of the North and South Anna rivers (p. 159, note 5); as for the rampart muskets, their great weight and recoil made them too unwieldy for use on the field of honor (p. 87, note 2). Most significantly, it may have been William Taliaferro, brother of Mrs. Joseph Jones, not Francis Taliaferro, a first cousin once removed, whose pants figured so heavily in the life of Congressman Madison. Though we are relieved to know that Madison's involvement was limited to picking up the leather breeches from the tailor (p. 51, note 4), it is disappointing not to be told their size. Happily this is the only important lapse in the incredible industry and meticulous scholarship of the editors. With a sharp eye for the irrelevant and farfetched, they have generously squandered their magnificent editorial talents by assembling and massively annotating every document remotely connected —and sometimes unconnected—with Madison during the ten months from March through December of 1781, a period "unmarked by any significant event in the life of Madison or in the history of the Confederation Congress of which he was a member" (p. xv).

The pages of this volume constitute an imperfect verbal democracy, for while the editors believe that every scrap of Madisonia has a natural right to be included, they make some words more equal than others. The treatment of documents of unequal importance is remarkable. Only twelve days after the final ratification of the Articles of Confederation, Madison claimed that Congress possessed "general and implied" powers and yet proposed an amendment to the Articles authorizing Congress to employ the military force of the United States to compel delinquent or recalcitrant states to fulfill their federal engagements and to apply economic sanctions against "any of the Citizens thereof. . . ." The editors, who do not supply an introductory headnote giving the context and reasons for this document, perfunctorily note Madison's "first use of a phrase of great moment in our constitutional history," and mention in passing that sanctions against individuals was probably the chief nationalizing provision. So much for the most important document in the volume. But let one Simon Nathan complain, not to Madison but to the state governor, about Virginia's debt to him, and we get a page of footnoted explanation (p. 21). Madison's terse recommendation for adding an assistant and two clerks to the staff of the Superintendent of Finance merits forty-seven lines of annotation ranging from information on Spanish pieces-of-eight to George Bancroft's misinformation to President Grant concerning the nomination of Alexander T. Stewart for Secretary of the Treasury (pp. 171–172); but Madison's motion for complete nonintercourse with Great Britain, a regulation of commerce implied from the war power, merits no explanations or comment except as to stylistic drafting changes (pp. 22–25). Madison "shared little, if at all," in the discussions leading to the Franco-American consular convention, though the story is told in a lengthy footnote pegged to the following vital document, quoted here in full: "Com(mitte)e on plan of Consular Convention Randolph Elsworth Vandyk" (p. 201). But at least the document is in his hand. Perhaps the prize document of the collection is the one not included, the letter "not found," from the Virginia Delegates to Governor Jefferson; the 600-word editorial essay (pp. 139–140), which doesn't mention Madison, surmises that the letter was probably written by his congressional colleague, Joseph Jones (it was he who asked Madison to pick up Colonel Taliaferro's pants), to Jefferson or maybe William Fleming (not to be confused with William Murray—Dan's brother, or with William Taliaferro—Mrs. Jones' brother).

There are 174 documents in volume III, most of them not worthy of the lavish scholarship of the editors. Included are 21 letters by Madison himself, more than half of which were addressed to Edmund Pendleton; 37 letters to Madison, of which 21, weekly dispatches of war news from Virginia, were by Pendleton; 26 from the Virginia delegation and 28 to the delegation—mostly weekly exchanges with the governor of Virginia; 24 motions; and a miscellany of reports, expense accounts, and random notes by Madison on congressional activities. The documents are overwhelmingly concerned with military events—battles, captures at sea, and the movements of men and supplies, but there are also some documents on the creation of the national domain, the boundaries of the United States, diplomatic negotiations, and the administration of Congress. Good use has been made of the manuscript collection of the papers of the Continental Congress in the National Archives. There are few editorial headnotes, none of extended length.

The editors state in their regrettably brief preface that only twenty-two of the documents in the volume have appeared in whole or in part in previous collections of the writings of Madison. They are rightfully modest in not venturing to say whether anything has been gained by their prodigious labors, other than quantitatively. I reread the relevant sections of Irving Brant's grand biography and of Edmund Cody Burnett's *The Continental Congress.* Comparing them with what volume III has to offer, I conclude that neither could have been improved by the use of this volume. I wonder what purpose is served by the publication of Madison's papers on so huge a scale as this, with such fantastically detailed annotations whose total wordage probably exceeds that of the documents themselves.

The editors promise "some twenty volumes," but when they devote a whole volume to less than a year admittedly "unmarked by any significant event" in his life, we can anticipate being smothered by tons of trivia. Madison was thirty-one years old in 1781. A long life, to 1836, and the great years of constructive achievement lie ahead of the editors. If these ten months are worth a volume in the life of a young congressman, who in these pages remains a shadowy and relatively unproductive figure, will we get a book for each month of the life of the mature Constitution-maker and congressman, a book for each week of the Secretary of State, and a book for each day of the Presidency? Given their present rate of progress and incapacity to judge what is worthy of inclusion and of annotation, the editors have plunged headlong into making the profession of editing look purely pedantic. Volume III sometimes seems intended as a satire on the now flourishing industry of editing the papers of our great statesmen.

PART II

The First Amendment Freedoms

LIBERTY OF THE
PRESS FROM
ZENGER TO JEFFERSON

I

FREEDOM of the press, in the words of the Continental Congress of 1774, is essential to "the advancement of truth, science, morality and arts in general" and to the maintenance of "honorable and just modes" of conducting public affairs.[1] Central to the concept of a free press is freedom of political opinion, and at the core of that freedom lies the right to criticize the government. The acquittal of John Peter Zenger in 1735, in a prosecution for seditious libel, is celebrated, deservedly or not, because it "marked a milestone in the fight for the right to criticize the government."[2]

That right is indispensable to personal liberty and is inseparable from self-government. When any avenues of political expression are closed, government by consent of the governed may be foreclosed. If any information or opinion is denied expression, the formation of public policy has not been founded on a consideration of all points of view; as a result, the will of the majority cannot really be known. Accordingly, libertarian theory, such as that advanced by Zenger's counsel, presents a fairly systematic argument that defines and defends both freedom of the press and the right to criticize the government.

A broad libertarian theory emerged toward the close of the eighteenth century, first in England and then in America. It advocated the utmost freedom of political opinion by repudiating the concept that the government can be criminally assaulted—that is, seditiously libeled—simply by the expression of critical views that have a tendency (alleged to be bad) to diminish the public's esteem for the government. The new theory also advocated the same freedom for everyone, even those whose opinions were thought to be detestable, mocking, or pernicious; this included the village atheist and the local extremist, whether radical or reactionary.

II

Seventeenth-century libertarians had advanced a drastically different theory. They did not remotely question the propriety of punishing seditious libels, even though criminal prosecutions for criticism of the government were one of the principal means of muzzling political and religious dissent. Another such means was official censorship, enforced by a licensing system of "prior" or "previous" restraints. Anything published without a license was criminal. All manuscripts had to be submitted to crown officials empowered to expunge objectionable passages or to deny a license altogether. Milton's *Areopagitica* derives its fame from its author's incisive and eloquent arguments against censorship, the foremost target of seventeenth-century libertarianism. "Give me liberty," cried Milton, "to know, to utter, and to argue freely according to conscience, above all liberties" [3]—but his use of the personal pronoun is significant.

Milton's well-advertised tolerance did not extend to the thought that he hated. It extended only, as he specified, to "neighboring differences, or rather indifferences," which in 1644 meant Protestantism in its various forms. He explicitly excluded from his spectrum of neighboring opinions "Popery, and open superstition," which he thought "should be extirpat," and he banned also the "impious or evil" which "no law can possibly permit. . . ." He deplored royalist writings as "libell against the Parliament" and thought they should be censored; he himself later served as one of Cromwell's official censors. In the concluding section of his *Areopagitica*—a section seldom read or quoted today—Milton, after advocating a system of unlicensed printing, endorsed the sanctions of the criminal law for any abuse or licentiousness of the press: "Those which otherwise come forth (unregistered, although unlicensed), if they be found mischievous and libellous, the fire and the executioner will be the timeliest and the most effectual remedy that mans prevention can use." [4]

Roger Williams, a second great libertarian champion of the seventeenth century, in his imperishable defense of toleration, "The Bloudy Tenent, of Persecution, for cause of Conscience," exempted from the civil magistrate's jurisdiction all matters of conscience, even "scandalous" doctrines against the establishment. But he broke into

116

his argument to note parenthetically, "I speak not of scandal against the civil state, which the civil magistrate ought to punish. . . ." [5]

John Locke, the third in the trinity of seventeenth-century libertarians, believed that "no opinions contrary to human society, or to those moral rules which are necessary to the preservation of civil society, are to be tolerated by the magistrate." Advocating that the intolerant should not be tolerated, he proposed punishment of any who "will not own and teach the duty of tolerating all men in matters of mere religion." [6] In both his "Letter concerning Toleration" and his "Fundamental Constitutions of Carolina" he supported an extraordinary latitude for freedom of religion, yet took care to specify that no person should speak anything "irreverently or seditiously of the government or governors, or of state matters." [7] And he regarded the opinions of atheists and the political implications of Catholic doctrine as seditious. Like Milton, Locke opposed the licensing system, though with far greater success. The system, Locke contended, injured the printing trade, was administratively cumbersome, and was unnecessary because the common law gave adequate protection against licentiousness. In 1694 Locke drafted for the House of Commons a statement of eighteen reasons for terminating government censorship.[8] Not a single one of the eighteen, however, was a principled defense of freedom of the press or a philosophical argument for the free mind. The "prior restraint" licensing system finally died in England, but it died on grounds of expediency.

The common law's definition of criminal libels meant that the press was free from censorship in advance of publication, but was subject to subsequent punishment for bad or wrong sentiments about the government. As Chief Justice Holt stated in Tuchin's case in 1704, a "reflection on the government"—such as saying that corrupt officers administered its affairs—must be punished because it tended "to beget an ill opinion" of the government. "If people should not be called to account for possessing the people with an ill opinion of the government, no government can subsist, for it is very necessary for all governments that the people should have a good opinion of it." [9] No libertarian theorist challenged this proposition or progressed beyond the no-prior-restraints concept of freedom of the press until "Cato" burst upon the scene.

III

"Cato" was the joint pseudonym of the Whig political journalists, John Trenchard and Thomas Gordon. Their essays, first published in London newspapers beginning in 1720, were collected in four volumes that went through six editions between 1733 and 1755.[10] "No one," writes a historian familar with the sources, "can spend any time in the newspapers, library inventories, and pamphlets of colonial America without realizing that *Cato's Letters* rather than Locke's *Civil Government* was the most popular, quotable, esteemed source of political ideas in the colonial period." [11] "*Cato's Letters* was quoted in every colonial newspaper from Boston to Savannah," [12] and "the most famous" [13] of his letters was "Of Freedom of Speech: That the same is inseparable from Public Liberty." [14] Another letter of immense popularity was "Reflections upon Libelling," one of three essays on libel law and freedom of the press.[15]

Cato brought to his wide audience a bold, systematic theory of intellectual and political liberty. At the core of this theory stood the concept of freedom of expression. Free speech, Cato insisted, was "the Right of every Man, as far as by it he does not hurt and controul the Right of another; and this is the only Check which it ought to suffer, the only Bounds which it ought to know." He explained the relationship between free government and freedom of the press, arguing that they prospered together or died together. Government officials, he declared, were merely trustees of the people's interests, and it was the people "for whose Sake alone all publick Matters are, or ought to be, transacted. . . ." Accordingly, good and honest officials should welcome having their deeds openly examined. "Only the wicked Governors of Men dread what is said of them," and it was only they who complained about the licentiousness of the press and sought to restrain it. If the press misrepresented public measures, the wisest remedy was to represent the measures correctly, rather than to punish the mistake.[16] Libels rarely provoked causeless discontent against the government. The benefits from what the law called libels, by checking the conduct of officials, outweighed their mischiefs. Libels, thought Cato, were the inevitable result of a free press, "an Evil arising out of a much greater Good," [17] bringing advantages to society in the fields of liberty, property, government, religion, science, the arts, and general knowledge. He conceded that there was a risk in allowing freedom of expression; let men talk as they wished about government, philosophy, or religion, and they might reason seditiously, wrongly, or irreligiously. But restrain their opinions, and the results would be worse—injustice, tyranny, and ignorance.[18]

Cato did not wish to be misunderstood as arguing for the uncontrolled liberty of men to calumniate each other or the government. Libels against the government were "always base and unlawful," [19] especially when untrue, and should be punished as an abuse of liberty as long as England's good laws were prudently and honestly enforced.[20] Notwithstanding this genuflection by Cato toward the law, keeping him on its safe side, he made it abundantly clear in his essays that he thought the law of criminal libel was neither good nor prudently enforced; indeed, that it was quite dangerous to public liberty and to good government. He approved of libel prosecutions only in extreme cases, and even then only under a law which did not penalize criticism that could be proved to be true. On the grounds that the public had an interest in knowing the truth about public measures and men, Cato contended that truth should be admitted as a defense against a criminal-libel charge—in other words, a defendant who could prove the accuracy of his allegedly seditious utterance should be acquitted.[21]

The law, however, did not regard truth as a defense. On the contrary, the theory of the law was, the greater the truth, the greater the scandal against the government. Judges in libel cases reserved exclusively to themselves, as a matter of law, decision of the crucial question whether the defendant's remarks were libelous. Cato condemned the courts' practice of implying a criminal or seditious intention on the part of defendants by stretching the defendants' words to find in them a danger to the government. The best way to treat undeserved libels, said Cato, was to "laugh at them, and despise them," rather than to prosecute them.[22] Such prosecutions, he thought, represented far too great a threat to liberty. "I must own, that I would rather many Libels should escape, than the Liberty of the Press should be infringed. . . ."[23]

Cato's Letters was the high-water mark of libertarian theory until the close of the eighteenth century. In the American colonies, Cato was adored, quoted, and plagiarized. In fact, American libertarian theory, neither original nor independent, was at its best little more than an imitation of Cato. Benjamin Franklin, the towering figure among American printers and theorists, illustrates the point. His own writings on freedom of the press were trite, brief, vague, and philosophically on a par with his "Poor Richard" pieces.[24]

But Franklin, in 1721 and 1722, was the first American to reprint Cato's "Of Freedom of Speech" and "Reflections upon Libelling" essays.[25] He also published a four-part essay on the same topics by Cato's greatest American pupil, James Alexander.[26] Alexander was the lawyer-editor who contributed articles on freedom of the press to Zenger's *New-York Weekly Journal*, masterminded Zenger's legal defense, and edited the narrative of the trial. With the possible exception of *Cato's Letters*, this narrative was the most widely known source of libertarian thought in the English-speaking world during the eighteenth century. Alexander used to copy extensive selections from Cato for his private instruction, as well as reprinting them for the readers of the *New-York Weekly Journal*, which he edited. The paper in its early years carried frequent excerpts, references, and paraphrases from the "almost divine" Cato. The "Of Freedom of Speech" essay was republished, for the second time, in the issue immediately following the public burning of "seditious" copies of the paper at the order of the Governor's Council.[27] Shortly afterward, the leader of the Zenger party against Governor Cosby, Lewis Morris, read Cato's "Discourse upon Libels" to the General Assembly and Alexander ran it in the *Weekly Journal*.[28]

Even the defense of Zenger, as planned by James Alexander and presented by Andrew Hamilton, was substantially derived from Cato, who was the first to popularize the idea that truth should be admitted as a defense against a charge of criminal libel.[29] Moreover, Cato also provided the basis of the argument that "while men keep within the bounds of truth, I hope they may with safety both speak and write their sentiments of the conduct of men in power." [30] The only essential of Zenger's defense that could not be traced to Cato was Hamilton's appeal to the jury to decide for themselves, rather than be bound by the court's instructions, whether the defendant's words were libelous.[31] If freedom of the press was the palladium of public liberty, as the colonists were so fond of reiterating, *Cato's Letters* was its intellectual source and provided virtually the entire content of its philosophy as well.

IV

Although eighteenth-century American libertarian theory was extraordinarily inventive in many areas—producing, for example, the ideas for a written fundamental law, bills of rights, a federal system, and constitutional conventions—American thought on freedom of the press remained stationary after the 1730's. Indeed, in some respects it stagnated and even regressed. From the time of the Zenger defense until the response to the Sedition Act, there were certainly no innovations in libertarian theory on freedom of the press. And practice, of course, lagged behind theory. In the 1720's, when Trenchard and Gordon wrote *Cato's Letters*, Samuel Mulford was summarily expelled from the New York Assembly for having suggested that the people ought to clean out some of the members of that body; [32] Benjamin Franklin's brother was jailed in Boston for insinuating in his newspaper that the provincial government was not taking effective action against coastal pirates; [33] the Reverend John Checkley was convicted in Massachusetts for distributing a book critical of Calvinist doctrines; [34] two Philadelphians were pilloried for daring to "speak evil of dignitaries"; [35] and, also in the

a special verdict, the jury would be leaving to the court as a matter of law, a ruling on the main question whether the words were criminal per se.) He urged instead that the jury should return a general verdict, deciding the law as well as the facts.[42]

Hamilton did not appreciate that truth is a mischievous, often an illusory, standard that often defies knowledge or understanding and cannot always be established by the rules of evidence. He did not appreciate that one man's truth is another's falsehood or that political opinions, which notoriously differ, may not even be susceptible of proof. Nor did he appreciate that a jury in a case of seditious libel is a court of public opinion (often synonymous with public prejudice), and is hardly adequate as an instrument for measuring the truth of an accusation that the government, or its policies, or its officials, may be unjust, tyrannical, or repugnant to the public interest.

When judges were dependent tools of the state, a jury of one's peers and neighbors seemed a promising bulwark against the tyrannous prosecution of seditious libel by the administration and its judges. But later events proved that juries with the power of ruling on the guilt or innocence of alleged libels could be as influenced by prevailing passions as were judges, when deciding the fate of defendants who had expressed unpopular sentiments. In England, where the power of juries in libel cases was secured by Fox's Libel Act of 1792, the most repressive prosecutions were, with very few exceptions, successful.[43] In America only one verdict of "not guilty" was returned in the numerous prosecutions under the Sedition Act which entrusted criminality to the jury and admitted truth as a defense.[44]

Embattled libertarians of the eighteenth century belatedly discovered that they had mistaken a prop of straw for one of brick when they accepted Hamilton's position instead of repudiating the concept of seditious libel. His argument, which hinged on the fact that public opinion was opposed to the administration, had its limitations as a libertarian defense of the press and, despite the jury's verdict, left the law unchanged. Indeed, judging from its impact on the bench, Hamilton's argument was like the stagecoach ticket inscribed: "Good for this day only." As late as 1804 Chief Justice Morgan Lewis of New York—a Jeffersonian, no less—was of the opinion that truth does not constitute a defense against a charge of criminal libel.[45]

Alexander's report of the Zenger trial saved Hamilton's argument for posterity. The account was reprinted in America, as well as in England, at politically strategic moments. It was reprinted in 1770 in New York, for example, when Alexander McDougall was prosecuted for seditious libel; and it appeared in 1799 in Boston, during the Sedition Act controversy.[46] The Zenger case became famous partly because it was so well publicized and partly because it was so isolated a phenomenon. Except for an obscure trial of a New Yorker in 1745 for "singing in praise of the Pretender," [47] and another insignificant prosecution in Virginia at about the same time,[48] Zenger's case was the last of its kind under the "royal judges." Altogether, there were probably not more than half a dozen prosecutions for seditious libel in the whole of the American colonial period.[49] Indeed, the maligned judges were virtually angels of self-restraint when compared with the intolerant public—or when compared with the oppressive governors who, acting in a quasi-judicial capacity with their councils, were more dreaded and active instruments of suppression than the common-law courts.

The most suppressive body by far, however, was that acclaimed bastion of the people's liberties, the popularly elected assembly. That the law bore down harshly on verbal crimes in colonial America was the result of the inquisitorial propensities of the governors and legislatures, which vied with each other in ferreting out slights upon the government. The law of seditious libel was enforced in America primarily by the provincial assemblies, exercising their power to punish alleged "breaches of parliamentary privilege." Needing no grand jury to indict and no petty jury to convict, the assemblies zealously sought to establish the prerogative of being as immune to criticism as the House of Commons they all emulated. An assembly might summon, interrogate, and fix criminal penalties against anyone who had supposedly libeled its members, its proceedings, or the government generally. Any words, spoken or printed, that were imagined to have a tendency to impeach an assembly's behavior, question its authority, derogate from its honor, affront its dignity, or defame its members individually or collectively, were regarded as seditious and punishable as a breach of parliamentary privilege.[50]

Had John Peter Zenger attacked the New York General Assembly instead of Governor Cosby, he would have been summarily convicted at the bar of the house and then jailed, and in all likelihood he would have remained unknown to posterity. Happily, he was tried before a jury. Hamilton's argument was especially appealing because his defendant symbolized the popular cause. It should be remembered that the grand jury, despite the administration's urgings, refused to indict Zenger, and that the Assembly refused to cooperate with the Governor's Council at every step of the prosecution. When, for example, the Council requested the Assembly's concurrence in its order that four issues of the *New-York Weekly Journal* "be burnt by the hands of the Common Hangman," and that their printer be prosecuted, the Assembly ordered "that the said . . . request lie on the table." [51] Moreover, the Court of Quarter Sessions, the lower house of the city's legislature, formally protested the actions of the Governor's Council. The Court, which comprised the mayor and aldermen of the city, argued that it was duty bound to protect liberty of the press, and it noted: ". . . an Assembly of the Province and several Grand Juries have refused to meddle with the papers when applied to by the Council. . . ."[52]

The Zenger case at best gave the press the freedom to print the "truth"—if the truth were not directed against the legislature. The power of the legislature to punish nonmembers as well as members for alleged breach of privilege—criticism of the assembly—enabled it to control the press. Indeed, long after the right to publish without first obtaining government approval or license had been won, the provincial legislatures continued to regard the unlicensed publication of their votes and proceedings as a breach of privilege. This information, of the most vital interest to the public, could be printed only after first being submitted to the speaker of the house for his examination and signature.

V

That the Zenger case did not emancipate the press in colonial New York is suggested by subsequent events. The contrast between the Assembly's behavior in 1747 and in 1753 is especially illuminating. In 1747 Governor George Clinton ordered James Parker, the colony's official printer, not to publish the Assembly's angry remonstrance against his policies. Unanimously, the legislators voted that it was "the undoubted Right of the People of this Colony, to know the Proceedings of their Representatives." The Assembly commanded Parker to print its remonstrance in order that the people might be apprised of their representatives' "firm Resolution to preserve the Liberty of the Press."[53] The legislature's professed commitment to the principle of a free press was abandoned a few years later, in 1753, when a printer, Hugh Gaine, believing the royal instructions to the new governor and the latter's speech to the Assembly to be matters of public interest, published them in his New-York Mercury. The Assembly, upon learning that Gaine had "presumed" to print part of its proceedings without license, summoned him to its bar and demanded to know by what authority he had dared to breach its privileges. Gaine, intimidated, most abjectly humbled himself. He had done wrong, he claimed, only out of ignorance; profusely sorry for having given offense, he "humbly asked their pardon." Mollified by this proper display of contrition, the Assembly magnanimously released Gaine after formal censure, a warning, and exaction of the costs of the case.[54]

In 1756 James Parker became the next victim of parliamentary privilege. He had published in his *New-York Gazette* an article on the distressed condition of the people in Orange and Ulster counties, and the house saw the article as "greatly reflecting" upon it and calculated "to irritate the People of this Colony against their Representatives. . . ." Parker and his associate, William Weyman, were voted to be guilty of a "high misdemeanour" and contempt of authority. Taken into custody by the sergeant at arms of the house, they were interrogated before the bar. Parker, a most cooperative witness, revealed that the offensive article had been written by the Reverend Hezekiah Watkins of Newburg. The publishers confessed their fault for printing the article, denied any intention of giving affront, and humbly begged the pardon of the honorable house. The honorable house kept its prisoners in jail for a week before discharging them. The Reverend Mr. Watkins, who was promptly arrested, confessed his authorship but pleaded that he had acted out of a mistaken zeal for the welfare of the people rather than from disrespect for the house. He was heartily sorry, he declared, and pleaded to be forgiven. He was jailed anyway. The next day he was officially reprimanded, forced to pay the costs, and then discharged.[55]

In 1758 the speaker of the house received a letter from one Samuel Townsend, a justice of the peace in Queen's County, asking legislative relief for certain refugees quartered on Long Island. The speaker, presenting the letter to the house, termed it "insolent," whereupon that body commanded Townsend's appearance. When he daringly failed to show up, he was cited for contempt and a warrant was issued for his arrest. He was hauled before the bar and examined in the usual intimidating fashion, but he showed no signs of repentance. The Assembly then voted that, because his letter reflected on its "Honour, Justice and Authority," he was guilty of a "high Misdemeanour and a most daring Insult." The gloomy prison in which Townsend found himself provoked him to reconsider his position. He sent a petition expressing his deep sorrow for having written the letter that had inadvertently cast reflection on the house. He also promised faithfully to avoid committing such misdeeds in the future, and he concluded by asking for the house's "Compassion." Moved by this respectful submission from a judge, the Assembly released him from jail and discharged him, with an official reprimand from the speaker.[56]

As New York approached the revolutionary controversy, its press was only as free as its legislature permitted. In practice, all political comment was tolerated as long as criticism did not anger the people's representatives. The courts were merely a formal threat against unfettered discussion, as the Zenger case demonstrated. It was the legislature, with unlimited discretion to punish supposed breaches of parliamentary privilege, that actively exercised repressive power. The frequency of the cases and the incidence of punishment hardly suggest tyranny, but the house's arbitrary use of its prerogative did have a smothering effect on the free expression of opinion relating to legislative matters and measures. Libertarian theorists had argued that freedom of speech and press would have the salutary effect of checking evil or incompetent rulers and stimulating responsible government. But in New York the legislature never permitted this libertarian theory to be practiced. The royal governor, his policies, and his administration were almost always fair game for popular disapprobation; the Zenger case proved that, but little more. In the struggle of the Assembly for independence from the governor, most anti-administration criticism played into the hands of the Assembly and the "popular" party. "Freedom of the press," in other words, was a useful instrument for the expansion of legislative prerogative, but in any clash between parliamentary privilege and liberty of discussion the victory went to parliamentary privilege, which was deemed the superior right.

The limited experience of colonial New York with broad freedom of the press matched the limited thinking of libertarian theorists on the scope of permissible expression. No one even dared to criticize the Assembly's restraints on the press. No one suggested that the press's freedom ought not to be fixed by the extent to which a jury's emotions might be swayed. And even Andrew Hamilton himself, in his defense of Zenger, had admitted that a "false" charge against the government merited punishment. "For as it is truth alone which can excuse or justify any man for complaining of a bad administration," Hamilton declared, "I as frankly agree that nothing ought to excuse a man who raises a false charge or accusation, even against a private person, and that no manner of allowance ought to be made to him who does so against a public magistrate." [57] Similarly, James Alexander acknowledged in the columns of Zenger's paper, before the trial, "That Abuses that disolve Society, and sap the Foundations of Government, are not to be sheltered under the Umbrage of the Liberty of the Press." [58] In 1737, in the midst of an essay on freedom of the press, Alexander confessed that "to infuse into the minds of the people an ill opinion of a just administration, is a crime that deserves no mercy. . . ." [59]

The colonial understanding of the scope of free expression was further revealed in 1753 by an editorial in *The Independent Reflector*, a New York magazine that was the voice of libertarian thought of mid-century America. When an opposition journal refused to publish an essay composed by one of *The Independent Reflector's* regular contributors, the editor, William Livingston, published this credo on liberty of the press: "A Printer ought not to publish every Thing that is offered to him; but what is conducive of general Utility, he should not refuse, be the Author a Christian, Jew, Turk or Infidel. Such Refusal is an immediate Abridgement of the Freedom of the Press. When on the other Hand, he prostitutes his Art by the Publication of any Thing injurious to his Country, it is criminal,—It is high Treason against the State. The usual Alarm rung in such Cases, the common Cry of an Attack upon the LIBERTY OF THE PRESS, is groundless and trifling. The Press neither has, nor can have such a Liberty, and whenever it is assumed, the Printer should be punished." [60]

The most willing tool of the crown could hardly have disagreed with this definition of a free press by the republican patriots from the colony identified with Zenger. On the other hand, there could be no greater danger to the right of the open political debate than the vague crime of constructive treason, especially if it could be committed by mere words. Even a crown lawyer knew that the law ruled out treason in any case where words against the government were unconnected with some treasonous project for carrying them out; such words were criminally punishable only as a seditious libel. The severity of the remarks by New York's Whig lawyer-editor is revealed by the fact that seditious libel was a misdemeanor, treason a capital crime.

A few years after the publication of this credo on the liberty of the press, James Parker, who had been *The Independent Reflector*'s printer and editor, wrote a broadside opposing a stamp tax on newspapers that was being proposed by the New York Assembly (1759). Parker announced that in countries "where Liberty truly reigns, every one hath a Privilege of declaring his Sentiments upon all Topicks with the utmost Freedom, provided he does it with proper Decency and a just Regard to the Laws." [61] Yet "the Laws" provided for the punishment of words that tended, however remotely, to disturb the peace, to lower the government in the esteem of the public, or to breach parliamentary privilege. Parker's statement was a neat way of saying that all opinions short of illegal ones were free— an epitome of the American view of the matter.

The New York General Assembly, which had intimidated a printer and his journeyman in 1766 for inadvertently publishing an address of the house with two typographical errors,[62] proved that it was capable of dealing effectively even with a radical of the patriot party. In December 1769, the Assembly had voted to supply provisions for the King's troops in New York City in return for Governor Cadwallader Colden's signature on an act authorizing needed bills of credit. Three days later a handbill, addressed "To the Betrayed Inhabitants of New-York" and signed by a "Son of Liberty," was broadcast throughout the city. The author condemned the Assembly for abandoning the liberties of the people by passing the provisions bill, and called upon the public to rise against unjust measures. The Assembly retaliated by declaring the handbill to be "a false seditious and infamous Libel," and by calling upon the Governor to offer rewards for information leading to the discovery of the author or authors. The provisions bill had passed the Assembly by a bare majority, but the resolves against the seditious writer passed unanimously. Governor Colden gladly complied with the Assembly's request and issued proclamations offering a reward of £150.[63]

Dazzled by so much money, a journeyman printer in the shop of James Parker betrayed his employer, declaring him the printer of "To the Betrayed." Parker, who in 1756 had been jailed for a week by the Assembly for printing a reflection, was now charged with having published a seditious libel. He was arrested and brought before the Governor and Council. His apprentices and journeymen were taken into custody for questioning at the same time. Their testimony substantiated that of the informer, and also revealed that one Alexander McDougall had corrected the proofs at the printing office. Parker himself balked at naming the author, but he could not withstand the threats of imprisonment and dismissal from his post as comptroller of the post office. He made a deal with the Council. He received immunity from prosecution and a guarantee against loss of his post, in return for identifying the author and pledging to appear against him as a government witness.[64]

The man identified by Parker was Alexander McDougall, a local merchant who was one of the commanders of the Sons of Liberty. Later McDougall would serve in both the First and Second Continental Congresses and as a major general during the Revolution. He died in 1786 a pillar of conservatism, the first president of the Bank of New York and founder and head of the New York Society of Cincinnati. In February 1770, however, he was arrested on a charge of seditious libel against the Assembly. With Parker as a witness of McDougall's authorship, the legislature had a sure-fire case and turned the prisoner over to the common-law courts. McDougall, on examination before Chief Justice Daniel Horsmanden, remained silent except to demand a trial by jury. Bail was set at the inordinately high sum of £500, which McDougall refused to pay. He preferred a martyr's prison while awaiting the action of the grand jury.

McDougall remained in jail for two and a half months. His imprisonment did more to publicize the cause of liberty of the press than any event since Zenger's trial. Alexander's account of that trial was republished for the first time in New York since 1736, and Parker's paper and John Holt's *New York Journal* courageously plumped for McDougall and for freedom of discussion. The editor and the prisoner against whom he was to testify each wrote hortatory articles urging all the colonies to enact statutes abolishing the "tyrannical Tenets" of the common law of seditious libel—which was invariably associated with the infamous Star Chamber. Yet the concept of seditious libel, the idea that political criticism could be a crime, was never attacked. Beneath the epithetical rhetoric was only the proposition that truth be accepted as a defense.[65]

The New York Mercury, however, defended the common law and backed the Assembly against McDougall.[66] The editor of conservatism's voice was Hugh Gaine, who in 1753 had been forced by the Assembly to humble himself in order to avoid prosecution for having printed its proceedings without prior license. Notwithstanding Gaine's policy, the McDougall case as managed by the Sons of Liberty became America's equivalent of the Wilkes case in England.[67] Indeed, McDougall himself consciously posed as the American Wilkes, and turned his imprisonment into a theatrical triumph, while his supporters used the issue of the free press as an anti-administration weapon. Forty-five, the number of the *North Briton* which had earned Wilkes his conviction for seditious libel, became the talismanic symbol of libertarianism and of the American cause against England. On the forty-fifth day of the year, for example, forty-five Liberty Boys dined in honor of McDougall on forty-five pounds of beef from a forty-five-month-old bull, drank forty-five toasts to liberty of the press and its defenders, and after dinner marched to the city jail to salute McDougall with forty-five cheers. On one particularly festive liberty day, forty-five songs were sung to him by forty-five virgins (every one of whom, reported a damned Tory, was forty-five years old).[68]

At the end of April, McDougall, attended by a mob of his partisans on the way from prison to court, was finally brought before the grand jury, which indicted him as the author of a seditious libel against the Assembly. It was the only indictment of its kind against a popular leader during the Revolutionary controversy, and the first of its kind in twenty-five years. Yet the unique fact that the prosecution was supported by every branch of the government, particularly the Assembly, makes the indictment understandable. So does the fact that the grand jurors were carefully picked from the "most . . . opulent & substantial gentlemen of the city." The trial was set for the next session of the court, in July. McDougall, this time paying the huge bail assessed against him, was released from prison. On July 2, just before the trial, James Parker, the star witness of the prosecution and the only one who could testify from personal knowledge that McDougall had written the seditious broadside, suddenly died. With his death the case against the defendant vanished. The trial was postponed till October and then again indefinitely. But if McDougall gloated over the turn of events that promised him a discharge from the indictment, he failed to consider the power of a revengeful Assembly.

With the collapse of the common-law prosecution, the Assembly resolved to punish McDougall on its own authority. Late in 1770, he was arrested on a warrant from the speaker by order of the house. After a week in jail, he was brought before the bar by the sergeant at arms. Speaker John Cruger then informed him that he was charged with having libeled the house and asked whether he was guilty or not. McDougall refused to plead to the charge until, he declared, he was informed of the identity of his accusers and the evidence against him. Cruger interrupted to threaten that he would be held in contempt for addressing the house without its prior leave, but Assemblyman George Clinton interceded on the prisoner's behalf, with the result that McDougall was permitted to give his reasons for not pleading. He explained that he had no counsel, that the case was still pending in the courts, and that the Assembly itself had already declared the broadside to be a seditious libel and its author guilty—in other words, he feared incriminating himself. Moreover, he added, the Assembly, having initiated the prosecution against him, was now acting as his judge and jury. This it had no power to do, particularly when it would be placing him under double jeopardy because he was still answerable at common law. For these reasons, McDougall declared, he would not answer the question. Representative John de Noyelles interjected that the house had the power to extort his answer and threatened infliction of *peine forte et dure,* a form of torture, recognized in English law, to force a suspect to plead one way or the other just so the trial might then proceed. McDougall braved de Noyelles' barbaric threat and obstinately refused to plead to the charge, thereby stymieing the proceedings.

The members fell to arguing among themselves whether they might coerce a prisoner to answer an incriminating question or even take jurisdiction of a case still pending in the courts. George Clinton, though he originally had voted for the resolution to prosecute McDougall's seditious libel, now supported him on technical grounds. (Clinton observed, however, that if the Assembly were not a party to the common-law indictment it would have full power over McDougall and, if necessary to make him plead, might even throw him out of the window.) The Assembly finally agreed to investigate the extent of its own powers in the case. McDougall was then ordered to state in writing his objections against entering a plea. He did so, and his statement provoked Speaker Cruger to announce that McDougall had reflected on the honor and dignity of the house. The members then voted that McDougall's fresh libels were in contempt of their parliamentary privilege and demanded that he beg for

PART II / *The First Amendment Freedoms*

pardon. His refusal prompted another vote sentencing him to an indeterminate period in prison. Only five members of the Assembly, in-including Clinton, opposed the sentence. McDougall obtained a writ of habeas corpus, but to no avail; the sheriff—who was ordered not to honor such a writ—notified the court that the matter was not within its jurisdiction, because the prisoner had been committed for breach of privilege. The court deferred to the legislature and McDougall remained in jail. Meanwhile the Assembly accepted a committee report, based on precedents of the House of Commons, supporting the lawfulness of its authority and actions in the case. Thus once more an American legislature endorsed the principle that it possessed an unbounded prerogative when personal liberty and freedom of expression were involved. McDougall finally was released when the legislative session ended. He had served nearly three months in jail. The common-law charge against him was dismissed, and America's Wilkes won his freedom.[69]

VI

No cause was more honored by rhetorical declamation and more dishonored in practice than the cause of freedom of expression during the Revolutionary period, from the 1760's through the War for Independence. The irony of the period might best be portrayed by a cartoon depicting the tarring and feathering of a Tory speaker or printer under a banner run up by the patriots inscribed, "In Liberty's Cause." Yankee Doodle's Liberty Boys vociferously claimed for themselves the right to freedom of expression which they denied their opponents, revealing an extraordinarily narrow understanding of the liberty of the press. But there was nothing in their heritage or experience which fitted them for a broader understanding. It is not surprising, even if ironical, that when the New York Sons of Liberty rode out to smash Tory presses they were led by Alexander McDougall, who in 1770 had been jailed for criticizing the provincial assembly. Nor is it surprising that the Continental Congress, in its Quebec Declaration in 1774, advertised as one of the virtues of freedom of the press that it made possible the "diffusion of liberal sentiments on the administration of government. . . ."[70] Illiberal—that is, loyalist—sentiments were simply suppressed during the Revolution. It was not, regrettably, an object of the Revolution "to get rid of the English common law on liberty of speech and of the press."[71]

Indeed, the Revolution wrought no change whatever in the common law, nor did it effect any breakthroughs in the field of libertarian thought on freedom of political opinion. Republican forms of government had been established; the first written constitutions had been framed; the first bills of rights, having the force of fundamental law, had been adopted; even the first constitutional guarantees of freedom of speech and press had been specified. But law and theory remained the same. They were epitomized best in a statement by Sir William Blackstone: "The liberty of the press is indeed essential to the nature of a free state; but this consists in laying no previous restraints upon publications, and not in freedom from censure for criminal matter when published. Every freeman has an undoubted right to lay what sentiments he pleases before the public; to forbid this is to destroy the freedom of the press; but if he publishes what is improper, mischievous, or illegal, he must take the consequences of his own temerity." [72]

To be sure, the principle of a free press, like flag, home, and mother, had no enemies in America after the Revolution. Only seditious libels, licentious opinions, and malicious falsehoods were condemned. The question, therefore, is not whether freedom of the press was favored, but what it meant and whether its advocates would extend it to a political opponent whose criticism cut to the bone on issues that really mattered. Jefferson once remarked that he did not care whether his neighbor said that there are twenty gods or no God, because "It neither picks my pocket nor breaks my leg." [73] But in drafting a constitution for Virginia in 1776 he considered proposing that freedom of religion "shall not be held to justify any seditious preaching or conversation against the authority of the civil government." [74] And in the same year he helped frame a statute on treasonous crimes, punishing anyone who "by any word" or deed defended the cause of Great Britain.[75] Apparently political opinions could break his leg or pick his pocket. What, then, did Jefferson mean by freedom of the press? He and his contemporaries supported an unrestricted public discussion of issues, but "unrestricted" meant merely the absence of censorship in advance of publication; although no one needed a government license to express himself, everyone was accountable under the criminal law for abuse of the right to speak or publish freely. Significantly, neither Jefferson himself nor anyone else in the United States, prior to 1798, extended his "overt acts" test to freedom of political opinion.

Jefferson had devised that test when seeking a way to insure the free exercise of religion. In one of his most enduring and noble achievements, the Act for Establishing Religious Freedom, which became law in Virginia in 1786, he declared that "to suffer the civil magistrate to intrude his powers into the field of opinion, and to restrain the profession or propagation of principles, on supposition of their ill tendency, is a dangerous fallacy, which at once destroys all religious liberty, because he being of course judge of that tendency, will make his opinions the rule of judgment, and approve or condemn the sentiments of others only as they shall square with or differ from his own; that it is time enough for the rightful purposes of civil government for its officers to interfere when principles break out into overt acts against peace and good order. . . ." [76] The overt-acts test applied in Jefferson's words, only to "opinions in matters of religion," although its principle should have been as relevant in cases of political opinion, and had been specifically extended to such cases by many English theorists.

Before 1798, the avant-garde among American libertarians staked everything on the principles of the Zenger case, which they thought beyond improvement. They believed that no greater liberty could be conceived than the right to publish without restriction, if only the defendant could plead truth as a defense in a criminal prosecution for libel, and if the criminality of his words might be determined by a jury of his peers rather than by a judge. The substantive law of criminal libels was unquestioned. But libertarians who accepted Zengerian principles painted themselves into a corner. If a jury returned a verdict of "guilty" despite a defense of truth, due process had been accorded and protests were groundless, because the substance of the law that made the trial possible had not been challenged.

American acquiescence in the common-law definition of a free press was so widespread that even the frail Zengerian principles seemed daring, novel, and had few adherents. It was not until 1790 that the first state, Pennsylvania, took the then radical step of adopting the Zengerian principles,[77] which still left the common law of seditious libel intact. The Pennsylvania provision was drafted by James Wilson who, in the state convention that ratified the Constitution, declared without challenge by any of the ardent proponents of a bill of rights that "what is meant by the liberty of the press is that there should be no antecedent restraint upon it; but that every author is responsible when he attacks the security or welfare of the government. . . ." The mode of proceeding, Wilson added, should be by prosecution.[78] The state constitutional provision of 1790 reflected this proposition, as did state trials before and after 1790.[79]

Delaware and Kentucky followed Pennsylvania's lead in 1792,[80] but elsewhere the status quo prevailed. In 1789 William Cushing and John Adams worried about whether the guarantee of a free press in Massachusetts ought to mean that truth was a good defense to a charge of criminal libel, but they agreed that false publications against the government were punishable.[81] In 1791, when a Massachusetts editor was prosecuted for a criminal libel against a state official, the

Supreme Judicial Court divided on the question of truth as a defense, but agreed, like the Pennsylvania judges,[82] that the state constitutional guarantee of a free press was merely declaratory of the common law in simply prohibiting a licensing system.[83]

The opinions of Jefferson, the acknowledged libertarian leader in America, and of Madison, the father of the Bill of Rights, are especially significant. In 1783, when proposing a new constitution for Virginia, Jefferson exempted the press from prior restraints but carefully provided for prosecution—a state trial—in cases of false publication.[84] In 1788, when urging Madison to support a bill of rights to the new federal Constitution, Jefferson made the same recommendation.[85] Madison construed it in its most favorable light, observing: "The Exemption of the press from liability in every case for *true facts* is . . . an innovation and as such ought to be well considered." [86] But, on consideration, he did not add the truth-as-a-defense principle to the amendment on the press which he offered when proposing a bill of rights to Congress.[87] Yet Madison's phrasing appeared too broad for Jefferson, who stated that he would be pleased if the press provision were altered to exclude freedom to publish "false facts . . . affecting the peace of the confederacy with foreign nations" [88]— a clause whose suppressive possibilities can be imagined in the context of a foreign-policy controversy like the one on Jay's Treaty.

Madison fortunately ignored Jefferson's proposal, but there is no warrant for the belief that he dissented from the universal American acceptance of the Blackstonian definition of a free press. In 1788, at the Virginia ratifying convention, Madison remained silent when George Nicholas, one of his closest supporters, declared that the liberty of the press was secure because there was no power to license the press; [89] Madison was silent, too, when John Marshall rose to say that Congress would never make a law punishing men of different political opinions "unless it be such a case as must satisfy the people at large." [90] In October of 1788, when replying to Jefferson's argument [91] that powers of the national government should be restricted by a bill of rights, Madison declared that "absolute restrictions in cases that are doubtful, or where emergencies may overrule them, ought to be avoided." [92] When Madison proposed an amendment in Congress guaranteeing freedom of the press, he did not employ the emphatic language of the Virginia ratifying convention's recommendation that freedom of the press should not be subject to abridgment "by any authority of the United States." [93] As Madison introduced the amendment, it omitted the important clause, "by any authority of the United States," [94] which would have covered the executive and judiciary as well as Congress; the omitted clause, in other words, would have prohibited the federal courts from ex-

135

ercising any common-law jurisdiction over criminal libels. As ratified, the First Amendment declared only that Congress should make no law abridging the freedom of speech or press.

What did the amendment mean at the time of its adoption? First of all (if the amendment is analyzed by focusing on the phrase, "the freedom of the press"), it was merely an assurance that Congress was powerless to authorize restraints in advance of publication. On this point the evidence for the period from 1787 to 1791 is uniform and nonpartisan. For example, Hugh Williamson of North Carolina, a Federalist signatory of the Constitution, used freedom of the press in Blackstonian or common-law terms,[95] as did Melancthon Smith of New York, an anti-Federalist. Demanding a free-press guarantee in the new federal Constitution, despite the fact that New York's constitution lacked that guarantee, Smith argued that freedom of the press was "fully defined and secured" in New York by "the common and statute law of England," making a state constitutional provision unnecessary.[96] No other definition of freedom of the press by anyone anywhere in America before 1798 has been discovered. There was no dissent from the proposition that the punishment of a seditious libeler did not abridge the proper or lawful freedom of the press.[97]

Nevertheless, the injunction of the First Amendment was not intended to imply that a sedition act might be enacted without abridging "the freedom of the press." A sedition act would not be an abridgment, but that was not the point of the amendment. To understand its framers' intentions, the amendment should not be read with the focus on the meaning of "the freedom of the press." It should not, in other words, be read merely to mean that Congress could impose no prior restraints. It should be read, rather, with the stress on the opening clause, "Congress shall make no law. . . ." The injunction, that is, was intended to prohibit any Congressional regulation of the press, whether by means of a licensing act, a tax act, or a sedition act. The framers meant Congress to be totally without power to enact legislation respecting the press. They intended a federal system in which the national government could exercise only such powers as were specifically enumerated, or were necessary and proper to carry out those enumerated. Thus James Wilson declared that, because the national government had "no power whatsoever" concerning the press, "no law . . . can possibly be enacted" against it; thus Alexander Hamilton, referring to the demand for a free-press guarantee, asked, ". . . why declare that things shall not be done which there is no power to do?" [98] The illustrations may be multiplied fiftyfold. In other words, no matter what was meant or understood by freedom of speech and press, the national government, *even in the absence of the First Amendment*, could not make speech or press a legitimate subject of restrictive legislation. The amendment itself was superfluous. To quiet public apprehension it offered an added security that Congress would be limited to the exercise of its delegated powers. The phrasing was intended to prohibit the possibility that those powers might be used to abridge speech and press. From this view of the matter, the Sedition Act of 1798 was unconstitutional.

That act was also unnecessary as a matter of law, however necessary it was as a matter of Federalist Party policy. It was unnecessary because the federal courts exercised jurisdiction over nonstatutory or common-law crimes against the United States. At the Pennsylvania ratifying convention, James Wilson had declared that, whereas Congress could enact no law against the press, a libel against the United States might be prosecuted in the state where the offense was committed—under Article III, Section 2, of the Constitution, which refers to the judicial power of the United States. A variety of common-law crimes against the United States were in fact tried in the federal courts during the first decade of the courts' existence.[99] There were even a couple of common-law indictments in the federal courts for the crime of seditious libel.[100] All the early Supreme Court judges, including several who had been influential in the Philadelphia Convention, or in the state ratifying conventions, or in the Congress that passed the Judiciary Act of 1789, assumed the existence of a federal common law of crimes.[101] Ironically, it was a case originating as a federal prosecution of Connecticut editors for seditious libels against President Jefferson that finally resulted in a ruling by a divided Supreme Court, in 1812, that there was no federal common law of crimes.[102]

There was unquestionably a federal common law of crimes at the time of the Sedition Act. Why, then, was the Act passed if it was not legally needed? Because even in England, where the criminal courts exercised an unquestioned jurisdiction over seditious libels, it was politically advisable in the 1790's to declare public policy in unmistakable terms by the enactment of sedition statutes.[103] Legislation helped ensure effective enforcement of the law, stirred public opinion against the law's intended victims, and in every way served Federalist Party objectives. The Federalists, hoping to control public opinion and elections, emulated the British model. A federal statute was expedient also because the Republicans insisted that libels against the United States might be tried only by the *state* courts, which were not so trustworthy in some states as the federal courts.

This suggests another original purpose of the First Amendment. We have noted that a constitutional guarantee of a free press did not per se preclude a sedition act, but the prohibition on Congress did, although it left the federal courts free to try cases of seditious libel. It now appears that the prohibition on Congress was motivated far less by a desire to give immunity to political expression than by a solicitude for states' rights and the federal principle. The primary purpose of the First Amendment was to reserve to the states an exclusive authority, as far as legislation was concerned, in the field of speech and press.

This is clear enough from the countless states' rights arguments advanced by the anti-Federalists during the ratification controversy; it is explicitly clear from the Republican arguments during the Sedition Act controversy. In the House debates on the bill, Albert Gallatin, Edward Livingston, John Nicholas, and Nathaniel Macon all agreed (to quote Macon on the subject of liberty of the press) that "The States have complete power on the subject. . . ." [104] Jefferson's Kentucky Resolutions of 1798 expressed the same proposition,[105] and so did Madison's "Address of the General Assembly to the People of the Commonwealth of Virginia" in 1799.[106]

It is possible that the opponents of the Sedition Act did not want or believe in state prosecutions, but argued for an exclusive state power over political libels because such an argument was tactically useful as a means of denying national jurisdiction, judicial or legislative. If so, how shall we explain the Republican prosecution in New York in 1803 against Croswell, a Federalist editor, for a seditious libel against President Jefferson? [107] How shall we explain the Blackstonian opinions of the Republican judges in that case? [108] How shall we explain Jefferson's letter to the governor of Pennsylvania in the same year? The President, enclosing a newspaper piece that attacked him unmercifully, urged a "few prosecutions" because they "would have a wholesome effect in restoring the integrity of the presses." [109] How shall we explain Jefferson's letter to Abigail Adams in 1804 in which he said: "While we deny that Congress have a right to controul the freedom of the press, we have ever asserted the right of the states, and their exclusive right to do so." [110] And if exclusive state power was advanced not as a principle but as a tactic for denying federal jurisdiction, how shall we explain what Jefferson's opponents called his "reign of terror": [111] the common-law indictments in 1806 in the United States Circuit Court in Connecticut against six men charged with seditious libel of the President? [112] How shall we explain his letter of 1807 in which he said of the "prosecutions in the Court of the U.S." that they could "not lessen the useful freedom of the press," if truth were admitted as a defense? [113]

VII

British libertarian theory provides an instructive contrast. English lawyers, pamphleteers, and ministers had progressed beyond Cato and Zengerian principles. Abandoning the concept of verbal political crimes, they embraced the overt-acts test as a measurement of the scope of permissible freedom of expression, and they cleaved the air with impassioned yet elaborate analyses of freedom of the press and the right to criticize the government. The most notable English statement was Robert Hall's *An Apology for the Freedom of the Press and for General Liberty*,[114] published in 1793, when men were being jailed in wholesale batches for political opinions that were condemned as false, dangerous, and subversive. Hall's position was that all men should have an absolute liberty to discuss "every subject which can fall within the compass of the human mind," and he meant what he said without any ifs or buts. He flatly denied the power of the government to punish the mere expression of political opinions. Distinguishing words, sentiment, and opinions from "conduct" or "behavior," Hall demanded that only the latter be regarded as criminal.[115] He sought to make the crime of sedition, like that of treason, depend upon nonverbal, overt acts. He made an otherwise commonplace point—that freedom of expression is to be cherished as a step to the truth—by noting that opinions possessing a social value were frequently mixed with error and falsehoods. Publications, he wrote, "like every thing else that is human, are of a mixed nature, where truth is often blended with falsehood, and important hints suggested in the midst of much impertinent or pernicious matter; nor is there any way of separating the precious from the vile, but by tolerating the whole." [116] This observation was original and cogent when such leading American libertarians as John Adams and Thomas Jefferson believed, even in time of calm, that falsehoods published against the government were criminal. Hall's courage and the libertarian character of his thought must be measured in the context of the repressive prosecutions that were sweeping England when he wrote:

[Government] being an institution purely human, one would imagine it were the proper province for freedom of discussion in its utmost extent. It is surely just that every one should have a right to examine those measures by which the happiness of all may be affected. . . . Under pretence of its being seditious to express any disapprobation of the *form* of our government, the most alarming attempts are made to wrest the liberty of the press out of our hands. . . . An inquiry respecting the comparative excellence of civil constitutions can be forbidden on no other pretence than that of its tending to sedition and anarchy. This plea, however, will have little weight with those who reflect to how many ill purposes it has already applied; and that when the example has been introduced of suppressing opinions on account of their imagined ill tendency, it has seldom been confined within any safe or reasonable bounds. . . . The law hath amply provided against overt acts of sedition and disorder, and to suppress mere opinions by any other method than reason and argument, is the height of tyranny. Freedom of thought being intimately connected with the happiness and dignity of man in every stage of his being, is of so much more importance than the preservation of any constitution, that to infringe the former, under pretence of supporting the latter, is to sacrifice the means to the end.[117]

The closest American approximation to British libertarianism before 1798 was reflected, somewhat uncertainly, in a Congressional debate of 1794. President Washington, having in mind the Democratic societies of western Pennsylvania, referred critically, in a Congressional message, to "certain self-created societies" that had urged resistance against the whiskey excise.[118] The Senate, in a formal response to the President, declared that the activities of these societies had injured the government and helped foment the insurrection. A motion by Senator Aaron Burr to expunge this passage in the Senate's response was defeated.[119] In the House, however, the Republicans, after a four-day debate, managed to expunge the reference to "self-created societies." The House simply expressed its great concern that any misrepresentations of the government so serious as to foment the insurrection should have been made by anyone.[120] A Virginia trio, Representatives William B. Giles, John Nicholas, and James Madison, in conducting their successful fight to water down the statement, expressed the libertarian position.

Giles, who spoke first, declared that the motion to express the House's "reprobation of the self-created societies" was intended "to censure the Democratic societies." Defending the right of free association, whether for religious, political, philosophical, or other purposes, he stated that Congress was not constitutionally empowered "to attempt checking or restraining public opinion." If any societies had acted illegally, they were punishable under the law. But the House simply had no "business to pass random votes of censure." [121] The response by William Smith, a South Carolina Federalist, sharpened the controversy and made the debate a precursor of the elaborate controversy on the floor of the House four years later when the Sedition Act was at issue. Smith, alleging that he was a friend to freedom of the press, believed that "the dissemination of improper sentiments . . . subversive of good order" was a suitable object of the House's reprobation. The matter in question was not the legality of the self-created societies, but the mischievous consequences of their calumnies against the government.[122]

Nicholas, in reply, repeated Giles's point that censure was beyond the powers of the House. In a statement marked by confusion, he declared: "It was wrong to condemn societies for particular acts. . . . I cannot agree to persecution for the sake of opinion." [123] It was a poor libertarian argument that could not distinguish acts from opin-

ions, particularly when the societies stood accused of having provoked an actual insurrection. Later, Nicholas arose to answer a
contention that the existence of libel prosecutions proved that
calumnious attacks on government were just objects of reprehension.
He failed wholly to assault libel prosecutions, thereby revealing how
impoverished or stunted was his libertarian thought in comparison to
the arguments he was to make only four years later. In 1794 he
merely contended that it was not fair to compare the censure of a
society with the prosecution of a libel, because in the latter case the
accused party had an opportunity to defend himself. The Democratic
societies had no such opportunity. They were accused, said Nicholas,
of never having once said a good word about government policies.
"If these societies had censured every proceeding of Government,
there would have been," he remarked, "the greatest reason for taking
some measures." But they had taken no notice whatever of many
acts of the government.[124] Aside from its unintended sinister implication, Nicholas' argument was confused and fatuous.

Giles, in a rambling speech, passingly reflected a genuine libertarian
position. "Many people who condemn the proceedings of the Democratic societies, yet will not choose to see them divested of the
inalienable privilege of thinking, of speaking, of writing, and of
printing. Persons may condemn the abuse in exercising a right, and
yet feel the strongest sympathy with the right itself. Are not Muir
and Palmer, and the other martyrs of Scotch despotism, toasted from
one end of the Continent to the other? And why is it so? These men
asserted the right of thinking, of speaking, of writing, and of printing." [125] The significance of this statement lies in Giles's condemnation of the convictions of Thomas Muir and the Reverend T. Fyshe
Palmer for the crime of seditious libel. Their notoriously unfair, even
brutal, trials in Scotland in 1793 were the result of their outspoken
campaign for annual parliaments and universal suffrage.[126] Given the
facts of these cases, and the severe sentences, Giles's statement should
not be stretched from an obvious censure of the two trials to a
repudiation of all trials for seditious libel. Moreover, he never took
the trouble of explaining what he meant by freedom of speech and
press. Indeed, Fischer Ames observed in reply that Giles "had been
occupied in refuting what nobody had asserted, and in proving what
nobody had denied." Ames himself spoke warmly of freedom of
speech and press, attacking only, he said, its abuses.[127]

Madison responded that the people, in forming the Constitution,
had retained all rights not delegated, making Congress powerless to
legislate on certain subjects. "Opinions," he stated, "are not the objects of legislation. You animadvert on the abuse of reserved rights:
how far will this go? It may extend to the liberty of speech, and of
the press. . . . If we advert to the nature of Republican Government,

141

we shall find that the censorial power is in the people over the Government, and not in the Government over the people." [128] That proposition, a few years later, served as the basis for a powerful libertarian argument against the concept of seditious libel. In 1794, however, Madison merely proceeded to restate the seventeenth-century argument that truth would prevail over error, making it unnecessary to proceed against the publications of the societies in question.

The Republicans rewrote the offensive passage in the House's response to President Washington, but it should be remembered that at no point had the Federalists proposed action against the publications or opinions of the "self-created societies." Publications and opinions were not the subject of repressive legislation until 1798. Only then did the new libertarian theories emerge.

Before then, a clear opportunity presented itself for the development of the libertarian argument. In 1796 New York had a new "McDougall case." The victim was William Keteltas, a Republican lawyer and member of the local Democratic Society. Keteltas had been present at the unfair and juryless trial of two Irish ferrymen who were convicted for allegedly insulting an alderman by refusing to ferry him off-schedule. Outraged by the proceedings in the Court of General Sessions, Keteltas published a newspaper article denouncing the tyranny of the trial magistrates—the mayor and five aldermen. He demanded a grand-jury investigation and impeachment of the guilty officials by the State Assembly. When the grand jury went fishing and the Assembly took up whitewashing, Keteltas aimed his blistering newspaper comments against the Assembly itself. That august body, smarting from his censure, which it took to be a seditious insult, summoned him to appear before its bar. Keteltas had to answer for his articles, which were condemned as "highly injurious to the honor and dignity" of the Assembly and as "calculated to create distrust and destroy the confidence" of the people in their representatives. [129]

Before the bar of the house, Keteltas admitted authorship of the offensive articles. The Assembly promptly and without debate found him guilty of "a misdemeanor and contempt of the authority of this House." When Keteltas refused to humble himself by admitting his wrong and asking pardon, the house immediately ordered him jailed. [130]

The case presented a perfect opportunity for a libertarian argument in defense of Keteltas. The issue was raised in precisely the right terms by Representative John Bird, a Republican member of the Assembly, who demanded: "Shall we attempt to prevent citizens from thinking? from giving their opinion on acts of the legislature? Shall we stop freedom of the press?" [131] Bird's questions were not only asked in vain; they were virtually unique, almost eccentric, certainly ignored or forgotten, and unsupported by any argument in development of the theme. Keteltas became a popular hero among the Jeffersonian faithful in New York, and his case became a *cause célèbre*. Yet freedom of the press and the right of the citizen to criticize his government played no part in the extensive argument in Keteltas' behalf. Not even Keteltas himself, an experienced politician and lawyer, spoke to the issue, although while in prison he published five articles protesting the "unconstitutional, tyrannical, and illegal" proceedings of the Assembly.[132]

In the last article he discoursed at length on "freedom of speech," but did so exclusively in the context of a discussion of parliamentary privilege. That is, he spoke only of the right of the legislator's freedom of debate. Not once did he allude to his own right, or that of the people, to debate public matters—let alone have the same scope of freedom of political expression as members of the house. His defense was based on the narrow argument that he had not breached any of the privileges of the house and that the house could not lawfully deprive any citizen of his liberty without benefit of grand-jury proceedings and trial by jury. An anonymous supporter, signing himself "Camillus Junius" after a hero of the ancient Roman Republic, trenchantly put forth the same argument in the press.[133] The assault on the power of the Assembly to punish citizens for alleged breaches of privilege was surely a significant libertarian action. But equally revealing was the total absence of discussion of Representative Bird's questions about the right of the citizen to criticize his government.

Keteltas, who was freed on a writ of habeas corpus as soon as the legislature ended its session, later brought unsuccessful suit for false imprisonment against the speaker of the house. The Assembly supported its speaker by a vote of 88 to 1, and the court ruled against Keteltas. A "Spectator" concluded his report of the trial by remarking: ". . . the freedom of the press is taken away, and personal liberty is no longer secure in the state of New York." [134] Other than Bird's, this was the only reference to freedom of the press that emerged from the case.

Thus, as late as 1794 and 1796, as the Congressional debates on self-created societies and the Keteltas case reveal, American libertarian theory was in a state of arrested development on the crucial question of the right of the citizen to criticize his government without being accused of a verbal political crime. "Freedom of the press" was invoked, to be sure, but the phrase was not self-defining, its meaning was neither self-evident nor static, and its mere utterance *ex vi termini* was neither a sovereign remedy nor adequate to support a libertarian theory. Pithy slogans and glittering generalities reflected sentiment and perhaps a principle, but not a theory. Bird's sloganeering, Keteltas' evasions, Nicholas' inconsistency, and Madison's ultimate

143

reliance on the federal principle together with Milton's truth-shall-prevail-over-error, can scarcely be compared, for libertarian qualities, freshness, or boldness, to the arguments of Cato or Alexander, let alone Robert Hall.

VIII

Then, in 1798, there was a sudden breakthrough in American libertarian thought on freedom of political expression. The change was abrupt, radical, and transforming, like that caused by an underwater volcano erupting its lava upward from the ocean floor to form a new island. The Sedition Act, which was a thrust in the direction of a single-party press and a monolithic party-system, triggered the libertarian surge among the Republicans. The result was the emergence of a new peak of libertarian thought, jutting out of a stagnant Blackstonian sea.

The Federalists in 1798 believed that true freedom of the press would benefit if truth—*their* truth—were the measure of freedom. Their infamous Sedition Act was, in the words of Gilbert and Sullivan, the true embodiment of everything excellent. It was, that is, the very epitome of libertarian thought since the time of Zenger's case—indicating that American libertarianism went from Zengerian principles to the Sedition Act in a single degeneration. Everything that the libertarians had ever demanded was incorporated in the Sedition Act: a requirement that criminal intent be shown; the power of the jury to decide whether the accused's statement was libelous as a matter of law as well as of fact; and truth as a defense, which was an innovation not accepted in England until 1843.[135] By every standard the Sedition Act was a great victory for libertarian principles of freedom of the press—except that libertarian standards abruptly changed, because the Republicans immediately recognized a Pyrrhic victory.

The Sedition Act provoked them to develop a new libertarian theory. It began to emerge when Congressmen Gallatin, John Nicholas, Nathaniel Macon, and Edward Livingston argued against the enactment of the Sedition bill.[136] It was further developed by defense counsel, most notably George Blake, in Sedition Act prosecutions.[137] It reached its most reflective and systematic expression in tracts and books that are now unfortunately rare and little known, even by historians. The main body of original Republican thought on the scope, meaning, and rationale of the First Amendment is to be found in George Hay's tract, *An Essay on the Liberty of the Press*;[138] in Madison's *Report* on the Virginia Resolutions for the Virginia House of Delegates;[139] in the book, *A Treatise Concerning Political En-*

quiry, and the Liberty of the Press, by Tunis Wortman of New York; [140] in John Thomson's book, *An Enquiry, Concerning the Liberty, and Licentiousness of the Press;* [141] and in St. George Tucker's appendix to his edition of Blackstone's *Commentaries*, [142] a most significant place for the repudiation of Blackstone on the liberty of the press. Of these works, Wortman's philosophical book is pre-eminent; it is an American masterpiece, the only equivalent on this side of the Atlantic to Milton and Mill.

The new libertarians abandoned the straitjacketing doctrines of Blackstone and the common law, including the recent concept of a federal common law of crimes. They scornfully denounced the no-prior-restraints definition. Said Madison: ". . . this idea of the freedom of the press can never be admitted to be the American idea of it," because a law inflicting penalties would have the same effect as a law authorizing a prior restraint. "It would seem a mockery to say that no laws shall be passed preventing publications from being made, but that laws might be passed for punishing them in case they should be made." [143] As Hay put it, the "British definition" meant that a man might be jailed or even put to death for what he published, provided that no notice was taken of him before he published. [144]

The old yardstick for measuring the scope of freedom was also rejected by the new libertarians. "Liberty" of the press, for example, had always been differentiated from its "licentiousness," which was the object of the criminal law's sanctions. "Truth" and "facts" had always divided the realm of lawfulness from "falsehoods," and a similar distinction had been made between "good motives" and "criminal intent." All such distinctions were now discarded, on the ground that they did not distinguish and therefore were not meaningful standards that might guide a jury or a court in judging an alleged verbal crime. The term "licentiousness," wrote Thomson, "is destitute of any meaning"; it was used, according to him, by those who wished "nobody to enjoy the Liberty of the Press but such as were of their own opinion." [145] The term "malice," in Wortman's view, was invariably confused with mistaken zeal or prejudice. [146] It was merely an inference drawn from the supposed evil tendency of the publication itself, and just a further means of punishing the ex-citement of unfavorable sentiments against the government even when the people's contempt of the government was richly deserved. The punishment of "malice," or intent to defame the government, con-cluded Madison, necessarily struck at the right of free discussion, be-cause critics intended to excite unfavorable sentiments. [147] Finding criminality in the tendency of words was merely an attempt to erect public "tranquility . . . upon the ruins of Civil Liberty," wrote Wortman. [148]

The wholesale abandonment of the common law's limitations on the press was accompanied by a withering onslaught against the constrictions and subjectivity of Zengerian principles. The Sedition Act, Hay charged, "appears to be directed against falsehood and malice only; in fact . . . there are many truths, important to society, which are not susceptible of that full, direct, and positive evidence, which alone can be exhibited before a court and a jury." [149] If, argued Gallatin, the administration prosecuted a citizen for his opinion that the Sedition Act itself was unconstitutional, would not a jury, composed of the friends of that administration, find the opinion "ungrounded, or, in other words, false and scandalous, and its publication malicious? And by what kind of argument or evidence, in the present temper of parties, could the accused convince them that his opinions were true?" [150] The truth of opinions, the new libertarians concluded, could not be proved. Allowing "truth" as a defense and thinking it to be a protection for freedom, Thomson declared, made as much sense as letting a jury decide which was "the most palatable food, agreeable drink, or beautiful color." [151] A jury, he asserted, could not give an impartial verdict in political trials. Madison agreed, commenting that the "baleful tendency" of prosecutions for seditious libel was "little diminished by the privilege of giving in evidence the truth of the matter contained in political writings." [152]

The renunciation of traditional concepts reached its climax in the assault on the idea that there was such a thing as a crime of seditious libel. That crime, Wortman concluded, could "never be reconciled to the genius and constitution of a Representative Commonwealth." [153] He and the others constructed a new libertarianism, genuinely radical because it broke sharply with the past and advocated an absolute freedom of political expression. One of the major tenets of this new libertarianism was that a free government cannot be criminally attacked by the opinions of its citizens. Hay, for example, insisted that freedom of the press, like chastity, was either "absolute" [154] or did not exist. Abhorring the very concept of verbal political crimes, he declared that a citizen should have a right to "say everything which his passions suggest; he may employ all his time, and all his talents, if he is wicked enough to do so, in speaking against the government matters that are false, scandalous and malicious," [155] and yet he should be "safe within the sanctuary of the press" even if he "condemns the principle of republican institutions . . . censures the measures of our government, and every department and officer thereof, and ascribes the measures of the former, however salutary, and conduct of the latter, however upright, to the basest motives; even if he ascribes to them measures and acts, which never had existence; thus violating at once, every principle of decency and truth." [156]

In brief, the new libertarians advocated that only "injurious conduct," as manifested by "overt acts" or deeds, rather than words, should be criminally redressable.[157] They did not refine this proposition except to recognize that the law of libel should continue to protect private reputations against malicious falsehoods. They did not even recognize that under certain circumstances words may immediately and directly incite criminal acts.

This absolutist interpretation of the First Amendment was based on the now familiar, but then novel and democratic, theory that free government depends for its very existence and security on freedom of political discourse. The scope of the amendment, according to this theory, is determined by the nature of the government and its relationship to the people. Because the government is the people's servant, exists by their consent and for their benefit, and is constitutionally limited, responsible, and elective, it cannot, said Thomson, tell the citizen: "You shall not think this, or that upon certain subjects; or if you do, it is at your peril." [158] The concept of seditiousness can exist only in a relationship based on inferiority, when people are subjects rather than sovereigns and their criticism implies contempt of their master. "In the United States," Madison declared, "the case is altogether different." [159] Coercion or abridgment of unlimited political opinion, Wortman explained, would violate the very "principles of the social state"—by which he meant a government of the people.[160] Because such a government depended upon popular elections, all the new libertarians agreed that the widest possible latitude must be maintained to keep the electorate free, informed, and capable of making intelligent choices. The citizen's freedom of political expression had the same scope as the legislator's, and had the same reasons behind it.[161] That freedom might be dangerously abused, but the people, if exposed to every opinion, would decide men and measures wisely.

This brief summary of the new libertarianism barely does justice to its complexity and sophistication, but should at least suggest its boldness, originality, and democratic character. The new libertarianism developed, to be sure, as an expediency of self-defense on the part of a besieged political minority that was struggling to maintain its existence and its right to function unfettered. But the new libertarians established, virtually all at once and in nearly perfect form, a theory justifying the rights of individual expression and of opposition parties. That the Jeffersonians in power did not always adhere to their new principles does not diminish the enduring nobility and rightness of those principles. It proves only that the Jeffersonians set the highest standards of freedom for themselves and posterity. Their legacy was the idea that there is an indispensable condition for the development of free men in a free society: the state must be bitted and bridled by a bill of rights that is to be construed in the most generous terms and whose protections are not to be the playthings of momentary majorities. That legacy deepened and enriched American libertarian theory, but it did not surmount the resistance of the law. Ultimate victory in the courts and statutes belonged to Alexander Hamilton's restatement of Zengerian principles.[162]

Hamilton, a supporter of the Sedition Act and of prosecutions for criminal libel, believed that the law of libel should be governed by the principles of the Zenger case, in order to protect the legitimate freedom of the press. In 1804 he was permitted by his Jeffersonian opponents in New York, who were then in power, to make political capital and legal history by advocating these old principles. The state indicted Harry Croswell, an obscure Federalist editor, for the common-law crime of seditious libel against President Jefferson. Croswell's crime was his publishing of the accusation that Jefferson had paid to have Washington denounced as a traitor and Adams as an incendiary. Chief Justice Morgan Lewis, a Jeffersonian, refused Croswell the opportunity of introducing evidence to prove the truth of his statements. In instructing the jury, Lewis told the jurors that their only duty was to determine whether the defendant had in fact published the statements as charged; that they must leave to the court, as a matter of law, the determination of the statements' libelous characer. Lewis, in other words, charged the jury that the law of New York was the law as laid down by Chief Justice DeLancey in the Zenger case.

On the appeal of Croswell's conviction, before the highest court of the state, Alexander Hamilton played the role of Andrew Hamilton, eloquently championing the cause of freedom of the press. That freedom, he said (in words that were even more restrictive than those of his precursor or of the Sedition Act), "consists in the right to publish, with impunity, truth, with good motives, for justifiable ends, though reflecting on government, magistracy, or individuals." The Sedition Act itself did not require proof of "good motives, for justifiable ends," but Alexander Hamilton's position, of course, seemed a shining standard of libertarianism when compared with the reactionary views of Chief Justice Lewis—or of the prosecutor, Attorney General Ambrose Spencer, another Jeffersonian. Spencer argued from Blackstone (not Tucker's version), and declared that a libel, even if true, was punishable because of its dangerous tendency. The former prosecutor had become a member of the Supreme Court of Judicature by the time it decided the case. Had Spencer not been ineligible to participate in the decision, the repressive opinion reexpressed by Chief Justice Lewis would have commanded a majority. Instead, the court divided evenly, two against two. The opinion of Judge James Kent expressed Hamilton's position.

In the following year, 1805, the state legislature enacted a bill allowing the jury to decide the criminality of an alleged libel and permitting truth as a defense, if published "with good motives and for justifiable ends." It is this standard that has prevailed in the United States.

NOTES

1 "To the Inhabitants of the Province of Quebec," October 24, 1774, in *Journals of the Continental Congress, 1774–1789,* Worthington Chauncey Ford et al., eds. (Washington, 1904–37), I, 108.

2 William O. Douglas, *The Right of the People* (Garden City, N. Y., 1958), p. 38.

3 *Areopagitica,* William Haller, ed., in *The Works of John Milton,* Frank A. Patterson, gen. ed. (New York, 1931–38), IV, 346.

4 *Ibid.,* IV, 320–321, 349, 353. For Milton as a censor, see William C. Clyde, *The Struggle for the Freedom of the Press from Caxton to Cromwell* (London, 1934), pp. 79–80, 172–173.

5 "The Bloudy Tenent, of Persecution, for cause of Conscience," in *The Writings of Roger Williams,* Samuel L. Caldwell, ed. (Providence, R. I., 1866–74), III, 136.

6 "A Letter concerning Toleration," in *The Works of John Locke,* 11th ed. (London, 1812), VI, 45, 46.

7 *Ibid.,* VI, 51–52; and "Fundamental Constitutions of Carolina," Section 103, in *The Federal and State Constitutions, Colonial Charters, and Other Organic Laws,* Francis Newton Thorpe, ed. (Washington, 1909), V, 2784.

8 For the eighteen reasons, see Lord Peter King, *The Life and Letters of John Locke* (London, 1858), pp. 202–209.

9 *Rex* v. *Tuchin* (1704), in *A Complete Collection of State Trials to 1783,* comp. by Thomas Bayly Howell (London, 1816–28), XIV, 1128.

10 "Cato" (John Trenchard and Thomas Gordon), *Cato's Letters: Or, Essays on Liberty, Civil and Religious* (London, 1733–1755), 4 vols. A judicious abridgment of *Cato's Letters,* ably edited and introduced by David L. Jacobson, has recently been published in the American Heritage Series under the title, *The English Libertarian Heritage: From the Writings of John Trenchard and Thomas Gordon* (Indianapolis, 1965).

11 Clinton Rossiter, *Seedtime of the Republic* (New York, 1953), p. 141.

12 Elizabeth Cristine Cook, *Literary Influences in Colonial Newspapers* (New York, 1912), p. 81.

13 Rossiter, *Seedtime of the Republic,* p. 299.

14 No. 15, February 4, 1720, in *Cato's Letters,* 6th ed. (London, 1755), I, 96–103.

15 "Reflections upon Libelling," No. 32, June 10, 1721, in *Cato's Letters,* I; "Discourse upon Libels," No. 100, October 27, 1722, in *Cato's Letters,* III; and "Second Discourse upon Libels," No. 101, November 3, 1722, in *Cato's Letters,* III. A sampling of the Boston press shows that No. 15 was reprinted in *The New England Courant,* July 9, 1722; in the *Boston Gazette,* April 21, 1755, April 26, 1756, November 9, 1767, May 6, 1771, and August 14, 1780; in the *Massachusetts Spy,* March 7 and March 28, 1771. No. 32 was reprinted in *The New England Courant,* September 11, 1721; in the *Boston Gazette,* April 26, 1756, and May 6, 1771; and the *Boston Post-Boy,* September 27, 1773. For citations to Zenger's *New-York Weekly Journal,* see notes 27 and 28, below.

[16] "Of Freedom of Speech," No. 15, in *Cato's Letters*, I, 96–103.

[17] "Reflections upon Libelling," No. 32, in *Cato's Letters*, I, 252.

[18] "Discourse upon Libels," No. 100, in *Cato's Letters*, III, 295–297.

[19] "Reflections upon Libelling," No. 32, in *Cato's Letters*, I, 252.

[20] "Discourse upon Libels," No. 100, in *Cato's Letters*, III, 299.

[21] "Reflections upon Libelling," No. 32, in *Cato's Letters*, I, 247.

[22] "Discourse upon Libels," No. 100, in *Cato's Letters*, III, 297–298.

[23] "Reflections upon Libelling," No. 32, in *Cato's Letters*, I, 252–253.

[24] See, for example, "An Apology for Printers," in *The Writings of Benjamin Franklin*, Albert Henry Smyth, ed. (New York, 1905–07), II, 172–179; and "An Account of the Supremest Court of Judicature of the State of Pennsylvania, Viz, The Court of the Press," 1789, *ibid.*, X, 36–40.

[25] *The New England Courant*, September 11, 1721, and July 9, 1722.

[26] *The Pennsylvania Gazette* (Philadelphia), November 10–December 8, 1737, Nos. 466–469. Reprinted in Zenger's *New-York Weekly Journal*, December 19, 1737–January 9, 1738.

[27] *New-York Weekly Journal*, February 18 and November 11, 1734.

[28] *Ibid.*, December 9, 1734.

[29] The origin of the principle that truth should be a defense is sometimes attributed to the Zenger defense, but the idea can be found earlier in *The Thoughts of a Tory Author, concerning the Press*, attributed to Joseph Addison (London, 1712), pp. 25–26.

[30] James Alexander, *A Brief Narrative of the Case and Trial of John Peter Zenger, Printer of the New-York Weekly Journal*, Stanley Nider Katz, ed. (Cambridge, Mass., 1963), p. 87. A literal reprint of the first edition of the trial narrative, as published by the Zenger press in New York in 1736, appears in Livingston Rutherfurd, *John Peter Zenger, His Press, His Trial, and a Bibliography of Zenger Imprints* (New York, 1904). The Katz edition, which presents a modernized version, is cited . . . because it is easily available to readers, is superbly annotated, has an excellent introduction, and includes many valuable related documents.

[31] The first voicing of the principle that the jury should decide the law as well as the facts in a case of seditious libel is sometimes attributed to the Zenger defense, but the principle was explicitly stated in 1692 by William Bradford during his trial for seditious libel in Philadelphia. See *New-England's Spirit of Persecution Transmitted to Pennsilvania . . . in the Tryal of Peter Boss, George Keith, Thomas Budd, and William Bradford . . . 1692* (Philadelphia, 1693), pp. 33–34. Thomas Maule, who was tried for seditious libel in Boston in 1696, also claimed that the jury should decide the law as well as the facts. See Theo. Philanthes (Thomas Maule), *New-England Persecutors Mauld with Their Own Weapons . . . Together with a Brief Account of the Imprisonment and Tryal of Thomas Maule of Salem, for Publishing a Book . . .* (New York, 1697), pp. 61–62.

[32] *Journal of the Votes and Proceedings of the General Assembly of the Colony of New-York, 1691–1765* (New York, 1764–66), I, 443.

[33] Isaiah Thomas, *The History of Printing in America* (Worcester, Mass., 1810), II, 217; and Clyde Augustus Duniway, *The Development of Freedom of the Press in Massachusetts* (New York, 1906), pp. 98–99.

[34] Edmund F. Slafter, *John Checkley: or the Evolution of Religious Tolerance in Massachusetts Bay* (Boston, 1897), I, 56–66.

[35] David Paul Brown, *The Forum: Or, Forty Years Full Practice at the Philadelphia Bar* (Philadelphia, 1856), I, 262–265.

[36] *Ibid.*, I, 285–286; and *Minutes of the Provincial Council of Pennsylvania* (Harrisburg, Pa., 1838–40), III, 392.

[37] John P. Roche, "American Liberty: An Examination of the 'Tradition' of Freedom," in *Shadow and Substance: Essays on the Theory and Structure of Politics* (New York, 1964), p. 11:

[38] John Kelly, "Criminal Libel and Free Speech," *Kansas Law Review*, VI (1958), 306.

[39] *Minutes of the Provincial Council of Pennsylvania*, I, 143.

[40] *Ibid.*, III, 392.

[41] Alexander, *A Brief Narrative* . . . , Katz, ed., pp. 62, 68, and 69–74.

[42] *Ibid.*, pp. 75, 78, 91–93, and 99.

[43] More trials for seditious utterances were reported in Howell's *State Trials* for the two years following Fox's Libel Act than had been reported for the whole of the 18th century before that time. Within a year of the statute the attorney general declared that he had on file 200 informations for seditious libel. Thomas Erskine May, *The Constitutional History of England Since the Accession of George III, 1760–1860* (New York, 1880), II, 142–150.

[44] The American Sedition Act cases are too familiar to require review. For an excellent treatment, see James Morton Smith, *Freedom's Fetters: The Alien and Sedition Laws and American Civil Liberties* (Ithaca, N.Y., 1956). Smith reports the single acquittal on p. 185.

[45] *People v. Croswell*, 3 Johnson (N.Y.), 336 (1804). Lewis' opinion is reported *ibid.*, 394–411.

[46] For a bibliography of 18th-century reprints, see Rutherfurd, *John Peter Zenger*, pp. 249–253.

[47] MS Minutes, New York Court of Quarter Sessions, 1732–62, p. 181, cited in Julius Goebel, Jr., and T. Raymond Naughton, *Law Enforcement in Colonial New York, a Study in Criminal Procedure (1664–1776)* (New York, 1944), p. 99, note.

[48] Thomas, *The History of Printing in America*, II, 143–144. The Virginia case ended in an acquittal. In the McDougall case of 1770, discussed below, the common-law prosecution, which was never brought to trial, was instigated by the legislature.

[49] There were probably more prosecutions for oral utterances of a seditious nature than there were for seditious libels or publications, but there is no way of estimating the number of the former, because most of them were tried before inferior courts whose records are, with few exceptions, unpublished. Goebel and Naughton, however, systematically examined the manuscript records of the inferior courts of New York, and reported that there were only "occasional exceptional" prosecutions for seditious oral utterances during the whole of the colonial period up to 1776. See their *Law Enforcement in Colonial New York*, pp. 98–99.

[50] Between 1706 and 1720 there were four such cases in New York. In one case nine citizens, and in another seventeen grand jurors, were arrested for seditious reflections on the Assembly. In each of the other two cases the victim of the Assembly's wrath was one of its own members—Lewis Morris in 1710, and Samuel Mulford in 1720. See *Journal of the Votes and Proceedings of the General Assembly of the Colony of New-York*, I (1706), 211; (1710), 283; (1717), 411; (1720), 443. Mary Patterson Clarke makes this guarded understatement: "Literally scores of persons, probably hundreds, throughout the colonies were tracked down by the various messengers and sergeants and brought into the house to make inglorious submission for words spoken in the

heat of anger or for writing which intentionally or otherwise had given offense." See her *Parliamentary Privilege in the American Colonies* (New Haven, Conn., 1943), p. 117.

51 Alexander, *A Brief Narrative* . . . , Katz, ed., pp. 43–44.

52 *Ibid.*, pp. 44–46.

53 *Journal of the Votes and Proceedings of the General Assembly of the Colony of New-York*, II, 173, 192, 193, and 198.

54 *Ibid.*, II, 358–359.

55 *Ibid.*, II, 487–489.

56 *Ibid.*, II, 551–555.

57 Alexander, *A Brief Narrative* . . . , Katz, ed., p. 84. See also p. 77.

58 *New-York Weekly Journal*, November 4, 1734.

59 *The Pennsylvania Gazette*, December 1, 1737.

60 "Of the Use, Abuse, and LIBERTY OF THE PRESS," in *The Independent Reflector*, August 30, 1753. See William Livingston and Others, *The Independent Reflector or Weekly Essays on Sundry Important Subjects*, Milton M. Klein, ed. (Cambridge, Mass., 1963).

61 November 1759, quoted in "James Parker versus New York Province," Beverly McAnear, ed., *New York History*, XXXII (1941), 322.

62 Thomas, *The History of Printing in America*, II, 302–303.

63 *The Documentary History of the State of New York*, Edmund B. O'Callaghan, ed. (Albany, N.Y., 1849–51), III, 528–536.

64 *New-York Gazette; or The Weekly Post-Boy*, February 12, February 26, December 24, 1770; *The New York Journal; or, the General Advertiser*, February 15, 1770. On McDougall's case, see Thomas Jones, *History of New York during the Revolutionary War*, E. F. de Lancey, ed. (New York, 1879), I, 24–33, 426–435; Isaac Q. Leake, *Memoir of the Life and Times of General John Lamb* (Albany, N.Y., 1850), pp. 60–73; *Historical Memoirs from 16 March 1763 to 9 July 1776 of William Smith*, William H. W. Sabine, ed. (New York, 1956), pp. 71–81; Dorothy Rita Dillon, *The New York Triumvirate* (New York, 1949), pp. 106–123.

65 *The Weekly Post-Boy*, February 12, 19, and 26, March 19 and April 9, 1770; *The New York Journal*, March 1 and 15, 1770, and January 26, 1771.

66 See, for example, the "Dougliad" articles, in the *New-York Gazette; and the Weekly Mercury*, April 9–June 25, 1770.

67 See George Nobbe, *The North Briton: A Study in Political Propaganda* (New York, 1939); George Rudé, *Wilkes and Liberty* (New York, 1962); and Robert R. Rea, *The English Press in Politics, 1760–1774* (Lincoln, Neb., 1963).

68 *The New York Weekly Post-Boy*, February 19, 1770; *The New York Journal*, March 22, 26, and 29, 1770.

69 Microfilm copy of the *Journal of the Votes and Proceedings of the General Assembly of the Colony of New-York, 1769–1771*, Public Records Office, London, Document #953, C.O. 5/1219. Extracts of the Assembly's *Journal* for December 13, 1770, when McDougall was interrogated, appeared in *The New York Weekly Post-Boy*, December 24, 1770, and *The New York Mercury*, December 24, 1770. See also the *Post-Boy* for March 11 and 25, 1771, and *The New York Journal*, January 29 and February 21, 1771.

70 *Journals of the Continental Congress, 1774–1789*, I, 108.

71 Henry Schofield, "Freedom of the Press in the United States," in his *Essays on Constitutional Law and Equity* (Boston, 1921), II, 521–522. Schofield has been quoted with approval by Zechariah Chafee, Jr., in *Free Speech in the United States* (Cambridge, Mass., 1948), p. 20; quoted by the Supreme Court,

in *Bridges* v. *California,* 314 U.S. 252, 264 (1941); and endorsed by many scholars.

[72] Sir William Blackstone, *Commentaries on the Laws of England* (Oxford, 1765–69), IV, 151–152.

[73] Query XVII, "Religion," in *Notes on the State of Virginia,* William Peden, ed. (Chapel Hill, N.C., 1955), p. 159.

[74] "A Bill for new modelling the form of government and for establishing the Fundamental principles of our future Constitution," dated by Boyd as "before 13 June 1776," in *The Papers of Thomas Jefferson,* Julian P. Boyd, ed. (Princeton, 1950), I, 353. Jefferson copied this provision from a similar one in an earlier draft, then bracketed it out, and omitted it from a third draft. *Ibid.,* p. 347.

[75] "That the mere utterance of a political opinion is being penalized in these cases becomes even clearer in a statute such as that in Virginia, which declared the utterance of the opinion, or action upon it, to be equally offensive, providing a fine not exceeding £20,000 and imprisonment not exceeding five years 'if any person residing or being within this commonwealth shall . . . by any word, open deed, or act, advisedly and willingly maintain and defend the authority, jurisdiction, or power, of the king or parliament of Great Britain, heretofore claimed and exercised within this colony, or shall attribute any such authority, jurisdiction, or power, to the king or parliament of Great Britain.' " Willard Hurst, "Treason in the United States," *Harvard Law Review,* LVIII (1944), 267, quoting *The Statutes at Large Being a Collection of All The Laws of Virginia (1619–1792),* William W. Hening, ed. (J. & G. Cochran, 1821), IX, 170. For Jefferson's role, see Hurst, p. 251; and *The Papers of Thomas Jefferson,* Boyd, ed., I, 598.

[76] *The Papers of Thomas Jefferson,* Boyd, ed., II, 545–553.

[77] "That the printing-presses shall be free to every person who undertakes to examine the proceedings of the legislature, or any branch of government, and no law shall ever be made to restrain the right thereof. The free communication of thoughts and opinions is one of the invaluable rights of man; and every citizen may freely speak, write, and print on any subject, *being responsible for the abuse of that liberty.* In *prosecutions* for the publication of papers investigating the official conduct of officers or men in a public capacity, or where the matter published is proper for public information, the truth thereof may be given in evidence; and in all indictments for libels the jury shall have a right to determine the law and the facts, under the direction of the court, as in other cases." "Pennsylvania Constitution of 1790," Article IX, Section 7, in *The Federal and State Constitutions,* Thorpe, ed., V, 3100. Italics added.

[78] *Pennsylvania and the Federal Constitution, 1787–1788,* John Bach McMaster and Frederick D. Stone, eds. (Philadelphia, 1888), pp. 308–309.

[79] *Respublica* v. *Oswald,* 1 Dallas (Penn.) Reports 319 (1788); "Trial of William Cobbett," November 1797, in *State Trials of the United States during the Administrations of Washington and Adams,* Francis Wharton, ed. (Philadelphia, 1849), pp. 323–324; *Respublica* v. *Dennie,* 4 Yeates' (Penn.) Reports 267 (1805).

[80] "Delaware Constitution of 1792," Article I, Section 5, in *The Federal and State Constitutions,* Thorpe, ed., I, 569; and "Kentucky Constitution of 1792," Article XII, Sections 7–8, *ibid.,* III, 1274.

[81] "Hitherto Unpublished Correspondence Between Chief Justice Cushing and John Adams in 1789," Frank W. Grinnell, ed., *Massachusetts Law Quarterly,* XXVII (1942), 12–16. Adams, of course, signed the Sedition Act into law

and urged its enforcement; and Cushing, as a Supreme Court judge, presided over some of the Sedition Act trials and charged juries on the Act's constitutionality. See Smith, *Freedom's Fetters*, pp. 97–98, 152, 242, 267, 268, 271, 284, 311, 363, and 371.

[82] See cases cited above at note 79. The judges in Oswald's case were Thomas McKean, then a Federalist but subsequently a Republican, and George Bryan, an anti-Federalist and libertarian advocate of a national bill of rights.

[83] *Commonwealth* v. *Freeman*, reported in the *Independent Chronicle* (Boston), February 24 and March 3, 10, 17, 24, 1791.

[84] "Draught of a Fundamental Constitution for the Commonwealth of Virginia," in *The Papers of Thomas Jefferson*, Boyd, ed., VI, 304: "PRINTING PRESS shall be subject to no other restraint than liableness to legal prosecution for false facts printed and published." Boyd dates this document between May 15 and June 17, 1783.

[85] "A declaration that the federal government will never restrain the press from printing any thing they please, will not take away the liability of the printers for false facts printed." Jefferson to Madison, July 31, 1788, in *The Papers of Thomas Jefferson*, Boyd, ed., XIII, 442.

[86] "Madison's Observations on Jefferson's Draft of a Constitution for Virginia," October 1788, *ibid.*, VI, 316.

[87] Madison's original proposal, June 8, 1789, was: "The people shall not be deprived or abridged of their right to speak, to write, or to publish their sentiments; and the freedom of the press, as one of the great bulwarks of liberty, shall be inviolable." *The Debates and Proceedings in the Congress of the United States* (Washington, 1834), I, 451, 1st Cong., 1st Sess. Cited hereafter as *Annals of Congress*, the bookbinder's title.

[88] Jefferson to Madison, August 28, 1789, in *The Papers of Thomas Jefferson*, Boyd, ed., XV, 367.

[89] "The liberty of the press is secured. . . . In the time of King William, there passed an act for licensing the press. That was repealed. Since that time it has been looked upon as safe." *The Debates in the Several State Conventions on the Adoption of the Federal Constitution*, Jonathan Elliot, ed., 2nd ed., rev. (Philadelphia, 1941), III, 247.

[90] *Ibid.*, III, 560.

[91] Jefferson to Madison, July 31, 1788, in *The Papers of Thomas Jefferson*, Boyd, ed., XIII, 422–423.

[92] Madison to Jefferson, October 17, 1788, *ibid.*, XIV, 20.

[93] *The Debates in the Several State Conventions*, Elliott, ed., III, 656.

[94] See note 87, above.

[95] "There was a time in England when neither book, pamphlet, nor paper could be published without a license from government. That restraint was finally removed in the year 1694; and, by such removal, the press became perfectly free, for it is not under the restraint of any license. Certainly the new government can have no power to impose restraints." Hugh Williamson, "Remarks in the New Plan of Government," in *Essays on the Constitution of the United States*, Paul Leicester Ford, ed. (Brooklyn, N.Y., 1892), p. 394.

[96] Melancthon Smith, "An Address to the People of the State of New York," 1788, in *Pamphlets on the Constitution of the United States*, Paul Leicester Ford, ed. (Brooklyn, N.Y., 1888), p. 114.

[97] The brief and vague statement by Oswald in 1788 may be regarded by some as an exception to this proposition. Oswald, having been indicted for a criminal libel on a private party, published an address to the public in which he stated: "The doctrine of libel being a doctrine incompatible with law and

liberty, and at once destructive of the privileges of a free country, in the communication of our thoughts, has not hitherto gained any footing in *Pennsylvania. . . ."* Quoted in *Respublica* v. *Oswald*, 1 Dallas 319, at p. 320 (1788).

98 Wilson's statement at the Pennsylvania ratifying convention, quoted in *Pennsylvania and the Federal Constitution*, McMaster and Stone, eds., p. 308; Hamilton in *The Federalist* #84.

99 "Trial of Joseph Ravara" (1792), in *State Trials . . .*, Wharton, ed., pp. 90–92; "Trial of Gideon Henfield" (1793), *ibid.*, pp. 49–92; *United States* v. *Worrall*, 2 Dallas 384 (1798), *ibid.*, pp. 188–199; "Trial of the Northhampton Insurgents" (1799), *ibid.*, p. 476; "Trial of Isaac Williams" (1799), *ibid.*, pp. 652–654. See also *U.S.* v. *Smith* (1797), MS Final Record of the United States Circuit Courts of Massachusetts, 1790–1799, I, 242, 244 (Federal Records Center, Boston). Smith's case is reported in *Federal Cases* #16323, where the date is erroneously given as 1792. In Worrall's case, mentioned above, Justice Chase disagreed with his associate, Judge Peters, who supported the jurisdiction of the federal courts in cases of common-law crime. Chase, however, changed his opinion in *U.S.* v. *Sylvester* (1799), MS Final Record, I, 303, an unreported case.

100 A federal grand jury in Richmond presented Congressman Samuel J. Cabell for seditious libel in 1797. Prosecutions for seditious libel were also begun against Benjamin F. Bache of the Philadelphia *Aurora* and John Daly Burk of the New York *Time Piece*, in 1798, shortly before the enactment of the Sedition Act. See Smith, *Freedom's Fetters*, pp. 95, 183–184, and 188–220.

101 Supreme Court Justices known to have accepted jurisdiction in cases of common-law crimes included Wilson, Ellsworth, Paterson, Jay, Iredell, and Chase. See cases mentioned in note 99, above.

102 *U.S.* v. *Hudson and Goodwin*, 7 Cranch 32, at p. 34 (1812). Justice Johnson, speaking for the "majority," gave an unreasoned opinion. The case had been decided without arguments of counsel. W. W. Crosskey, *Politics and the Constitution* (Chicago, 1953), II, 782, claims that Chief Justice Marshall and Justices Story and Washington dissented from Johnson's opinion without noting the fact of their dissent on the record.

103 On the English legislation of the 1790's, see May, *The Constitutional History of England . . .*, II, 161–174. The Parliamentary debates and the texts of the Treasonable Practices Act and of the Sedition Act of 1795, known together as "The Two Acts," were published in London in 1796 under the title, *The History of the Two Acts*, and were imported into the United States and advertised under the title, *History of the Treason and Sedition Bills lately passed in Great Britain.* For the influence of the English experience and legislation on Federalist thought, see Manning J. Dauer, *The Adams Federalists* (Baltimore, 1953), pp. 157–159.

104 *Annals of Congress*, 5th Cong., 2nd Sess., p. 2152; see also, *ibid.*, Macon at p. 2106, Gallatin at p. 2163, Nicholas at p. 2142, and Livingston at p. 2153.

105 *The Debates in the Several State Conventions*, Elliot, ed., IV, 540–541.

106 *The Writings of James Madison*, Gaillard Hunt, ed. (New York, 1900–10), VI, 333–334.

107 *People* v. *Croswell*, 3 Johnson's (N.Y.) Cases 336 (1804).

108 Chief Justice Morgan Lewis, joined by Judge Brockholst Livingston, whom Jefferson appointed to the United States Supreme Court in 1806, explicitly defined freedom of the press in common-law terms. In 1805 the state legislature enacted a bill allowing truth as a defense if published "with good motives and for justifiable end," and allowing the jury to decide the whole

issue. The statute is reported at 3 Johnson's Cases 411–413, following the arguments of counsel and the judicial opinions.

[109] Jefferson to Governor Thomas McKean, February 19, 1803, in *The Writings of Thomas Jefferson*, Paul Leicester Ford, ed. (New York, 1892–99), IX, 451–452.

[110] Jefferson to Abigail Adams, September 4, 1804, *ibid.*, X, 90. In the eloquent First Inaugural Address, Jefferson declared, in a deservedly much-quoted passage: "If there be any among us who would wish to dissolve this Union or to change its republican form, let them stand undisturbed as monuments of the safety with which error of opinion may be tolerated where reason is left free to combat it." But in the Second Inaugural Address he spoke quite differently.

[111] "Hampden," *A Letter to the President of the United States, touching the Prosecutions under his Patronage, before the Circuit Court in the District of Connecticut* (New Haven, Conn., 1808), p. 28.

[112] *Ibid.*, pp. 8–12.

[113] Jefferson to Thomas Seymour, February 11, 1807, in *The Writings of Thomas Jefferson*, Ford, ed., IX, 90.

[114] First issued as a tract (London, 1793). The reprint cited here is from *The Miscellaneous Works and Remains of the Reverend Robert Hall*, John Foster, ed. (London, 1846), pp. 159–233. For other British precursors of the new American libertarianism, see "Father of Candor," *A Letter Concerning Libels, Warrants, the Seizure of Papers and Sureties for the Peace of Behaviour*, 7th ed. (London, 1771), pp. 20, 34, 71, and 161; Ebenezer Ratcliffe, *Two Letters Addressed to the Right Rev. Prelates* (London, 1773), p. 100; Andrew Kippis, *A Vindication of the Protestant Dissenting Ministers* (London, 1773), pp. 98–99; Francis Maseres, *An Enquiry Into the Extent of the Power of Juries* (1776), (Dublin, 1792), pp. 6, 13, 18, 22, 24, and 28; Jeremy Bentham, *A Fragment on Government* (London, 1776), p. 154; Capel Lofft, *An Essay on the Law of Libels* (London, 1785), pp. 60–61; James Adair, *Discussions of the Law of Libels As at Present Received* (London, 1785), pp. 27–28; Manasseh Dawes, *The Deformity of the Doctrine of Libels, and Informations Ex-Officio* (London, 1785), pp. 11–24, 28; and the celebrated argument of Thomas Erskine in defense of Tom Paine, in a trial for seditious libel, 1792, published as a contemporary tract and available in *Speeches of Thomas Lord Erskine*, Edward Walford, ed. (London, 1870), I, 309, 313.

[115] *An Apology for the Freedom of the Press . . .* , in *The Miscellaneous Works . . .* , Foster, ed., p. 172.

[116] *Ibid.*

[117] *Ibid.*, pp. 174, 176–177, and 179.

[118] *Annals of Congress*, 3rd Cong., 2nd Sess., p. 792, November 19, 1794.

[119] *Ibid.*, p. 794, November 21, 1794.

[120] *Ibid.*, pp. 946–947, November 28, 1794.

[121] *Ibid.*, pp. 900–901, November 24, 1794.

[122] *Ibid.*, pp. 901–902, November 24, 1794.

[123] *Ibid.*, p. 905, November 24, 1794.

[124] *Ibid.*, p. 911, November 25, 1794.

[125] *Ibid.*, p. 918, November 26, 1794.

[126] May, *The Constitutional History of England . . .* , II, 145–149.

[127] *Annals of Congress*, 3rd Cong., 2nd Sess., pp. 921, 924, November 26, 1794.

[128] *Ibid.*, p. 934, November 27, 1794.

[129] I am indebted to Professor Alfred Young for bringing the Keteltas case to my attention, and for permitting me to read his unpublished dissertation,

"The Democratic-Republican Movement in New York State, 1788–1797" (1958), which discusses the case at pp. 713–751. See also *Journal of the Votes and Proceedings of the General Assembly of New York*, 19th Sess., March 8, 1796, and *Greenleaf's New York Journal and Patriotic Register*, March 11, 1796.

130 *Ibid.*

131 *Greenleaf's New York Journal*, March 11, 1796.

132 *The Argus, or Greenleaf's New Daily Advertiser*, April 4, 5, 7, 8, and 12, 1796.

133 *Ibid.*, March 15 and April 6, 1796.

134 *The Time Piece* (New York), December 22, 1797.

135 Sir James Fitzjames Stephen, *A History of the Criminal Law of England* (London, 1883), II, 383; and Frank Thayer, *Legal Control of the Press* (Brooklyn, N.Y., 1950), pp. 17, 25, and 178.

136 *Annals of Congress*, 5th Cong., 2nd Sess., pp. 2102–2111, 2139–2143, 2153–2154, and 2160–2166.

137 *Independent Chronicle* (Boston), issues of March 4–7, April 8–11, April 11–15, and April 29–May 2, 1799, reporting the trial of Abijah Adams, editor of the *Chronicle*, for seditious libel against the state legislature of Massachusetts.

138 "Hortensius," *An Essay on the Liberty of the Press. Respectfully Inscribed to the Republican Printers Throughout the United States* (Philadelphia, 1799), 51 pp. Reprinted in Richmond, Va., in 1803 by Samuel Pleasants, Jr., but set in small type, in an edition of 30 pages. The latter edition is cited here. Hay also published, in 1803, a different tract with a similar title, *An Essay on the Liberty of the Press, Shewing, That the Requisition of Security for Good Behaviour from Libellers, is Perfectly Compatible with the Constitution and Laws of Virginia* (Richmond, Va., 1803), 48 pp.

139 The *Report* originally appeared as a tract of over 80 pages. The copy in the Langdell Treasure Room, Harvard Law Library, is bound together with the 1799 issue of Hay's *Essay*. Madison wrote the *Report* at the close of 1799; it was adopted on January 11, 1800, by the Virginia legislature, which immediately published it. It is reproduced in *The Debates in the Several State Conventions*, Elliot, ed., IV, 546–580, under the title, "Madison's Report on the Virginia Resolutions. . . . Report of the Committee to whom were referred the Communications of various States, relative to the Resolutions of the last General Assembly of this State, concerning the Alien and Sedition Laws." The *Report* is also available in *The Writings of James Madison*, Hunt, ed., VI, 341–406. The edition cited here is *The Virginia Report of 1799–1800, Touching the Alien and Sedition Laws; together with the Virginia Resolutions of December 21, 1798, The Debates and Proceedings thereon, in the House of Delegates in Virginia* (Richmond, Va., 1850); see pp. 189–237. This is a book of great value for its inclusion of the Virginia debates on the Sedition Act, at pp. 22–161. While those debates added little to the debates of the House of Representatives, the remarks of Republican speakers constitute another example of the new libertarianism.

140 (New York, 1800), 296 pp.

141 (New York, 1801), 84 pp.

142 Five vols. (Philadelphia, 1803), Vol. I, Part II, Note G, pp. 11–30 of Appendix.

143 *The Virginia Report of 1799–1800*, p. 220.

144 *An Essay on the Liberty of the Press* (1803 ed. of 1799 tract), p. 29; and *An Essay on the Liberty of the Press, Shewing* . . . (1803), p. 32. See note 138, above.

145 *An Enquiry, Concerning the Liberty, and Licentiousness of the Press*, pp. 6–7.

146 *A Treatise Concerning Political Enquiry*, p. 173.

147 *The Virginia Report of 1799–1800*, pp. 226–227.

148 *A Treatise Concerning Political Enquiry*, p. 253.

149 *An Essay on the Liberty of the Press* (1803 ed. of 1799 tract), p. 28.

150 *Annals of Congress*, 5th Cong., 2nd Sess., p. 2162.

151 *An Enquiry, Concerning the Liberty, and Licentiousness of the Press*, p. 68.

152 *The Virginia Report of 1799–1800*, p. 226.

153 *A Treatise Concerning Political Enquiry*, p. 262.

154 *An Essay on the Liberty of the Press* (1803 ed. of 1799 tract), pp. 23–24.

155 *Ibid.*, p. 25.

156 *An Essay on the Liberty of the Press, Shewing . . .* (1803 tract), p. 29.

157 Wortman, *A Treatise Concerning Political Enquiry*, pp. 140, 253; Thomson, *An Enquiry, Concerning the Liberty, and Licentiousness of the Press*, p. 79.

158 *An Enquiry, Concerning the Liberty, and the Licentiousness of the Press*, p. 22.

159 *The Virginia Report of 1799–1800*, p. 222.

160 *A Treatise Concerning Political Enquiry*, p. 29.

161 Thomson, *An Enquiry, Concerning the Liberty, and Licentiousness of the Press*, pp. 20, 22; Hay, *An Essay on the Liberty of the Press* (1803 ed. of 1799 tract), p. 26.

162 See *People* v. *Croswell*, 3 Johnson's (N.Y.) Cases 336 (1804).

FREEDOM IN TURMOIL:
THE SEDITION ACT ERA

I N 1798 the Fourth of July was commemorated in rather sinister fashion. While the officers of a New York military company drank to the toast "One and but one party in the United States," Federalist partisans in Newburyport, Massachusetts, publicly burned copies of the leading Republican newspaper in New England. On that same festive day the Senate, in the hope of controlling public opinion and crushing the opposition party, passed a bill making it a crime to criticize the government. The sponsor of the bill, Senator Lloyd, expressed anxiety to Washington—the bill might not be severe enough to muzzle "the lovers of Liberty, or, in other words, the Jacobins"; moreover, complained Lloyd, "I fear Congress will close the session without a declaration of War, which I look upon as necessary to enable us to lay our hands on traitors. . . ." In a similar spirit the president of Yale, in his Fourth of July Sermon, warned that if the author of the Declaration of Independence, then the Vice-President of the United States, were to have his way, the country would "see the Bible cast into a bonfire . . . our wives and daughters the victims of legal prostitution . . . our sons become the disciples of Voltaire, and the dragoons of Marat. . . ." Within a fortnight and even before the Sedition Act became law, the impatient administration arrested two opposition editors, Burke of the New York *Time Piece* and Bache of the Philadelphia *Aurora*, the nation's foremost Republican newspaper. A spirit of vigilantism flashed like summer lightning over a divided land that girded itself for war—abroad against the legions of Napoleon, at home against the subversion of its Jeffersonian minions. A crisis was in the making that jeopardized the nation's policies and free institutions.

The foreign crisis had been caused by French aggressions against American commerce and aggravated by Jay's Treaty. France, at war with England, not unjustifiably viewed Jay's Treaty as a pro-British instrument, a rebuff to an old ally and benefactor, even as diplomatic treachery. For Monroe, the American minister to France, had been deceived by the State Department and unwittingly misled the French on the course of Jay's mission. He had also induced them to promise compensation for their spoliations and repeal of their maritime decrees against American shipping. News of the treaty provoked France to recall her American ambassador and reinstitute her decrees with greater rigor than before, on the theory that American commerce deserved from France no greater respect than that offered by England and acquiesced in by the United States. Within a year the French sank or captured over three hundred American ships and refused recognition to Charles C. Pinckney, Monroe's successor —indeed, had ordered him out of France on threat of arrest. Such was the posture of Franco-American relations when John Adams was inaugurated.

President Adams, convinced that the differences with France, however serious, might be resolved by negotiation, resolutely determined upon a policy of peace with honor. He proposed a new diplomatic mission to Paris and wisely recommended defense measures during the emergency: an increased army (then only 3,500 men), creation of a permanent navy, convoys, and the arming of merchant ships. But the Republicans, despite their recent bellicosity against Great Britain, opposed all preparedness measures as unnecessarily provocative and contrary to the pacific intent of the new mission. A fierce party battle ensued in Congress. The Federalists, spurred by a war faction, tarred the obstructionist Republicans with charges of disloyalty and indulged in jingoistic saber rattling. The session ended in July with the failure of most major defense measures, chiefly because Congress was so closely divided. But the party debate had been so vituperative that a residue of hate remained. Jefferson, presiding over the Senate, commented to a friend: "You and I have formerly seen warm debates and high political passions. But gentlemen of different politics would then speak to each other, and separate the business of the Senate from that of society. It is not so now. Men who have been intimate all their lives, cross the streets to avoid meeting, and turn their heads another way, lest they should be obliged to touch their hats." When Congress reconvened in a tense atmosphere, partisan oratory was disrupted by a fistfight on the floor, and some Congressmen predicted "blood to be let" before the session ended.

In March of 1798 the President notified Congress that dispatches from the American envoys proved that the objects of the peace mission could not be accomplished "on terms compatible with the safety, the honor, or the essential interests of the nation." He would therefore permit merchant ships to arm for their own protection, and exhorted Congress speedily to enact defense measures proportionate to the dangers to national security. Adams neither wished war nor took any step that would provoke Congress to its declaration; but the Republicans fitfully described his message as "insane" and denounced him for incitement to belligerency on behalf of England's interests. The Republicans, however, were betrayed by their own distrust. Believing that the President had exaggerated the gravity of the situation, they induced Congress to request full disclosure of the envoys' dispatches. When Adams complied, the doubters were aghast to discover that he had muted the true state of affairs. The damning evidence of the humiliating and contumelious treatment of our envoys even alluded to a "French party in America." The envoys, after having been ignored for months, had been approached by unofficial agents of the French government—designated as Messrs. X, Y, and Z—who demanded outrageous gifts of money for high officials, an extravagant "loan" to France, and an apology for supposedly obnoxious statements made by President Adams. In addition the United States must pay all debts owed by France to American citizens and the cost of damages caused by French depredations on American commerce. Official negotiation would follow if these terms were met! After more months of degrading intrigue and diplomatic blackmail, the envoys gave up the mission as a hopeless failure.

France had been motivated by simple rapacity and arrogance, not by a desire to drive the United States into war, but she almost succeeded in doing just that. The "XYZ" disclosures, whose publication the Republicans sought to suppress, electrified the country. In the patriotic craze in support of the administration, "Millions for defense, but not one cent for tribute" became the national slogan, and the opposition dwindled to a distinctly beaten minority. War fever mounted, but no one lusted for hostilities except a small sect of ultra-Federalists who controlled the Senate. The President, the closely divided House, and the majority of the people would countenance only resistance against French aggression, not an offensive war.

Federalists of whatever hue shared a sinister understanding that national security and party supremacy might be insured if the country could be first frightened and then panicked. Both fear and panic, already present in the situation, were intensified by chilling stories in the Federalist press on the imminence of a French invasion and the dangers of subversive activities. The Republican opposition was identified as revolutionary Jacobins treasonably allied with the foreign enemy to overthrow the Constitution and cut the throats of true Americans. The Federalists were so obsessed with hate and convinced that anyone whose opinion differed must be a criminal subversive that they openly reviled even their fellow Congressmen.

For example, when Gallatin, the Republican leader of the House, discounted the possibility of an invasion, Speaker Dayton retorted that since his principles were those of "the furious hordes of democrats which threatened this country with subjugation," Gallatin could calmly watch "our dwellings burning, and might 'laugh at our calamities and mock when our fears came upon us.' " When Livingston of New York spoke against a Federalist system of tyranny that would destroy civil liberties, Allen of Connecticut lashed him for "intimate acquaintance with treason" and claimed that he "vomited" falsehood on "everything sacred, human and divine." The prime victim of abuse was the Vice-President himself, who observed: "It suffices for a man to be a philosopher and to believe that human affairs are susceptible of improvement, and to look forward, rather than back to the Gothic ages, for perfection, to mark him as an anarchist, disorganiser, atheist, and enemy of the government." To be an alien or even a naturalized citizen was equally stigmatizing. Was not Gallatin himself a Swiss, and were not Priestly, Cooper, Volney, Burk, Duane, Callender, and other foreign-born scholars and journalists the leaders of swarms of wild Irishmen, political refugees, and French apostles of sedition? It was necessary to "strike terror among these people," as Congressman Harper put it.

Between April and July of 1798, when Congress adjourned, the party program was adopted. In addition to mustering the forces of defense—enlisting an army, creating a navy, fortifying harbors, abrogating all treaties with France, authorizing the capture of armed French ships—Congress passed a series of repressive measures designed to intimidate the opposition, coerce conformity of opinion, and extend Federalist control of the government. The Naturalization Act increased the period of residence from five to fourteen years before citizenship could be granted to immigrants. The statute was a disappointment to ultra-Federalists who preferred "that nothing but birth should entitle a man to citizenship" or the right to vote and hold office. The Alien Act empowered the President to order, without assigning cause, the summary arrest and deportation of any foreigner, even the citizen of a friendly nation, whom he judged to be "dangerous" to the peace and safety of the nation or believed "suspect" of "secret machinations." A deported alien who returned without permission might be imprisoned indefinitely at the discretion of the President. The Republicans described the measure as a "refinement on despotism," while the Federalists claimed that "to *boggle* about slight forms" in time of danger courted national disaster.

The capstone of the new Federalist system was the Sedition Act, an expression of the easy rule of thumb offered by the party organ in the nation's capital, "He that is not for us, is against us." The same editor added: "Whatever American is a friend to the present administration of the American government, is undoubtedly a true republican, a true patriot. . . . Whatever American opposes the administration is an anarchist, a jacobin and a traitor. . . . It is *Patriotism* to write in favor of our government—it is Sedition to write against it." Given such a view of things, the Federalists believed that the government could be criminally assaulted merely by political opinions that had the supposed tendency of lowering the public esteem of the administration. Security lay in the elimination of political criticism and the creation of a one-party press, eventually a one-party system. Thus the Sedition Act made criminal any "false" or "malicious" statements against the President (but not the Vice-President), Congress, or the "government"—i.e., the administration—with intent to defame or excite the people's animosity. The Federalists had deliberately exploited the crisis in foreign relations for the sake of partisan advantage. To Jefferson, Madison explained that "the loss of liberty at home is to be charged to provisions against danger real or pretended from abroad."

As actually applied by the federal judges—all Federalists—the Sedition Act made criticism of the administration the test of criminality. Even in the course of the House debates, advocates of the measure clearly stated that the political opinion of the Republican opposition was to be outlawed. But only one congressman, Mathew Lyon of Vermont, was tried and convicted. For the crime of having published an address to his constituents in which he accused Adams of a "continual grasp of power" and an "unbounded thirst for ridiculous pomp," he was sentenced to four months and fined $1,000. Lyon's cruel treatment in jail was vividly described by the editor of one of the few Jeffersonian newspapers in New England, with the result that he too became a victim of the Sedition Act.

Altogether there were only about twenty-five arrests under the Sedition Act, fourteen indictments, and a dozen trials—all ending in conviction. Though few in number the prosecutions were selectively important, for among the victims were major Jeffersonian publicists like Thomas Cooper and the editors of four of the five leading Republican papers in the nation. The administration's sedition-net also closed around several minor journalists and a few village radicals. In one farcical case a town drunk, upon hearing a sixteen-gun salute in honor of the President who had just passed by, remarked: "I do not care if they fired through his ass." Another potential Robespierre who was jailed was the itinerant speaker who so fired his Dedham audience that they put up a liberty pole with a sign proclaiming:

> No Stamp Act, No sedition, No Alien Bills,
> No Land Tax; downfall to the Tyrants of
> America, peace and retirement to the
> President, Long Live the Vice President
> and the Minority.

The speaker and a local farmer who raised the liberty pole were convicted for having erected a "rallying point of insurrection and civil war."

Despite these prosecutions the repressive impact of the Sedition Act has been exaggerated. Countless citizens guarded their political expressions, but the "witchhunt" and "reign of terror" decried by the Republicans existed more by Federalist intention than by execution. Harassed Republican politicians and journalists simply refused to be intimidated and their popular support in the Middle Atlantic states and especially in the South was so great that the administration did not dare close their presses or tamper with free elections. By the time of the election of 1800 the number of Jeffersonian newspapers had even increased substantially, in spite of the Sedition Act—or perhaps because of it, as well as because of the high taxes accompanying brink-of-war defense policies. The Sedition Act was a measure of abortive tyranny. Its failure might have been predicted by any astute politician when Congressman Lyon, its first victim, was reelected while in prison.

The policies of the government—high taxes (even a stamp tax), repression, a standing army—convinced Old Dominion leaders of the need to resist another "Anglo-monarchic-aristocratic-military government." The nation must be roused to the danger, brought to its senses. Mass petitions of protest from many states were deluging Congress, but a more effective, statesmanly appeal must be made to the voters. The device hit upon by Jefferson was the adoption of formal resolutions by state legislatures. In *The Federalist* Hamilton himself had once argued that the states were "bodies of perpetual observation . . . capable of forming and conducting plans of regular opposition" should the central government exceed its powers and invade constitutional rights. The Vice-President secretly framed a series of resolutions which were adopted by the legislature of Kentucky in November 1798; a month later Virginia passed companion resolutions drawn by James Madison.

The Kentucky and Virginia Resolves were classic expressions of the Republican creed. They consisted of a spirited denunciation of Federalist policies, particularly the Alien and Sedition Acts, a defense of civil liberties and of the rights of a peaceable opposition, and an eloquent restatement of the most orthodox American constitutional theory, based on the concept of limited government. In a word they expressed the view that man is free because the government is not, is limited, rather, by regularized restraints upon power. What was controversial about the resolutions was their assertion that each state retained the right to judge for itself whether the central government had exceeded its powers. The other states, which were invited to join in a declaration of the unconstitutionality of the Alien and

Sedition Acts, either responded adversely or not at all. In the Southern states, where public opinion was agitated by the XYZ disclosures, a discreet silence was maintained rather than give the appearance of national disunity. In the North, where the Federalists viewed the Resolutions as little short of a declaration of war against the Union, the state legislatures censured their erring Southern sisters, defended Congressional policies, and maintained that the federal judiciary was the proper body to judge infractions of the Constitution—although judicial review over Congress was not yet established. A Supreme Court decision against the Sedition Act would have been welcomed by the Jeffersonians, obviating the need for their Resolutions; but the members of the Court, on circuit duty, had been enforcing the dread statute.

The disheartening state responses impelled counter-responses, lest silence be construed as the abandonment of doctrines considered vital for the preservation of constitutional liberty. The Second Kentucky Resolves, penned by Jefferson, contained the proposition that state "nullification" was the rightful remedy for an unconstitutional act of Congress. In later years Calhoun was to subvert the constitutional theories of Jefferson and Madison when he adopted them for a defense of slavery, whereas they had been reluctantly driven to "nullification" and "interposition" in defense of human rights.

General Alexander Hamilton, who was in actual command of the army, was certain—and even hopeful—that the Virginia Jacobins were about to rise in insurrection. Given the opportunity to "subdue a *refractory* and *powerful* State," he would head the army for Virginia, enforce the national laws, and "put Virginia to the Test of resistance." Hamilton, even before the XYZ disclosures that "delighted" him, had become the principal architect of American foreign and domestic policy because of his influence on the Federalist party and his control over a Cabinet which was disloyal to Adams. As soon as the United States was armed, Hamilton, echoed by his ultra-Federalist followers, wanted war, preferably as a result of French attack. War would unify the nation, make possible the execution of traitors and the electoral destruction of the opposition party, and in the event of "internal disorder" would justify the "subdivision" of Virginia into small states that could not menace the central government. A large army, whose officers were carefully screened for party loyalty, was the *sine qua non* of his plans. He got that army, although both he and it had to be "crammed" down Adams' throat by the Cabinet and Washington, the titular commander.

Virginia, however, failed to oblige Hamilton by rebellion, and Napoleon was equally uncooperative. As early as October 1798, Adams had predicted that there was "no more prospect of seeing a French army here than there is in Heaven." As for General Hamilton's fellow citizens, only a few Pennsylvania farmers armed to resist payment of direct taxes for the army, and they fired merely dirty looks when "conquered" by four brigades. What little satisfaction could be gained when the leaders of "Fries's Rebellion" were sentenced to death for treason was robbed by Adams' pardon.

Notwithstanding disappointments Hamilton envisioned military glories and conquests more grandiose than those of the Conquistadors. His army was not to be unused. Adams justifiably thought of him as an "artful, indefatigable and unprincipled intriguer," while a Republican journalist shrewdly wrote, "When a *little Alexander* dreams himself to be ALEXANDER THE GREAT . . . he is very apt to fall into miserable intrigues." Hamilton's plan, in which he was joined by Rufus King, the American minister in Great Britain, and Timothy Pickering, the Secretary of State, was the conquest and annexation of Louisiana and the Floridas. Even "the riches of Mexico and Peru," perhaps all of Latin America, beckoned invitingly for a liberator. Spain, the hapless ally of France, was to be despoiled, France herself forestalled from expansion in the Americas. Great Britain, in alliance with the United States, would provide the naval cover, while the United States would furnish the whole land force. "The command in this case," Hamilton modestly confided to Ambassador King, "would naturally fall upon me, and I hope I shall disappoint no favorable expectation." The British were ready to cooperate; Miranda, a South American revolutionary, promised the aid of his insurrectionary constituents; Pickering and McHenry, the Secretary of War, consented; and Hamilton, who did not recognize a real traitor when confronted by one, had enlisted the western commander, General Wilkinson, in the plan—Wilkinson who was a spy in the pay of Spain! All was in readiness, but John Adams had been ignored.

In February 1799, the President stunned the country, his Cabinet, the Congress, and most of all, Hamilton and the ultra-Federalists, by announcing his intention to make peace with France. Making public a letter from Talleyrand which stated France's desire to end "existing differences" and assured that an envoy would be received on the President's own terms, "with the respect due to the representative of a free, independent, and powerful nation," Adams nominated an envoy. Disbelief soured into consternation and rage among the Hamiltonians. Their leader had planned for a declaration of war by August, but peace with France signaled the end of everything—the crisis psychology which they had manipulated for party gain, the plans for new defense measures and more taxes, the thrilling little naval war that raged at sea, the British alliance, the glorious prospects of military conquest, the army itself, the expectation of victory in the next election. All fizzled like a soggy firecracker. Hamilton still wanted "to squint at South America," but the best that he and his followers could do was delay negotiations, first by pressing for a three-man mission, then by intriguing against the departure of the envoys. The President finally issued a personal order for their sailing and did all but place them aboard himself.

In later years he wrote, "I desire no other inscription over my gravestone than: 'Here lies John Adams, who took upon himself the responsibility of the peace with France. . . .'" His bold and courageous stroke, placing country above partisanship, earned him the enmity of the ultras whose factitiousness split the party and cost Adams his reelection. But the triumph of Jefferson and the restoration of national sanity represented the triumph of moderation. In that sense the triumph belonged also to Adams himself, a flinty, principled old patriot whom the British ambassador admitted was the last man to be "bullied into measures which he does not approve."

The crisis of 1798–1799 took shape when the latent authoritarianism within the Federalist party threatened to abort the development of a free and responsible government in the United States. Deterioration of relations with France created the opportunity and the cover for a thrust for power by a high-placed political elite with little or no faith in the capacity of the people for self-government. These men, who composed the ultra-Federalist faction, conceived of themselves as an aristocracy not of land and bloodline but of political virtue and fitness to rule—rule rather than govern. Impatient with political compromise and incapable of distinguishing dissent from disloyalty, they were prepared to use legal and military coercion to control public opinion for party purposes. They were prepared, too, to abandon a foreign policy of neutrality and nonintervention in exchange for foreign intrigues and military conquest. Even war was planned as an instrument of party policy. Distrustful of free elections, they were intolerant of free speech, freedom of the press, and a free political opposition. Their efforts to institutionalize vigilantism and repression were noxiously at variance with the elementary principles of an open society and the development of a political democracy.

The party had been in continuous mastery since the organization of the government under the Constitution. But Washington's retirement from politics had been followed by a hairline victory in the election of 1796, jarring the Hamiltonians into a realization that their personal power and domination of the nation's destiny faced a precarious future. Unable to accept gracefully the possibility of defeat, they exploited a crisis in foreign relations by advancing an extremist program calculated to burke the opposition.

When President Adams suddenly made peace with France, he

broke the Hamiltonians by destroying the basis of their program. Their savage campaign against him ended public confidence in the party which had already been weakened by the public reaction against the high cost of military preparations. A few instances of outrageous conduct on the part of soldiers against civilians gave substance to Republican propaganda which played on the popular fear of a standing army. Taxes and soldiers probably alienated more moderate voters from Federalism than did the Sedition Act prosecutions.

Adams deserved the credit for the Franco-American Convention of 1800, ratified in 1801, which gave the United States a desperately needed period of peace and reestablished the principle of neutrality in American foreign relations. He also paved the way for the return of national sanity. It was Jefferson, however, who reaped the credit. Certainly his election meant the conclusive repudiation of militarism and of a one-party system by the young American nation. The new President's inaugural address recharted the national course. The will of the majority, he declared, must prevail, but to be rightful it must be reasonable, respectful of the equal rights of the political opposition.

Let us, then, fellow-citizens [said Jefferson], unite with one heart and one mind. Let us restore to social intercourse that harmony and affection without which liberty and even life itself are but dreary things. And let us reflect that, having banished from our land that religious intolerance under which mankind so long bled and suffered, we have yet gained little if we countenance a political intolerance as despotic, as wicked, and capable of as bitter and bloody persecutions . . . every difference of opinion is not a difference of principle. We have called by different names brethren of the same principle. We are all Republicans, we are all Federalists. If there be any among us who would wish to dissolve this Union or change its republican form, let them stand undisturbed as monuments of the safety with which error of opinion may be tolerated where reason is left free to combat it. . . . Let us, then, with courage and confidence pursue our Federal and Republican principles, our attachment to the Union and representative government.

NO ESTABLISHMENT
OF RELIGION:
THE ORIGINAL
UNDERSTANDING

Introduction

THE First Amendment begins with the clause against an establishment of religion: "Congress shall make no law respecting an establishment of religion. . . ." There are two basic interpretations of what the framers intended by this clause.

The broader interpretation has been advanced in its most authoritative form by the Supreme Court in deciding the case of *Everson* v. *Board of Education* in 1947.[1] Justice Black, speaking for the majority, declared: "The 'establishment of religion' clause of the First Amendment means at least this: Neither a state[2] nor the Federal Government can set up a church. Neither can pass laws which aid one religion, aid all religions, or prefer one religion over another. Neither can force nor influence a person to go to or to remain away from church against his will or force him to profess a belief or disbelief in any religion. No person can be punished for entertaining or professing religious beliefs or disbeliefs, for church attendance or nonattendance. No tax in any amount, large or small, can be levied to support any religious activities or institutions, whatever they may be called, or whatever form they may adopt to teach or practice religion. Neither a state nor the Federal Government can, openly or secretly, participate in the affairs of any religious organizations or groups and vice versa. In the words of Jefferson, the clause against establishment of religion by laws was intended to erect 'a wall of separation between Church and State.' "[3]

The dissenting justices in the *Everson* case, while disagreeing with the majority on the question whether the "wall of separation" had in fact been breached by the practice at issue, concurred with the majority on the historical question of the intentions of the framers. Justice Rutledge's opinion, which was endorsed by all the dissenting justices, declared: "The Amendment's purpose was not to strike merely at the official establishment of a single sect, creed or religion, outlawing only a formal relation such as had prevailed in England and some of the colonies. Necessarily it was to uproot all such relationships. But the object was broader than separating church and state in this narrow sense. It was to create a complete and permanent separation of the spheres of religious activity and civil authority by comprehensively forbidding every form of public aid or support for religion." [4] Thus the heart of this broad interpretation is that not even government aid impartially and equitably administered to all religious groups is permitted by the First Amendment.

The second or narrow interpretation of the clause holds that it was intended to prevent the establishment by government of a single state church which would have preferences of any sort over other churches. In the words of a leading advocate of this interpretation, "establishment of religion" meant to Madison, Jefferson, and the members of the First Congress, "*a formal, legal union of a single church or religion with government, giving the one church or religion an exclusive position of power and favor over all other churches or denominations.*" [5] An advocate of this view would reject Justice Rutledge's contention that every form of public aid or support for religion is prohibited; he would also reject Justice Black's opinion that government cannot aid all religions nor levy a tax on behalf of religious activities or institutions. He might rephrase the debatable part of Justice Black's statement to read: "The establishment of religion clause of the First Amendment means this: Neither a state nor the Federal Government can set up a church. Neither can pass laws which aid one religion or prefer one religion over another. No tax can be levied to support any religious activities or institutions unless apportioned in some equitable form and without discrimination in any form or degree. Government participation in the affairs of any religious organization or groups is prohibited unless with the consent and approval of such. The very phrase, 'wall of separation between Church and State,' is ambiguous and misleading."

According to this view, the wall of separation was intended merely to keep the government from abridging religious liberty by discriminatory practices against religion generally, or against any particular sects or denominations; the wall was not intended, however, to enjoin the government from fostering religion generally or all such religious groups as are willing to accept government aid, whether in the form of tax support, promotional activities, or otherwise.

These two interpretations of the no-establishment clause are patently irreconcilable, yet almost every writer who has explored the evidence has concluded that the interpretation of his choice is historically "right," the other "wrong." The subject, apparently because of its implications for current public policy in the field of education, seems to transform into partisans all who approach it. Even scholars, who cultivate disinterestedness in the search for the truth, convince themselves that "history" speaks loudly, clearly, and in a single voice in behalf of one interpretation or the other.[6]

The issue is certainly more debatable than partisans on either side would have us believe. Yet the fact that each side can write with such complete assurance ought to give the other considerable pause. To a scholar the question is not which of the interpretations of the no-establishment clause "should" prevail, but which is historically more accurate. Yet historical investigation is hampered by the fact that the known sources are often unclear and always disappointingly incomplete (see Appendix). My review of the evidence available leads me to conclude that the truth in this matter is uncertain and ambiguous, a disconcerting conclusion to those who look to history for "answers." I believe, however, that a preponderance of the whole evidence indicates that the Supreme Court's interpretation is historically the more accurate one.

The Background

The Constitutional Convention

The Constitutional Convention of 1787 gave only slight attention to the subject of a Bill of Rights and even less to the subject of religion. In contrast to the Declaration of Independence and to many acts of the Continental Congress, the Constitution contained no references to God; the Convention did not even invoke divine guidance for its deliberations. Its only reference to religion was in reference to qualifications for federal office holders.[7] On August 20 Pinckney proposed that "no religious test or qualification shall ever be annexed to any oath of office under the authority of the U.S."[8] The proposal was referred to the Committee on Detail without debate or consideration by the Convention. When the committee reported ten days later, it ignored Pinckney's proposal. From the floor of the convention he moved it again. The chairman of the committee, Roger Sherman of Connecticut, stated that such a provision was "unnecessary, the prevailing liberality being a sufficient security against such tests."[9] However, two delegates, in unreported speeches, "approved the motion" by Pinckney, and when put to a vote, without further debate, it passed.[10] Rephrased by the Committee on Style, it was incorporated into Article VI, clause 3 of the Constitution: ". . . no religious test shall ever be required as a qualification to any office or public trust under the United States."

This clause "went far," according to one scholar, "in thwarting any State Church" in the United States.[11] The reasoning behind this thought is that, in the absence of the clause, Congress might have had the power to require an oath or subscription to the articles of faith of some particular church,[12] or to Protestantism, or to Christianity generally. But the scope of the protection was not defined by anyone at the time; that is, the implied ban against an establishment of religion is no aid in explaining the meaning of such an establishment.

There are no other references to the subject of religion at the Constitutional Convention. When George Mason of Virginia expressed a wish that the new Constitution "had been prefaced with a Bill of Rights," he offered no suggestions as to the contents of such a bill. Nor did Elbridge Gerry of Massachusetts who, agreeing with Mason, moved for a committee to prepare a Bill of Rights. This motion aroused opposition on the ground that the state bills of rights "being in force are sufficient." Mason rejoined, "The Laws of the U.S. are to be paramount to State Bills of Rights," but without further debate the motion that a Bill of Rights be prepared was put to a vote. It was defeated ten to zero, the delegates voting as state units.[13] Thus, on its face, the record of the Constitutional Convention is no guide in discerning the understanding of the framers as to establishments of religion.

On the other hand, the failure of the convention to provide for a Bill of Rights should not be misunderstood. The members of the convention did not oppose personal liberties; in the main they simply regarded a Bill of Rights as superfluous. The new national government possessed only expressly enumerated powers; no power had been granted to legislate on any of the subjects which would be the concern of a Bill of Rights. Since no such power existed, none could be exercised or abused, and therefore all provisions against that possibility were unnecessary. Of the many statements of this argument,[14] the most widely publicized was that of Hamilton in *The Federalist* where he concluded, simply: "For why declare that things shall not be done which there is no power to do? Why, for instance, should it be said that the liberty of the press shall not be restrained, when no power is given by which restrictions may be imposed?" [15]

The reasoning here is of the utmost significance in defining the powers of Congress in regard to religious establishments. There is abundant evidence to show the belief of the framers that Congress was bereft of any authority over the subject of religion.[16] Congress was powerless, therefore, even in the absence of the First Amendment, to enact laws which benefited one religion or church in particular or all of them equally and impartially. While it is important to try to understand the precise meaning of the First Amendment, this effort must be viewed within the larger framework of the Constitution.

The Ratification Controversy

From late 1787 through the following year, the political attention of the country was engrossed by the proposed Constitution which was submitted to state conventions for ratification. A torrent of speeches, essays, articles, and pamphlets poured forth from partisans on both sides. Opponents of ratification feared most of all that the centralizing tendencies of a consolidated national government would extinguish the rights of states and individuals. The failure of the new instrument to provide for a Bill of Rights was the most important single objection, and the Constitution would probably not have received the requisite number of state votes for ratification had not Federalist leaders like Madison pledged themselves to seek amendments constituting a Bill of Rights as soon as the new government went into operation. Indeed, six of the thirteen original states accompanied their instruments of ratification with recommendations for amendments which would secure specified fundamental personal liberties.[17]

In the light of these facts it is astonishing to discover that the debate on a Bill of Rights was conducted on a level of abstraction so vague as to convey the impression that Americans of 1787–1788 had only the most nebulous conception of the meanings of the particular rights they sought to insure. The insistent demands for the "rights of conscience" or "trial by jury" or "liberty of the press" by the principal advocates of a Bill of Rights were not accompanied by a reasoned analysis of what these rights meant, how far they extended, and in what circumstances they might be limited. Many opponents of ratification discovered that to denounce the omission of a Bill of Rights was a superb tactic, one which provided a useful mask for less elevating, perhaps even sordid, objections relating to such matters as taxation and commerce.

One cannot assume that there was no necessity for careful definition, on the ground that the meanings of specific rights were widely known and agreed to by all. They were not. Not even trial by jury, which was protected by more state constitutions than any other right, had the same meaning and scope from state to state.[18] Moreover, there were substantial differences in the character and number of the rights guaranteed by the various states.[19] Several state conven-

173

tions in ratifying the Constitution even recommended amendments to protect rights not known in their own constitutions.[20] Whatever the explanation, the fact is that in the tens of thousands of words exchanged during the ratification controversy on the subject of a Bill of Rights, no illumination can be gained as to the understanding and content attached at that time to particular rights.

This generalization applies to the subject of religious establishments. An awareness of the need for precision and analysis in discussing the subject might be expected, considering the variety of historical experiences with establishments before and after independence and considering the diversity of relevant state constitutional and statutory provisions. At the very least, one would expect frequent expressions of fear and concern on the subject. Yet the startling fact is that it was rarely mentioned at all and then only very briefly. One searches in vain for a definition in the rhetorical effusions of leading advocates of a Bill of Rights and in the debates of the state ratifying conventions.[21]

The debates of the ratifying conventions of Delaware, New Jersey, and Georgia are nonexistent. Moreover, each ratified unconditionally and without proposing any amendments. Nothing, therefore, can be said of opinion in those states.

In Connecticut, which also ratified without recommendations for amendments, the fragmentary record of the debates shows only that Oliver Wolcott, briefly mentioning the value of the clause against test oaths, said: "Knowledge and liberty are so prevalent in this country, that I do not believe that the United States would ever be disposed to establish one religious sect, and lay all others under legal disabilities." [22] Similarly, Ellsworth, writing in a tract, referred to the fact that religious tests for office were always found in European nations where one church is established as the state church.[23] Neither Ellsworth nor Wolcott, both Federalists, believed that Congress could legislate on the subject of religion.

In Pennsylvania, the convention ratified unconditionally after voting against a series of amendments, constituting a Bill of Rights, proposed by the minority. These defeated amendments, while protecting the "rights of conscience," contained no provision respecting an establishment of religion,[24] which Pennsylvania never experienced. Tench Coxe, a Federalist tract writer, used the words "established church" when pointing out that only members of the Church of England could hold office in Great Britain.[25] Anti-ratificationists from the town of Carlisle proposed that "none should be compelled contrary to his principles or inclination to hear or support the clergy of any one established religion." [26] "Centinel," who also recommended a bill of rights, proposed more broadly in the language of the state constitution that "no man ought, or of right can be compelled to attend any religious worship, or erect or support any place of worship, or maintain any ministry, contrary to or against his own free will and consent. . . ." [27]

Massachusetts, which maintained an establishment of religion at the time of ratification, was the first state to ratify with amendments, but the only rights mentioned were those of the criminally accused.[28] No person in the state convention or in anti-ratificationist tracts alluded to an establishment of religion. This would be an astonishing fact, considering the opposition within the state to the establishment there existing, unless there was an undisputed understanding that Congress had no power over religion.

Maryland ratified without amendments,[29] although fifteen had been recommended, including a proposal "That there be no national religion established by law; but that all persons be equally entitled to protection in their religious liberty." [30] Maryland's constitution permitted an establishment of religion, though none existed. All fifteen defeated amendments were designed chiefly to protect state governments from infringement by the national.[31] They failed not because the Federalist-dominated convention of Maryland disagreed with them but because it wished to ratify unconditionally for the purpose of demonstrating confidence in the new system of government.[32] The same may be said of Pennsylvania and all other states which ratified without recommending amendments.

South Carolina's debates do not allude to the subject of an establishment, and the convention's recommendations of amendments to the Constitution did not relate to a Bill of Rights.[33] The state maintained an establishment at the time.

New Hampshire's debates are nonexistent. Though the state maintained an establishment, its instrument of ratification included among recommendations for amendments the following: "Congress shall make no laws touching Religion, or to infringe the rights of Conscience." [34]

In Virginia, where the most crucial struggle against establishments of religion had ended in victory just three years before the state ratifying convention met, only two speakers during the course of the lengthy debates alluded to an establishment. Edmund Randolph, defending the Constitution against Patrick Henry's allegation that it endangered religious liberty, pointed out that Congress had no power over religion and that the exclusion of religious tests for federal office-holders meant "they are not bound to support one mode of worship, or to adhere to one particular sect." He added that there were so many different sects in the United States "that they will prevent the establishment of any one sect, in prejudice to the rest, and forever oppose all attempts to infringe religious liberty." [35] Madison, also addressing himself to Henry's general and unsupported accusation, argued at this time that a "multiplicity of sects" would secure freedom of religion, but that a Bill of Rights would not. He pointed out that the Virginia Declaration of Rights (which guaranteed "the free exercise of religion, according to the dictates of conscience") would not have exempted the people "from paying for the support of one particular sect, if such sect were exclusively established by law." If a majority were of one sect, liberty would be poorly protected by a Bill of Rights. "Fortunately for this commonwealth," he added, "a majority of the people are decidedly against any exclusive establishment. I believe it to be so in the other states. There is not a shadow of right in the general government to intermeddle with religion. Its least interference with it would be a most flagrant usurpation. . . . A particular state might concur in one religious project. But the United States abound in such a variety of sects, that it is a strong security against religious persecution; and it is sufficient to authorize a conclusion that no one sect will ever be able to outnumber or depress the rest." [36]

Nonetheless, Madison and his party could not muster sufficient votes to secure Virginia's ratification of the Constitution without accepting a recommendation for amendments which were first submitted by Patrick Henry. Henry's amendments, including a Declaration of Rights, were read before the convention, but not reported in its record of proceedings; the reporter states that they "were nearly the same as those ultimately proposed by the Convention" [37] after perfunctory endorsement by a committee on amendments. Among the recommended amendments was a provision that "no particular religious sect or society ought to be favored or established, by law, in preference to others." [38]

In New York, Thomas Tredwell, an anti-ratificationist, made the only reported reference to an establishment, in his speech favoring a Bill of Rights: "I could have wished also that sufficient caution had been used to secure to us our religious liberties, and to have prevented the general government from tyrannizing over our consciences by a religious establishment—a tyranny of all others most dreadful, and which will assuredly be exercised whenever it shall be thought necessary for the promotion and support of their political measures." [39] The New York debates were fully reported until the closing days of the convention when John Lansing, an anti-ratificationist leader, introduced a Bill of Rights to be prefixed to the Constitution. Although debate began on this subject on July 19, 1788, and continued intermittently through July 25 when Lansing's Bill of Rights was adopted, not a single word of the debate is reported. [40] Thus there is no indication of the meaning attached by the convention to its recommendations, which included a provision "that no

Religious Sect or Society ought to be favored or established by Law in preference of others." [41] This language was similar to that used in the state constitution of 1777 which abolished establishments of religion in New York.

North Carolina, which had abolished its establishment in 1776, recommended an amendment like that of Virginia and New York.[42] The subject first arose in the convention when a delegate, Henry Abbot, expressing concern about the possibility of the general government's infringing religious liberty, asserted that "some people" feared that a treaty might be made with foreign powers to adopt the Roman Catholic religion in the United States. "Many wish to know what religion shall be established," he added. He was "against any exclusive establishment; but if there were any, I would prefer the Episcopal." In the next breath, he expressed a belief that the exclusion of religious tests was "dangerous," because Congressmen "might all be pagans." [43]

James Iredell answered Abbot's fears by pointing out that the exclusion of a religious test indicated an intent to establish religious liberty. Congress was powerless to enact "the establishment of any religion whatsoever; and I am astonished that any gentleman should conceive they have. Is there any power given to Congress in matters of religion? . . . If any future Congress should pass an act concerning the religion of the country, it would be an act which they are not authorized to pass, by the Constitution, and which the people would not obey." [44] Governor Samuel Johnston agreed with Iredell and concluded: "I hope, therefore, that gentlemen will see there is no cause of fear that any one religion shall be exclusively established." [45] The Reverend David Caldwell, a Presbyterian minister, then spoke in favor of a religious test which would eliminate "Jews and pagans of every kind." [46] Samuel Spencer, the leading anti-Federalist, took Caldwell's statement as endorsing the establishment of "one particular religion" which Spencer feared would lead to persecution. He believed that religion should stand on its own "without any connection with temporal authority." [47] William Lenoir agreed with Spencer but warned that federal ecclesiastical courts might be erected and they "may make any establishment they think proper." [48] Richard Dobbs Spaight, who had been a delegate to the Federal Convention, answered: "As to the subject of religion, I thought what had been said [by Iredell] would fully satisfy that gentleman and every other. No power is given to the general government to interfere with it at all. Any act of Congress on this subject would be a usurpation." [49]

When Rhode Island's convention tardily met to ratify the Constitution, eight states had already ratified the Bill of Rights. Accordingly Rhode Island's recommendation for an amendment against an

177

establishment,⁵⁰ modeled after those of New York, Virginia, and North Carolina, was a superfluous flourish which had no effect on the framing of the First Amendment.

Conclusions

Scanty as they are, the relevant data drawn from the period of the ratification controversy have been described in full. What conclusions do they yield?

1) No state or person favored an establishment of religion by Congress. On the few occasions when an establishment was mentioned by a convention delegate or a contemporary writer, the individual spoke either against its desirability and/or against the likelihood that there would be one.

2) The evidence does not permit a generalization as to what was meant by an establishment of religion. To be sure, most of the few references to an establishment expressly or in context referred to the preference of one church or sect or religion above others. Clearly, however, this fact taken by itself proves little. For example, Coxe of Pennsylvania had merely said that in England, where there was an "established church," only its members could hold office. From this statement we can conclude only that Coxe thought that the exclusive support of one church or denomination by the government, such as the Episcopal Church enjoyed in England, constituted an established church. There is no argument about that, but did he distinguish between an established *church* and an establishment of *religion?* Did he understand an establishment of religion to be government support of all church denominations or of one only? Coxe's brief statement provides no answers to these questions, and the same may be said of the statements by the other speakers on the subject. Madison, for example, was simply saying to those who believed that religious liberty was endangered by the proposed national government, "Not even your worst fears shall come to pass." As for the recommendations for amendments by Virginia, New York, North Carolina, and Rhode Island, they are not clarifying. They do not even necessarily indicate that preference of one sect over others was all that was comprehended by an establishment of religion. They do indicate that preference of one sect over others was something so feared that there was a political necessity to assuage that fear by specifically making it groundless.

3) As at the Constitutional Convention, there was during the ratification controversy a widespread understanding in the states that the new central government would have no power whatever to legislate on the subject of religion. This by itself does not mean that any person or state understood an establishment of religion to mean any

government aid to any or all religions or churches. It means rather that religion as a subject of legislation was reserved exclusively to the states.

Drafting and Ratification

Drafting the No-Establishment Clause

At the first session of the First Congress, Representative Madison on June 8, 1789, proposed for House approval a series of amendments to the Constitution.[51] He accompanied his presentation with a lengthy speech explaining his action and defending the value of a Bill of Rights, but he did not discuss the proposal relating to an establishment of religion. It read: "The civil rights of none shall be abridged on account of religious belief or worship, nor shall any national religion be established, nor shall the full and equal rights of conscience be in any manner, or on any pretext, infringed." [52]

"National religion" has ambiguous connotations. It might have meant quite narrowly a nationwide preference for one sect over others or, more broadly, preference for Christianity, that is, for all Christian denominations over non-Christian religions. Proponents of the narrow interpretation of the no-establishment clause see in the word "national" proof of their contention that nothing more was intended than a prohibition against the preference for one church or religion over others. Madison did not at this time or later, when the proposal was debated, clearly explain what he meant by the clause, "nor shall any national religion be established."

Taken in the context of Madison's recommended amendments it seems likely that "national" in this case signified action by the national government, for his next recommendation proposed a restriction upon the powers of the states: "No State shall violate the equal rights of conscience, or the freedom of the press, or the trial by jury in criminal cases." [53]

In other words, the term "national" was probably intended to imply that the prohibition against an establishment of religion—whatever that meant—applied to Congress only and not to the states. Perhaps the word "national" was really superfluous, but Madison probably felt that it would allay apprehensions on the part of those states which maintained their own establishments of religion. In any case, if there is any validity to the argument that "national" signified the intention to prohibit only the establishment of a single religion or sect, the fact remains that the word was deleted and does not appear in the final version of the amendment, thereby indicating that Congress rejected that intention and meant something broader by its ban on an establishment of religion.

Without debate, Madison's recommendations for amendments were referred for consideration to a select committee of the House, composed of one member from each state, including Madison.[54] Although we know nothing of the committee's deliberations, which took one week, its report to the House shows that Madison was the dominating figure, because his amendments were kept intact with but slight changes in phraseology in the interests of brevity. From the proposal on religion the commitee deleted the clause on "civil rights" and the word "national." The proposed amendment then read: "No religion shall be established by law, nor shall the equal rights of conscience be infringed." [55] The report of the select committee to the House was merely a redrafting of the original proposals; no explanation of changes was included.

The House, sitting as a Committee of the Whole, began and ended its debate on the amendment on August 15. Our only account of the debate, in the *Annals of Congress,* is probably more in the nature of a condensed and paraphrased version than it is a verbatim report.[56] The account is brief enough to be given here in full:

Saturday, August 15

AMENDMENT TO THE CONSTITUTION

The House again went into a Committee of the Whole on the proposed amendments to the constitution, Mr. Boudinot in the chair.

The fourth proposition being under consideration, as follows:

Article 1. Section 9. Between paragraphs two and three insert "no religion shall be established by law, nor shall the equal rights of conscience be infringed."

Mr. Sylvester had some doubts of the propriety of the mode of expression used in this paragraph. He apprehended that it was liable to a construction different from what had been made by the committee. He feared it might be thought to have a tendency to abolish religion altogether.

Mr. Vining suggested the propriety of transposing the two members of the sentence.

Mr. Gerry said it would read better if it was, that no religious doctrine shall be established by law.

Mr. Sherman thought the amendment altogether unnecessary, inasmuch as Congress had no authority whatever delegated to them by the constitution to make religious establishments; he would, therefore, move to have it struck out.

Mr. Carroll.—As the rights of conscience are, in their nature, of peculiar delicacy, and will little bear the gentlest touch of governmental hand; and as many sects have concurred in opinion that they are not well secured under the present constitution, he said he was much in favor of adopting the words. He thought it would tend more towards conciliating the minds of the people to the Government than almost any other amendment he had heard proposed. He would not contend with gentlemen about the phraseology, his object was to secure the substance in such a manner as to satisfy the wishes of the honest part of the community.

Mr. Madison said, he apprehended the meaning of the words to be, that Congress should not establish a religion, and enforce the legal observation of it by law, nor compel men to worship God in any manner contrary to their conscience. Whether the words are necessary or not, he did not mean to say, but they had been required by some of the State Conventions, who seemed to entertain an opinion that under the clause of the constitution, which gave power to Congress to make all laws necessary and proper to carry into execution the constitution, and the laws made under it, enabled them to make laws of such a nature as might infringe the rights of conscience, and establish a national religion; to prevent these effects he presumed the amendment was intended, and he thought it as well expressed as the nature of the language would admit.

Mr. Huntington said that he feared, with the gentleman first up on this subject, that the words might be taken in such latitude as to be extremely hurtful to the cause of religion. He understood the amendment to mean what had been expressed by the gentleman from Virginia; but others might find it convenient to put another construction upon it. The ministers of their congregations to the Eastward were maintained by the contributions of those who belonged to their society; the expense of building meeting-houses was contributed in the same manner. These things were regulated by by-laws. If an action was brought before a Federal Court on any of these cases, the person who had neglected to perform his engagements could not be compelled to do it; for a support of ministers, or building of places of worship might be construed into a religious establishment.

By the charter of Rhode Island, no religion could be established by law; he could give a history of the effects of such a regulation; indeed the people were now enjoying the blessed fruits of it. [Intended as irony.] He hoped, therefore, the amendment would be made in such a way as to secure the rights of conscience, and a free exercise of the rights of religion, but not to patronize those who professed no religion at all.

Mr. Madison thought, if the word national was inserted before religion, it would satisfy the minds of honorable gentlemen. He believed that the people feared one sect might obtain a pre-eminence, or two combine together, and establish a religion to which they would compel others to conform. He thought if the word national was introduced, it would point the amendment directly to the object it was intended to prevent.

Mr. Livermore was not satisfied with that amendment; but he did not

181

wish them to dwell long on the subject. He thought it would be better if it was altered, and made to read in this manner, that Congress shall make no laws touching religion, or infringing the rights of conscience.

Mr. Gerry did not like the term national, proposed by the gentleman from Virginia, and he hoped it would not be adopted by the House. It brought to his mind some observations that had taken place in the conventions at the time they were considering the present constitution. It had been insisted upon by those who were called antifederalists, that this form of Government consolidated the Union; the honorable gentleman's motion shows that he considers it in the same light. Those who were called antifederalists at that time complained that they had injustice done them by the title, because they were in favor of a Federal Government, and the others were in favor of a national one; the federalists were for ratifying the constitution as it stood, and the others not until amendments were made. Their names then ought not to have been distinguished by federalists and antifederalists, but rats and antirats.

Mr. Madison withdrew his motion, but observed that the words "no national religion shall be established by law," did not imply that the Government was a national one; the question was then taken on Mr. Livermore's motion, and passed in the affirmative, thirty-one for, and twenty against it.[57]

Present-day proponents of both the narrow and the broad interpretations of the no-establishment clause are quick to see in this House debate conclusive proof for their respective points of view. But in fact it proves nothing conclusively. It was apathetic and unclear: ambiguity, brevity, and imprecision in thought and expression characterize the comments of the few members who spoke. That the House understood the debate, cared deeply about its outcome, or shared a common understanding of the finished amendment is doubtful.

Not even Madison himself, dutifully carrying out his pledge to secure amendments, seems to have troubled to do more than was necessary to get something adopted in order to satisfy popular clamor and deflate anti-Federalist charges. Indeed, Madison agreed with Sherman's statement that the amendment was "altogether unnecessary, inasmuch as Congress had no authority whatever delegated to them by the constitution to make religious establishments. . . ." The difficulty, however, lies in the fact that neither Sherman, Madison, nor anyone else took the trouble to define what they were talking about. What were "religious establishments"? And what did the select committee on amendments intend by recommending that "no religion shall be established by law"? Madison's statement that the words meant "that Congress should not establish a religion" hardly showed the clarity for which we might have hoped.

It should be observed, however, that on two occasions he commented in such a way as to give considerable force to the arguments of those who defend the narrow interpretation of the no-establishment clause. In his answer to Sherman, made after Carroll's comment, Madison declared that the amendment was intended to satisfy "some of the State Conventions" which feared that Congress "might infringe the rights of conscience, and establish a national religion. . . ." At the time he spoke he had the recommendations from four states. That of New Hampshire, drafted by the same Livermore who was present in Congress and took an essential part in the debate, was very much in line with his own thinking. But the recommendations from Virginia, New York, and North Carolina used the language of no-preference-to-one-sect. If Madison's intent was merely to yield to their requests, whatever may have been his own ideas on the subject, he was by necessary implication construing the proposal in such a way as to lend validity to the narrow interpretation of the First Amendment.

That such was his intent seems possible in view of his response to Huntington of Connecticut. The reporter present tells us of Madison: "He believed that the people feared one sect might obtain a pre-eminence, or two combine together, and establish a religion to which they would compel others to conform. He thought that if the word national was introduced, it would point the amendment directly to the object it was intended to prevent." Here, Madison himself used the language of no-preference or preeminence.

Justice Rutledge, however, read the exchange between Huntington and Madison as proving "unmistakably that 'establishment' meant public 'support' of religion in the financial sense." [58] If Huntington was in fact referring to private, voluntary support of religion—which is not at all certain—Rutledge's conclusion was correct, but even so it proved only what no one would deny: an established religion is a governmentally supported one. That does not prove that government aid to all sects and religions is an establishment of religion, for on the basis of the evidence thus far there is reason to believe that "establishment" was restricted in its meaning to support of just one sect or "two combined together" as Madison put it. Yet we know from other evidence (reviewed later) that Madison himself did not regard the element of preference as indispensable to the idea of an establishment of religion. If *all* sects combined together with preference to none and the government supported all, the result would in his mind be an establishment.

In addition, there is no certainty that Huntington was referring to private, voluntary contributions for the support of religion. He was speaking of the situation of those whose congregations were "to the Eastward." If he meant Rhode Island, which had no semblance of an establishment and which is east of Huntington's Connecticut, then Justice Rutledge was correct in concluding that he was concerned about the possibility of private, voluntary support of religion being construed as an establishment. That Huntington meant this, however, seems impossible: 1) the amendment as then worded could not possibly be twisted to cover any case but an establishment "by law"; 2) there is probably no recorded instance in history when anyone alleged that private, voluntary support of religion was an establishment by law; and 3) if this interpretation is accepted, Madison's answer to Huntington would make no sense whatever, for Madison replied that misconstruction would be avoided by placing the word "national" before the word "religion," whereas if he meant to assure Huntington that privately supported religion would not be construed as an establishment, the word "public" instead of "national" would have been more to the point.

Huntington's ambiguous statement probably referred not to Rhode Island but to the Eastern States (contrasted with Southern and Middle) such as his own, where taxes for religion were euphemistically called "contributions" [59] and were regulated by parish bylaws. He was therefore probably expressing a fear that state establishments might be interfered with by Congress. If so, Madison's reply makes sense, for he was saying that the proposed amendment restricts Congress but not the states. Even his use of the language of no-preference makes sense if construed as a reply in kind to Huntington's *ironic* reference to the effects in Rhode Island of the lack of an establishment. That is, Madison may have been saying, in effect, "what the people fear, Mr. Huntington, is not the situation in Rhode Island but that in Connecticut where one sect has obtained a pre-eminence, or two, the Congregationalists and Episcopalians, have combined together and compel others to conform." If this was what Madison meant, then his use of the language of no-preference was calculated to reveal one intent of the proposed amendment but not its only intent.

Livermore's motion for a change of wording apparently expressed what Madison meant by his use of the word "national" and satisfied the Committee of the Whole. The proposed amendment, adopted by a vote of 31 to 20, then read: "Congress shall make no laws touching religion, or infringing the rights of conscience." But a few days later, on August 20, when the House took up the report of the Committee of the Whole and voted clause by clause on the proposed amendments, an additional change was made. Fisher Ames of Massachusetts moved that the amendment read: "Congress shall make no law establishing religion, or to prevent the free exercise thereof, or to infringe the rights of conscience." [60] Without debate this was adopted by the necessary two-thirds of the House. Apparently there was a feeling that the draft of the clause based on Livermore's motion might not satisfy the demand of those who wanted something said specifically against establishments of religion. The amendment as submitted to the Senate reflected a stylistic change which gave it the following reading: "Congress shall make no law establishing religion, or prohibiting the free exercise thereof, nor shall the rights of conscience be infringed."

The Senate began debate on the House amendments on September 3 and continued through September 9. The debate was conducted in secrecy and no record exists but for the bare account of motions and votes in the *Senate Journal*. According to the record of September 3, three motions of special interest here were defeated on that day.[61] These motions were clearly intended to restrict the ban in the proposed amendment to establishments preferring one sect above others. The first motion would have made the clause in the amendment read: "Congress shall make no law establishing one religious sect or society in preference to others. . . ." After the failure of a motion to kill the amendment, a motion was made to change it to read: "Congress shall not make any law infringing the rights of conscience, or establishing any religious sect or society." The last defeated motion restated the same thought differently: "Congress shall make no law establishing any particular denomination of religion in preference to another. . . ."

The failure of these three motions, each of which clearly expressed a narrow intent, would seem to show that the Senate intended something broader than merely a ban on preference to one sect. Yet, if anything is really clear about this problem of "meaning" and "intent" it is that nothing is clear; when the Senate returned to the clause six days later, the House amendment was changed to read: "Congress shall make no law establishing articles of faith or a mode of worship, or prohibiting the free exercise of religion. . . ." Like the three previously defeated motions, this has the unmistakable meaning of limiting the ban to acts which prefer one sect over others or which, to put it simply, establish a single state church.[62]

We are indebted to the Senate's wording for provoking the House to action which would make *its* intent clear, as the next step in the drafting of the amendment reveals. In voting on the Senate's proposed amendments, the House accepted some and rejected others. Among those rejected was the Senate's article on religion. To resolve the disagreement between the two branches the House proposed a joint conference committee. The Senate refused to recede from its position but agreed to the proposal for a conference committee. The committee, a strong and distinguished one, consisted of Madison as chairman of the House conferees, joined by Sherman and Vining, and Ellsworth as chairman of the Senate conferees, joined by Paterson and Carroll. Four of the six men had been influential members of the Constitutional Convention. The House members of the conference committee flatly refused to accept the Senate's version of the amendment on religion, indicating that the House would not be satisfied with merely a ban on preference of one sect or religion over others. The Senate conferees abandoned the Senate version, and the amendment was redrafted to give it its present phraseology. On September 24, Ellsworth reported to the Senate that the House would accept the Senate's version of the other amendments provided that the amendment on religion "shall read as follows: 'Congress shall make no laws respecting an establishment of religion, or prohibiting the free exercise thereof. . . .' " [63] On the same day, the House sent a message to the Senate verifying Ellsworth's report.[64] On the next day, September 25, the Senate by a two-thirds vote accepted the condition laid down by the House.[65] Congress had passed the no-establishment clause.

Conclusions

The one fact which stands out from this review of the drafting of the amendment is that Congress very carefully considered and rejected the phraseology which spells out the narrow interpretation. The House's rejection of the Senate's version of the amendment shows that the House's intention, though by no means revealed in its own ambiguous and imprecise debates, was *not* to frame an amendment which banned only Congressional support to one sect, church, denomination, or religion. The Senate three times defeated versions of the amendment embodying the narrow interpretation, on a fourth vote adopted such a version, and finally abandoned it in the face of uncompromising hostility by the House. The amendment was definitely intended to mean something broader than the narrow interpretation which some scholars have given it. At bottom the amendment was an expression of the fact that the framers of the Constitution had not intended to empower Congress to act in the field of religion. The "great object" of the Bill of Rights, as Madison explicitly said when introducing his draft of amendments to the House, was to "limit and qualify the powers of Government" [66] for the purpose of making certain that the powers granted could not be exercised in forbidden fields, such as religion.

The history of the drafting of the no-establishment clause does not provide us with an understanding of what was meant by "an establishment of religion." To argue, however, as proponents of the narrow interpretation do, that the amendment permits Congressional aid and support to religion in general or to all churches without discrimination, leads to the impossible conclusion that the First Amendment added to Congress' power. There is nothing to support such a conclusion. Every bit of evidence goes to prove that the First Amendment, like the others, was intended to restrict Congress to its enumerated powers. Since Congress was given no power by the Constitutional Convention to legislate on matters concerning religion, Congress has no such power even in the absence of the First Amendment. It is therefore unreasonable to believe that an express prohibition of power—"Congress shall make no law respecting an establishment of religion"—vests or creates the power, previously nonexistent, of supporting religion by aid to one or all religious groups. The Bill of Rights, as Madison said, was not framed "to imply powers not meant to be included in the enumeration." [67]

Ratification of the First Amendment

Little or no new light on the meaning of the no-establishment clause is available as a result of the deliberations of the state legislatures to which the amendments to the Constitution were submitted for ratification. Records of state debates are nonexistent; private correspondence, newspapers, and tracts are no help.

Nine states summarily approved the Bill of Rights by mid-June of 1790.[68] Virginia, Massachusetts, Connecticut, and Georgia had not yet taken action; indeed, the last three states took no action until 1939 when, on the sesquicentennial anniversary of the Constitution, they belatedly ratified the Bill of Rights.

Of the three states which failed to ratify the Bill of Rights until 1939, Georgia took the position that amendments were unnecessary until experience under the Constitution showed the need for them.[69] Connecticut's lower house voted to ratify in 1789 and again the following year, but the state senate, apparently in the belief that a Bill of Rights was superfluous, adamantly refused. Yankee Federalists in the state seem to have thought that any suggestion that the Constitution was not perfect would add to the strength of the anti-Federalists. The same sentiment was prevalent in Massachusetts. There Federalist apathy to the Bill was grounded on satisfaction with the Constitution as it was, unamended, while the anti-Federalists were more interested in amendments which would weaken the national government and strengthen the states than in protecting personal liberties. The Bill of Rights was caught between conflicting party interests, and as a result Massachusetts failed to act on the proposed amendments.

The circumstances surrounding ratification in Virginia are of particular interest for this discussion. In that state, ratification was held up for nearly two years while the amendment was attacked as inadequate, and the eight state senators who opposed it explained their vote publicly in these words: "The 3d amendment [our First Amendment] recommended by Congress does not prohibit the rights of conscience from being violated or infringed: and although it goes to restrain Congress from passing laws establishing any national religion, they might, notwithstanding, levy taxes to any amount, for the support of religion or its preachers; and any particular denomination of christians might be so favored and supported by the General Government, as to give it a decided advantage over others, and in process of time render it as powerful and dangerous as if it was established as the national religion of the country. . . . This amendment then, when considered as it relates to any of the rights it is pretended to secure, will be found totally inadequate. . . ."[70]

Taken out of context and used uncritically, this statement by the eight Virginia state senators has been offered as proof that the no-establishment clause had only the narrowest intent, was so understood by the Virginia legislators, and was ultimately approved by the state with only that narrow intent attached. Because the eight senators who favored a broader ban were ultimately defeated, the conclusion is drawn that the amendment did not purport to ban government aid to religion generally or to all sects without discrimination. However, examination of the intricate party maneuverings and complex motives in the Virginia ratification dispute sheds a different light on the senators' statement.

Virginia's anti-Federalists, led by Patrick Henry and United States Senators Richard Henry Lee and William Grayson, had opposed the ratification of the Constitution for a variety of reasons. Chief among these was the belief that the Constitution established too strong a central government at the expense of the states. For example, the anti-Federalists wanted amendments to the Constitution which would restrict Congress' commerce and tax powers. It is true enough that they were also in the forefront of the movement for amendments which would protect personal liberties, but there is considerable reason to suspect that many cried out against the absence of a Bill of Rights more for the purpose of defeating the Constitution than of actually getting such a Bill of Rights.

When Congress had considered amending the Constitution, the anti-Federalists sought to secure amendments which would aggrandize state powers, but in this effort they failed. In the ratification controversy, therefore, the strategy of Virginia's anti-Federalists was to defeat the proposed Bill of Rights in order to force Congress to reconsider the whole subject of amendments. The Federalists, on the other hand, eagerly supported the Bill of Rights in order to prevent additional amendments which might hamstring the national government.

On November 30, 1789, Virginia's lower house, dominated by the Federalists, "and without debate of any consequence," [71] quickly passed all the amendments proposed by Congress. But the opposition party controlled the state senate. "That body," reported Randolph to Washington, "will attempt to postpone them [the amendments]; for a majority is unfriendly to the government." [72] As a member of the Virginia lower house reported to Madison, the senate was inclined to reject the amendments not from dissatisfaction with them, but from apprehension "that the adoption of them at this time will be an obstacle to the chief object of their pursuit, the amendment on the subject of direct taxation." [73] As Randolph had predicted, the senate, by a vote of eight to seven, did decide to postpone final action on what are now the First, Sixth, Ninth, and Tenth Amendments until the next session of the legislature, thereby allowing time for the electorate to express itself. It was on this occasion that the eight senators in question made their statement on the alleged inadequacy of the amendment, bidding for electoral support against an allegedly weak Bill of Rights by presenting themselves as champions of religious liberty and advocates of separation between government and religion.

Madison remained unworried by this tactic, confidently predicting that the action of the senators would boomerang against them. "The miscarriage of the third article [the First Amendment], particularly, will have this effect," he wrote to Washington.[74] His confidence is explainable on several counts.

First, he knew that the First Amendment had the support of the Baptists, the one group most insistent upon demanding a rigid and absolute separation between government and religion.[75] Second, he knew that the eight senators did not come before the electorate with clean hands. Like Henry and Lee, who laid down their strategy for them, they had consistently voted against religious liberty and in favor of taxes for religion. Their legislative record on this score was well known. By contrast, the seven senators who favored ratification of the First Amendment had stood with Jefferson and Madison in the fight between 1784 and 1786 against a state establishment of religion and for religious liberty.[76] Finally, Madison reasoned that the statement by the eight senators was an inept piece of propaganda with little chance of convincing anyone, because it was obviously misleading and inaccurate. The eight senators alleged that "any particular denomination of Christians might be so favored

189

and supported by the general government, as to give it a decided advantage over others . . ."—a construction of the First Amendment which not even proponents of the narrow interpretation would accept—and they also asserted that the amendment "does not prohibit the rights of conscience from being violated or infringed . . ."—whereas anyone might read for himself the positive statement in the amendment that Congress shall not abridge the free exercise of religion.

In the end, Madison's confidence proved justified. On December 15, 1791, after a session of inaction on the Bill of Rights, the state senate finally ratified without a record vote. In the context of anti-Federalist maneuverings, there is every reason to believe that Virginia supported the First Amendment with the understanding that it had been misrepresented by the eight senators. There is no reason to believe that Virginia ratified with the understanding that the amendment permitted any government aid to religion.

What conclusions can one come to, then, in connection with ratification of the First Amendment by the states? In Virginia, the one state for which there is some evidence, we can arrive only at a negative conclusion: the evidence does not support the narrow interpretation of the no-establishment clause. In nine other states there was perfunctory ratification, with no record of the debates, and in the remaining three states there was inaction. In the absence of other evidence, therefore, it is impossible to say on the basis of ratification alone just what actually was the general understanding of the no-establishment clause.

Meaning of the Clause

By now the difficulty of trying to explain exactly what was intended by the no-establishment clause should be obvious. What was meant by an establishment of religion? Was the prohibition in the First Amendment intended only to ban preference for one church? Or was it designed to ban nondiscriminatory government support to all religious bodies and to religion generally? Here an examination of the American experience with establishments of religion is essential.

This experience was in many respects unique, for it did not always follow the pattern of European precedent. Yet many scholars, perhaps unaware of this fact, have arbitrarily assigned to the phrase "an establishment of religion" its European meaning only. As a consequence, there has been a good deal of misunderstanding.

A prime example may be found in what is probably the fullest and best documented study in support of the narrow interpretation of the no-establishment clause.* The book by James O'Neill advocates the idea that the clause in question does not ban aid to religion generally or to all churches without discrimination. Yet there is nothing in it on the subject of establishments of religion in colonial America, nor on the nature of the establishments which existed after the Revolution and at the time of the framing of the First Amendment. Indeed, except for a brief glance at the abortive plan in Virginia to reintroduce an establishment in 1784, the author did not discuss this aspect of colonial or state history in the seventeenth and eighteenth centuries at all. He was, therefore, able to conclude in capital letters that an establishment of religion has always and everywhere meant what he finds it means in Europe and in an encyclopedia: "A SINGLE CHURCH OR RELIGION ENJOYING FORMAL, LEGAL, OFFICIAL, MONOPOLISTIC PRIVILEGE THROUGH A UNION WITH THE GOVERNMENT OF THE STATE. That is the meaning given in the *Encyclopaedia Britannica*. The phrase has been used this way for centuries in speaking of the established Protestant churches of England, Scotland, Germany, and other countries, and of the established Catholic Church in Italy, Spain, and elsewhere. There is not an item of dependable evidence . . . which shows that the term means, or ever has meant, anything else." [77]

The *Encyclopaedia Britannica* and the European precedents notwithstanding, there is abundant evidence that the European form of an establishment was not the only form in America and that the European meaning of establishment of religion was not the only meaning in America. Indeed, at the time of the framing of the Bill of Rights all state establishments which still existed in America were *multiple* establishments of *all* churches, something unknown in European experience.

The Colonial Experience

On the eve of the Revolution, establishments of religion in the European sense existed only in the Southern colonies of Virginia, Maryland, North Carolina, South Carolina, and Georgia, where the Church of England or Episcopalian Church was the state church. Attendance upon its services was legally required, and all persons, regardless of belief or affiliation, were taxed for the support of the established church. Taxes so collected were spent to build and main-

---

* This memorandum was prepared in 1958. In 1964 a book was published that superseded O'Neill's as the fullest and best documented study in support of the narrow interpretation. See Chester James Antieau *et al.*, *Freedom from Federal Establishment: Formation and Early History of the First Amendment Religion Clauses* (Milwaukee, 1964). Nothing in this book persuades me to alter my view of the evidence.

tain church buildings and pay salaries of Episcopalian clergy. These Southern establishments were therefore comparable to European counterparts.

The record in Rhode Island, Pennsylvania, Delaware, and New Jersey is equally clear: [78] these four colonies never experienced any establishment of religion. In the colonies of New York, Massachusetts, Connecticut, and New Hampshire, however, the pattern of establishment was diversified and uniquely American.

New York. New York's colonial history of church-state relationships provides the world's first example of an establishment of religion radically different from the European type, an establishment of religion in general—or at least of Protestantism in general—and without preference to one church over others. When the English conquered New Netherlands in 1664, renaming it New York in honor of its new proprietor, the Duke of York (James II), they found that the Dutch Reformed Church (Calvinist) was exclusively established as the state church. The "Duke's Laws" of 1664, in the form of instructions to his governor, disestablished the Dutch Reformed Church and established in its place a multiplicity of churches. Any church of the Protestant religion could become an established church. In a sense, of course, this was an exclusive establishment of one religion, Protestantism, but the system involved a multiple establishment of several different Protestant churches, in sharp contrast to all European precedents which provided for the establishment of one church only.

Under the "Duke's Laws" every township was obliged publicly to support some Protestant church and a minister. The denomination of the church did not matter. Costs were to be met by a public tax: "Every inhabitant shall contribute to all charges both in Church and State." [79] A local option system prevailed. Each town, by a majority vote of its householders, was to select the denomination to be established locally by electing a minister of that denomination. The head of the state was the head of all the churches. Upon proof that a minister was Protestant, he was inducted into his pastorate by the governor representing the state. In other words, this was an establishment of religion in which there was a formal, legal, official union between government and religion on a nonpreferential basis and without the establishment of any individual church. "Here is an establishment without a name." [80]

In effect, the "Duke's Laws" allowed the Dutch Reformed Church to remain the established church in most localities, since the Dutch for a while were the most numerous among the settlers. Yet others dominated in a few towns, and as the religious composition of the population changed through constant immigration, the established church of different localities changed. In addition, the system was the only establishment of religion at the time which permitted a very considerable religious liberty to all, including non-Protestants, and on this score too it was unique.

In 1683 the system of multiple establishment was explicitly confirmed by a "Charter of Liberties" enacted by the New York Assembly. This "Charter" stated that "the Churches already in New York do appear to be privileged Churches. . . . Provided also that all other Christian Churches, that shall hereafter come and settle in the province, shall have the same privileges." [81]

However, in 1686 the Catholic James II instructed Dongan, royal governor of New York and also a Catholic, to establish the Episcopalian Church of England as the state church of the colony, thereby singling out that church for preferential treatment. Services of the state church were to be based on the Anglican Book of Common Prayer; sacraments were to be administered according to Anglican rites. The ecclesiastical jurisdiction of the entire province was vested in the Archbishop of Canterbury; the governor was empowered to remove ministers. Despite these instructions, however, Governor Dongan took no steps to establish the Church of England. A successor, Governor Fletcher, did try to implement the royal instructions, but the colonial assembly at that time refused to enact the needed statute. In 1693, however, the assembly grudgingly enacted what one historian has called "a bill for a religious establishment of an entirely nondescript character, the like of which is not to be found elsewhere." [82] The act stated that in the places thereinafter named, "there shall be called, inducted, and established a good, sufficient, Protestant Minister." One such minister was for New York City, one for Richmond County, and two for Westchester and Queens Counties. The ministers were to be supported by public taxes.

In effect, the act of 1693 seemed to have established the Episcopalian Church in the four localities named, but not a word in the act referred to that church. The legislature which passed the measure, to the governor's wrath, resolved in 1695 that the act permitted a "dissenting protestant minister" to be called to a church within the geographic limits of the act, and "he is to be paid and maintained as the act directs." [83] In other words, non-Anglican Protestants in the four localities could pay their taxes for the support of their own local church, and churches not of the Church of England were in fact built; they and their ministers were maintained by local taxation within the four localities after the act of 1693. Lewis Morris, himself a strong Church of England man, shortly before becoming Chief Justice of the province, admitted in 1711 that the act of 1693 was "very loosely worded. The Dissenters claim the benefit of it as well as we." [84] As a result there was constant argument—the royal governors and the Church of England on one side, the assembly and non-Anglican Protestants on the other—concerning the disposition of tax funds for the support of religion.

Finally, in 1731, the provincial court of New York decided the controversy in a case involving the Jamaica Church of Queens. The church had been built by a town tax as a Presbyterian edifice in 1699. Episcopalians, backed by the governor, seized and took possession of the church on the ground that any property for religious purposes built by public funds must belong to the Church of England as the only established church under the act of 1693. After several years of Episcopalian control, the Presbyterians again took the church. The Episcopalians then sued for possession, again arguing that a publicly supported church could belong to none but the Church of England. The court ruled in favor of the Presbyterians, allowing them to hold the church and collect taxes for its maintenance and for the salary of the minister.[85] Thus a formal judicial decision by the highest court of the province shows that 1) a multiple establishment of religion existed in New York, and 2) an establishment of religion in New York did not simply mean state preference to one religion or sect over others; it meant public support of religion on an impartial or nonpreferential basis.

Worthy of note also is the way in which the system of multiple establishment in New York had changed since its initiation by the "Duke's Laws" of 1664. In the beginning, townspeople by majority vote selected a church as the established church of the town, to be supported by the taxes of everyone regardless of church affiliation. By 1731, however, the multiple establishment had come to mean not only that the several Protestant churches were established, but that in each town with a heterogeneous religious population there were likely to be several different established churches, each supported by the taxes of its own communicants. This system remained in operation down to the Revolution, and in 1775 Alexander Hamilton, New York's leading citizen, was able to define "an established religion" as "a religion which the civil authority engaged, not only to protect, but to support." [86]

New England. There is a widespread belief that the New England colonies, excepting Rhode Island, maintained exclusive establishments of the Congregational church. To those who hold this view it will come as a surprise to learn that multiple establishments were legally permissible and that dual establishments existed in fact.

In Massachusetts, the major and archetypal New England colony, the Congregational church was not established by name after 1692. The General Court's act of that year provided for an establishment of religion on a town basis by simply requiring every town to maintain an "able, learned and orthodox" minister, to be chosen by the voters of the town and supported by a tax levied on all taxpayers.[87] As a matter of law it was theoretically possible for several different denominations to benefit from the establishment. Since the Congregationalists were the overwhelming majority in nearly every town, however, they reaped the benefits of the establishment of religion. Except in Boston, the law operated to make theirs the privileged church, which unquestionably was the purpose of the statute, and non-Congregationalists, chiefly Episcopalians, Baptists, and Quakers, were for a long time taxed for the support of Congregationalism.

The growing number of dissenters forced concessions, however, so that the Congregational church from 1724 to 1833 was obliged to retreat "until the other denominations in the Commonwealth were on an equal footing with it." [88] The retreat began in 1727 when the Episcopalians won the statutory right of having their religious taxes turned over for the support of their own churches.[89] Town treasurers after that date were legally obligated to give to Episcopalian churches the monies paid into the town treasuries for the support of public worship. By coincidence, the Connecticut legislature passed a similar act on behalf of the Episcopalian churches in the same year, 1727.[90] During 1728 and for a short time after that in Massachusetts, and possibly for several years after 1729 in Connecticut, it even seems that "the constable collected rates from all, applying those from dissenters to the support of their own ministers, thus making all the churches a concern of the state" [91]—creating, in other words, a clear, multiple establishment in practice.

Massachusetts in 1729 exempted Quakers and Baptists from all taxes for the payment of ministerial salaries; then in 1731 and 1735 each denomination was respectively exempted from sharing the taxes for building new churches.[92] Until then, presumably, Quakers and Baptists in Massachusetts were subject to public assessments for the cost of erecting their own meetinghouses. After those dates, tax exemption statutes on their behalf were periodically renewed, so that members of these denominations were not supposed to pay religious taxes for the benefit of Congregational churches or of their own. There were many abuses to this system of tax exemption, which also prevailed in Connecticut; many Quakers and Baptists in both colonies were unconscionably forced to pay for the support of Congregationalist churches as a result of a variety of complicated legal technicalities as well as outright illegal action. Even Episcopalians who lived too far from a church of their own denomination to attend its services were taxed for the support of the Congregational churches in both colonies. But these abuses of both the letter and spirit of the law do not alter the basic fact that after 1727 the establishments of religion in both colonies meant government support of two churches, Congregationalist and Episcopalian, without specified preference to either.

The situation did not substantially differ in New Hampshire, which had no official church. The town system of establishment operated to benefit the Congregational church exclusively down to the middle of the eighteenth century. New Hampshire, however, did not systematically require the payment of rates by dissenters nor concern itself with the support of their ministers. Quakers, Episcopalians, Presbyterians, and Baptists were exempt from supporting the local established church, which, because of Congregationalist dominance, was usually Congregationalist. In some towns, however, Episcopalians and Presbyterians were authorized to establish their own parishes and to use town authority to collect taxes for their churches. The pattern of establishment was bewilderingly diverse by the eve of the Revolution. Some towns maintained dual establishments, others multiple establishments, with free exercise for dissenters.[93] Thus in New England there was no single provincial establishment supported by all, or even by the taxes of its own members alone.

Early State Constitutions

The Revolution triggered a long pent-up movement for disestablishment of religion in several of the states, and expressions against an establishment in three states which had never experienced an establishment of any kind during the colonial period. A fourth state which had never had establishment, Rhode Island, did not adopt a state constitution and therefore had no provision on the subject.

New Jersey provided by its constitution of 1776 that no person should "ever be obliged to pay tithes, taxes, or any other rates, for the purpose of building or repairing any other church or churches, place or places of worship, or for the maintenance of any minister or ministry, contrary to what he believes to be right, or has deliberately or voluntarily engaged himself to perform." [94] Pennsylvania's provision in its constitution of 1776 was equally broad: ". . . no man ought or of right can be compelled to attend any religious worship, or erect or support any place of worship, or maintain any ministry, contrary to, or against, his own free will and consent." [95] But Delaware, the last of the states which in their colonial experience had never had even the semblance of an establishment, used narrow language in its constitution of 1776, providing: "There shall be no establishment of any one religious sect in this State in preference to another." [96] In 1792, however, Delaware adopted a new constitution and substituted the much broader language used by Pennsylvania.[97]

In New York, where a multiple establishment had been maintained in New York City and three adjoining counties, the long history of an insistence by the Church of England that it was rightfully the only established church influenced the writing of the clause against establishments in the constitution of 1777. The system of multiple establishments of religion was ended by the following words, reflecting the stubborn determination of non-Episcopalians never to admit, even by implication, that there had ever been an exclusive or preferential establishment of the Church of England: "That all such parts of the said common law, and all such of the said statutes and acts aforesaid, or parts thereof, *as may be construed to establish or maintain any particular denomination of Christians or their ministers . . . be, and they hereby are, abrogated and rejected.*" [98]

In six states pro-establishment parties were forced to make concessions to the growing sentiment against any establishments. In these states, the concessions took the form of a compromise: four states replaced single or exclusive establishments by instituting multiple establishments, while two states substituted multiple establishments for dual ones. The evidence relating to each of the six proves that, while it lasted, an establishment of religion was not restricted in meaning to a state church or to a system of public support of one sect alone; instead, an establishment of religion meant public support of several or all churches, with preference to none.

Three of these six states were in New England. Massachusetts adopted its constitution in 1780. Article III of its Declaration of Rights commanded the legislature to authorize the "several towns, parishes, precincts, and other bodies politic, or religious societies, to make suitable provision, at their own expense, for the institution of the public worship of God, and for the support and maintenance of public Protestant teachers of piety, religion, and morality. . . ." Clause two of Article III empowered the legislature to make church attendance compulsory. Clause three provided that the towns, parishes, etc., were to have the right of electing their ministers. Clause four was the principal one relevant to the problem under inquiry; it stated: "And all moneys paid by the subject to the support of public worship, and all the public teachers aforesaid, shall, if he require it, be uniformly applied to the support of the public teacher or teachers of his own religious sect or denomination, provided there be any on whose instructions he attends; otherwise it may be paid towards the support of the teacher or teachers of the parish or precinct in which the said moneys are raised." A fifth clause even provided that "no subordination of any one sect or denomination to the other shall ever be established by law." [99] In the context of Article III, the fifth clause, against preference, proves that, constitutionally speaking, the several churches of the establishment were on a non-

197

preferential basis. Clearly, establishment in Massachusetts meant government support of religion and of several different churches in an equitable manner. As in colonial days, the Congregationalists were the chief beneficiaries of the establishment, primarily because they were by far the most numerous and because they resorted to various tricks to fleece non-Congregationalists out of their share of religious taxes. But the fact remains that Baptist, Episcopalian, Methodist, Unitarian, and even Universalist churches were publicly supported under the establishment after 1780.[100] The establishment in Massachusetts lasted until 1833.

In New Hampshire the state constitution of 1784, by Article VI of its Declaration of Rights, created a statewide multiple establishment with the guarantee that no sect or denomination should be subordinated to another.[101] As in Massachusetts, which was the model for New Hampshire, all Protestant churches benefited. The multiple establishment ended in 1819.

Connecticut's story is also like that of Massachusetts. Before the Revolution a dual establishment had been maintained, with provisions for tax exemption for Quakers and Baptists; after the Revolution a multiple establishment was created. Connecticut, like Rhode Island, adopted no constitution at this time; its establishment was regulated by the "Act of Toleration" of 1784 which was in force when the Bill of Rights was framed. By this statute, no sect was to be subordinated to any other; religion was to be publicly supported; religious taxes in each town were divided among the various Protestant churches in proportion to the amounts paid by their respective members. The establishment lasted until 1818.[102]

In Maryland, Georgia, and South Carolina "an establishment of religion" meant very much what it did in the three New England states which maintained multiple establishments. In Maryland, where the Church of England had been exclusively established, the constitution of 1776 provided that no person could be compelled "to maintain any particular place of worship, or any particular ministry," thus disestablishing the Episcopalian church. But the same constitution provided for a new establishment of religion: "yet the Legislature may, in their discretion, lay a general and *equal tax*, for the support of the Christian religion; leaving to each individual the power of appointing the payment over of the money, collected from him, to the support of any particular place or worship or minister. . . ." [103] "Christian" rather than "Protestant" was used in Maryland because of the presence of a large Catholic population, thus insuring nonpreferential support of all churches existing in the state. In 1785 the Maryland legislature apparently sought to exercise its prescribed discretionary power to institute nonpreferential support, but "a huge uproar arose against the measure" and it was denounced as a new establishment and decisively beaten.[104] The power to enact a multiple establishment was taken from the legislature by a constitutional amendment in 1810 which provided that "an *equal* and *general* tax or any other tax . . . for the support of *any religion*" was not lawful.[105]

Georgia's constitution of 1777 tersely effected the disestablishment of the Church while permitting a multiple establishment of all churches without exception: "All persons whatever shall have the free exercise of their religion; . . . and shall not, unless by consent, support any teacher or teachers except those of their own profession." [106] "This, of course, left the way open for taxation for the support of one's own religion," says the historian of eighteenth-century church-state relationships in Georgia, "and such a law was passed in 1785" [107] although similar bills had failed in 1782 and 1784. According to the 1785 law, all Christian sects and denominations were to receive tax support in proportion to the amount of property owned by their respective church members, but it is not clear whether this measure even went into operation. What is clear is that an establishment of religion meant government tax support to all churches, with preference to none. The constitution in effect at the time of the framing of the Bill of Rights was adopted in 1789. Its relevant provision declared that no persons should be obliged "to contribute to the support of any religious profession but their own," thereby permitting a multiple establishment as before. In the state constitution adopted in 1798, however, Georgia separated church and state by a guarantee against any religious taxes and by placing the support of religion on a purely voluntary basis.[108]

South Carolina's was the sixth state constitution providing for a multiple establishment of religion, in 1778. Article XXVIII most elaborately spelled out the details for the maintenance of the "Christian Protestant religion" as "the established religion of this State." Adult males forming themselves into any religious society of a Protestant denomination were declared to be "a church of the established religion of this State," on condition of: subscribing to a belief in God; promising to worship him publicly; a belief in Christianity as "the true religion"; and a belief in the divine inspiration of the Scriptures. It was specifically guaranteed that "no person shall, by law, be obliged to pay towards the maintenance and support of a religious worship that he does not freely join in, or has not voluntarily engaged to support." [109] State support of all Protestant churches, without preference, continued in South Carolina until a new constitution reflecting the influence of "the discussions over the Federal Constitution and its Bill of Rights" [110] was adopted in 1790 with no provisions whatever for public support of religion.[111]

The constitutions of North Carolina and Virginia did not provide for an establishment of religion of any kind. North Carolina, in 1776, by very broadly guaranteeing that the support of religion was a voluntary, individual matter, banned all state support and disestablished the Church of England.[112] By contrast, Virginia's constitution of 1776 was noncommittal on the subject of an establishment.

At the close of 1776 the Church of England was for all practical purposes disestablished in Virginia by a statute which 1) forever exempted all nonmembers from taxes for its support, and 2) suspended for one year the collection of any taxes from Church of England members. The suspension of religious taxes for members was renewed in 1777 and 1778; in 1779, the old colonial statute levying those taxes was repealed. Thus the Church of England received no government support after 1776. But the statute of 1776 which initiated the end of the exclusive establishment expressly reserved for future decision the question whether religion ought to be placed on a private, voluntary basis or be supported on a nonpreferential basis by a new "general" assessment.[113]

In 1779 a bill for support on a nonpreferential basis was introduced; at the same time, however, Jefferson's "Bill for Religious Freedom" was introduced, providing, in part, "That no man shall be compelled to frequent or support any religious worship, place, or ministry whatsoever. . . ."[114] The principle underlying this provision was Jefferson's belief that religion was a personal matter between the individual and God and not rightfully a subject under the jurisdiction of the civil government. By contrast, Patrick Henry's "General Assessment Bill" was predicated on the supposition, expressed in its preamble, that the state must encourage religion. This bill stipulated that the Christian religion should be "the established religion," that societies of Christians organized for the purpose of religious worship should in law be regarded as churches of the established religion, each to have its own "name or denomination" and each to share the tax proceeds assessed on tithable personal property and collected by county sheriffs. Every person was to designate the church of his membership and that church alone would receive his taxes; money collected from persons not designating membership was to be divided proportionately among all churches of his county.[115]

Confronted by two diametrically opposed bills, the Virginia legislature was deadlocked. Neither bill could muster a majority until in 1784 the Presbyterian clergy, attracted by the prospect of state support for their own church, became converted to an establishment which they had hitherto opposed. Henry reintroduced his general assessment plan under the title, "A Bill Establishing a Provision for the Teachers of the Christian Religion," in which the stated purpose was to require "a moderate tax or contribution annually for the support of the Christian religion, or of some Christian church, denomination or communion of Christians, or for some form of Christian worship." [116] A resolution in favor of the bill was passed against the opposition of a minority led by Madison.

Only the notes of Madison's speech against the measure remain. These show that he argued that religion is a matter of private rather than civil concern and that taxes in support of religion violated religious liberty. The true question, he declared, was not, "Is religion necessary?" but rather, "Are religious establishments necessary for religion?" to which he argued in the negative.[117] Through masterly political maneuvering, Madison got Henry out of the legislature by supporting his election as governor and then managed to get a final vote on the bill postponed until the next session of the legislature, nearly a year later, in November of 1785. In the meanwhile, he brought his case to the people by writing his famous "Memorial and Remonstrance Against Religious Assessments." The political effect of this widely distributed pamphlet was staggering; it caused literally thousands of people, including the Presbyterians, to change their minds on the assessment bill, and resulted in the election of a legislature with an overwhelming majority against it. The new legislature let the bill die unnoticed, and by a vote of 67 to 20 enacted instead Jefferson's bill for religious freedom with its provision against government support of religion.

Conclusions

The struggle in Virginia outlined above is usually featured in accounts of the history of separation of church and state in America. No doubt historians focus their attention on the Virginia story because the sources are uniquely ample,[118] the struggle was important and dramatic, and the opinions of Madison, the principal framer of the Bill of Rights—not to mention those of Jefferson—were fully elicited. As a result, the details of no other state controversy over church-state relationships are so familiar. If, however, one is concerned with attempting to understand what was meant by "an establishment of religion" at the time of the framing of the Bill of Rights, the histories of the other states are equally important, notwithstanding the stature and influence of Jefferson and Madison as individuals. Indeed, the abortive effort in Virginia to enact Patrick Henry's assessment bill is less important than the fact that five states actually had constitutional provisions authorizing general assessments for religion, and a sixth (Connecticut) provided for the same by statute. Had the assessment bill in Virginia been enacted, it would simply have increased the number of states maintaining multiple establishments from six to seven.

In no state or colony, of course, was there ever an establishment of religion which included every religion without exception. Neither

Judaism, Buddhism, Mohammedanism, nor any religion but a Christian one was ever established in America. In half of the six multiple establishments existing in 1789, Protestantism was the established religion; in the other half, Christianity was. It may therefore be argued that the concept of a multiple establishment is fallacious, and that exclusive establishments of one religion existed in every colonial or state precedent. Such a statement would be true so far as it goes, but alone it is a misleading half-truth.

In each of the six states where multiple establishments existed, the establishment included the churches of every denomination and sect with a sufficient number of adherents to form a church. There were a few isolated towns or counties in each of the states where the letter of the law was not followed, particularly where a congregation of a sect such as the Quakers conscientiously opposed compulsory tax support of even their own church, but such cases were comparatively rare. In general, where Protestantism was established, it was synonymous with religion; there were either no Jews and Catholics or too few of them to make a difference; and where Christianity was established, as in Maryland which had many Catholics, Jews were scarcely known.

Clearly, the provisions of these six states show that to understand the American meaning of "an establishment of religion" one cannot arbitrarily adopt a definition based on European experience. In every European precedent of an establishment, the religion established was that of a single church. Many different churches, or the religion held in common by all of them, i.e., Christianity or Protestantism, were never simultaneously established by any European nation. Establishments in America, on the other hand, both in the colonial and early state periods, were not limited in nature or in meaning to state support of one church. *An establishment of religion in America at the time of the framing of the Bill of Rights meant government aid and sponsorship of religion, principally by impartial tax support of the institutions of religion, the churches.*

Not one of the six American states maintaining establishments of religion at that time preferred one church to others in their constitutional law. Even in New England where the Congregational church was dominant as a result of numerical superiority, there were constitutional and legal guarantees against subordination or preference. Such an establishment can hardly be called an exclusive or preferential one, as in the case where only one church, as in all European precedents, was the beneficiary. The uniqueness of the American experience justifies defining an establishment of religion as *any support of religion by government*, whether the support be to religion in general, to all churches, some churches, or one church.

Madison and Jefferson

The opinions of Jefferson and Madison are, of course, of particular importance. Jefferson, who was most responsible for converting Madison to the cause of amending the Constitution by adding a Bill of Rights, wrote the Statute of Religious Liberty in Virginia which placed the support of religion on a private basis; and he first used the celebrated phrase, "a wall of separation between church and state," to explain the establishment-of-religion clause. Madison led the fight against the general assessment bill in Virginia and was by far the most important draftsman of the First Amendment. The generation of the framers knew more about the opinions of Jefferson and Madison on the meaning of an establishment of religion than about those of anyone else. While their thinking on the subject cannot be taken as representative of their whole generation, it was surely the most influential. Moreover, these two were nearly the only men among the framers to express themselves on establishments of religion in the period after as well as before the adoption of the First Amendment. For these reasons and because their opinions have been variously interpreted, a review of the record is worthwhile.

Madison's Views

Madison's "Memorial and Remonstrance Against Religious Assessments," written in 1785, certainly shows that he regarded the general assessment bill as an establishment of religion. He refers to it again and again as "the establishment proposed by the bill," "ecclesiastical establishments," "the establishment in question," "the proposed establishment," and so on.[119] The bill's supporters admitted that it was an establishment of religion, as its very name indicated: "A Bill Establishing a Provision for Teachers of the Christian Religion." However, proponents of the narrow interpretation say that the bill provided for an exclusive establishment of one religion, Christianity, and therefore that Madison's opposition shows merely that he was only against government support of one religion.

That only Christian churches were to be tax-supported cannot be denied, even though every known religious group in the state would have been established by the bill and even though there were no non-Christian congregations in the state. Nevertheless, it does not follow that Madison opposed the bill simply because it did not establish other religions also.

He opposed the bill because it created an establishment of religion. What kind it created did not matter to him, nor how inclusive or exclusive. He opposed the bill because as a matter of principle he opposed any kind of an establishment of religion. Had he opposed the bill only because it established the Christian religion exclusively, his arguments would have been directed, quite simply, to the reasons for amending the bill so as to include all religions. He made no such argument. He opposed the bill in whole, not in part. Indeed, at only one point in his "Memorial and Remonstrance" did he mention the bill's exclusive character: "Who does not see that the same authority which can establish Christianity, in exclusion of all other Religions, may establish with the same ease any particular sect of Christians, in exclusion of all other Sects?" [120]

It is significant that this sentence occurs in the course of an argument in which he seeks to convince his readers that the way to avoid the consequences of an infringement of liberty is to deny, on its first appearance, "the principle" which supports the infringement. The whole passage shows that Madison was not opposing the establishment because it was exclusively a Christian one. He was opposing, rather, what in his mind was a threat to liberty deriving from an unwarranted exercise of power in a domain forbidden to government.

That there can be no doubt of this is evident from the fourteen other reasons for opposing the bill. Each was applicable to a bill supporting religion in general. The Reverend John Courtney Murray, S.J., though he did not approve of Madison's opinions, granted the correctness of Justice Rutledge's statement that the "Remonstrance" discloses Madison's opposition to "every form and degree of official relation between religion and civil authority. For him religion was a wholly private matter beyond the scope of civil power either to restrain or support." [121] Father Murray added that the theme of the "Remonstrance" is that religion "must be absolutely free from governmental restriction and likewise *absolutely 'free' from governmental aid.* . . . For Madison, as for John Locke, his master, religion could not by law be made a concern of the commonwealth as such, deserving in any degree of public recognition or aid, for the essentially theological reason that religion is of its nature a personal, private, interior matter of the individual conscience, having no relevance to the public concerns of the state." [122]

In the same year as the "Remonstrance," 1785, Madison also expressed himself strongly against an abortive plan of the Continental Congress to set aside public land in each township in the western territories for the support of religion—any religion.[123] In 1790, prior to the adoption of the Bill of Rights, Madison in Congress gave the following reason for omitting ministers from enumerated occupations in a census bill: "As to those who are employed in teaching and inculcating the duties of religion, there may be some indelicacy in singling them out, as the general government is proscribed from interfering, in any manner whatever, in matters respecting religion; and it may be thought to do this, in ascertaining who, and who are not ministers of the gospel." [124] Surely, one who opposed non-preferential land grants for religious purposes and who objected to a federal census report of ministers cannot be regarded as an opponent of only that public aid to religion which failed to provide for non-Christians. Indeed, Madison's constitutional scruples on this matter were so refined that he even regarded as unconstitutional such governmental, legal, or financial supports to religion as Presidential proclamations of Thanksgiving, tax exemptions for religious institutions, chaplains for Congress and the armed services, incorporation of churches by the federal government in the District of Columbia, and the grant of lands to a church.

While Madison was President, he vetoed a land-grant bill intended to remedy the peculiar situation of a Baptist church which had, through a surveying error, been built on public land. Congress sought to rectify the error by permitting the church to have the land rather than buy it or be dispossessed. Here was no making of broad public policy, yet President Madison saw a dangerous precedent, and he vetoed the bill on the ground that it "comprises a principle and precedent for the appropriation of funds of the United States for the use and support of religious societies, contrary to the article of the Constitution which declares that 'Congress shall make no law respecting a religious establishment.'" [125]

Incidentally, it is interesting and perhaps significant that Madison, known as the "father" of the Constitution and the Bill of Rights, should in a formal message to Congress have misquoted the First Amendment in the particular way he did, using "religious establishment" synonymously with "an establishment of religion," although the former, unlike the latter, does not technically imply an act of government. The point is, of course, that Madison never altered his early view, which was widely shared by the other framers of the Constitution, that Congress had no power to legislate on any matters concerning religion. His use of "religious establishment" instead of "establishment of religion" shows that he understood the clause in the First Amendment to mean that Congress shall make no law touching or "respecting" religious institutions or religion. He misquoted the First Amendment in the same way in another veto message against a Congressional bill which would have incorporated a church in the District of Columbia, [126] showing that he regarded even simple recognition, without financial support, to be within the ban against an establishment of religion.

As a Congressman, Madison served in 1789 on a joint committee which created Congressional chaplaincies. There is no record of that date to indicate his objection to such chaplaincies, but in a letter of

1822 to Edward Livingston he stated that he had not approved at that time or later: "I observe with particular pleasure the view you have taken of the immunity of religion from civil jurisdiction, . . . This has always been a favorite principle with me; and it was not with my approbation, that the deviation from it took place in Congress, when they appointed Chaplains, to be paid from the National Treasury." [127]

In Madison's "Detached Memoranda," written after he retired from the Presidency in 1817, he expressed concern that the "danger of silent accumulations & encroachments by Ecclesiastical Bodies have [*sic*] not sufficiently engaged attention in the U.S." [128] He asked, "Is the appointment of Chaplains to the two Houses of Congress consistent with the Constitution, and with the pure principle of religious freedom?" By way of answer he replied: "In strictness the answer on both points must be in the negative. The Constitution of the U.S. forbids everything like an establishment of a national religion. The law appointing Chaplains establishes a religious worship for the national representatives, to be performed by Ministers of religion, elected by a majority of them; and these are to be paid out of the national taxes. Does not this involve the principle of a national establishment, applicable to a provision for a religious worship for the Constituent as well as of the representative Body, approved by the majority, and conducted by Ministers of religion paid by the entire nation?"

Madison continued: "The establishment of the chaplainship to Congress is a palpable violation of equal rights, as well as of Constitutional principles. . . . If Religion consists in voluntary acts of individuals, singly, or voluntarily associated, and it be proper that public functionaries, as well as their Constituents should discharge their religious duties, let them like their Constituents, do so at their own expense." [129] He classified chaplainships for the army and navy "in the same way," as forbidden "establishments" or an "establishment of a national religion." [130] Clearly a man who considered unconstitutional the use of public funds for the support of interfaith invocations and benedictions—and nothing could be more nonpreferential or lacking in exclusiveness—would also consider unconstitutional the use of public funds for any other purpose respecting religion.

It is significant too that Madison called the public support of chaplaincies "an establishment of a *national* religion," and he repeated the idea when adding that the chaplaincies involved "the principle of a *national* establishment." The phrase "national religion" appears in Madison's first draft of the First Amendment, and when the word "national" was dropped by the House drafting committee he suggested in debate that it be restored. Some have construed his use of "national" to mean that he sought merely to prohibit the establishment by Congress of a single state church or Congressional preference for one church or religion over others. But the evidence indicates that Madison's use of the word "national" in 1789 was intended to distinguish an act of the national government from that of a state, without regard to the preferential or nonpreferential character of the national act on a matter respecting religion. In his "Detached Memoranda" he discussed the establishment of religion clause as if the word "national" still remained in it, yet he continued to interpret the meaning of the clause with the most extraordinary latitude.

In his "Detached Memoranda" Madison also stated that "Religious proclamations by the Executive recommending thanksgivings and fasts are shoots from the same root with the legislative acts reviewed [the chaplaincies]." [131] It should be noted that he was here discussing so innocuous an act as a Presidential recommendation for a day of thanksgiving, another extreme example of nonpreference on a matter respecting religion. He regarded such recommendations as violating the First Amendment: "They seem," he wrote, "to imply and certainly nourish the erronious [sic] idea of a *national* religion [Madison's italics]." [132] Although Madison as President proclaimed several days for fast and thanksgiving, it is relevant to remember the extenuating circumstances that he was chief executive during the time a war was fought on national soil. And as he pointed out in his letter of 1822 to Livingston, while he "found it necessary" to deviate from "strict principle" by his proclamations, "I was always careful to make the Proclamation absolutely indiscriminate, and merely recommendatory; or, rather mere *designations* [Madison's italics] of a day on which all who thought proper might unite in consecrating it to religious purposes, according to their own faith and forms."

In the same letter he warned that the danger of an "alliance or coalition between Government and Religion . . . cannot be too carefully guarded against. . . . Every new and successful example therefore of a *perfect separation* between ecclesiastical and civil matters is of importance . . . religion and Government will exist in greater purity, without than with the aid of Government." [133] His stress on a "perfect separation" appears also in his "Detached Memoranda" where he noted: "Strongly guarded as is the separation between Religion and Government in the Constitution of the United States the danger of encroachment by Ecclesiastical Bodies, may be illustrated by precedents. . . ." One of his illustrations was the "attempt in Kentucky, for example, where it was proposed to exempt Houses of Worship from taxes." [134] Madison believed that any semblance of support to religion by government was unconstitutional.

Jefferson's Views

Jefferson fully shared Madison's opinions on the subject of an establishment of religion. But unlike Madison he did not in his writings expressly state what he understood an establishment to mean, except in regard to Presidential proclamations of a quasi-religious character such as thanksgiving. What he meant by an establishment must on the whole be inferred from the dozens of instances when he, like Madison, committed himself without exception to the principle of private, voluntary support of religion and stated that government had no jurisdiction in a realm exclusively belonging to individual conscience. If, as President, like Madison he countenanced the use of public funds for Congressional and military chaplaincies or for proselytizing activities among the Indians, his inconsistency was trivial and may be dismissed on the traditional ground of *de minimis*. A partial review of the evidence will indicate the identity of their points of view.

Jefferson's most quoted statement on the subject of an establishment appears in his Presidential letter to the Danbury (Connecticut) Baptist Association on January 1, 1802. Upon declaring that religion was "solely between man and his God," he added: ". . . I contemplate with sovereign reverence that act of the whole American people which declared that their legislature should 'make no law respecting an establishment of religion, or prohibiting the free exercise thereof,' thus building a wall of separation between church and state." [135] The usual treatment of Jefferson's Danbury Baptist letter by those who seek to weaken its force is either to minimize it or to argue that he was here concerned only with the rights of conscience, and that these would not be endangered by treating all religions equally.[136] Neither approach is valid.

The rights-of-conscience argument ignores the fact that Jefferson quoted the establishment clause in the very sentence in which he spoke of a wall of separation, indicating that he was concerned with more than protection of the free exercise of religion. In any case, Jefferson most assuredly did believe that the right of conscience was violated by government support of all religions. His Statute of Religious Freedom expressly asserts that "even the forcing him [any man] to support this or that teacher of his *own* religious persuasion, is *depriving* him of the comfortable *liberty* of giving his contributions . . . . no man shall be compelled to frequent or support *any* religious worship place, or ministry whatsoever. . . ." [137]

The second technique of robbing the Danbury letter of its clear intent to oppose any government support of religion is to belittle it as a "little address of courtesy" containing a "figure of speech . . . a metaphor." [138] Or, as one commentator suggests, the letter was scarcely "deliberate" or "carefully considered"; it was rather "not improbably motivated by an impish desire to heave a brick at the Congregationalist-Federalist hierarchy of Connecticut. . . ." [139] Jefferson, however, had powerful convictions on the subject of establishments and religious freedom, and he approached discussion of it with the greatest solemnity. Indeed, on the occasion of writing this letter he was so concerned with the necessity of expressing himself with deliberation, precision, and care that he went out of his way to get the approbation of the Attorney-General of the United States. Sending him the letter before dispatching it to Danbury, Jefferson asked his advice as to its contents and explained: "Averse to receive addresses, yet unable to prevent them, I have generally endeavored to turn them to some account, by making them the occasion, by way of answer, of sowing useful truths and principles among the people, which might germinate and become rooted among their political tenets. The Baptist address, now enclosed, admits of a condemnation of the alliance between Church and State, under the authority of the Constitution. It furnishes an occasion, too, which I have long wished to find, of saying why I do not proclaim fastings and thanksgivings, as my predecessors did." [140] On the matter of proclaiming fast and thanksgiving days, Jefferson departed from the precedents of Washington and Adams, and went further even than Madison, by utterly refusing on any occasion to recommend or designate a day for worship, citing as a reason, among others, the clause against establishments of religion.[141]

Religion and Education

It remains only to review the evidence involving the views of Madison and Jefferson in relation to establishments of religion and public aid to education, particularly aid to the University of Virginia. Most of the data in this regard relate to Jefferson. Except for Madison's association with him in planning and governing the state university, there is no evidence available of an explicit expression by Madison on religion and education. The closest approximation comes in his Presidential veto of the bill to incorporate a church in the District of Columbia. In his veto message of February 21, 1811, he not only declared that the bill violated the establishment-of-religion clause, but added that it was also objectionable because it provided for educational support of the poor of the church. Such a provision, he said, might be considered as "a precedent for giving religious societies as such a legal agency in carrying into effect a public and civil duty." [142] In other words, Congress could not empower a religious institution to carry out the public duty of educating children. On the basis of this reasoning, there is good cause for believing that

Madison would think it unconstitutional for government to allow religious schools to carry out the public duty of educating children in nonsectarian subjects.

It is argued by proponents of the narrow interpretation of the no-establishment clause that Jefferson favored cooperation between government and religion in the field of public education. The contention is that Jefferson advocated the use of public funds in Virginia in 1814 for a school of theology for the training of clergymen; that he approved of quite elaborate arrangements in the University of Virginia for the students of private theological schools to share the facilities of the university; that he recommended a room in the university to be used for religious worship; and that he did not protest against the use by Virginia of tax monies on behalf of religious education.[143]

An analysis of the whole of Jefferson's work in relation to education, however, seems to demonstrate that Jefferson opposed public support of religious education and supported a system of public education quite uninfluenced by religion. Such an analysis has been made by Roy J. Honeywell in his book, *The Educational Work of Thomas Jefferson*.[144] For one reading this book in search of expressions on religion in education, the most striking impression is of the neglect Jefferson accorded religion. On matters of education he was a complete secularist. In 1779, the year he introduced his bill for religious liberty, placing the support of religion on a private, voluntary basis, he submitted to the legislature, in his capacity as governor, a "Bill for the More General Diffusion of Knowledge." [145] This bill constituted a comprehensive plan for public education at the primary and secondary levels. Religious instruction was completely absent from the proposed curriculum at a time when it was featured prominently in schools everywhere else. This omission of religious instruction was deliberate on Jefferson's part, for he wrote in his *Notes on the State of Virginia,* in 1785, "Instead therefore of putting the Bible and Testament into the hands of the children, at an age when their judgments are not sufficiently matured for religious enquiries, their memories may here be stored with the most useful facts from Grecian, Roman, European and American history." [146]

Religion was also conspicuously absent from Jefferson's 1817 plan, submitted in his "Bill for Establishing a System of Public Education." In the enumeration of subjects to be taught, only secular ones were mentioned, and Jefferson specified that ministers should not serve as "visitors" or supervisors; he provided that "no religious reading, instruction or exercise, shall be prescribed or practised" in violation of the tenets of any sect or denomination.[147] It could scarcely be more apparent that Jefferson opposed the teaching of religion in the public schools, and that he carried his principle of separation between church and state into the field of education.

Such evidence as can be cited to the contrary relates entirely to the field of higher education, specifically to Jefferson's plans for the state University of Virginia which he was instrumental in founding. But even in regard to higher education, only evidence that is carefully selected and hence misleading can count him in favor of public aid to religion. Jefferson's first proposal in the field of higher education was made in 1779 when he was state governor—a "Bill for the Amending of the Constitution of the College of William and Mary." The bill stated that the college as then organized consisted of "one school of sacred theology, with two professorships therein, to wit, one for teaching the Hebrew tongue, and expounding the holy scriptures; and the other for explaining the commonplaces of divinity, and controversies with heretics." There were six other professorships divided among a school of philosophy, one of classical languages, and one for teaching Indians reading, writing, "the catechism and the principles of the Christian religion." Jefferson proposed to abolish both the school of theology with its professorships of religion and the school for teaching Indians. In place of the latter he proposed that a missionary be selected by the newly constituted faculty whose "business shall be" not to teach religion but "to investigate their [Indian] laws, customs, religions, traditions, and more particularly their languages. . . ." Thus Jefferson's missionary was to be an anthropologist charged with reporting his findings to the faculty and preserving his reports in the college library. In place of the school of theology and the professorships of religion, he proposed simply a professorship "of moral philosophy" and another "of history civil and ecclesiastical." [148]

Jefferson's proposed bill failed because of Episcopalian opposition, but in the same year, 1779, he and Madison as visitors of the college instituted such changes as could be made by executive authority without legislative approval. In 1821 he summarized the changes by writing, "When I was a visitor, in 1779, I got the two professorships of Divinity . . . put down, and others of law and police, of medicine, anatomy, and chemistry, and of modern languages substituted. . . ." [149] A comparable statement appears in his *Notes on the State of Virginia* where he states less personally that the visitors "excluded" the school of divinity.[150]

Although the College of William and Mary was a public institution, supported by state taxes, Jefferson was never satisfied with the education it offered; failing to achieve adequate reform of the college, he turned to the establishment of a new institution, a state university. He also attempted to transform Albemarle Academy, a private school, into an institution offering instruction from the primary grades through college and postgraduate training. The new institution was to be supported in part by public funds. At no point in the entire curriculum before postgraduate or professional training was there any provision for religious education. One of the "professional schools," however, was to be devoted to "Theology and Ecclesiastical History," to which would come the "ecclesiastic" as would the "lawyer to the school of law." [151]

Here is one piece of evidence that indicates Jefferson's support of the use of tax funds on behalf of religious education, although only at the graduate level. It is not irrelevant to add, however, that the proposed institution was privately supported and endowed, though aided by public funds. More to the point is the fact that never again, after the failure of this proposal, did Jefferson renew it. As Honeywell states, "In 1814 he proposed among the professional schools a professorship of theology and ecclesiastical history. By the advice of Dr. [Thomas] Cooper, he omitted theology from all future proposals of subjects to be taught." [152] In 1818, for instance, his proposed curriculum for the newly authorized state university included ten professorships and thirty-four subjects, none of them relating to religion.[153]

This curriculum, which was adopted, was laid out in a report written by Jefferson as chairman of the Commissioners for the University of Virginia. Madison was also a member of the commission. The report stated: "In conformity with the principles of our Constitution, which places all sects of religion on an equal footing . . . we have proposed no professor of divinity. . . . Proceeding thus far without offence to the Constitution, we have thought it proper at this point to leave every sect to provide, as they think fittest, the means of further instruction in their own peculiar tenets." [154] The report also stated: "It is supposed probable, that a building . . . may be called for in time, in which may be rooms for religious worship . . . for public examinations, for a library. . . ." [155] It is clear from the extraordinarily conditional phrasing of this sentence that Jefferson and Madison were seeking to fend off an anticipated barrage of criticism against the university as a godless institution. In fact, they were under constant pressure from pro-religious groups to make suitable provision for theological training and religious worship at the university. The supposedly probable room which might in time be needed as a place in part for worship was a concession to those who, as Jefferson reported in a letter to Dr. Cooper, used the absence of a professorship of divinity to spread the idea that the university was "not merely of no religion, but against all religion." [156]

Opposition to the secular character of the university, resulting in a postponement of the beginning of instruction until 1825, forced additional concessions to religious interests. On October 7, 1822, Jefferson, as rector of the university, and the Board of Visitors, which included Madison, proposed in the most reluctant language to accept a suggestion "by some pious individuals . . . to establish their religious schools on the confines of the University, so as to give their students ready and convenient access and attendance on the scientific lectures of the University; . . ." The report noted that the religious schools would also offer places for regular students of the university to worship as they pleased, "But always understanding that these schools shall be independent of the University and of each other." And the report concluded that if the legislature questioned "what here is suggested, the idea will be relinquished on any surmise of disapprobation which they might think proper to express." [157] The legislature did not, however, take the eager hint to scrap the plan which involved no public expense.

A month later, Jefferson explained in his letter to Dr. Cooper that to silence the calumny that the university was atheistic, "In our annual report to the legislature, *after stating the constitutional reasons against a public establishment of any religious instruction*, we suggested the *expediency* of encouraging the different religious sects to establish, *each for itself*, a professorship of their own tenets, on the confines of the University. . . ." [158] In 1824, shortly before the opening of the first classes, the Board of Visitors, Jefferson and Madison being present, adopted formal regulations which provided that the "religious sects of this State" might "establish within, or adjacent to, the precincts of the University, schools for instruction in the religion of their own sect. . . ." Students of the university were "free, and expected to attend religious worship" at the "establishment" of their choice, on condition that they did so in the mornings prior to attending classes which began at 7:30 A.M. The same regulations also provided for the use of one of the university's rooms for worship as well as for other purposes, although the students were enjoined by the regulations of the previous paragraph to attend services in the theological seminaries surrounding the university.

The superficial resemblance between these provisions and current programs of "released time" is deceiving, for it is clear that no part of the regular school day was involved. Possibly the proposal that a room belonging to the university be used for worship was intended originally as a makeshift arrangement until the various sects established their own schools of theology. Yet, although none in fact did so until several decades later, the room belonging to the university was not in practice permitted by Jefferson to be used for religious purposes. On April 21, 1825, writing as rector of the University on behalf of the Board of Visitors, he rejected a proposal to hold religious services on university property on *Sundays*. He pointed out that the Board of Visitors had already turned down an application

213

to permit a sermon to be preached in one of the rooms, on the ground that "the buildings of the University belong to the state, that they were erected for the purposes of an University, and that the Visitors, to whose care they are commd [commanded or committed] for those purposes, have no right to permit their application to any other." He took the position that the legislature had failed to sanction a proposal to use university facilities for worship and that, consequently, an alternative plan had been adopted "*superseding* the 1st idea of permitting a room in the Rotunda to be used for religious worship. . . ." The alternative plan was the one permitting the different sects to establish their own divinity schools, without public aid, independently of the university.[159]

R. Freeman Butts summarized the matter most aptly when he wrote: "At a time when, in most colleges and universities of the country, ministers were presidents and common members of boards of control, daily chapel attendance was compulsory, courses in religion were required, and professors of theology and doctors of divinity had a prominent place on the faculties, the University of Virginia stood out sharply in contrast with its loyalty to the principle of separation of church and state." [160] Butts added that the university did not even appoint a chaplain until 1829 and then only after Madison, following Jefferson as rector, had provided that the cost of maintaining the chaplain be paid by the students themselves on a voluntary basis. "Being altogether voluntary," declared Madison, "it would interfere neither with the characteristic peculiarity of the University, the consecrated principle of the law, nor the spirit of the country." [161]

The evidence, therefore, dictates the conclusion that in the field of education, as elsewhere, Jefferson and Madison opposed public aid and support of religion. As they understood the First Amendment and the provisions of their state constitution, the prohibition against an establishment of religion meant no public aid or support of all or any religious institutions or groups. In short, they believed that the Constitution of the United States and that of Virginia rendered both the federal and state governments absolutely powerless to act in matters respecting religion.

Appendix

The Nature of the Evidence

The principal sources for an inquiry like this should be 1) the records of the First Congress, which framed and submitted for ratification the first ten amendments to the United States Constitution, and 2) the records of the state legislatures which engaged in the process of ratification.

One would think that it would merely be necessary to read the debates and minutes of the First Congress and of the state legislatures to determine the answers to the questions under study, because the members of these bodies were in the most immediate sense the "framers" of the Bill of Rights. However, the sources for the study of Congress' part are incomplete and yield few definite answers, while sources for the work of the state legislatures are nonexistent.

As to Congress: no official records were kept of the debates in either the Senate or House. Since the Senate during the First Congress met in secret session, no reporters were present to take even unofficial notes of the proceedings. A valuable record of the proceedings of the Senate for this time is *The Journal of William Maclay*,[162] United States Senator from Pennsylvania, 1789–1791. Unfortunately, however, Maclay was not present during most of the time the Senate debated the Bill of Rights, and he mentions the subject merely in passing. No account of the debates exists, and the only Senate document we have is a meager record of action taken on motions and bills, *the Journal of the First Session of the Senate of the United States of America*.[163]

The situation for the House is considerably better, but unsatisfactory. We have a House Journal, comparable to that for the Senate, and what is more important, a version of the debates, since, unlike the Senate, the House permitted entry to reporters who took shorthand notes. These unofficial reports, however, which were published in the contemporary press, have numerous deficiencies. The reporters took notes on the debates "and rephrased these notes for publication. The shorthand in use at that time was too slow to permit verbatim transcription of all speeches, with the result that a reporter, in preparing his copy for the press, frequently relied upon his memory as well as his notes and gave what seemed to him the substance, but not necessarily the actual phraseology, of speeches. Different reportings of the same speech exhibited at times only a general similarity, and details recorded by one reporter were frequently omitted by another." [164] Volume One of *The Debates and Proceedings in the Congress of the United States*, commonly known by its binder's title as the *Annals of Congress*, was published in 1834.[165] The information it includes about Senate proceedings is "only an abstract of the scanty record that was written in the Senate's journal." [166] The House debates as recorded in the *Annals of Congress* for the first session of the First Congress, which framed the Bill of Rights, are based chiefly on the account reported for a contemporary newspaper known as Lloyd's *Congressional Register* (despite its name, an ordinary newspaper). The reports of these House debates "were so condensed" by the compilers of the *Annals of Congress* "that much information about the debates was omitted entirely or was presented only in garbled form." [167]

Thus, our record of the House debates does not necessarily reveal all that was said about the Bill of Rights, nor is the report necessarily accurate as far as it goes. Accordingly, quotations from the *Annals of Congress* purporting to represent a speaker's words must be regarded with some skepticism, a fact of particular importance in cases where slight changes in phraseology may shift the speaker's meaning, as in the debate on the establishment-of-religion clause. Finally, there is no known record of the minutes of the special House committee on amendments; it was this committee which, using Madison's original proposals, drafted the version of the Bill of Rights submitted to the House for approval. Nor is there any record extant of the minutes of the joint Senate-House conference committee which worked out a compromise draft between Senate and House versions of the proposed amendments.

Nor is much enlightenment to be had from other sources. The fact that Congress was drafting a Bill of Rights during the summer of 1789 prompted no analytical comment by the press which published the House debates. Moreover, as another historian who has scoured the sources has pointed out, "The finished amendments were not the subject of any special newspaper comment, and there is little comment in the available correspondence." [168]

As far as the records of the state legislatures which ratified the Bill of Rights are concerned, the situation is altogether hopeless. No records were kept of the debates which might illuminate what the people of the various states understood to be the meanings of the various parts of the Bill of Rights. Nor has any scholar who has worked over the contemporary newspapers uncovered anything particularly revealing as to these meanings. Incredible as it may seem today, public interest in the proposed amendments was desultory, and public discussion of them largely confined to generalities, in contrast to the searching character of the earlier discussion of the Constitution proper.

Every schoolboy knows that the Constitution nearly failed of adoption by the states because it had no Bill of Rights, and that the promise of immediate amendments to rectify that situation was necessary to secure the requisite number of votes for ratification. Yet if we turn back to the controversy over ratification, expecting to find deeply considered arguments on the meaning of the various rights which ought to be guaranteed, we are again disappointed. In a flood of campaign literature, the lack of a Bill of Rights was denounced, specific suggestions were made as to the contents of such a document, but no one thought it necessary to spell out the scope and the limits of these rights.

Nor is more to be learned from the debates in the state ratifying conventions. To be sure, only the debates for six of the thirteen states are fully reported, but on the matters which concern this memorandum, little of value emerges even from these debates. Several of the state ratifying conventions submitted bills of rights in the form of proposed amendments to the new Constitution, but in no state was there considerable or meaningful discussion of the amendments. They were usually the result of unrecorded deliberations of special committees whose reports were adopted quite perfunctorily.[169]

If we go back even further in time to the framing of the first state constitutions, several of which included bills of rights, the sources are equally disappointing as the basis for any definitive statement as to the meaning of the provisions.

Private correspondence, diaries, and other papers of the framers constitute, of course, another relevant source, but such manuscripts as have been published prove in the main to be of only peripheral help. Only meager results can be derived from still another possible source, the reported decisions of the early state courts, most of whose work remains unpublished and unstudied.

It must be said, therefore, that the insubstantial, even flimsy, records which we know at present scarcely permit confident pronouncements. Such conclusions as may be drawn from the available evidence must certainly be regarded as merely suggestive and subject to change if and when fresh sources are unearthed. Work is presently under way which promises to yield new data. In 1954 the National Historical Publications Commission, a federal body charged by Congress with the responsibility of planning and recommending publication of historical documents by the government, announced plans "for the publication by the Commission of documentary histories of (a) the ratification of the Constitution and the Bill of Rights, and (b) the work of the First Federal Congress, 1789–91." [170] The plan is to present these two documentary histories exhaustively, in six and fourteen volumes respectively. Among the data to be included are debates, to be published as definitively as possible, the relevant pamphlet literature, and the letters and diaries of members of Congress. It is to be regretted that the project does not also call for a systematic search for the literary remains of every member of each of the state conventions which ratified the Constitution, and of each member of the state legislatures to which the first ten amendments were submitted for adoption. Only when such a canvass of the sources has been completed and the results published will it be possible, perhaps, to state with assurance what the Bill of Rights meant to its framers.

NOTES

[1] 330 U.S. 1.

[2] The states were not restricted by the First Amendment at the time of its adoption; it applied only against the national government. Beginning in 1925, the Supreme Court has ruled that the freedoms protected against national infringement by the First Amendment are protected against state infringement by the Fourteenth, ratified in 1868. Thus, Justice Black's statement in 1947 on the restrictions imposed upon the states by the establishment-of-religion clause was not intended to represent either the intentions of the framers, in 1789, or the constitutional law of the matter at that early date. As far as the United States Constitution is concerned, the states were free to erect and maintain establishments of religion before the adoption of the Fourteenth Amendment.

[3] 330 U.S. 1, 15.

[4] *Ibid.*, 31–32.

[5] J. M. O'Neill, *Religion and Education Under the Constitution* (New York, 1949), p. 56.

[6] So distinguished a constitutional authority as Professor Edward S. Corwin, for example, concluded a brief survey of the sources by affirming, without the slightest trace of doubt, that the Supreme Court's unanimous agreement on the unconstitutionality of government aid to "all religions" is "untrue historically." "In a word," added Corwin, "what the 'establishment of religion' clause of the First Amendment does, and all that it does, is to forbid Congress to give any religious faith, sect, or denomination preferred status. . . ." He concludes that, "The historical record shows beyond peradventure that the core idea of 'an establishment of religion' comprises the idea of preference; and that any act of public authority favorable to religion in general cannot, without manifest falsification of history, be brought under the ban of that phrase." Corwin, "The Supreme Court As National School Board," *Law and Contemporary Problems*, xiv (Winter 1949), 10, 20.

[7] Several scholars declare that the germ of the no-establishment clause derived from a proposal allegedly advanced by Charles Pinckney of South Carolina on May 29: "The legislature of the United States shall pass no law on the subject of religion. . . ." See Leo Pfeffer, *Church, State, and Freedom* (Boston, 1953), pp. 110, 145; Anson Phelps Stokes, *Church and State in the United States* (New York, 1950), I, 526–527. Pinckney's proposal appears in Madison's *Notes* as part of a comprehensive plan of Union submitted to the Convention by Pinckney. Jonathan Elliot, ed., *The Debates in the Several State Conventions on the Adoption of the Federal Constitution . . . In Five Volumes* (Philadelphia, 1941), v, 131. However, the Pinckney plan has been revealed to be spurious. Neither it nor the proposal banning laws on religion was ever presented to the Convention; in 1818 or later a copy of the Pinckney plan was added by Madison to his original *Notes*, which were not published until 1840. Charles Warren, *The Making of the Constitution* (Boston, 1928), pp. 142–143. Pfeffer's book, mentioned above, is particularly recommended to

readers as the most authoritative constitutional history of America's experience with the double-faceted principle of religious liberty and separation of government and religion.

[8] Elliot, *Debates*, v, 446.

[9] *Ibid.*, v, 498.

[10] *Ibid.*

[11] Stokes, I, 527. See also Pfeffer, p. 110.

[12] See letter of Madison to Edmund Randolph, April 10, 1788, quoted in Stokes, I, 524.

[13] Elliot is in error on this point; see Charles C. Tansill, ed., *Documents Illustrative of the Formation of the Union of the American States* (Washington, 1927), p. 716.

[14] For example: Elliot, *Debates*, III, 203–204, 450, 600 (Randolph and Nicholas in Virginia); IV, 149 (Iredell in North Carolina); IV, 315–316 (C. C. Pinckney in South Carolina); and II, 78 (Varnum in Massachusetts). For the very influential statements by Wilson of Pennsylvania, see *ibid.*, II, 436 and 453; also John Bach McMaster and Frederick D. Stone, eds., *Pennsylvania and the Federal Constitution, 1787–1788* (Lancaster, Pa., 1888), pp. 313–314. See also McKean in *ibid.*, p. 377; Ellsworth in Paul L. Ford, ed., *Essays on the Constitution of the United States* (Brooklyn, 1892), pp. 163–164; Williamson, "Remarks," *ibid.*, p. 398 (N. C.); and Hanson, "Remarks on the Proposed Plan," in P. L. Ford, ed., *Pamphlets on the Constitution of the United States* (Brooklyn, 1888), pp. 241–242 (Md.).

[15] *The Federalist*, any edition, #84.

[16] The whole concept of a federal system of distributed powers, with the national government possessing only limited, delegated powers, forms the principal evidence. In addition consider the following specific comments which are illustrative rather than exhaustive. Wilson of Pennsylvania in response to the allegation that there was no security for the rights of conscience: "I ask the honorable gentlemen, what part of this system puts it in the power of Congress to attack those rights? When there is no power to attack, it is idle to prepare the means of defense." Elliot, II, 455. Randolph of Virginia asserted that "no power is given expressly to Congress over religion," and added that only powers "constitutionally given" could be exercised, in Elliot, III, 204, and see also *ibid.*, 469. Madison of Virginia: "There is not a shadow of right in the general government to intermeddle with religion." Elliot, III, 330. Iredell of North Carolina: "If any future Congress should pass an act concerning the religion of the country, it would be an act which they are not authorized to pass, by the Constitution, and which the people would not obey." Elliot, IV, 194. Spaight of North Carolina: "As to the subject of religion . . . No power is given to the general government to interfere with it at all. Any act of Congress on this subject would be a usurpation." Elliot, IV, 208.

[17] Massachusetts, New Hampshire, Virginia, New York, North Carolina, and Rhode Island.

[18] See Elliot, *Debates*, II, 112, 114 (Gore and Davis in Massachusetts); III, 468 (Randolph in Virginia); IV, 145, 150 (Iredell and Johnston in North Carolina); also Wilson of Pennsylvania in McMaster and Stone, eds., *Pennsylvania and the Constitution*, pp. 309, 353, 406. On the variety of early state procedures concerning the rights of accused persons, see generally Charles Fairman, "The Supreme Court and Constitutional Limitations on State Government Authority," *University of Chicago Law Review*, XXI (Autumn 1953), 40–78 passim. Charles Warren points out that in civil cases, the citizens of four states had been deprived of jury trial in the seven-year period before the Constitution

was framed, in *Congress, the Constitution and the Supreme Court* (Boston, 1925), p. 81.

[19] For example, only seven of the thirteen states had separate Bills of Rights in their constitutions; several states maintained establishments of religion which were prohibited by others; six states did not constitutionally provide for the right to the writ of habeas corpus. See generally Francis Newton Thorpe, *The Constitutional History of the United States* (Chicago, 1901), II, 199–211, for a table on state precedents for the federal Bill of Rights.

[20] For example, Massachusetts recommended the right to indictment by grand jury but did not provide for it in its own constitution; Virginia and North Carolina recommended constitutional protection for freedom of speech which they did not protect in their respective constitutions; and New York recommended protections against compulsory self-incrimination and double jeopardy, neither of which were constitutionally protected by New York.

[21] Elliot, *Debates*, reports in detail the debates of five states (Massachusetts, New York, Virginia, North Carolina, and South Carolina) and in very fragmentary fashion the debates of three others (Maryland, Pennsylvania, and Connecticut). McMaster and Stone (see note 14 above) collected the extant Pennsylvania debates together with pamphlets and essays from that state, while P. L. Ford collected important essays and pamphlets from all the states (see note 14 above).

[22] Elliot, *Debates*, II, 202.

[23] Ford, ed., *Essays*, p. 168.

[24] McMaster and Stone, pp. 421, 424, 461, 480.

[25] Ford, ed., *Pamphlets*, p. 146.

[26] McMaster and Stone, p. 502.

[27] *Ibid.*, p. 589. "Centinel" was either Samuel or George Bryan.

[28] Tansill, ed., pp. 1018–1020.

[29] *Ibid.*, pp. 1021–1022.

[30] Elliot, *Debates*, II, 553.

[31] Philip A. Crowl, *Maryland During and After the Revolution* (Baltimore, 1943), p. 156; Albert W. Werline, *Problems of Church and State in Maryland* (South Lancaster, Mass., 1948), pp. 143–168.

[32] *Ibid.*, chap. 6, passim.

[33] Tansill, ed., pp. 1022–1024.

[34] *Ibid.*, p. 1026.

[35] Elliot, *Debates*, III, 204.

[36] *Ibid.*, III, 330. See also the similar statement by Zachariah Johnson at III, 645–646.

[37] *Ibid.*, III, 593.

[38] *Ibid.*, III, 659 and Tansill, p. 1031.

[39] Elliot, *Debates*, II, 399.

[40] *Ibid.*, II, 410–412.

[41] Tansill, p. 1035.

[42] *Ibid.*, p. 1047 and Elliot, *Debates*, IV, 244.

[43] Elliot, *Debates*, IV, 191–192.

[44] *Ibid.*, p. 194.

[45] *Ibid.*, pp. 198–199.

[46] *Ibid.*, p. 199.

[47] *Ibid.*, p. 200.

[48] *Ibid.*, p. 203.

[49] *Ibid.*, p. 208.

[50] Tansill, p. 1053.

51 *The Debates and Proceedings in the Congress of the United States.* Compiled from Authentic Materials, by Joseph Gales (Washington, 1834), I, 448–459. This source, commonly known by its bookbinder's title as the *Annals of Congress,* will hereafter be cited as *Annals.*

52 *Annals,* I, 451.

53 *Ibid.,* I, 452.

54 In addition to Madison the committee included three other signers of the Constitution: Abraham Baldwin of Georgia, Roger Sherman of Connecticut, and George Clymer of Pennsylvania. Also on the committee were Aedanus Burke of South Carolina, the only anti-Federalist, and Nicholas Gilman of New Hampshire, Egbert Benson of New York, Benjamin Goodhue of Massachusetts, Elias Boudinot of New Jersey and John Vining of Delaware, who was chairman. *Annals,* I, 691.

55 *Annals,* I, 757.

56 See Appendix.

57 *Annals,* I, 757–759.

58 *Everson* v. *Board of Education,* 330 U.S. 1, at note 34.

59 Under Connecticut's Toleration Act of 1784, a non-Congregationalist who wished to be exempt from the tax for the support of the town Congregational Church was permitted to pay his tax to the church which he regularly attended upon obtaining a certificate proving that he "*contributes* his share and proportion to supporting the public worship and ministry thereof. . . ." See M. Louise Greene, *The Development of Religious Liberty in Connecticut* (Boston, 1905), p. 372. The use of "contribution" as a euphemism or synonym of tax appeared in other states as well. In Virginia, for example, the resolution of the state legislature designed to carry out a motion for a general assessment for religion provided: "That the people . . . ought to pay a moderate tax or *contribution* annually, for the support of the Christian religion. . . ." Quoted in Stokes, I, 389.

60 *Annals,* I, 796.

61 *Journal of the First Session of the Senate of the United States* (Washington, 1820), p. 70.

62 *Ibid.,* p. 77. It is interesting, however, to note that a Baptist memorial of 1774 used similar language: ". . . the magistrate's power extends not to the establishing any articles of faith or forms of worship, by force of laws." Yet the Baptists were advocates of extreme separation of government and religion, and they opposed nondiscriminatory government aid to all sects—proving once again how infuriatingly ambiguous language can be. For the Baptist statement, see Pfeffer, p. 91. For Baptist views, see Stokes, I, 306–310, 353–357, and 368–375.

63 *Journal of the Senate,* p. 86.

64 *Ibid.,* p. 87.

65 *Ibid.,* p. 88.

66 *Annals,* I, 454.

67 Madison to Jefferson, October 17, 1788, in *The Writings of James Madison,* Gaillard Hunt, ed. (New York, 1910), V, 271.

68 David M. Matteson, "The Organization of the Government under the Constitution," in Sol Bloom, Director General, *History of the Formation of the Union Under the Constitution* (Washington, 1943), pp. 317–319.

69 *Ibid.,* pp. 325–328.

70 *Journal of the Senate of the Commonwealth of Virginia; Begun and Held in the City of Richmond, on Monday, the 18th Day of October, . . . 1789* (Richmond, 1828) [Binder's title, *Journal of the Senate, 1785 to 1790*], p. 62.

Quoted by John Courtney Murray, "Law or Prepossessions," *Law and Contemporary Problems*, XIV (Winter 1949), 43, and quoted by Corwin, "Supreme Court as National School Board," *ibid.*, p. 12. The statement by the eight Virginia senators was revived and quoted by an advocate of the narrow interpretation of the establishment-of-religion clause, in "Brief for Appellees," pp. 51–54, filed in the case of *McCollum* v. *Board of Education*, 333 U.S. 203 (1948). Both Murray and Corwin quoted the brief, rather than the *Journal of the Senate*, and drew their conclusions on this matter from the brief alone, without investigating the context of the statement by the eight senators.

[71] E. Randolph to Washington, December 6, 1789, quoted by Matteson, p. 321.

[72] *Ibid.*

[73] Hardin Burnley to Madison, December 5, 1789, quoted by Irving Brant, *James Madison, Father of the Constitution* (Indianapolis, 1950) p. 286.

[74] Matteson, pp. 321–322; Madison to Washington, November 20, 1789, quoted in Brant, *Madison, Father of the Constitution*, p. 287.

[75] Brant, *Madison, Father of the Constitution*, p. 287.

[76] *Ibid.*, pp. 286–287 and 491, note 16, for the voting records.

[77] O'Neill, *Religion and Education Under the Constitution*, p. 204.

[78] When New Jersey became a royal province in 1702 the Crown and the Royal Governor assumed half-heartedly that the Church of England had been established, though there was not at the time a single Episcopalian Church in the colony. ". . . the establishment was simply taken for granted without any law or decree on which to base it. The colonial legislature had never enacted such a law, nor did it afterward supply the deficiency . . . . in point of fact the Church of England never was established in New Jersey by either Crown or legislature." Sanford Cobb, *The Rise of Religious Liberty in America* (New York, 1902), p. 408. No tax was ever levied for the support of religion in New Jersey.

[79] Quoted in Cobb, p. 326. Cobb's excellent account of church-state relations in colonial New York is on pp. 301–361. The account here is based on it.

[80] *Ibid.*, p. 327.

[81] Quoted in Cobb, pp. 333–334.

[82] *Ibid.*, p. 338.

[83] *Ibid.*, p. 340.

[84] *Ibid.*, p. 339.

[85] *Ibid.*, pp. 345–348.

[86] "Remarks on the Quebec Bill," *Works of Alexander Hamilton*, J. C. Hamilton, ed., II, 131, quoted in Stokes, I, 510.

[87] Jacob C. Meyer, *Church and State in Massachusetts . . . to 1833* (Cleveland, 1930) p. 10.

[88] *Ibid.*, pp. 13–14.

[89] *Ibid.*, pp. 14, 16–17, 71–72.

[90] Greene, pp. 200–201; Cobb, pp. 269–270.

[91] Cobb, p. 298. See also his statements pp. 234–235 and 270. See also Meyer, pp. 14–15. Cf. Greene, pp. 216–218.

[92] Meyer, p. 15.

[93] Charles B. Kinney, *Church and State: The Struggle for Separation in New Hampshire, 1630–1900* (New York, 1955), pp. 58–62, 72–82.

[94] Francis N. Thorpe, *The Federal and State Constitutions, Colonial Charters, and Other Organic Laws of the States . . .* (Washington, 1909), V, 2597.

[95] *Ibid.*, V, 3082.

[96] *Ibid.*, I, 567.

[97] *Ibid.*, I, 570.
[98] *Ibid.*, V, 2636. Italics added.
[99] *Ibid.*, III, 1890–1891.
[100] See Meyer for details, beginning with chap. 4.
[101] Thorpe, IV, 2454. See Kinney, pp. 83–108.
[102] See Kinney, cited in note 93 above, and Greene, cited in note 59, above.
[103] Thorpe, III, 1689.
[104] Allan Nevins, *The American States During and After the Revolution* (New York, 1927), p. 431; Werline, cited in note 31 above, pp. 169–186.
[105] Thorpe, III, 1705.
[106] *Ibid.*, II, 784.
[107] Reba C. Strickland, *Religion and the State in Georgia in the Eighteenth Century* (New York, 1939), p. 164, also 166.
[108] Thorpe, II, 789.
[109] *Ibid.*, II, 801.
[110] *Ibid.*, VI, 3253–3257.
[111] Stokes, I, 434.
[112] Thorpe, VI, 3264.
[113] *Ibid.*, V, 2793.
[114] Stokes, I, 393. Jefferson in 1776 had written a draft of a constitution for Virginia which included a similar provision: ". . . nor shall any be compelled to frequent or maintain any religious institution."
[115] Hamilton J. Eckenrode, *The Separation of Church and State in Virginia* (Richmond, 1910), pp. 58–61.
[116] *Ibid.*, p. 86.
[117] *Writings*, Hunt, ed., II, 88. See Brant, *James Madison, the Nationalist* (Indianapolis, 1948), pp. 344–345.
[118] In 1785, the same year the general assessment bill was debated in Virginia, both Maryland and Georgia, as noted in the text above, also considered general assessment bills; little is known about their history.
[119] Stokes, I, 799–800.
[120] *Ibid.*, p. 390; Brant, *The Nationalist*, p. 345.
[121] Murray, "Law and Prepossessions," L. & C.P., p. 28, quoting J. Rutledge, in *Everson* case, 330 U.S. 1, 39–40 (1947).
[122] Murray, p. 29. Italics added.
[123] *Writings*, Hunt, ed., II, 145, letter to Monroe, May 29, 1785, and see Brant, *Nationalist*, p. 353.
[124] Quoted in Brant, *Father of Constitution*, p. 272.
[125] James D. Richardson, ed., *A Compilation of the Messages and Papers of the Presidents* (Washington, 1896–), I, 490. Message of February 28, 1811.
[126] *Ibid.*, I, 489.
[127] Letter to Livingston, July 10, 1822, in *Writings*, IX, 100.
[128] Elizabeth Fleet, ed., "Madison's 'Detached Memoranda,'" *William and Mary Quarterly*, III (1946), 554.
[129] *Ibid.*, pp. 558–559.
[130] *Ibid.*, pp. 559–560.
[131] *Ibid.*, p. 560.
[132] *Ibid.*
[133] *Writings*, IX, 100–103.
[134] "Detached Memoranda" (cited in note 128 above), p. 555.
[135] Quoted in Stokes, I, 335; available in any edition of Jefferson's writings.
[136] O'Neill, p. 81.
[137] Quoted in Stokes, I, 393.

[138] O'Neill, pp. 83, 81–82.

[139] Corwin, "The Supreme Court as National School Board," *Law and Contemporary Problems*, XIV (Winter 1949), 14.

[140] *Works of Thomas Jefferson*, P. L. Ford, ed. (New York, 1904), IX, 346–347.

[141] See Stokes, I, 490–491 and 335–336.

[142] Richardson, ed., *Messages of Presidents*, II, 489–490.

[143] O'Neill, pp. 76–77, 205–206.

[144] Harvard Studies in Education (Cambridge, Mass., 1931).

[145] *Ibid.*, pp. 10–11 and Appendix A, pp. 199–205.

[146] *Notes on the State of Virginia*, William Peden, ed. (Chapel Hill, 1955), 147.

[147] Honeywell, pp. 233–235.

[148] *Ibid.*, pp. 54–55 and Appendix A, pp. 205–209.

[149] *Ibid.*, pp. 55–56, quoting letter to J. C. Cabell, February 22, 1821.

[150] *Notes on the State of Virginia*, p. 151.

[151] Honeywell, pp. 15–16, 39–42, and Appendix E, Letter to Peter Carr, September 7, 1814, pp. 222–227.

[152] *Ibid.*, p. 125.

[153] *Ibid.*, pp. 252–253.

[154] *Ibid.*, Appendix J, p. 256.

[155] *Ibid.*, p. 249.

[156] *Ibid.*, p. 125; and R. Freeman Butts, *The American Tradition in Religion and Education* (Boston, 1950), p. 126.

[157] Quoted in Butts, pp. 124–125. Italics added.

[158] *Ibid.*, p. 126.

[159] *Ibid.*, pp. 127–129, quoting letter to A. S. Brockenborough, April 21, 1825, citing Jefferson Papers (MSS), Library of Congress, vol. 229, folio 40962. Italics added.

[160] *Ibid.*, p. 130.

[161] *Ibid.*

[162] Edgar S. Maclay, ed., *Journal of William Maclay* (New York, 1890).

[163] Printed by Thomas Greenleaf (New York, 1789).

[164] *A National Program for the Publication of Historical Documents*. A Report to the President by the National Historical Publications Commission (Washington, 1954), p. 92.

[165] "Compiled from Authentic Materials," by Joseph Gales (Washington, 1834).

[166] *A National Program* (see note 164 above), p. 93.

[167] *Ibid.*, p. 93.

[168] David M. Matteson, "The Organization of the Government under the Constitution," in Sol Bloom, Director General, *History of the Formation of the Union Under the Constitution* (Washington: United States Constitution Sesquicentennial Commission, 1943), p. 316.

[169] *Ibid.*, pp. 317–328; Rodney L. Mott, *Due Process of Law* (Indianapolis, 1926), pp. 152–153.

[170] *A National Program*, p. vii.

SCHOOL PRAYERS
AND THE
FOUNDING FATHERS

WHAT was the original intention of the First Amendment's injunction against laws "respecting an establishment of religion"? That question is being asked once again in the wake of the U.S. Supreme Court decision against the nonsectarian prayer prescribed by the New York State Board of Regents for daily recitation in the schools. The hostile reaction to the decision reveals how little the establishment clause is understood, how welcome to certain groups are the many breaches in the "wall of separation" between religion and government. These breaches are the more easily justified if the Court, as its critics insist, has really misread, indeed perverted, the intentions of the framers of the First Amendment. But the critics are wrong, their history faulty.

No one, of course, would really permit his judgment of a contemporary church-state issue to be determined by an antiquarian examination of the original meaning of the clause against establishments of religion. There is, to be sure, a comforting assurance in having the authority of the past coincide with present legislative preferences, and it is an old American custom to invoke the names of the framers to buttress an argument. However, it is also an old American custom to dismiss the framers when it becomes clear that they cannot be conscripted into service. After all, one can always argue that what passed for wisdom in their era may very well by now have passed out of date. Even so, few would openly reject the principles on which the Constitution was based.

The principle that government and religion be kept separate is not directly, at least not yet, under attack by the critics of the Court's recent decision. Their tactic is to argue that the purpose of separation was merely to prevent government *preference* of one religious group over another, so as to insure religious liberty for all.

The stakes in the current controversy are large: the question of federal and state aid (as well as tax-supported bus rides) to sectarian schools accounts for much of the Catholics' bitterness against the Court. The school-prayer decision was quickly condemned, for example, by the national Catholic weekly *America*, as a "stupid decision . . . a decision that spits in the face of our history." And William Buckley, Jr., prominent Catholic layman and the editor of the *National Review*, states in his nationally syndicated column, "The First Amendment to the Constitution was not designed to secularize American life, merely to guard against an institutionalized pre-eminence of a single religion over others on a national scale."

The implied outlawing of Bible-reading, Christmas plays, and religious songs in the public schools, public crèches, and released-time programs, has also united many Protestant spokesmen in similar criticism of the decision, despite their usually outspoken declarations in favor of separation of church and state and against public aid to sectarian schools. Thus, Reinhold Niebuhr, the distinguished Protestant theologian and political liberal, protested that the Court did not follow "what the First Amendment intended." California's Bishop James A. Pike has used even stronger language, charging that the Court's decision "has just deconsecrated the nation." He urged that the decision be overridden by a constitutional amendment which would insert in place of "establishment of religion" in the First Amendment, the phrase ". . . the establishment of any denomination, sect, or other organized religious association. . . ." The First Amendment, according to Pike, "merely meant to prevent the establishment of a particular religion or the suppression of a particular religion."

This narrow view of the meaning of the establishment clause has also been supported by one of our leading constitutional scholars, Professor Edward S. Corwin, who concluded a sketchy survey of the historical sources by affirming that the Court's interpretation of the First Amendment as making government aid to religion in general unconstitutional is "untrue historically." "In a word," Professor Corwin added, "what the 'establishment of religion' clause of the First Amendment does, and all that it does, is to forbid Congress to give any religious faith, sect, or denomination preferred status. . . . The historical record shows beyond peradventure that the core idea of 'an establishment of religion' comprises the idea of preference; and that any act of public authority favorable to religion in general cannot, without manifest falsification of history, be brought under the ban of that phrase." Justice Potter Stewart, the only dissenter in the school-prayer case, indicated his agreement with this interpretation when he pointed out that the Court was not confronted by "the establishment of a state church" or an "official religion."

In defense of the Court, and out of respect for history, the errone-ous nature of the narrow interpretation of the establishment clause should be exposed. According to that interpretation—as we have seen from the above quotations—the wall of separation was not meant to enjoin the government from fostering religion generally or from helping all such religious groups as are willing to accept government support or aid, whether in the form of tax benefits, promotional activities, or direct subsidy. Now, it is true that the framers did not speak loudly, clearly, and in a single voice on behalf of the broad interpretation adopted by the Court in the school-prayer case. But the preponderance of the evidence certainly supports the broad inter-pretation as historically more accurate.

Justice Black, the Court's spokesman in the school-prayer case, advanced the broad interpretation in its most authoritative form in the school-bus case of 1947. He then declared:

The "establishment of religion" clause of the First Amendment means at least this: Neither a state nor the Federal government can set up a church. Neither can pass laws which aid one religion, aid all religions, or prefer one religion over another. Neither can force nor influence a person to go to or to remain away from church against his will or force him to profess a belief or disbelief in any religion. No person can be punished for enter-taining or professing religious beliefs or disbeliefs, for church attendance or non-attendance. No tax in any amount, large or small, can be levied to support any religious activities or institutions, whatever they may be called, or whatever form they may adopt to teach or practice religion. Neither a state nor the Federal government can, openly or secretly, par-ticipate in the affairs of any religious organizations or groups and vice versa. In the words of Jefferson, the clause against establishment of reli-gion by law was intended to erect "a wall of separation between Church and State."

The dissenting justices in the school-bus case, while disagreeing with the majority on the question of whether the "wall of separa-tion" had in fact been breached by the practice at issue, nevertheless concurred with the majority view of the intentions of the framers. Justice Rutledge's opinion, which was endorsed by all the dissenting justices, declared: "The Amendment's pupose was not to strike merely at the official establishment of a single sect, creed or religion, outlawing only a formal relation such as had prevailed in England and some of the colonies. Necessarily it was to uproot all such rela-tionships. But the object was broader than separating church and state in this narrow sense. It was to create a complete and permanent separation of the spheres of religious activity and civil authority by comprehensively forbidding every form of public aid or support for religion." In other words, according to the broad interpretation,

227

even government aid that is impartially and equitably administered to all religious groups is barred by the First Amendment.

The debate in the First Congress, which drafted the Bill of Rights, provides support neither for the broad nor the narrow interpretation. Yet the drafting history of the clause, in contrast to the debate, is revealing. In the House, the prohibitory phrase was aimed against laws "establishing religion." In the Senate, three motions, each of which clearly expressed a narrow intent, were introduced and defeated. All were explicitly directed against laws preferring one religious "sect" or "denomination" above others. Although their defeat would seem to show that the Senate intended something broader than merely a ban on preference to one sect, it finally did adopt a narrow prohibition: "Congress shall make no law establishing articles of faith or a mode of worship. . . ." But the Senate's wording provoked the House to clarify its intent; for the House rejected the Senate's article on religion. To resolve the disagreement between the two branches, the House proposed a joint conference committee. The six-man committee—four of whom had been influential members of the constitutional convention—included James Madison as chairman of the House conferees, and Oliver Ellsworth (later Chief Justice) as chairman of the Senate conferees. The House members flatly refused to accept the Senate's version of the amendment on religion, indicating that the House would not be satisfied with merely a ban against the preference of one sect or religion over others. The Senate conferees then abandoned the Senate version, and the amendment was redrafted to give it the phraseology which has come down to us: "Congress shall make no law respecting an establishment of religion, or prohibiting the free exercise thereof. . . ."

The one fact which stands out from this review of the drafting of the amendment is that Congress very carefully considered and rejected the phraseology which spells out the narrow interpretation. At bottom the amendment was an expression of the intention of the framers of the Constitution to prevent Congress from acting in the field of religion. The "great object" of the Bill of Rights, as Madison explicitly said when introducing his draft of amendments to the House, was to "limit and qualify the powers of Government" for the purpose of making certain that none of the powers granted could be exercised in forbidden fields. And one such forbidden field was religion.

The history of the drafting of the no-establishment clause does not provide a clear understanding of what was meant by the phrase "an establishment of religion." To argue, however, as proponents of the narrow interpretation do, that the amendment permits government aid and support to religion in general or to all churches without discrimination, leads to the impossible conclusion that the First Amendment *added* to Congress's powers. There is nothing to support this notion. Every bit of evidence we have goes to prove that the First Amendment, like the others, was intended to *restrict* Congress to its enumerated powers. Since Congress was given no power by the Constitutional Convention to legislate on matters concerning religion, and therefore could not support all religious groups non-preferentially, Congress would have had no such power even in the absence of the First Amendment. It is therefore unreasonable to suppose that an express prohibition of power—"Congress shall make no law respecting an establishment of religion"—vests or creates the power, previously nonexistent, of supporting religion by aid to one or all religious groups. The Bill of Rights, as Madison said, was not framed "to imply powers not meant to be included in the enumeration."

Madison and his colleagues were not merely logicians or hair-splitting lawyers. Nor were they abstract theoreticians. If they did not carefully define what they meant by an establishment of religion, the reason is simply that they knew from common experience what they were talking about. At the time of the framing of the First Amendment, six states maintained or authorized establishments of religion. By that amendment, Congress was denied the power to do what those states were doing—and since the adoption of the Fourteenth Amendment, the states have been included in the ban. "An establishment of religion" meant to the framers what it meant in those states. Thus, reference to the American *experience* with establishments of religion at the time of the framing of the Bill of Rights is essential for any understanding of what the framers intended.

The American experience was in many respects unique, for it did not always follow the pattern of European precedents. Persons unaware of this fact have arbitrarily assigned to the phrase, "an establishment of religion," its European meaning only. James M. O'Neill, for example, whose *Religion and Education under the Constitution* presents the best argument on behalf of the narrow interpretation of the establishment clause, ignored the American establishments and therefore concluded, in capital letters, that "an establishment of religion" has always and everywhere meant what he found it meant in Europe and in the *Encyclopaedia Britannica:* " 'A SINGLE CHURCH OR RELIGION ENJOYING FORMAL, LEGAL, OFFICIAL, MONOPOLISTIC PRIVILEGE THROUGH A UNION WITH THE GOVERNMENT OF THE STATE. . . .' The phrase has been used this way for centuries in speaking of the established Protestant churches of England, Scotland, Germany, and other countries, and of the established Catholic Church in Italy, Spain, and elsewhere. There is not an item of dependable evidence . . . which shows that the term means, or ever has meant, anything else."

The encyclopedia and the European precedents notwithstanding, there is abundant evidence that the European form of an establishment was not the American form, and that the European meaning of establishment was not the American meaning. The American Revolution triggered a pent-up movement for the separation of church and state. Four states had never experienced establishments of religion. Of the remaining states, three completely abolished their establishments during the Revolution, and the other six—Massachusetts, New Hampshire, Connecticut, Maryland, South Carolina, and Georgia—converted to comprehensive or multiple establishments. Significantly, *every one of the six states explicitly provided that no sect or denomination should be subordinated to any other;* all denominations enjoyed equal status before the law on a wholly nonpreferential basis. It is true that in no state was there an establishment which took in every religion without exception. Neither Judaism, Buddhism, Mohammedanism, nor any religion but a Christian one was ever established in America. In half of the six multiple establishments existing in 1789, Christianity was the established religion; Protestantism was specified in the other half.

In each of the six states where plural establishments existed, they included the churches of *every* denomination and sect with a sufficient number of adherents to form a church. There were probably a few isolated towns or counties in each of the states where the letter of the law was not followed, particularly where a congregation of some sect like the Quakers conscientiously opposed compulsory tax support even of their own church; but such cases were comparatively rare. In general, where Protestantism was established, it was synonymous with religion; there were either no Jews or Catholics, or too few of them to make a difference; and where Christianity was established, as in Maryland which had many Catholics, Jews were scarcely known. It would be a misleading half-truth, therefore, to argue that exclusive establishments of one religion existed in each of the six states; it would miss the novel equalitarianism of the American establishments.

The provisions of these six states show beyond doubt that to understand the American meaning of "an establishment of religion" one cannot arbitrarily adopt a definition based on European experience. In every European precedent of an establishment, the religion established was that of a single church. It never happened in any European nation that many different churches, or the religion held in common by all of them—i.e., Christianity or Protestantism—were simultaneously established. Establishments in America, on the other hand, both in the colonial and early state periods, were not limited in nature or in meaning to state support of one church. An establishment of religion in America at the time of the framing of the Bill of Rights meant government recognition, aid, or sponsorship of religion, principally through impartial or nonpreferential tax support to the churches. The framers of the First Amendment understood "an establishment of religion" to mean what their experience showed them it meant.

Madison, for example, who is known justifiably as the "father of the Constitution and of the Bill of Rights," explicitly characterized as an establishment of religion Virginia's proposed "General Assessment Bill" of 1784, which would have underwritten all the existing churches by the taxes of their adherents. He opposed the bill in principle, not because it did not also provide for the establishment of religious groups that did not then exist in Virginia. Madison's constitutional scruples were so refined on the question of establishments of religion that he regarded as unconstitutional such legal recognition of financial aids as Presidential proclamations of Thanksgiving, tax exemptions for religious societies, chaplains for Congress and the armed services if paid from government funds, incorporation of churches by the federal government in the District of Columbia, and nonpreferential land grants for the support of religion generally. Jefferson shared the same views. As rector of the University of Virginia, a state-supported institution, he refused to permit Sunday religious services to be performed on university property. And it is not without current interest that, as President, Jefferson refused even to designate or recommend a day of thanksgiving or prayer, on the theory that even so innocuous and interdenominational an act violated the establishment clause.

These early Presidents were deeply religious men, but they opposed any government aid, however beneficent and equitable, to religion. They reasoned that religion should remain a voluntary and private matter, the exclusive concern of the individual and his Creator. Any "alliance or coalition between Government and Religion," advised the aged Madison, "cannot be too carefully guarded against." He argued for a *"perfect separation,"* believing that "religion and Government will exist in greater purity, without than with the aid of Government."

Thus the legislative evolution of the establishment clause, the experience with establishments at the time of its drafting, and the

231

opinions of Madison and Jefferson (as well as of other framers) demonstrate the validity of the Supreme Court's interpretation of the original intention of the framers.

The policy of the First Amendment embodies the wisdom gathered from American colonial and European experience. Since that policy, like a vaccine, is preventive in character, and since that wisdom is subtle, the majority, who benefit from it most, often fail to credit the source of their good fortune. Impatiently they dismiss the ancient warnings that the time to take alarm is at the first experiment with their liberties. In the school-prayer case, the Court was quite sensitive to the dangers of such experimentation, but this has unfortunately not always been true of its decisions. From the time that it enunciated the broad interpretation in the school-bus case and yet found no constitutional breach in the wall—provoking Justice Jackson to note that the majority opinion reminded him of Byron's Julia who "whispering, 'I will ne'er consent,'—consented"—the Court has been extremely inconsistent, even erratic, in its interpretation of the establishment clause.

The public, which has little patience with legal distinctions, has a right to be appalled at the contradictory results of the Court's various decisions on the establishment clause: New York's released-time program of religious education for public school children, New Jersey's subsidized bus-rides for parochial school children, and Massachusetts' Sunday closing or blue laws are not, the Court has ruled, violations of the establishment clause. Yet New York's brief, nondenominational school prayer—"Almighty God, we acknowledge our dependence upon Thee, and we beg Thy blessings upon us, our parents, our teachers, and our country"—the Court has declared unconstitutional. That Justice Black, the author of the school-bus decision (constitutional) is also the author of the school-prayer decision (unconstitutional) only adds to the public's confusion.

Even more confusing is Justice Douglas' record. In his opinion for the Court in the released-time case, he spoke of America as a religious nation "whose institutions presuppose a Supreme Being," called approving attention to the many trivial breaches in the wall of separation and remarked, with seeming sarcasm, that a "fastidious atheist or agnostic could even object to the supplication with which the Court opens each session: "God save the United States and this Honorable Court." Now, in his well-publicized concurring opinion in the school-prayer case, Justice Douglas clearly indicates his belief that that supplication, like the New York Board of Regents prayer, is unconstitutional.

The Court has reaped the scorn of a confused and aroused public because it has been inconsistent; moreover, its past compromises failed to prepare the public for a principled decision. The school-prayer decision, however impolitic, is sound, constitutionally and historically, and has the effect of reinforcing the framers' original injunction against any form of an establishment of religion. One may hope that the Court, having now decided rightly, will shun a policy of appeasement, and that this decision will serve not merely as another incident in a history of vacillation, but as a strong reconnection with the principles and intentions of the framers.

PART III

And Other Civil Rights

"EXOTIC FRUIT":
THE RIGHT AGAINST
COMPULSORY SELF-
INCRIMINATION IN
COLONIAL NEW YORK

with Lawrence H. Leder

T
HE Bill of Rights epitomizes one of our history's most noble
and enduringly important themes, the triumph of individual liberty,
yet has been strangely one of the most neglected subjects. Although
constitutional guarantees of personal liberty go to the heart of American political philosophy, there is no satisfactory study of the origins
and framing of the first state bills of rights and few studies of particular rights. The American origins of the right against compulsory
self-incrimination are especially shrouded in obscurity.

That fact is all the more striking because the courts have assured
us, again and again, that our understanding in this instance is quite
dependent upon history. Chief Justice Warren, for example, noting
that the right against self-incrimination "was hard-earned by our
forefathers," stated that the "reasons for its inclusion in the Constitution—and the necessities for its preservation—are to be found
in the lessons of history." [1] However, the lessons of history have
hardly been made abundantly clear by historians, despite the reliance
of jurists upon them. Over half a century ago when the Supreme
Court, in *Twining* v. *New Jersey*, resorted to "every historical test
by which the meaning of the phrase [self-incrimination] can be
tried," the justices were forced to "pass by the meager records of the
early colonial time, so far as they have come to our attention, as
affording light too uncertain for guidance." [2] The question before
the court at that time was whether the right against compulsory self-
incrimination was "a fundamental principle of liberty and justice
which inheres in the very idea of free government" and therefore
must be included within the conception of due process of law. The

decision, which was adverse to the right, was founded upon "history." The court's historical analysis was shallow and inaccurate, although the blame lies more with historians than with the justices.[3]

In 1935, when R. Carter Pittman published a pioneering article on the American background of the right against compulsory self-incrimination, he observed that tangible causes could be singled out for the inclusion of the various provisions in the original bills of rights "with the exception of ,the privilege against self-incrimination."[4] Pittman's superficial survey, although highly suggestive, contained many inaccuracies and left many gaps. He did not even mention the right's history in New York, which was one of the four states proposing protection of the right in the federal Constitution. Neither historians nor judges understood why New York recommended such an amendment when it did not protect the right in its own constitution. New York's inconsistency remains a mystery.

That mystery is deepened by the confident assertion of eminent legal historians that the right was unknown in colonial New York. In 1944, Julius Goebel and T. Raymond Naughton published their mammoth and erudite *Law Enforcement in Colonial New York: A Study in Criminal Procedure (1664–1776)*. Based on an apparently exhaustive research in manuscript sources, the book has all the characteristics of a definitive study and an intimidating tone. The introduction bristles with caveats against the writing of legal history by "laymen"—historians without legal training who neither use nor understand the manuscript minute books, pleadings, briefs, and judgment rolls, tasks "for which the lawyer alone is trained." A "certain pedantic attachment to truth" forced the authors to "speak sharply regarding the well-intentioned efforts of amateurs in the law to re-create a part of culture that only the technician is equipped to handle."

Goebel and Naughton assert that "the existence before the Revolution of a privilege of defendants is an illusion. The fruit grown from the seed of the maxim *nemo tenetur prodere seipso* [no man is bound to accuse himself] was an exotic of Westminster Hall, and of it neither the local justices in England nor in New York had eaten, or if they had, they took good care to keep their knowledge to themselves." That the "privilege against self-incrimination did not develop" in New York, was the result of "a prevailing indifference" to the privilege even in England. There had been a "great to-do" in the mother country during the early seventeenth century over the ex officio oath in ecclesiastical procedure. There had also been protests by disgruntled subjects that the secular adoption of this proceeding involved a similar infraction of fundamental right. Yet, "nothing had come of the protest."

Goebel and Naughton are as misleading about the right in New

York as they are wrong about its existence in England. They belittle the history of the right in England and allege the "failure" of its advocates "to carry over notions about self-incrimination to temporal justice." At the same time they convincingly develop the thesis that the criminal law of colonial New York was an extremely sophisticated duplication of the "practices and forms of the English central courts." From the beginning of the eighteenth century, New York's criminal courts were peopled by men with excellent legal training who conducted their work as skillfully as their counterparts in England; since their "intellectual home . . . centered in the dingy streets about the Inns of Court, they read and cited what lawyers did at home." They prized English law books, "because it was from English precedent that provincial law was built." The standard of practice in the highest court of the colony became "really comparable" with that in King's Bench, while the inferior criminal jurisdiction was "administered in much the same way as . . . in English Quarter Sessions." [5]

If, therefore, the right against compulsory self-incrimination was entrenched and respected in England, its existence in New York should be expected, its absence astonishing. That England provided the model, places English history, English law books, and English criminal practice at the source of any understanding of the right in New York.

Maitland's epigram, that the "seamless web" of history is torn by telling a piece of it,[6] is borne out by any effort to explain the origins of the right against self-incrimination. The American origins may derive largely from the inherited English common-law system of criminal justice. But the English origins, so much more complex, spill over legal boundaries and reflect the many-sided religious, political, and constitutional issues which racked England during the sixteenth and seventeenth centuries: the struggles for supremacy between Anglicanism and Puritanism, between Parliament and King, between limited government and arbitrary rule, and between freedom of conscience and suppression of heresy and sedition. Even within the more immediate confines of law, the history of the right against self-incrimination is enmeshed in broad issues: the contests for supremacy between the accusatory and the inquisitional systems of procedure, the common law and the royal prerogative, and the common law and its canon- and civil-law rivals. Against this broad background the origins of the concept that "no man is bound to accuse himself" (*nemo tenetur seipsum prodere*) must be understood and its legal development traced.

The concept seems to have been the indirect product of the common law's accusatory system and of its opposition to rival legal systems which employed inquisitorial procedures. Toward the close of the sixteenth century, just before the concept first appeared in England on a sustained basis, all courts of criminal jurisdiction habitually sought to exact self-incriminatory admissions from persons suspected of or charged with crime. Although defendants in Crown cases suffered from this and many other harsh procedures, even in the common-law courts, the accusatory system afforded a degree of fair play not available under the inquisitional system. The double jury of the accusatory system was becoming a safeguard for the defendant. The grand jury or jury of accusation made a definite and formal charge against him that was judged by the trial jury of his peers. The confrontative, oral, and public character of the accusatory system benefited the defendant. The judge, although usually the Crown's hatchetman, at least in theory sat as an impartial arbiter between the prosecution and the defense, sworn to do justice under God and the law. Indeed, the rationale for refusing counsel to the accused was that none was needed when an English judge was present to protect his rights and give counsel when necessary. In practice the system around 1600 worked very strongly to the disadvantage of the accused, but it embodied if only in theory a great ideal of fair play and equality between parties in the determination of guilt or innocence, an ideal that in time would become meaningful. Moreover, torture was never sanctioned by the common law, although employed as an instrument of royal prerogative until 1641.[7]

By contrast, torture for the purpose of detecting crime and inducing confession was regularly authorized by the Roman codes of the canon and civil law. "Abandon hope, all ye who enter here" well describes the chances of an accused person under inquisitorial procedures characterized by presentment based on mere rumor or suspicion, indefiniteness of accusation, the oath ex officio, secrecy, lack of confrontation, coerced confessions, and magistrates acting as accusers and prosecutors as well as "judges." This system of procedure, by which heresy was most efficiently combatted, was introduced into England in the thirteenth century by ecclesiastical courts.[8]

The use of the oath ex officio by prerogative courts, particularly by the ecclesiastical Court of High Commission as reconstituted by Elizabeth and directed by Archbishop Whitgift, resulted in the defensive claim that "no man is bound to accuse himself." The High Commission, an instrument of the Crown for maintaining religious uniformity under the Anglican establishment, used the canon law *processus per inquisitionem*, but made the oath ex officio, rather than torture, the crux of its procedure. Men suspected of "heretical opinions," "seditious books," or "conspiracies," were summoned before the High Commission without being informed of the accusation against them or the identity of their accusers. Denied due process of law by common-law standards, suspects were required to take an oath to answer truthfully to interrogatories which sought to establish guilt for crimes neither charged nor disclosed.[9]

A nonconformist victim of the High Commission found himself thrust between hammer and anvil: refusal to take the oath, or having taken it, refusal to answer the interrogatories, meant a sentence for contempt and invited Star Chamber proceedings; to take the oath and respond truthfully to questioning often meant to convict oneself of religious or political crimes and, moreover, to supply evidence against nonconformist accomplices; to take the oath and then lie meant to sin against the Scriptures and risk conviction for perjury.

To the Puritan victims, salvation in this world as well as in the next seemed to hinge upon crippling the High Commission in the performance of its duties. Powerless to redefine the substantive law which made their activities criminal, the Puritans turned to legal obstructionism. They challenged the High Commission's jurisdiction and procedures, concentrating their attack on the oath ex officio whose use as a method of incriminatory examination made that court so effective. They convinced themselves that the oath was immoral and illegal, a vague contention at first supported by little more than Scriptural inferences. But common lawyers of the Puritan party, led by James Morice, Robert Beale, and Nicholas Fuller, originated the daring and novel argument that the oath, although sanctioned by the Crown, was unconstitutional because it violated Magna Carta, which limited even the royal prerogative.[10]

The argument had myth-making qualities for it was one of the earliest to exalt Magna Carta as the talismanic symbol and source of English constitutional liberty. As yet there was no contention that one need not answer incriminating questions after accusation by due process according to common law. But a later generation would use substantially the same argument—"that by the Statute of Magna Carta . . . for a man to accuse himself was and is utterlie inhibited" [11]—on behalf of the contention that one need not involuntarily answer incriminating questions even after he had been properly accused.

In Elizabeth's time royal opposition had accounted for Parliament's failure to convert Puritan grievances against the High Commission into a statute. Elizabeth's policy was continued by James I who, at the Hampton Court Conference, rejected the Puritan protest against the oath "whereby men are forced to accuse themselves." The Puritans persisted, therefore, in their litigious tactics, the only course left open to them. Fuller's case (1607) presented for the first time before a common-law court the argument that not even the royal prerogative could lawfully authorize a proceeding in conflict with

Magna Carta. Although the court avoided a decision on the oath ex officio, which originally precipitated the case, liberty of the subject and the idea of constitutional government were advanced against compulsory self-incrimination.[12]

Under Chief Justice Edward Coke the common-law courts, with the sympathy of Commons, vindicated the Puritan tactic of litigious opposition to the High Commission. The deep hostility between the canon- and common-law systems expressed itself in a series of writs of prohibition issued by Coke and his colleagues, staying the Commission's proceedings. Coke, adept at creating legal fictions which he clothed with the authority of resurrected "precedents" and inferences from Magna Carta, grounded a number of these prohibitions on the allegedly ancient common-law rule that no man is bound to accuse himself criminally.[13]

The dismissal of Coke, the appointment to the bench of more pliable supporters of the prerogative, the increasingly arbitrary rule of the Stuarts, and the rise of Archbishop William Laud resulted in a slackening by the common-law courts of their attack on the inquisitorial procedures of the ecclesiastical courts. In the 1630's the High Commission and the Star Chamber, which employed similar procedures, reached the zenith of their powers. But in 1637 the oath was refused and denounced by a flinty, principled, Puritan agitator, John Lilburne. His well-publicized, recalcitrant opposition to criminatory questioning focused England's attention upon the alleged injustice and illegality of such practices. In 1641 the Long Parliament, dominated by the Puritan party and common lawyers, condemned the sentences against Lilburne and others, abolished the Star Chamber and the High Commission, and prohibited ecclesiastical authorities from administering any oath obliging one "to confess or to accuse himself or herself of any crime."[14]

The new statutory right against compulsory self-incrimination applied before ecclesiastical courts only. Ironically the common-law courts continued to ask incriminating questions and to bully men into answering them. However, the rudimentary idea of a broad right against self-incrimination was lodged in the imperishable opinions of Coke, publicized by Lilburne and the Levellers, and firmly associated with Magna Carta. That the idea was beginning to take hold of men's minds is evident from the case of the Twelve Bishops in 1642. Impeached by the House of Commons on a charge of high treason, they were asked whether they had signed a document that constituted proof of their crime. The bishops, who as members of ecclesiastical tribunals had never honored a Puritan's plea that he be permitted to remain silent to an incriminating question, refused to answer because "neither were they bound to accuse themselves."[15] Their Puritan prosecutors did not press the question.

Lilburne was again the catalytic agent in the development of the right against self-incrimination. At his various trials for his life, in his testimony before investigating committees of Parliament, and in his ceaseless tracts, he dramatically popularized the demand, so vigorously championed by the Leveller party, that a right against self-incrimination be accorded general legal recognition. Lilburne, in fact, educated the courts, the government, and the public on the fundamentals of fair play in criminal procedures from arrest through trial. His career illuminates how the right against self-incrimination developed not only in conjunction with a whole gamut of fair procedures associated with "due process of law" but also with demands for freedom of conscience and expression.[16]

After Lilburne's time the right became entrenched in English jurisprudence, even under the judicial tyrants of the Restoration. For example, at the trial of one of the Regicides in 1660, the court asked the defendant whether he had voted in favor of the execution of the King, but instructed him, "You are not bound to answer me, but if you will not, we must prove it." In 1679, a defense witness in one of the trials for the "Popish Plot" was protected from answering the question whether he was a priest because his answer might "make him accuse himself." By the end of Charles II's reign, "there is no longer any doubt, in any court" about the general establishment of the right against self-incrimination. A generation later, as the state became more secure and fairer treatment of the criminally accused became possible, the old practice of bullying the prisoner for answers gradually died out.[17]

By the early eighteenth century the accused was no longer put on the stand at all: he could not give evidence in his own behalf even if he wished to, although he was permitted to tell his story, unsworn. It was felt unfair to expose him to cross-examination under oath or to the irresistible temptation to perjury. More important, his interest in the case made his testimony untrustworthy. Consequently the prisoner was regarded as incompetent to be a witness for himself.[18]

After the first quarter of the eighteenth century, the English history of the right centered primarily upon the preliminary examination of the suspect and the legality of placing in evidence various types of involuntary confessions. Incriminating statements made by suspects at the preliminary examination could be used against them at their trials; a confession, even though not made under oath, sufficed to convict. Yet suspects could not be interrogated under oath. One might be ensnared into a confession by the sharp and intimidating tactics of the examining magistrate; but there was no legal obligation to answer an incriminating question—nor, until 1848, to notify the prisoner of his right to refuse answer. That a suspect might unwittingly incriminate himself at his preliminary examination is not proof

243

that the right did not exist. He simply had no right to be warned that he need not answer, and his answers, given in ignorance of his right, might certainly be used with devastating effect against him. By the 1740's, however, the courts were willing to consider the exclusion of confessions that had been under duress. At no time in the history of Anglo-American jurisprudence has a voluntary confession been regarded as improper evidence or conflicting with the right against self-incrimination. The right has always existed as a protection against involuntary or compulsory self-incrimination by vesting an option to refuse answer. A confession extorted by threats or solicited by promises has, since the mid-eighteenth century, been viewed by the law more as unreliable evidence, and therefore excludable, than as an infringement of the right against self-incrimination.[19]

The existence of the right against self-incrimination in England was scarcely unnoticed by English law writers, a fact that would be taken for granted had not Goebel and Naughton circulated a contrary impression. They also stressed heavily the influence of English law books on the development of New York colonial law generally and the imitative character of criminal procedure in particular. "No one who has examined the memoranda and citations of any first-rate New York lawyer of the 1730's can doubt the general availability or spread of these sources or the competency to use them." For nearly everything done in the New York Supreme Court, precedent can be found in William Hawkins's *Pleas of the Crown*, while the New York City Sessions Court "treads as closely as it may the path of the superior court" and the local justices of the peace find some manual like Dalton or Nelson to be the magistrate's *vade mecum*. Since the "patterns of practice were cut after the designs of Hawkins, Hale and the *Crown Circuit Companion*," defiance of these tutelary geniuses was "exceptional." "The course of the typical criminal trial in New York during the eighteenth century," concluded Goebel and Naughton, can be plotted with the *Office of the Clerk of Assize* in one hand and Hawkins's *Pleas of the Crown* in the other.[20]

Since the New York bar so avidly followed the English law books and precedents, Goebel and Naughton are justified in concluding that a strong prima facie case against the existence of the right could be constructed *if* it were passed over in those books. "It is obviously idle to imagine that a 'principle' which even Baron Gilbert forbears to mention, should have been cosseted in our own courts." [21] But Gilbert did not forbear to mention the principle, nor did other writers, relied upon by New York colonial lawyers, ignore it.

Geoffrey Gilbert's *Law of Evidence*, published in 1756, is described by Goebel and Naughton as the first work on the subject with any analytic merit.[22] Gilbert, the Lord Chief Baron of the Exchequer, after noting that the best evidence is a confession, added: "but then this Confession must be voluntary and without Compulsion; for our Law in this differs from the Civil Law, that it *will not force any Man to accuse himself;* and in this we do certainly follow the Law of Nature, which commands every Man to endeavour his own Preservation; and therefore Pain and Force may compel Men to confess what is not the Truth of Facts, and consequently such extorted Confessions are not to be depended on."[23] The phrasing, "our Law . . . will not force any Man to accuse himself," embodies the traditional English expression of the right against self-incrimination. Gilbert stated the principle in the most general terms, without exceptions, and grounded it on the Enlightenment's most appealing rationale, the "Law of Nature." By mid-eighteenth century, the principle was so self-evident and customary that no further explanation was required.

Goebel and Naughton state that Gilbert's *Law of Evidence* was used in New York "not long after publication." In fact it was used even before publication. On February 5, 1753, William Smith, Jr., one of the luminaries of the New York bar, received from John McEvers, a fellow attorney, a manuscript volume "supposed to be done by Baron Gilbert." Smith copied 173 pages of the manuscript, including the passage against self-accusing, quoted above, and in the margin later wrote, "Note this book is now printed under title Law of Evidence in 8 vo. 1 June 1756."[24] Smith not only knew of the right, from many sources in addition to Gilbert, but as a historian, councilor, and lawyer, he respected the right.

Gilbert's book has been singled out for special consideration only because its alleged silence on the subject has been offered by Goebel and Naughton as proof that the right was not "cosseted" in New York's English-minded courts. Yet almost any law book that touched criminal law might be used to prove that the right was known. In the most widely used law dictionary of the eighteenth century, the broad proposition is stated under "evidence," with support by appropriate references to Coke's *Institutes*, Hobbes's *Leviathan*, and the *State Trials*, that "the witness shall not be asked any Question to accuse himself." The author of the dictionary restated that proposition in a popular book, *Every Man His Own Lawyer*, the seventh edition of which was published in New York by Hugh Gaine in 1768. Michael Dalton's *The Countrey Justice*, a book that also went through many editions and that Goebel and Naughton refer to as a *vade mecum* for local magistrates in New York, stated that the offender should not be examined upon oath "for by the Common

Law, Nullus tenetur seipsum prodere." The same principle was expressed in slightly different Latin—"Nemo debet seipsum accusare" —in what was probably the most widely used manual for justices of the peace. There were at least eight American editions in the eighteenth century, in six of which, including both New York editions, it is given as "a general rule, that a witness shall not be asked any question, the answering of which might oblige him to accuse himself of a crime." The language is identical to that used in the classic *Pleas of the Crown* by William Hawkins, first published in 1716, which was exactly quoted, too, by other popular manuals for justices of the peace.[25]

From Edmond Wingate's *Maximes of Reason* of 1658, which includes perhaps the earliest discussion under the heading, "Nemo tenetur accusare seipsum"—copies were in the libraries of such eminent New York lawyers as James Alexander, Joseph Murray, and William Smith—to William Blackstone's *Commentaries*, the principle of the right against self-incrimination was recognized by the English law writers as well as by the English courts.[26] The logic of Goebel and Naughton leads us, therefore, to expect its recognition by the bench and bar of New York. It *was* so recognized, if not "cosseted" or pampered.

The evidence for its recognition is not abundant, for the trial records, unfortunately, prove little. As Goebel and Naughton state, only a few trials are reported and those "execrably" so; the judgment rolls and *posteas* "are nearly always silent on what was said or proffered at trial, and the judicial minutes at best ordinarily furnish only a list of documents or the names of those who testified." Since "statements respecting testimony are rarely to be found in minutes of the provincial courts or the records of trials," a generalization about the nonexistence of the right against self-incrimination in New York should be regarded as suspect. Historians who "cleave to a scintilla of evidence theory" are properly reprimanded by Goebel and Naughton; they disapprove of those who take a proposition as proven with the minimum of citation, who bottom a rule on a single case, or refer to statutes only when stating a judicial practice. "This is the way of advocacy, not of scholarship. . . . The ends of legal history are not served by the mere establishment of a *prima facie* case."[27]

The injunction, a sound one, has not been observed by Goebel and Naughton in their discussion of the right against self-incrimination. By way of proving the nonexistence of that right, they instance the case of a man who was incriminatingly questioned at his trial about the contradictory confessions he had made in his preliminary examination. "This case of course concerned a slave [one of the defendants in the Negro Plot to burn the city in 1742], but we have

246

not noticed any special tenderness for white persons charged with felony, and it is not unlikely that similar tactics were used against them. There are numerous cases where the minutes reveal the reading at trial of a prisoner's confession." [28] The passage illustrates the "scintilla of evidence theory" in practice and a badly mistaken assumption that the right against self-incrimination is nonexistent in a jurisdiction that accepts in evidence the confession of the accused.

At the risk of repetition, it should be understood that the right exists against *compulsory* self-incrimination and, except at the preliminary examination after 1848, had to be claimed by the prisoner. That the bench did not need to caution him on his right to refuse answer to an incriminating question proves nothing, contrary to Goebel and Naughton. Nor does the fact that there were "occasional" instances, down to the Revolution, of the ancient practice of questioning the defendant upon his arraignment in order to secure his submission. The scintilla of evidence theory is glaringly adopted in the proposition that the general "indifference to any privilege against self-incrimination probably embraced witnesses generally although we have found but one case." [29]

In a different connection, Goebel and Naughton declare that while it is impossible to determine whether the conduct of trials at Quarter Sessions resembled that in the superior courts, "if the case of Penn and Mead at Old Bailey is typical the proceedings were exactly similar," and presumably they illustrate the sessions in colonial New York.[30] In that case, the Quaker defendants, upon finding their meetinghouse padlocked by the authorities, held public worship in the street. At their trial, on a charge of "tumultuous assembly," William Mead successfully invoked the right against self-incrimination. After a witness stated that he had not seen Mead at the street-meeting, the bench asked, "What say you, Mr. Mead, were you there?" To this question Mead responded: "It is a maxim in your own law, 'Nemo tenetur accusare seipsum,' which if it be not true Latin, I am sure it is true English, 'That no man is bound to accuse himself.' And why dost thou offer to insnare me with such a question?" "Sir, hold your tongue," replied the judge, "I did not go about to insnare you." The question was dropped.[31]

The right first became an issue in New York during the Earl of Bellomont's investigation into the administration of his predecessor, Governor Benjamin Fletcher. It is both revealing and significant that the issue arose as a result of the inquisitorial tactics of a prerogative court, here the court of governor and Council, in a case heavy with political implications. The right had arisen in England as a shield against inquisitions into crimes that were essentially political and religious in nature. Thus a scrutiny of the records of courts, which employed regularized common-law procedures, yields little data about the emergence of the right. Goebel and Naughton, in other words, searched the wrong records. The investigations of the governor and Council or of the Assembly, bodies which tended to employ inquisitorial procedures, might be expected to produce protests that would eventually culminate in the right's acceptance.

A victim of Bellomont's effort to discredit his predecessor, Henry Beekman, an assemblyman who had been close to Fletcher, had been instrumental in securing the passage of the Bolting Act of 1694 by which New York City lost its monopoly of the bolting and packing of flour. Beekman was summoned in 1698 by Bellomont to be examined on his connection with the charge that the approval of the act by Fletcher and certain councilors had been purchased. Instructed to answer questions under oath, Beekman refused. Threatened with imprisonment "without baile or mainprize" should he persist in his contemptuous refusal to take his oath without giving a "lawful" reason, he was finally "persuaded" to take the oath and answer the questions. That Beekman's case was not exceptional would appear from the accusations filed with the Board of Trade against Bellomont by the London correspondent of the New York merchants, John Key: that Bellomont "has tendered extrajudicial oaths to severall of His Majtys subjects requiring them to make answer to such questions he should ask them, and upon their refusall to swear has threatned to committ them into custody." In one case he imprisoned two merchants, who had "farmed the excise," for refusing to "discover upon oath what profits they had made by that farme." [32]

New York merchants understandably objected to testifying against themselves, particularly when they suspected that political motives were behind the governor's inquisition. Nicholas Bayard, one of Fletcher's most intimate associates who had been ousted from the Council by Bellomont, complained in London to the Board of Trade about the latter's administration. He cited Bellomont's "undue method in forcing witnesses to swear, and instanced in his requiring Colonel Beckman [*sic*] . . . to make oath to answer whatever should be asked him (tho' he were himself concerned in the business of that Enquiry) with threats to send him to Gaol in case he refused." Bayard's protest, in other words, was that Beekman had been forced to incriminate himself. In defending Bellomont, Thomas Weaver, his agent in London, made the interesting point that both he and the attorney general of the province agreed that "Beekman was obliged (as any man might be, especially in matters of state or other high concernment) to give evidence in what did not concerne himself criminally (which was all required of him)." [33] Thus, Weaver, later a councilman and attorney general, and, if his word may be

248

relied upon, James Graham, the Attorney General of New York under Bellomont, explicitly acknowledged that a man might not be forced to testify against himself in a criminal matter, not even by the governor and Council.

In 1702 William Atwood, the Chief Justice of New York, and Samuel Shelton Broughton, the new attorney general, also acknowledged the right in connection with the sensational treason trial of Bayard and Hutchins. The death of Bellomont had kindled Bayard's hope of returning to power against the Leislerians who controlled the government. To ingratiate himself with the new governor, Lord Cornbury, Bayard drew up addresses accusing Lieutenant Governor John Nanfan, Chief Justice Atwood, and members of the Council, of nefarious actions. Nanfan retaliated by arresting Bayard on a charge of treason under a statute of 1691 which provided that anyone who by arms "or otherwise" endeavored to "disturb the peace" should be deemed a traitor. For a crime which at worst was a mere misdemeanor, a seditious libel, Bayard found himself in 1702 on trial for his life along with his confederate, Alderman John Hutchins.[34]

In the initial stage of the case, Nanfan and the Council employed inquisitorial tactics to gather evidence about the addresses; several suspects refused to produce copies on demand. The Council, upon receiving an opinion from Attorney General Broughton, decided to prosecute them for contempt. Broughton believed that because the addresses "were not criminal or illegal" the suspects could be forced to produce copies without incriminating themselves. Although the Council thought the addresses criminal, it sought only to incriminate the authors of the addresses. Bayard, his son, and Hutchins were shortly arrested. Bayard, complaining to friends in England, noted that Hutchins had been jailed for treason, without bail, until he produced copies of the addresses which the Council "were pleased to call Libells." After the conviction of the defendants, Bayard's friends petitioned the Board of Trade and charged that an attempt had been made to force Hutchins to incriminate himself in a criminal matter. Sir Edward Northey, Attorney General of England, informed the Board of Trade that "it appears by the warrant for committing Hutchins that the Council required him to produce a libell he is charged to be author of *which was to accuse himself* and his refusing to produce it is alledged as part of his Crime." After the Privy Council annulled the sentences, Chief Justice Atwood defended his conduct in the case, and sought to justify the Council's requirement that Hutchins produce the addresses. Although Atwood's statement of the facts differs from Bayard's, the significant point is his denial that Hutchins had been forced to incriminate himself: "But since he was not committed for *High Treason*, as he might have been, and there wanted no Evidence against him; this, surely, may answer the Objection against requiring him to produce Papers which might tend to accuse himself." [35]

The right against self-incrimination next became an issue in New York politics as a result of merchant protest against Governor William Burnet's efforts to outlaw the fur trade between Albany and Quebec. When a prohibitory act of 1720 proved unenforceable because of the sheriff's inability to supervise the frontier, the legislature adopted an amendment in 1722 authorizing civil and military officers to exact from any suspected persons an oath of purgation that they had not in any way traded with the French. Refusal to take the oath automatically convicted one of the crime of illicitly trading, the penalty for which was a £100 fine.[36] The statute certainly compelled the guilty to incriminate themselves, a fact which its opponents used as the basis of their objections to the Board of Trade.

Stephen DeLancey, Adolph Philipse, and Peter Schuyler cared little about abstract principle, but they recognized a good issue with which to mask their interest in the fur trade. John Sharpe, their London agent, argued that the statute of 1722 was illegal because the party suspected "was by a very extraordinary Oath, made liable either to accuse himself or to suffer very great Penalties." A fur trader, John Peloquin, giving evidence at the hearing, mentioned that he had bought skins from the French and was asked when he had done so. Sharpe interposed to say that Peloquin's "answering that Question might be of ill consequence to himself, if it were since the passing [of] the said Acts; and said he believed their Lordships did not expect Mr. Peloquin should accuse himself." Their Lordships changed the subject. Subsequently they recommended to the Privy Council that Governor Burnet be urged to halt the undesirable trade by other methods. The Board specified its objections: "There is an Oath imposed upon all Traders whereby they are obliged to accuse themselves or else to be under the greatest temptation to perjury." New York enacted a new statute regulating the fur trade by a tax device. The oath was conspicuously absent from its provisions.[37]

On the other hand, the purgative oath that in effect compelled self-incrimination was a frequent feature of New York legislation during the colonial period. The right against self-incrimination was indeed an illusion, as Goebel and Naughton declare, if the laws from 1701 to 1759 are considered. The first act employing the oath of purgation, with a proviso that those refusing to take it should be subject to double the normal penalties imposed on the guilty, was intended to detect and deter evasion of the militia laws. Legislation of this kind was used against those suspected of selling liquor to the Indians, exporting specie, taking seamen's notes for liquor or food, entertaining slaves, stealing furs from Indians, selling liquor to servants, failing to report imported copper money, trading with the Iroquois for certain articles, and giving credit to servants.[38] In all these cases, the statutes fixed criminal penalties for the refusal of a suspect to take the oath of purgation. Some declared that such a refusal automatically established guilt for the crime suspected; others provided for special fines and/or imprisonment. The purgative oath, like the oath ex officio of an earlier time, was an iron trap for the guilty: the mere requirement of it ensured conviction for perjury, or contempt, or the crime suspected. Even the innocent could suffer, particularly conscientious objectors. However, the purgative oath was authorized by the legislature only once after 1759 and passed into disuse before the outbreak of the Revolution. The ever increasing professionalization of the bar, the growing familiarity with "the liberty of the subject" and English rights, and the protests against compulsory self-accusing all contributed to the respectability of the right against incriminating oneself.

William Smith, Jr.'s, *History of the Late Province of New-York*, published in 1757, contained a scathing passage against oaths of purgation. When the Assembly had tendered such an oath to Robert Livingston in 1701, Smith wrote, "Mr. Livingston, who was better acquainted with English law and liberty than to countenance a practice so odious, rejected the insolent demand with disdain." [39]

Three years later, Smith's father had occasion to place himself on record against self-incrimination. The elder William Smith, who had learned his law at the Inns of Court, was one of the colony's most distinguished attorneys, had served as provincial attorney general, and in 1760 declined the chief justiceship, although he accepted a seat on the high court in 1763. In 1760, Councilor Smith, in a report on illicit trading by many of the colony's leading merchants, declared that the master of one vessel had given information against others, but he, "being Particeps Crimin[is] can not be compelled to answer. On this [we?] therefore only observed that if upon further Enquiry sufficient Proofs can be gained of the Fact, the Offenders ought to be prosecuted." Unlike the earlier instance in 1702, when Chief Justice Atwood had prevented David Jamison from testifying on behalf of Bayard because Jamison "is *particeps criminis*, for which reason he cannot be allowed to be an evidence," the 1760 case of the master involved one who could not be *compelled*. Jamison, as an alleged party to the crime, could not be *allowed* because his interest in the case had disqualified him. The master was not disqualified for interest, but protected against self-incrimination.[40]

John Tabor Kempe, the attorney general, did not wholly agree with Smith's opinion, which might deprive the prosecution of testimony needed to convict. In 1762, on the basis of information provided by informers, sixteen prominent men were charged with trading with the enemy. In preparation for the trial of two of the merchants, Kempe drafted a long brief in which he indicated his intention to call a number of witnesses who might be disqualified from testifying because of interest or excused because they were parties to the crime. Kempe carefully wrote out the arguments by which he intended to show that such persons were not necessarily incompetent to testify and, indeed, might even be compelled to testify. These witnesses, he declared, even if parties to the crime, could be obliged to give evidence against others, "for the convictions of the persons on tryal will be attended with no punishment corporal or pecuniary to the witness—and he is not obliged to accuse himself." To the objection that no person should be compelled to swear against his own interest, Kempe noted: "He may—the Court of Chancery every day compels the party on oath to discover his own frauds. The rule that a witness shall not be compelled to swear to his own detriment goes not farther, than that he shall not be compelled to accuse himself of a crime." Finally, he wrote, "every person being a *participis criminis*, may be a witness either for or against his accomplices, if he has not been indicted for the offence (2 Hawk. P.C. 432)." Thus, at three points in his brief, the attorney general, whose opinions Goebel and Naughton highly prize, acknowledged the principle of the right against self-incrimination.[41]

Not all the ship captains, whom Kempe had sworn as witnesses, were willing to testify. Captain William Dobbs, for example, simply refused to answer questions and was committed. Captain William Paulding, in the same case, at first refused to be sworn, saying, "he understood he was not to declare anything that might affect himself." He was then told that he had the King's pardon, "whereupon he declared he would not accept the pardon." Although he permitted himself to be sworn, he refused to answer questions. The court ordered him committed. The jury, however, "without going from the Bar" found the defendants not guilty. The same occurred when Captain Theunis Thew refused to testify. He too was pardoned in order to prevent him from incriminating himself, but he remained silent to the questions and was committed. Dobbs, Paulding, and Thew were fined heavily for their respective contempts. In the case of Paulding, the right against self-incrimination had been expressly invoked by the witness and was respected by the Crown via the offer of a pardon. That same offer was extended to Thew to safeguard him from self-incrimination. The case hardly bears out the allegation that the right was an illusion in New York.[42]

That illusion is finally dispelled by the facts of the McDougall case. In December of 1769 a handbill addressed "To the Betrayed Inhabitants of New-York," signed by a "Son of Liberty," was broadcast throughout the city. The author criticized the legislature for voting provisions for the King's troops and called upon the public to rise against unjust measures that subverted American liberties. The legislature condemned the handbill as a seditious libel and offered a reward for information leading to discovery of "Son of Liberty's" identity. A journeyman printer in the shop of James Parker, publisher of the *New-York Gazette or the Weekly Post-Boy*, betrayed his employer as the printer of the broadside.[43]

On February 7, 1770, the governor and Council summoned Parker and his employees. Having once before been jailed by the Assembly for publishing a reflection on its members, Parker was a reluctant witness. Claiming that he would be "wrecked" if he answered the Council's questions, he asked for immunity in exchange for his cooperation. He remained reluctant even after being informed that he was not being asked to incriminate *himself*. He was then threatened with the loss of his position in the post office and warned of his "danger"—punishment for contempt. Yet he was not threatened criminally for a refusal to incriminate himself. Giving Parker an opportunity to reconsider, the Council brought in Anthony Carr, one of his journeymen. Carr, testifying under oath, denied knowledge of the identity of the author of "To the Betrayed," although he admitted that the offensive piece had been printed at Parker's. Councilman William Smith recorded in his diary that Carr was then told "at my Instance as Parker had been before, that he need not answer so as to accuse himself." Nevertheless, Carr was bullied and finally broke down, naming as author one Captain Alexander McDougall. Carr's brother, John, also a journeyman printer in Parker's office, was next sworn and "told he was not bound to accuse himself." John Carr willingly corroborated Anthony's testimony. Parker was then recalled. Upon being told that the Council knew everything about the writing and printing of the libel, he accepted the offer of a pardon and confessed his role and McDougall's authorship. He was then sworn and his examination taken down.[44]

McDougall, a popular leader of the radical party in the controversy with Britain, was arrested for seditious libel and jailed when he refused to pay bail. He turned his arrest into a theatrical triumph, consciously posing as America's John Wilkes while the Sons of Liberty converted his prosecution into a weapon for the patriot cause. William Smith, having refused Governor Cadwallader Colden's request that he assist Attorney General Kempe in the prosecution of "an unpopular suit," anonymously published in Parker's paper a defense of McDougall, based chiefly upon liberty of the press, in which he censured the Star Chamber practice of examining "even the accused." The manuscript version of the article, considerably shortened for publication, declared that "to the eternal scandal of this inquisition they examined sometimes the Party himself and even accepted against himself." [45]

When Parker, the principal witness for the Crown, died, the trial of McDougall was postponed a number of times. Finally the legislature, impatient for revenge, resolved to punish him on its authority. McDougall was summoned before the bar of the House on December 13, 1770. Charged with having written "To the Betrayed," he was asked whether he was in fact the author. McDougall refused to answer, claiming the rights against self-incrimination and against double jeopardy. The minutes of the Assembly's proceedings show his reply, in part, to be: "That as the Grand Jury and House of Assembly had declared the Paper in Question to be a Libel, he could not answer to the Question." [46]

McDougall, in a letter to the press written from prison, more fully reported his statement as follows: "First, that the Paper just read to me, had been declared by the Honourable House to be a Libel; that the Grand Jury for . . . New-York, had also declared it to be a Libel, and found a Bill of Indictment against me as the Author of it; therefore that I could not Answer a Question that would tend to impeach myself, or might otherwise be improper for me to answer." For McDougall's insistence that the House could not try him on a criminal charge still being prosecuted in the courts, the Assembly voted him guilty of contempt and remanded him to prison for the remainder of its session, which continued for nearly three months. About a week after his release, the Sons of Liberty met to celebrate the anniversary of the repeal of the Stamp Act. One of the many toasts on that festive occasion was to Alexander McDougall; another was, "No Answer to Interrogatories, when tending to accuse the Person interrogated." McDougall's case not only popularized but made respectable the right against self-incrimination.[47]

The impact of McDougall's case is evident from the history of the use of oaths against suspects after 1770. Goebel and Naughton assert that the legislature authorized oaths of purgation "until the very eve of the Revolution." Their proof is not only inaccurate; it omits evidence to the contrary. They cite enactments of 1770 and 1774 as evidence of the continued use of "this purgation procedure," but neither contained an oath of purgation.

The 1770 act authorized the examination "on oath" of any person suspected of concealing the assets of the estate of an insolvent debtor, but the oath was simply the usual one to tell the truth. The 1774 act is supposed to strikingly illustrate "the parallel between this purgation procedure and the ecclesiastical forms against which the English Puritans had so bitterly inveighed." But this act against "excessive and deceitful gambling" simply made winners liable to suits for the recovery of their spoils; and suspects were obliged "to answer under Oath such Bill or Bills as shall be preferred against them for discovering the Sum and Sums of Money or other Thing so won at Play as aforesaid." Goebel and Naughton, having rather freely quoted this section of the statute, move on to the "inescapable" conclusion that in New York Province there was "no attempt made to privilege a defendant . . . but on the contrary, a great deal was done to make sure that in one form or other his testimony would be secured and that it would count against him. The shadowy protection offered by the rule that a confession could not be under oath, was quite offset in the cases where he could be convicted on a confession alone and by those where he was required to trap himself by a purging oath." But the oath authorized in the 1774 act against gambling was not an oath of purgation. None was provided for, and the act itself was more a manifestation of Puritanism than of the ecclesiastical forms against which the English Puritans had inveighed. More important, Goebel and Naughton neglect to inform their readers that the next paragraph of the very same act provided that a person who confessed his winnings and repaid them "shall be acquitted, indemnified and discharged from any further or other Punishment, Forfeiture, or Penalty which he or they may have incurred by the playing for or winning such Money." Confession, in other words, "purged" him of his offense; it did not trap or incriminate him, for the statute—in the section omitted by Goebel and Naughton— provided for complete immunity. Then, as now, self-incrimination meant to expose oneself to "Punishment, Forfeiture, or Penalty," in the absence of which one cannot incriminate himself.[48]

The practice of providing immunity, which protects against self-incrimination, was begun by the legislature, significantly enough, in the first statute requiring an oath—but not an oath of purgation—that was passed after the McDougall case. This act of 1772 against private lotteries authorized justices of the peace to examine suspects under oath. Those who answered truthfully were "exempted from . . . Penalty, and from all Prosecutions in virtue of this Act." In the following year there was a reenactment of a statute of 1750 against selling liquor to servants or extending them "large" credit. The original statute contained an oath of purgation; the reenactment of 1773 made no mention of any kind of oath.[49]

In 1773, however, a new statute, overlooked by Goebel and Naughton, virtually authorized a purgative oath, though none was literally prescribed. To catch petty vandals, the legislature provided that a person caught in the vicinity when a trespass, such as the breaking of windows, was committed, "shall be deemed guilty thereof" even if not an abettor, unless he gave evidence for the conviction of the parties "really guilty" or declared under oath that he was at the scene accidentally and did not know the identity of the real offenders. The obnoxious procedures authorized by this statute, the first and last of its kind since 1759, were the subject of a complaint to the Board of Trade, which recommended disallowance by the Privy Council. Mr. Jackson, the attorney for the Crown, specifically censured the act as being "improper in that it provides for a Purgation by Oath in a criminal Matter, which is . . . contrary to the Genius of the Laws of this Country." The Privy Council, noting that Jackson's argument possessed "Weight," voted on July 6, 1774, to disallow the act despite its "useful" objective. The New York Assembly, *prior* to the disallowance, reenacted the statute against private lotteries, once again ensuring immunity against prosecution to persons who confessed their guilt under a simple oath to tell the truth. In 1775 a new act on trespasses was passed without the objectionable procedures of the act that had been disallowed—and without reference to oaths of any kind by the suspect.[50]

When two years later New York adopted its first state constitution, no guarantee of the right against self-incrimination was included. Nor was there a declaration of rights or its equivalent. However, the constitution provided that the pre-Revolutionary common and statutory law of England should continue to be "the law of this State," excepting only that part concerning English authority over New York or the establishment of religion. Goebel and Naughton describe this article in the constitution of 1777 as a "terse bill of rights," reasoning that constitutional rights were imbedded in the common law. The right to vote, the free exercise of religion, representation by counsel, and a qualified freedom from bills of attainder were expressly guaranteed, probably because they were unprotected or inadequately protected at common law; but the right to indictment and trial by jury, which were also expressly mentioned in the constitution, were surely secured by common law. Why they were singled out above all other common-law rights is inexplicable, since the courts were enjoined to "proceed according to the course of the common law" and citizens were additionally protected by the standard "law of the land" or due process clause.[51]

Although the right against self-incrimination was not mentioned, neither were the rights to freedom of speech and press, bail, or the writ of habeas corpus; nor was any protection specified against unreasonable searches and seizures, ex post facto laws, or double jeopardy. The absence of express guarantees cannot be construed to indicate the absence of the rights themselves. One could no more reasonably argue that the omission of a guarantee against compulsory self-incrimination proved that it did not exist or was regarded without respect than he could argue that the right to the writ of habeas corpus was illusionary because it was not protected by name. In its enumer-

256

ation of rights, New York's constitution was framed in an incredibly haphazard fashion, with no discernible principle of selection. However, the omnibus clause—the adoption of the common law—was insurance against the need for careful or complete enumeration.

In 1786, the legislature of New York passed "An Act Concerning the Rights of the Citizens of this State," which became known as the state's bill of rights.[52] The right against self-incrimination was once again passed over, but so too were every one of the rights, mentioned above, that had been omitted from the original constitution, excepting the right to reasonable bail. Several provisions of Magna Carta were included; the right to grand jury proceedings was more carefully defined; and there were guarantees of free elections, the right to petition, free speech for members of the legislature, taxation by consent of the governed, and immunity against the quartering of troops. But freedom from unreasonable searches and seizures, the right to the writ of habeas corpus, freedom of the press, and other vital rights received no recognition. Once again there was no discernible principle of selection, for most of the rights protected were already secured by the common law. The enumeration of some but not of others defies explanation and reveals a certain carelessness in the performance of the task. It was not until 1821 that New York, when framing its first true bill of rights, systematically enumerated all the traditional rights, including many that had been protected by custom and practice, such as the right against self-incrimination.

In 1788, the ratifying convention of New York proposed a series of amendments to the new federal Constitution. Among the proposals was one ensuring "that, in all criminal prosecutions, the accused . . . should not be compelled to give evidence against himself." Unfortunately the record of the state convention's debates offers no illumination of the reasons for this or of any other proposal included in the suggested federal bill of rights. The debates are fully reported through July 2, when a bill of rights was first mentioned in a speech by Thomas Tredwell, an anti-Federalist delegate who expressed apprehension about the danger of tyranny on the part of the new federal courts. None could say, he declared, whether their proceedings would be according to the common law or the "civil, the Jewish, or Turkish law," and he warned darkly about the history of inquisitions in the Star Chamber Court of England. Tredwell's is the last reported speech on any subject. The proceedings of the convention are thereafter reported in brief minutes. We know little more than that on July 7, John Lansing, one of the anti-Federalist leaders, reported a proposed bill of rights, that it was debated on July 19, and was passed on July 26.[53]

It is certain, however, that New York's recommended bill of rights, which included a provision on the right against self-incrimination, was the product of an interstate anti-Federalist committee of correspondence. As early as June 9, a letter to John Lamb, as head of "the federal Republican Committee of New York," from George Mason, chairman of the Republican Society of Virginia, concurred in Lamb's suggestion of a "free correspondence on the Subject of amendments." George Mason, Patrick Henry, and William Grayson kept Lamb informed of the nature and progress of proposed amendments in the Virginia convention, while Lamb kept in touch with Eleazar Oswald of Pennsylvania's minority and Rawlins Lowndes of South Carolina, Joshua Atherton of New Hampshire, and Timothy Bloodworth of North Carolina, all leading anti-Federalists. The Pennsylvania minority, whose dissenting report was circulated in New York, had proposed an amendment, securing the right against self-incrimination, copied verbatim from Article 8 of the Virginia Declaration of Rights of 1776. Copies of Virginia's declaration were forwarded to Lamb by Henry on June 9 and to Robert Yates by Mason on June 21.[54]

Lansing's original proposal of a bill of rights, made July 7, consisted of three sections: one securing the rights of life and liberty in general, another vesting sovereignty in the people, and the third a verbatim statement of Article 8 of the Virginia Declaration of Rights. On July 19, Melancthon Smith proposed three amendments, constituting a bill of rights, presumably the same three. Excepting a comment by John Jay to the effect that no bill of rights was needed, there appears to have been no debate on the motion. On its passage, Smith moved adoption of "the Virginia amendments," doubtless the entire package proposed by the Virginia convention which on June 25 had voted for ratification, with recommended amendments, including a provision copied from Article 8. The only debate in New York occurred on the question of whether the amendments were to be recommended or made conditional. Thus, the right against self-incrimination was recommended by the New York convention, notwithstanding its absence in the state's own constitution, under the influence of Virginia. It is revealing, however, that the right against self-incrimination was unquestionably accepted by the New Yorkers, both anti-Federalists and Federalists, as a desideratum in the procedures to be followed in federal criminal prosecutions. There is nothing in the circumstances surrounding the New York proposal to doubt that the right was a traditional and respected part of the state's common-law system of criminal procedure. One may suspect the motives of the anti-Federalists in demanding that a bill of rights be affixed to the new federal Constitution, but not the substantive merit of the provisions selected for inclusion in that bill of rights.[55]

New York's history may not disprove the allegation by the Supreme Court, in *Twining* v. *New Jersey*, that the right against self-incrimination was not such a fundamental principle of liberty and justice that it inheres in the very idea of a free government. But the court was correct in stating that the right "had become embodied in the common law" of all the states at the time of the formation of the Union, New York included. Nor is it without significance that the right was accepted, historically, both in Britain and New York, before most other rights, including the rights to freedom of press, speech, and worship and a whole cluster of procedural rights such as benefit of counsel and freedom from unreasonable search and seizure, double jeopardy, and bills of attainder. History, far from degrading the right against self-incrimination, exalts it in comparison with most other rights, in New York as in England, at least as far as precedence is concerned.

NOTES

[1] *Quinn* v. *U.S.*, 349 U.S. 155, 161 (1955). In *Maffie* v. *U.S.*, 209 F. 2nd 225, 227 (1954), Chief Judge Magruder declared: "Our forefathers, when they wrote this provision into the Fifth Amendment of the Constitution, had in mind a lot of history which has been largely forgotten today." Similarly Justice Frankfurter has stated: "The privilege against self-incrimination is a specific provision of which it is peculiarly true that 'a page of history is worth a volume of logic.'" *Ullmann* v. *U.S.*, 350 U.S. 422, 438 (1956). See also *Brown* v. *Walker*, 161 U.S. 591, 596–597 (1896).

[2] 211 U.S. 78, 108, 110 (1908). The Court stressed data from the period 1776 to 1789, pointing out that five of the original thirteen states (North Carolina, 1776; Pennsylvania, 1776; Virginia, 1776; Massachusetts, 1780; New Hampshire, 1784) secured the right against self-incrimination from legislative or judicial change, while four states (Virginia, 1788; New York, 1788; North Carolina, 1789; Rhode Island, 1790) ratified the Constitution with recommendations for an amendment protecting the right against self-incrimination. The Court also pointed out that the Maryland Constitution of 1776 gave qualified protection to the right. The Court failed to note that Delaware's Constitution of 1776 protected the right without qualification, as did Vermont's Constitution of 1777. Every state that included a declaration of rights in its original constitution protected the right against self-incrimination. The four states whose ratifying conventions recommended constitutional protection for the right against self-incrimination were the last four to ratify.

[3] E.g., at one point in Justice Moody's opinion, when reviewing the origins of the right, he alleged that the trial of Anne Hutchinson in Massachusetts proved that the Massachusetts authorities were "not aware of any privilege against self-incrimination or conscious of any duty to respect it." *Twining* v. *N.J.*, 211 U.S. 78, 103 (1908). Yet the trial of John Wheelwright in the same year by the same authorities proves the contrary. See [John Winthrop], "A Short Story of the Rise, Reign, and Ruine of the Antinomians, Familists and Libertines, that Infected the Churches of New England" (London, 1644), in Charles Francis Adams, ed., *Antinomianism in the Colony of Massachusetts Bay, 1636–1638* (Boston, 1894), pp. 193–195. See also the correspondence between Governor Bradford and the Reverends Partich, Reynor, and Chauncey,

in William Bradford, *History of Plymouth Plantation* (1650), Massachusetts Historical Society, *Collections*, Ser. 4, III (Boston, 1856), 390–397.

[4] R. Carter Pittman, "The Colonial and Constitutional History of the Privilege against Self-Incrimination in America," *Virginia Law Review*, XXI (1934–35), 763.

[5] Julius Goebel, Jr., and T. Raymond Naughton, *Law Enforcement in Colonial New York: A Study in Criminal Procedure (1664–1776)* (New York, 1944), xxxvi, xxxvii, 656–657, xxiii, xxviii, 59.

[6] Frederic William Maitland, "A Prologue to a History of English Law," in *Select Essays in Anglo-American Legal History* (Boston, 1907), I, 7.

[7] Sir James Fitzjames Stephen, *A History of the Criminal Law of England* (London, 1883), I, 319–357. On torture, see David Jardine, *A Reading on the Use of Torture in the Criminal Law of England . . .* (London, 1837).

[8] See A[dhémar] Esmein, *A History of Continental Criminal Procedure*, John Simpson, trans. (London, 1914), 3–12, 78–94; John Henry Wigmore, *A Treatise on the Anglo-American System of Evidence in Trials at Common Law . . .*, 2nd ed. (Boston, 1923), IV, sec. 2250, 795–803. For a detailed and excellent study, see Mary Ballantine Hume (Mrs. Mary Maguire), "The History of the Oath *Ex Officio* in England" (unpubl. Ph.D. diss., Radcliffe College, 1923), chaps. 1–2.

[9] See Roland G. Usher, *The Rise and Fall of the High Commission* (Oxford, 1913), and Hume, "History of the Oath," chap. 3.

[10] Hume, "History of the Oath," chap. 4 and, by the same author, Mary Hume Maguire, "Attack of the Common Lawyers on the Oath *Ex Officio* as Administered in the Ecclesiastical Courts in England," in *Essays in History and Political Theory in Honor of Charles Howard McIlwain* (Cambridge, Mass., 1936), pp. 199–229. See also Faith Thompson, *Magna Carta: Its Role in the Making of the English Constitution, 1300–1629* (Minneapolis, 1948), pp. 205–230.

[11] Robert Beale, "A Collection Shewinge what Jurisdiction the Clergie Hathe Heretofore Lawfully Used" (ca. 1590), quoted by Thompson, *Magna Carta*, p. 222.

[12] "The Millenary Petition," 1603, in J. R. Tanner, ed., *Constitutional Documents of the Reign of James I . . .* (Cambridge, 1930), 59; Roland G. Usher, "Nicholas Fuller: A Forgotten Exponent of English Liberty," *American Historical Review*, XII (1906–07), 743–760.

[13] See Charles H. Randall, Jr., "Sir Edward Coke and the Privilege against Self-Incrimination," *South Carolina Law Quarterly*, VIII (1956), 417–453; and Maguire, "Attack of the Common Lawyers," pp. 220–228.

[14] M. A. Gibb, *John Lilburne, The Leveller: A Christian Democrat* (London, 1947), pp. 42–54; St. 16 Car. I, c. II, sec. 4 (1641). See Hume, "History of the Oath," pp. 196–199, and Wigmore, *Treatise on Evidence*, IV, 808–809.

[15] Proceedings against the Twelve Bishops, 1642, in T. B. Howell, ed., *Cobbett's Complete Collection of State Trials . . .* (London, 1809–26), IV, 76. See also The Trial of the King, 1649, in *ibid.*, IV, 1101, where Holder objected to his having to give evidence against Charles I, and the court, "finding him [Holder] already a Prisoner, and perceiving that the Questions intended to be asked him, tended to accuse himself, thought fit to wave his Examination." This is the first time the right against self-incrimination was extended to a witness as well as the accused.

[16] See generally, Gibb, *Lilburne*, and Harold W. Wolfram, "John Lilburne: Democracy's Pillar of Fire," *Syracuse Law Review*, III (1952), 213–258.

[17] Scroop's Trial, 1660, in Howell, ed., *State Trials*, V, 1039; Whitebread's

Trial, 1679, in *ibid.*, VII, 361; Wigmore, *Treatise on Evidence*, IV, 815; Stephen, *History of the Criminal Law*, I, 440.

[18] Wigmore, *Treatise on Evidence*, I, sec. 575; and William Searle Holdsworth, *A History of English Law* (London, 1903-[38]), IX, 193-196.

[19] Stephen, *History of the Criminal Law*, I, 216-228 and 441; E. M. Morgan, "The Privilege against Self-Incrimination," *Minnesota Law Review*, XXXIV (1949-50), 17-19 and cases there cited. See also the quotation from [Geoffrey Gilbert], *The Law of Evidence by a Late Learned Judge* (London, 1756), note 23 below, and Wigmore, *Treatise on Evidence*, II, secs. 818-819, 823. Cf. Goebel and Naughton, *Law Enforcement*, pp. 653-659, and passim.

[20] Goebel and Naughton, *Law Enforcement*, pp. xxviii, 56, 59-60, 284, 573. William Hawkins, *A Treatise of the Pleas of the Crown* . . . , 2nd ed. (London, 1724-26).

[21] Goebel and Naughton, *Law Enforcement*, pp. 656-657.

[22] *Ibid.*, p. 628. The date of publication is incorrectly given by Goebel and Naughton as 1754.

[23] Gilbert, *Law of Evidence*, pp. 139-140. A fifth edition published in Philadelphia in 1788, contained the identical passage at p. 137.

[24] Goebel and Naughton, *Law Enforcement*, p. 628, note; "A Treatise on Evidence," William Smith Papers, IX, 127-128, New York Public Library, New York.

[25] Giles Jacob, *A New Law-Dictionary*, 2nd ed. (London, 1732), under the title of "Evidence." The identical provision is also in the 8th edition of 1762. Giles Jacob, *Every Man His Own Lawyer* . . . , 7th ed. (New York, 1768), p. 93; Michael Dalton, *The Countrey Justice* (London, 1677 ed.), chap. 164, p. 411. The same passage appears in the London edition of 1742, chap. 164, p. 380; [No author], *Conductor Generalis: Or the Office, Duty, and Authority of Justices of the Peace* . . . , 2nd ed. (Philadelphia, 1749). The Latin of *Conductor Generalis* was probably copied from William Nelson, *The Office and Authority of a Justice of Peace* . . . , 4th ed. (London, 1714), p. 253; *Conductor Generalis* . . . (New York, Hugh Gaine, 1788), p. 139, and (New York, John Patterson, 1788), p. 169. The other editions were published in Philadelphia, 1722, 1749, and 1792; in Woodbridge, N.J., 1764 and 1794; and in Albany, 1794. The quoted material appeared in all editions except the first two of Philadelphia. Hawkins, *Pleas of the Crown*, 2nd ed., II, chap. 46, sec. 20, p. 433; [Richard Burn], *An Abridgment of Burn's Justice of the Peace* . . . (Boston, 1773), p. 123, and Richard Starke, *The Office and Authority of a Justice of Peace* . . . (Williamsburg, Va., 1774), p. 146.

[26] Edmond Wingate, *Maximes of Reason: Or, the Reason of the Common Law of England* (London, 1658), sec. 125, pp. 486-487; Paul M. Hamlin, *Legal Education in Colonial New York* (New York, 1939), pp. 173, 179, 184; Sir William Blackstone, *Commentaries on the Law of England* (Oxford, 1765-69), III, chap. 7, p. 101, chap. 23, p. 370; IV, chap. 22, p. 293. By the mid-18th century, the right against self-incrimination was recognized even in courts of equity, mainly as a result of the opinions of Lord Chancellor Hardwicke. See, e.g., *Smith v. Read*, 1 Atk. 526, 527 (1737); *Duncalf v. Blake*, 1 Atk. 52 (1737); *Baker v. Pritchard*, 2 Atk. 387 (1742); and *Harrison v. Southcote*, 1 Atk. 528 (1751). Equity precedents go back at least as early as *Trevor v. Lesguire*, Finch 73 (1673) and *Bird v. Hardwicke*, 1 Vern. 109 (1682). The respect accorded to the right is abundantly clear from the Parliamentary debates in 1742 following the refusal of Nicholas Paxton, the Solicitor of the Treasury, to answer incriminatory questions before an investigating committee. Commons passed a bill of "indemnity" immunizing incriminatory testimony against prosecution,

but the bill failed in the House of Lords. John, Lord Carteret, the Secretary of State, in opposing the bill, declared: "It is an established maxim, that no man can be obliged to accuse himself, or to answer any questions which may have any tendency to discover what the nature of his defence requires to be concealed." The Duke of Argyle, in a speech favoring the bill, acknowledged "that *no man is obliged to accuse himself*, and that the constitution of Britain allows no man's evidence to be extorted from him to his own destruction." He described the right as one "of the first principles of English law." "Debate on a Motion for Indemnifying Evidence," May 20, 1742, in Samuel Johnson, ed., *Debates in Parliament* (London, 1787), II, 123, 142.

27 Goebel and Naughton, *Law Enforcement*, pp. 628–629, 641, xxxi.

28 *Ibid.*, p. 654.

29 *Ibid.*, pp. 656, 659.

30 *Ibid.*, p. 556.

31 Trial of William Penn and William Mead, 1670, in Howell, ed., *State Trials*, VI, 957–958.

32 "Calendar of Council Minutes, 1668–1773," New York State Library, *Bulletin 58 (March 1902) History 6* (Albany, 1902), 132; Philip L. White, *The Beekmans of New York in Politics and Commerce, 1647–1877* (New York, 1956), pp. 87–88, 91–92; Lawrence H. Leder, *Robert Livingston, 1654–1728, and the Politics of Colonial New York* (Chapel Hill, 1961), pp. 130–132; New York Council Minutes, June 25, 1698, VIII, 55–56, N.Y. State Library, Albany, N.Y.; John Key, "Heads of Accusation against the Earl of Bellomont," March 11, 1700, in E. B. O'Callaghan and B. Fernow, eds., *Documents Relative to the Colonial History of the State of New-York* (Albany, 1853–87), IV, 622.

33 Proceedings of Lords of Trade, January 20, 1698–99 in O'Callaghan and Fernow, eds., *Documents*, IV, 467, 468.

34 *Rex* v. *Bayard*, 1702, in Howell, ed., *State Trials*, XIV, 471–506; Leder, *Robert Livingston*, pp. 174–177.

35 Samuel Bayard to Adderly and Lodwick, January 27, 1701–02, in O'Callaghan and Fernow, eds., *Documents*, IV, 945; New York Council Minutes, January 21, 26, 1701–02, VIII, 302–303, 305; Nicholas Bayard to Adderly and Lodwick, January 28, 1701–02, in O'Callaghan and Fernow, eds., *Documents*, IV, 947; Sir Edward Northey to Board of Trade, April 25, 1702, in *ibid.*, p. 954 (italics added); "The Case of William Atwood, Esq." (1703), New-York Historical Society, *Collections* (New York, 1881), p. 269.

36 Leder, *Robert Livingston*, pp. 251–254. Commissioners of Statutory Revision, *The Colonial Laws of New York from the Year 1664 to the Revolution* . . . (Albany, 1894), II, 8–10, 98.

37 Journal of Board of Trade, May 5, 12, 1725, Representation of Board of Trade, June 16, 1725, in O'Callaghan and Fernow, eds., *Documents*, V, 748, 750, 763. Commrs. of Stat. Rev., *Colonial Laws*, II, 281–287.

38 Commrs. of Stat. Rev., *Colonial Laws*, I, 454–455 (chap. 95, October 18, 1701). Goebel and Naughton, *Law Enforcement*, p. 657, state that the first statute employing a purgatory oath was passed in 1709. For the acts after 1701, see *Colonial Laws*, I, 657–658 (chap. 187, May 24, 1709), 678–679 (chap. 196, September 24, 1709), 681 (chap. 197, October 11, 1709), 764 (chap. 250, December 10, 1712), 830 (chap. 282, September 4, 1714), 889–890 (chap. 317, June 30, 1716); II, 245 (chap. 463, November 10, 1725), 710 (chap. 568, September 30, 1731), 954 (chap. 651, December 16, 1737), 962 (chap. 655, December 16, 1737); III, 243–244 (chap. 734, October 29, 1742), 730–731 (chap. 869, July 1, 1748), 757–758 (chap. 881, November 24, 1750), 1097–1098 (chap. 979, July 5, 1755); IV, 349–350 (chap. 1086, March 7, 1759).

39 William Smith, *The History of the Late Province of New-York* (New York, 1829), I, 139.

40 Report of Committee of Council, December 24, 1760, New York Colonial Manuscripts, LXXXIX, 54 (5), New York State Library; Howell, ed., *State Trials*, XIV, 503.

41 "Note of Recognizances taken by Mr. Justice Horsmanden relating to illicit trade," John Tabor Kempe Papers, Box "B" (under Augustus Bradley), New-York Historical Society, New York; Manuscript Brief, "The King agt. Waddell Cunningham and Thomas White," 1763, Pleadings, Pl. K 1023, pp. 8, 10, Hall of Records, New York County, New York City.

42 Minute Book of the Supreme Court of Judicature, October 19, 1762, to April 28, 1764, entries for October 28, 1763, p. 273, and October 26, 1763, p. 289, Engrossed Minutes, Hall of Records, New York County.

43 Leonard W. Levy, *Legacy of Suppression: Freedom of Speech and Press in Early American History* (Cambridge, Mass., 1960), pp. 78–79.

44 Diary entry of Wednesday, February 7, 1770, William H. W. Sabine, ed., *Historical Memoirs, from 16 March 1763 to 9 July 1776, of William Smith, Historian of the Province of New York . . .* (New York, 1956), pp. 74–75.

45 Levy, *Legacy of Suppression*, pp. 81–82; [William Smith] "Copy of a late letter from an eminent Counsellor," *New-York Gazette: or, the Weekly Post-Boy*, March 19, 1770; William Smith, "Copy of a late letter from an eminent Counsellor," William Smith Papers, Folder # 204–9, New York Public Library.

46 *Journal of the Votes and Proceedings of the General Assembly of the Colony of New York, 1769–1771*, Colonial Office Papers, Class 5, Vol. 1219, p. 8, Public Record Office, London (microfilm), Doc. # 953. Also available in *New-York Gazette; and the Weekly Mercury*, December 24, 1770.

47 Alexander McDougall, "To The Freeholders," *New-York Gazette: or the Weekly Post-Boy*, December 24, 1770; *ibid.*, March 25, 1771.

48 Goebel and Naughton, *Law Enforcement*, pp. 658, 659; Commrs. of Stat. Rev., *Colonial Laws*, V, 130, 621, 623; *Brown* v. *Walker*, 161 U. S. 591 (1896) and *Ullmann* v. *U.S.*, 350 U.S. 422 (1956).

49 Commrs. of Stat. Rev., *Colonial Laws*, V, 354, 583–584; III, 757–758.

50 *Ibid.*, V, 237–239, 458, 639, 642, 874; W. L. Grant and James Munroe, eds., *Acts of the Privy Council of England, Colonial Series* (London, 1908–12), V, 399–400.

51 Articles 13, 33–35, 38, 41, N. Y. Constitution of 1777, in Francis Newton Thorpe, ed., *The Federal and State Constitutions, Colonial Charters, and Other Organic Laws . . .* (Washington, 1909), V, 2632–2637; Goebel and Naughton, *Law Enforcement*, xvii, 57, 325.

52 Charles Z. Lincoln, *The Constitutional History of New York . . .* (Rochester, 1906), I, 728.

53 Jonathan Elliot, ed., *The Debates in the Several State Conventions on the Adoption of the Federal Constitution . . .*, 2nd ed. rev. (Philadelphia, 1941), I, 328, 400, 410–413.

54 George Mason to John Lamb, June 9, 1788; Patrick Henry to John Lamb, June 9, 1788; William Grayson to John Lamb, June 9, 1788; John Lamb to Governor Clinton, June 17, 1788; John Lamb to New Hampshire, June 6, 1788; Joshua Atherton to John Lamb, June 11, 1788; Rawlins Lowndes to John Lamb, June 21, 1788; Joshua Atherton to John Lamb, June 23, 1788; Timothy Bloodworth to John Lamb, July 1, 1788; Draft "Amendments to the New Constitution of Government" in hand of Charles Tillinghast, Lamb's son-in-law, John Lamb Papers, Box 5, New-York Historical Society. Also, George

Mason to John Mason, September 2, December 18, 1788, George Mason Papers, 1766–1788, pp. 245, 249, New York Public Library.

[55] "Proceedings of the Convention of the State of New York in a Committee of the Whole," July 7, 1788, John McKesson Papers, Box 3, New-York Historical Society; Gilbert Livingston's Notes on the New York Ratifying Convention, Gilbert Livingston Papers, Box 2, New York Public Library; Levy, *Legacy of Suppression,* pp. 214–237, and passim.

THE RIGHT AGAINST
SELF-INCRIMINATION:
HISTORY AND
JUDICIAL HISTORY

B Y now we all know the notorious fact: the Supreme Court has flunked history. The justices stand censured for abusing historical evidence in a way that reflects adversely on their intellectual rectitude as well as on their historical competence. Professors of constitutional history charge that the justices frequently use "law office history," which is merely a function of ex parte advocacy. The Court artfully selects historical facts from one side only, ignoring contrary data, in order to support, rationalize, or give the appearance of respectability to judgments resting on other grounds. Alfred H. Kelly, who aimed his sharpest barbs at the liberal activists, claimed that the Court's historical scholarship is simplistic, manipulative, and devoid of balance or impartiality. He referred to the Court's "historical felony," "amateurish historical solecism," "mangled constitutional history," and its practice of confusing the writing of briefs with the writing of history—all of which "runs wild" in the Court's opinions. Kelly also questioned whether history as written by the Court is reconcilable with historians' history.[1]

Since Charles Fairman demolished Justice Black's opinion in the *Adamson* case [2] on the question whether the Fourteenth Amendment was intended to incorporate the Bill of Rights as limitations on the states, scholars have regularly criticized the Court's use of history.[3] Paul L. Murphy preceded Kelly in condemning "law office history" and described one opinion as having relied on "a shockingly inaccurate use of historical data." [4] Alexander M. Bickel negated the Court's reading of the history of the first section of the Fourteenth Amendment on the question of racial segregation.[5] Historical evidence has also been mustered to disprove the Court's assertion that the free speech clause of the First Amendment was intended to supersede the common law of seditious libel.[6] Now it can be added that the Court's use of history in cases on the Fifth Amendment's self-incrimination clause fits a pattern that might charitably be described as historical incompetence, uncharitably as law-office history.

I

The most historically minded opinion on the Fifth Amendment was Justice Moody's in *Twining* v. *New Jersey*, decided in 1908.[7] *Twining*, which the Court recently abandoned,[8] runs counter to the general trend of decisions favoring a liberal construction of the Fifth Amendment. But the Court's use of history in *Twining* is representative, not of its viewpoint but of its historical knowledge. The question was whether the *right* against self-incrimination [9] was "a fundamental principle of liberty and justice which inheres in the very idea of free government" and therefore ought to be included within the concept of the due process of law safeguarded from state abridgment.[10] Relying on its version of history, the Court decided against the right. Justice Moody said that he had resorted to "every historical test by which the meaning of the phrase [of the Fifth Amendment] can be tried," [11] although he had to "pass by the meager records of early colonial time, so far as they have come to our attention, as affording light too uncertain for guidance." [12] But Moody did not pass by the 1637 trial of Anne Hutchinson which proved, he alleged, that the Massachusetts authorities were "not aware of any privilege against self-incrimination or any duty to respect it." [13] Four decades later Justice Black, in his famous *Adamson* dissent, exclaimed, "Of course not," because the court that tried Anne Hutchinson for heresy, believing that its religious convictions must be forced upon others, could not believe that dissenters had any rights worth respecting.[14] Black's outraged explanation is misleading. Incriminating interrogation was routine in 1637 on both sides of the Atlantic in all criminal cases. Nevertheless the Hutchinson case does not reveal that the judges were unaware of the right against self-incrimination or of a duty to respect it, because she did not claim it. She welcomed incriminating questions as an opportunity to reveal God's word as she saw it. What is significant is not that the court sought her incrimination but, rather, that she freely and voluntarily incriminated herself. Justice Moody did not know that the same Massachusetts court a few months earlier, when trying her brother-in-law John Wheelwright on similar charges, was put on the defensive by objections to its procedure and questioning. Governor Winthrop explained that his court neither meant to examine the defendant by compulsory means, such as by using an incriminating oath, nor sought to "draw matter from himselfe whereupon to proceed against him." [15] The maxim *memo tenetur seipsum prodere*—no one bound to accuse himself—was widely known among the Massachusetts Puritans.[16]

Moody said in *Twining* that the right was not in Magna Carta and that the practice of self-incriminatory examinations had continued for more than four centuries after 1215. That is true, but far short of the whole truth. As early as 1246, when the church introduced its inquisitorial oath-procedure into England, a procedure that required self-incrimination, Henry III condemned it as "repugnant to the antient Customs of his Realm" and to "his peoples Liberties." [17] In the early fourteenth century Parliament outlawed the church's incriminatory oath-procedure,[18] and when the King's Council emulated that procedure, Parliament protested and reenacted section 29 of Magna Carta.[19] One such reenactment, in 1354, for the first time used the phrase "by due process of law." [20] On its face the statute said nothing about self-incrimination. Seen in its context the statute condemned incriminating examinations, when conducted outside the common-law courts, as violations of Magna Carta or denials of due process. In *Twining* the Supreme Court failed to recognize that Magna Carta grew in meaning. Originally a feudal document protecting the barons, it became the talismanic symbol and source of the expanding liberties of the subject. Thus, in 1590 Robert Beale, the clerk of the Privy Council, declared that "by the Statute of Magna Carta and the olde lawes of this realme, this othe for a man to accuse himself was and is utterlie inhibited." [21] This became the view of other common-lawyers, of Chief Justice Edward Coke, and of Parliament.[22] To allege that Magna Carta did not outlaw compulsory self-incrimination is a mischievous oversimplification, a half-truth. The same can be said of the Court's *Twining* statement that the Petition of Right of 1628 did not address itself to the evil of compulsory self-incrimination. It did, in the passage censuring "an oath . . . not warrantable by the laws or statutes of this realm. . . ." That oath, which preceded interrogation, operated to coerce confessions from the opponents of the king's forced loan of 1626.[23]

The Court in *Twining* also found significance in the fact that compulsory self-incrimination was not condemned by the Stamp Act Congress, the First Continental Congress, or the Northwest Ordinance.[24] But the Stamp Act Congress mentioned only trial by jury among the many well-established rights of the criminally accused; failure to enumerate them all proved nothing. The Court failed to note that the First Continental Congress did claim that the colonists were "entitled to the common law of England," which had long protected the right against self-incrimination, nor did the Court note, or know, that Congress in 1778, in an investigation of its own, did respect that right.[25] The Northwest Ordinance did contain a guarantee of "judicial proceedings according to the course of the common law." [26] Indeed, the Supreme Court itself said in *Twining*, though without proof, that by 1776 the courts recognized the right even in the states whose constitutions did not protect it. Justice Moody mentioned six states whose constitutions provided such protection; but he neglected a seventh, Delaware, and an eighth, Vermont, not then a member of the Union.[27] What Moody did not recognize was that *every* state that had a separate bill of rights protected the right against self-incrimination. He noted that only four of the original thirteen states insisted that the right be incorporated in the new national Constitution, but he failed to note that these were the only states which ratified the Constitution with comprehensive recommendations for a national bill of rights.[28] Using Moody's yardstick, one could argue that the fundamental concept of due process of law was not fundamental at all because it did not appear in any of the thirteen state constitutions and was recommended by only one state ratifying convention. Moody remarked, inaccurately, that the principle that no person could be compelled to be a witness against himself "distinguished the common law from all other systems of jurisprudence." [29] If so, and if that principle was first elevated to constitutional status in America, and if it was safeguarded by every state having a bill of rights, and if it fit the several definitions of due process that Moody offered, there is no explaining the Court's finding that the right came into existence as a rule of evidence that was not "an essential part of due process." [30]

There are many other misleading or mistaken statements of history in *Twining*, but the point has been made: the opinion was founded on inaccurate and insufficient data. Contrary to the Court's assertion, the right against self-incrimination did evolve as an essential part of due process and as a fundamental principle of liberty and justice. Thus, Ben Franklin in 1735 called it a natural right ("the common Right of Mankind"), and Baron Geoffrey Gilbert, the foremost English authority on evidence at the time, called it part of the "Law of Nature." [31]

II

Other cases reveal the justices to be equally inept as historians even when conscripting the past into service for the defense and expansion of the Fifth Amendment. The most historically minded opinion of this kind was Justice Douglas' dissent in *Ullmann* v. *United States*, decided in 1956.[32] The seven-man majority, speaking through Justice

Frankfurter, sustained the constitutionality of Congress's Immunity Act of 1954. That act required that in certain cases involving national security, a federal court, on application approved by the attorney general, might require a witness to testify or produce records that might otherwise incriminate him, on condition that his revelations could not be used as evidence against him in any criminal proceeding. Frankfurter's opinion for the majority stressed the importance of history in interpreting the Fifth. History, he said, showed that it should be construed broadly, though he construed it narrowly, and he quoted Chief Judge Magruder's remark that "Our forefathers, when they wrote this provision into the Fifth Amendment of the Constitution, had in mind a lot of history which has been largely forgotten today." [33] Frankfurter himself observed that, "the privilege against self-incrimination is a specific provision of which it is peculiarly true that 'a page of history is worth a volume of logic.' " [34] But Frankfurter did not provide that page of history despite his rhetorical stress on its importance. He offered only the brief line that the Fifth was aimed against a recurrence of the Inquisition and of the Star Chamber. Though Frankfurter was the best and most historically minded scholar on the Court, he was apparently unaware of the several colonial precedents [35] in support of his argument that the right cannot be claimed if the legal peril, which is the reason for its existence, ceases.

Douglas' dissent, in which Black joined, is a splendid specimen of law-office history, yet most of his history was not even relevant to his conclusion that the Immunity Act violated the Fifth Amendment. Douglas's relevant data, which dealt with the concept of infamy, were unsound. He claimed that the act was unconstitutional because it was not broad enough: it did not protect against infamy or public disgrace. In support of this proposition he had to prove that the framers of the Fifth meant it to protect against disclosures resulting in public disgrace accompanied by noncriminal penalties like the loss of employment. Such evidence as history provides to support his proposition [36] was unknown to Douglas. *His* evidence was far-fetched, for he based his argument on the fact that protection against infamy is found in the ideas of Beccaria and the *Encyclopédistes* whom Jefferson read. But the Fifth Amendment was exclusively the product of English and American colonial experience. The influence of Continental theorists was nonexistent. As for Jefferson, he had nothing to do with the making of the Fifth. Indeed, he omitted protections against self-incrimination in the two model constitutions that he proposed for Virginia.[37]

Douglas's other evidence dealt not with the issue in question, immunity, but with the general origins of the Fifth. He referred to the Puritan hatred of the self-incriminatory oath ex officio used by the Star Chamber and its ecclesiastical counterpart, the High Commission. The hatred existed, but there were significant differences between the Star Chamber's use of the oath and the High Commission's. The High Commission required the suspect to take that oath to tell the truth as the first step of the examination, and then interrogated him orally without telling him the charges against him or the identity of his accusers. By contrast, the Star Chamber normally provided a bill of complaint, as specific as common-law indictment, and permitted the accused to have plenty of time to answer the charges in writing and with the advice of counsel; only then did the accused have to take the oath and be interrogated.[38] However, in Archbishop Laud's time, the power of examining parties under oath, as a Star Chamber lawyer recorded, "was used like a Spanish inquisition to rack men's consciences." [39] But that was exceptional in the Star Chamber, routine in the High Commission. The same Star Chamber lawyer stated that if "the matter in charge tendeth to accuse the defendant of some crime which may be capital; in which case *nemo tenetur prodere seipsum* [no man is bound to accuse himself]. . . ." And, "neither must it question the party to accuse him of crime." [40] The same rule applied to witnesses. In the High Commission, however, the inquisitional procedure conformed to a quite different rule: any person suspected, even if only by rumor, must answer the interrogatories, however incriminating. The maxim *nemo tenetur seipsum prodere*, from which the right against self-incrimination derived, did not operate in the High Commission.[41] For these reasons common-lawyers led by Robert Beale, James Morice, and Sir Edward Coke, who supported that maxim and assaulted the oath ex officio, did not attack the use of the oath by the Star Chamber.[42] Too often the Star Chamber is loosely identified as the symbol of arbitrary, inquisitional procedure, the opposition to which gave rise to the right against self-incrimination. Thus Justice Black in his *Adamson* dissent spoke of the Star Chamber practice of compelling people to testify against themselves, and the same thought is in Chief Justice Warren's opinion for the Court in the *Miranda* case which extended the right against self-incrimination to the police station.[43]

Black in *Adamson*, Douglas in *Ullmann*, and Warren in *Miranda* referred to John Lilburne's Star Chamber trial of 1637 and his refusal to take the oath.[44] As these justices imply, Lilburne was more responsible than any other single individual for the recognition by the common-law courts of the right against self-incrimination. If any one man deserves to be remembered as the father of the right, it was he. But not because of his opposition to the oath in 1637. He said then, "Before I swear, I will know to what I must swear," and the court examiner replied, "As soon as you have sworn, you shall, but not before." [45] The fact is that in this case the Star Chamber had abandoned its normal procedure. Rather, it followed High Commission procedure, demanding the oath first instead of providing the written complaint first. As a result Lilburne refused the oath, claiming that he was the first ever to have done so before the Star Chamber [46]—proof that its procedure in that 1637 case was exceptional. Moreover, Lilburne remained silent only to incriminating questions that were not germane to the issue.[47] Justice Douglas' quotations from Lilburne in 1648 and 1653 against the oath [48] were redundant. Douglas should have quoted statements by Lilburne that even in the *absence* of the oath and *after* common-law indictment, Magna Carta and the Petition of Right protected a man from being examined on interrogatories concerning himself—"concerning," which is far broader than "incriminating." [49] Douglas should also have quoted Lilburne's claim, made during his trial for treason in 1649, that even after common-law indictment and without oath, he did not have to answer questions "against or concerning myself." [50] At that trial Lilburne placed the right against self-incrimination squarely in the context of what he called "fair play," "fair trial," "the due process of the law," and "the good old laws of England." [51] Justice Douglas gave to John Lilburne a page of his opinion in *Ullmann*, straining the evidence and never knowing that history provided him with stronger facts with which to construct his one-sided argument.

Douglas' respect for evidence, particularly historical evidence, has frequently been minimal when he has a libertarian theme to defend. In his *Ullmann* opinion he grossly distorted the evidence concerning an important episode in the colonial history of the right against self-incrimination. He mentioned that Governor Bradford of Plymouth sought the advice of his ministers on the question, "How farr a magistrate may extracte a confession from a delinquente, to acuse himselfe of a capitall crime, seeing *Nemo tenetur prodere seipsum*." [52] Inexplicably, Douglas omitted the Latin phrase that both supported his argument and invalidated the generalization in *Twining*, based on the Anne Hutchinson case, that the right against self-incrimination was unknown. Three Plymouth ministers, Douglas said, were unanimous in concluding that the oath was illegal, and he quoted as "typical" only the answer of Ralph Partrich that the magistrate might not extract a confession "by any violent means," whether by oath or "punishment." [53] Douglas concealed the answer of Charles Chauncy who said, "But now, if the question be mente of inflicting bodly torments to extract a confession from a mallefactor, I conceive that in maters of higest consequence, such as doe conceirne the saftie or ruine of stats or countries, magistrats may proceede so farr to bodily torments, as racks, hote-irons, &c. to extracte a confession, espetially wher presumptions are strounge; but otherwise by no means." [54]

Chauncy would not force self-incrimination by oath, but he would employ torture in matters such as sedition or treason and perhaps heresy. Douglas' account also omits the fact that John Winthrop, who received the opinions of the elders and magistrates of Massachusetts Bay, New Haven, and Connecticut, as well as of Plymouth, recorded that "most" answered that in a capital case if one witness or "strong presumptions" pointed to the suspect, the judge could examine him "strictly, and he is bound to answer directly, though to the peril of his life." [55] Douglas stressed the Puritan opposition to the oath, yet Samuel Maverick, when petitioning the General Court of Massachusetts in 1649 for a remission of the fines imposed on him for his part in the Robert Child Remonstrance, declared, "your whole proceeding against us seemes to depend on our refusall to answer Interrogatories upon oath." [56]

However inept, ignorant, biased, or dishonest some justices may be as historians, the blame is less theirs than that of the professional historians. The Bill of Rights epitomizes one of our history's most noble and enduringly important themes, the triumph of individual liberty, yet has been one of the most neglected subjects of historical scholarship. There is no satisfactory study of the origins and framing of the first state bills of rights, nor of the national Bill of Rights; there are few studies of particular rights; and there was no book on the origins of the right against self-incrimination until 1968. [57] That latter fact is especially striking because the Court has assured us again and again that our understanding of the right is quite dependent upon history. Chief Justice Warren, for example, noting that the right "was hard-earned by our forefathers," declared that the "reasons for its inclusion in the Constitution—and the necessities for its preservation—are to be found in the lessons of history." [58] Yet the members of the Court, who understandably lack either the time or competence to do their own research, must turn to the work of lawyers for whatever illumination history might offer, because historians have defaulted. Chief Justice Warren, who denied—correctly, I think—that the Fifth is a historical relic, has had to rely primarily on the chapter in Wigmore's *Treatise on Evidence*, an unsympathetic account by one who regarded the Fifth as a historical relic. [59] Frankfurter's description of this classic, first published in 1904, as "a masterpiece of scholarship," [60] is well deserved; yet Wigmore made many errors and ignored the American origins of the Fifth. An excellent corrective, the essay by Mary H. Maguire, [61] which also treats only the English side of the story, was long the only account by a historian until Levy and Leder published an article in a journal of history, the *William and Mary Quarterly*,[62] which the Court apparently does not read. The justices read the law reviews. Except for the Levy-Leder article, the only account of the colonial background of the Fifth is the suggestive and much-cited, but shallow and unreliable, article published in 1935 in the *Virginia Law Review* by R. Carter Pittman of the Virginia bar.[63] Such is the scholarly literature on which the Court has based its own accounts.[64]

III

What illumination is available from the face of the Fifth? Its words include more than merely a right against self-incrimination, a phrase of modern origin. The clause in the Fifth is, "no person . . . shall be compelled in any criminal case to be a witness against himself." In some respects that formulation is quite broad, because it protects against more than just compulsory self-incrimination or even disclosures merely tending to provide a link in a chain of circumstantial evidence that might be the basis of a prosecution. A person can also be a witness against himself in ways that do not incriminate him. He may, in a criminal case, injure his civil interests or disgrace himself in the public mind. Thus the Fifth could be construed on its face to protect against disclosures that expose one to either civil liability or infamy. The Fifth could also be construed to apply to an ordinary witness as well as to the criminal defendant himself. In Virginia, where the right against self-incrimination first received constitutional status, it appeared in a paragraph relating to the accused only.[65] But the Fifth Amendment is not similarly restrictive, unlike its Virginia precedent and unlike the Sixth Amendment which explicitly refers to the accused, protecting him alone. The location of the clause in the Fifth, rather than in the Sixth, and its reference to "no person," made it applicable to witnesses as well as to the accused.

On the other hand, the clause has a distinctively limiting factor: it is restricted on its face to criminal cases. The phrase "criminal case" seems to some to preclude more than the invocation of the right in civil or equity cases. In the minds of some judges and legal scholars, no criminal case exists until a formal charge has been made against the accused by indictment, information, or complaint before a magistrate.[66] Under such an interpretation the right would have no existence until the accused is put on trial; before that, when he is taken into custody, interrogated by the police, or examined by a grand jury, he would not have the benefit of the right. Nor would he have its benefit in a nonjudicial proceeding like a legislative investigation or an administrative hearing. Moreover, despite what has been said about the language of the Fifth embracing a witness as well as the accused, some judges and legal scholars claim that its language protects only the accused.[67] Though the Supreme Court has held otherwise, the Court has also given the impression that the clause, if taken literally, does have that restrictive effect. But the Court refuses to take the clause literally. Of no other clause in the Constitution has the Court declared that it cannot mean what it seems to say. Thus, in *Counselman* v. *Hitchcock*, a major case on the Fifth decided in 1892, the Court held that the Fifth did protect ordinary witnesses, even in federal grand-jury proceedings.[68] Unanimously the Court declared, "It is *impossible* that the meaning of the constitutional provision can only be that a person shall not be compelled to be a witness against himself in a criminal prosecution against himself." [69] Although the Court did not explain why it was "impossible," the Court was right. Had the framers of the Fifth intended the literal, restrictive meaning, then their constitutional provision was a meaningless gesture because there was no need to protect the accused at his trial: he was not permitted to give testimony, whether for or against himself, at the time of the framing of the Fifth. Making the criminal defendant competent to be a witness in his own case, if he wanted to, was a reform of the later nineteenth century, beginning in the state courts with Maine's example in 1864, in the federal courts by an act of Congress in 1878.[70]

The Court has construed the clause as if its framers neither meant what they said nor said what they meant. Generally the Court has acted as if the letter killeth. Seeking the spirit and policy of the Fifth, the Court has, on the whole, given it an ever-widening, liberal interpretation, on the principle that "it is as broad as the mischief against which it seeks to guard." [71] In effect the Court has taken the position that the Fifth embodied the still evolving common law of the matter, rather than a precise rule of fixed meaning. State courts confronted by an even more restrictive constitutional clause, one expressly safeguarding only the criminal defendant, have also, and consistently, read it as if it were synonymous with broad common-law practices.[72] Indeed early state and federal decisions usually rested on the common law without reference to the constitutional provisions. In so doing the courts have been true to the intent of the framers of the Fifth and of its state constitutional equivalents. And in so doing the courts have also been true to the historical meaning of the right. The Supreme Court, in its liberal interpretations, has had the past on its side, but has not known it. Many apparent innovations are supported by old practices and precedents. Maybe Santayana was on the right track when he said that those who do not know history are doomed to repeat it.

IV

What, briefly, does history reveal about the scope and meaning of the Fifth? First, its framers meant to bequeath a large and still-growing principle. Madison, who introduced it, proposed the unqualified principle that no person should be a witness against himself.[73] Congress added the phrase, "in any criminal case," [74] probably—we are not sure—to permit the courts to compel a *civil* defendant to produce documents "against himself." [75] Such documents might injure his civil interest without infringing his traditional right not to produce them if they could harm him criminally.

Second, the right did extend to grand-jury proceedings. As early as 1681 John Somers, the Lord Chancellor of England, took that for granted.[76] His book on the grand jury was reprinted in Boston in 1720 and, on the eve of the Revolution, in New York in 1773. An early federal circuit court opinion, not cited in *Counselman* v. *Hitchcock*, also took for granted that the right extended to a witness before a federal grand jury.[77]

Third, that the right extended to witnesses, as well as to the accused, can be traced to English cases of 1649 and 1679. Protection of the witness was invariably stated in American manuals of legal practice throughout the eighteenth century, as well as in English treatises, including the familiar works by Hawkins and Blackstone.[78]

Fourth, the right extended to both witnesses and parties in civil as well as criminal cases if a truthful answer to the question might result in a forfeiture, penalty, or criminal prosecution. The proof consists of many English and early American state decisions.[79] In a little-known aspect of the famous case of *Marbury* v. *Madison*, Chief Justice Marshall asked the Attorney General of the United States, Levi Lincoln, what he had done with Marbury's missing commission which he had had in his possession when serving as acting secretary of state. The Attorney General, who probably had burned the commission, refused to incriminate himself by answering, and the Supreme Court sustained him, though he was a witness in a civil suit.[80]

Fifth, there are many early state cases and one federal one showing that a witness in a civil suit did not have to answer questions against himself even if his answers would not incriminate but would merely affect his civil interests or property rights adversely. These far-fetched precedents have been abandoned.[81]

Sixth, along the same lines, there are many early state cases show-ing that neither witnesses nor parties were required to answer against themselves if to do so would expose them to public disgrace or infamy.[82] The origins of so broad a right of silence can be traced as far back as sixteenth-century claims by Protestant reformers like William Tyndale and Thomas Cartwright in connection with their argument that no man should be compelled to accuse himself.[83] The idea passed to the common lawyers, including Coke,[84] was accepted even in the Star Chamber as well as English case-law,[85] and found ex-pression in Blackstone[86] and the American manuals of practice.[87] Yet the Supreme Court restricted the scope of the historical right when ruling that the Fifth did not protect against compulsory self-disgrace. Its decision to that effect in 1896[88] was oblivious to the history of the matter. In the 1956 *Ullmann* case reaffirming that precedent of 1896, Frankfurter for the Court stressed the importance of history, yet offered none, and, forgetting that the Constitution does not speak of merely a stunted right against self-incrimination, alleged that the "sole concern [of "the privilege against self-incrimination"] *as its name indicates*" [!] is with the danger of giving testimony lead-ing to the infliction of criminal penalties.[89] History was on the side of Douglas and Black, dissenting, with respect to the question whether the "privilege" embraced public infamy, but they did not know it.

Seventh, from the standpoint of history, that 1896 case and its reaffirmation in 1956 were correctly decided on the main question, whether a grant of full immunity supersedes the witness' right to refuse answer on grounds of self-incrimination. As early as 1698 a Connecticut statute required testimony by providing immunity against prosecution for self-incriminatory disclosures.[90] Among the later colonial precedents are cases of 1758, when the Pennsylvania Assembly granted a witness immunity in exchange for his testimony,[91] and of 1763, when the Supreme Court of Judicature of New York offered pardons to some ships' captains in order to force them to testify about illicit trading with the enemy.[92]

Eighth, history also supports the decision made by the Court for the first time in 1955 that the right extends to legislative investiga-tions.[93] As early as 1645 John Lilburne, relying on his own reading of Magna Carta and the Petition of Right, claimed the right, unsuc-cessfully, before a Parliamentary committee, and the notion became commonplace in Leveller literature thereafter. In the mid-eighteenth century the two houses of Parliament were divided on the validity of such a claim.[94] On these shores, there were numerous instances of a witness claiming the right during an investigation conducted by a colonial assembly. Some assemblies, like that of Pennsylvania in 1756, explicitly recognized the validity of such a claim;[95] others, like that of New York in 1770, did not.[96] In the latter instance the Sons of Liberty were provoked into drinking to the toast, "No Answer to Interrogatories, when tending to accuse the Person interrogated." [97] A stronger precedent grew out of the investigation in 1778 by the Continental Congress into the corrupt schemes of Silas Deane, the diplomat. Deane invoked the right against self-incrimination, and Congress, it seems, voted that it was lawful for him to do so.[98]

Ninth, history belies the "two sovereignties" rule, a stunting restriction upon the Fifth introduced by the Court in 1931, but recently abandoned. The rule was that a person could not refuse to testify on ground that his disclosures would subject him to prosecution in another sovereignty or jurisdiction. Thus he could be convicted of a federal crime on the basis of testimony that he was required to give in a state proceeding, or vice versa. In matters involving national supremacy, Congress at its discretion could grant immunity against state prosecution, but not vice versa, nor could one state immunize against a prosecution in another. The Court mistakenly alleged that the "two sovereignties" rule had the support of historical precedents. History clearly contradicted that rule as the Court belatedly confessed when wholly scrapping it in 1964.[99]

Tenth, history supports the 1897 rule of the Court that in criminal cases in the federal courts—this was extended in 1964 to the state courts, too—whenever a question arises whether a confession is incompetent because it is involuntary or coerced, the issue is controlled by the self-incrimination clause of the Fifth.[100] Partly because of Dean John H. Wigmore's intimidating influence and partly because of the rule of *Twining* denying that the Fourteenth Amendment extended the Fifth to the states, the Court until 1964 held that the coercion of a confession by state or local authorities violated the principle of due process of law rather than the right against self-incrimination.[101] Wigmore, the great master of evidence, claimed that the rule against coerced confessions and the right against self-incrimination had "no connection," the two being different in history, time of origin, principle, and practice. He was wrong.[102]

Finally, history is ambiguous on the controversial issue of current interest, whether the right against self-incrimination extends to the police station. When justices of the peace performed police functions and conducted the preliminary examination of suspects, the interrogation was inquisitorial in character, as it is in the interrogation room of the police station today, and it usually had as its object the incrimination of the suspect. Yet he could not be examined under oath, and he did have a lawful right to withhold the answer to incriminating questions. On the other hand he had no right to be apprised that he need not answer, nor be cautioned that his answers could be used against him—not until the mid-nineteenth century in England. However, the right against self-incrimination began as a protest against incriminating interrogation *prior* to formal accusation. That is, the maxim *nemo tenetur seipsum prodere* originally meant that no one was obligated to supply the evidence which could be used to indict him. Thus, from the very inception of the right, a suspect could invoke it at the earliest stages of his interrogation.[103] In its *Miranda* decision in 1966 the Supreme Court expanded the right beyond all precedent, yet not beyond its historical spirit and purpose. The Court ruled that the Fifth requires that the police fully and clearly apprise the suspect of his constitutional rights. He must understand that he has a right to remain silent, that his answers may be used against him, that he is entitled to counsel in the police station in order to protect his right under the Fifth, that he can forestall all questioning until counsel is present, that the state will provide counsel if he is indigent, and that he may not waive these rights except knowingly and intelligently.[104]

The ghost of John Lilburne wrote that opinion. Its purpose is to eliminate the inherently coercive and inquisitional atmosphere of the interrogation room and to guarantee that any incriminating admissions are made voluntarily. That purpose—to overcome inquisitions and insure that confessions are the product of free choice—is, historically, the heart of the Fifth, the basis of its policy. Even the guarantee of counsel to effectuate that purpose has precedent in a historical analogy: the development of the right to counsel originally safeguarded the right against self-incrimination at the trial stage of a prosecution. When the defendant lacked counsel, he had to conduct his own case, and though he was not put on the stand and did not have to answer incriminating questions, his failure to rebut accusations and insinuations by the prosecution prejudiced the jury, vitiating the right to silence. The right to counsel permitted the defendant's lips to remain sealed; his "mouthpiece" spoke for him.[105] In the *Miranda* case the Court extended the protection of counsel to the earliest stage of a criminal action, when the need is the greatest because the suspect is most vulnerable.

History, Frankfurter once wrote, presents a body of experience expressing the judgment of its time, but history does not save the Supreme Court "from the necessity for judgment in giving past history present application." [106] Whether the Court's opinions ought to rely upon the wisdom and insights of the past in relation to the right in question is not the issue here. The issue is whether the Court has used the evidence of history knowledgeably and responsibly in its Fifth Amendment opinions. It has not. Yet, without knowing it, by blunder or instinct the Court has handed down opinions that have had a strong ally in history in keeping the Fifth "as broad as the mischief against which it seeks to guard."

NOTES

[1] Alfred H. Kelly, "Clio and the Court: An Illicit Love Affair," in Philip B. Kurland, ed., *Supreme Court Review: 1965* (Chicago, 1965), pp. 119–158.

[2] *Adamson* v. *California*, 332 U.S. 46 (1947).

[3] Charles Fairman, "Does the Fourteenth Amendment Incorporate the Bill of Rights? The Original Understanding," *Stanford Law Review*, II (1949), 5–139.

[4] Paul L. Murphy, "Time to Reclaim: the Current Challenge of American Constitutional History," *American Historical Review*, LXIX (1963), 64–79. Murphy referred to *United States* v. *Curtiss-Wright Export Corp.*, 299 U.S. 304 (1936). He credited Howard J. Graham for the phrase "law office history."

[5] Alexander M. Bickel, "The Original Understanding and the Segregation Decision," *Harvard Law Review*, LXIX (1955), 1–43.

[6] Leonard W. Levy, *Legacy of Suppression: Freedom of Speech and Press in Early American History* (Cambridge, Mass., 1960). For a lucid discussion, see John Wofford, "The Blinding Light: the Uses of History in Constitutional Interpretation," *University of Chicago Law Review*, XXXI (1964), 502.

[7] *Twining* v. *New Jersey*, 211 U.S. 78 (1908). In my over-generalized reference to "the Fifth Amendment," I have followed the example of Erwin N. Griswold, *The 5th Amendment Today* (Cambridge, Mass., 1955) and many others. The Supreme Court has said, "Surely, in popular parlance and even in legal literature, the term 'Fifth Amendment' in the context of our time is commonly regarded as synonymous with the privilege against self-incrimination." *Quinn* v. *United States*, 349 U.S. 155, 163 (1955).

[8] *Malloy* v. *Hogan*, 378 U.S. 1 (1964).

[9] Jurists and legal commentators invariably speak of the "privilege" against self-incrimination. I refer to it as a "right" because it is one, having the same status, constitutionally, as free speech, trial by jury, benefit of counsel, and other guarantees of the Bill of Rights. A privilege is a revocable concession granted by the government to its subjects. In American constitutional theory, the rights of the people do not derive from the government; the Constitution, which secures those rights, is paramount to the government which it creates. To speak of the "privilege" against self-incrimination, degrades it, inadvertently or otherwise, in comparison to other constitutional rights.

[10] *Twining* v. *New Jersey*, 106.

[11] *Ibid.*, 110.

[12] *Ibid.*, 108.

[13] *Ibid.*, 103–04.

[14] *Adamson* v. *California*, 88.

[15] *A Short Story of the Rise, Reign, and Ruine of the Antinomians, Familists and Libertines, that Infected the Churches of New England* (London, 1649), reprinted in Charles Francis Adams, ed., *Antinomianism in the Colony of Massachusetts Bay, 1636–1638* (Boston, 1894), pp. 194, 195.

[16] (William Bradford), *Bradford's History "Of Plimoth Plantation"* (Boston, 1898), p. 465.

[17] E. G. Atkinson, ed., *Close Rolls of the Reign of Henry III, 1247–51* (London, 1922), pp. 221–222.

[18] Prohibition Formata de Statuto Articuli Cleri, in A. Luders *et al.*, eds., *Statutes of the Realm* (London, 1810), I, 209.

[19] I. S. Leadam and J. F. Baldwin, eds., *Select Cases before the King's Council, 1243–1482* (Cambridge, Mass., 1918), xxvi–xxvii, xliii, 33, 40, 74, 79–80, 94,

103, 105–06; James Fosdick Baldwin, *The King's Council in England during the Middle Ages* (Oxford, 1913), pp. 296–297.

20 *Rotuli Parliamentorium; ut et petitiones, et placita in Parliamento tempore Edwardi R. I* (*ad finem Henrici VII*) (London, 1767–77), II, 168, no. 28 (1347); 228, no. 16 (1351); 239, no. 19 (1352); 280, no. 37 (1363). *Statutes of the Realm,* I, 267, 5 Edw. III, chap. 9 (1331); 296, 15 Edw. III, chap. 3 (1341); 321, 25 Edw. III, chap. 4 (1352); 345, 28 Edw. III, chap. 3 (1354); 382, 37 Edw. III, chap. 18 (1363); 388, 42 Edw. III, chap. 3 (1368). On Magna Carta in the 14th century, see Faith Thompson, *Magna Carta, Its Role in the Making of the English Constitution, 1300–1629* (Minneapolis, 1948), chap. 3.

21 Robert Beale, "A Collection Shewinge what Jurisdiction the Clergie Hathe Heretofore Lawfully Used," British Museum, Cotton MSS, Cleopatra F. I., no. 1, *folio 18, recto.*

22 James Morice, *A briefe treatise of Oathes exacted by Ordinaries and Ecclesiasticall Judges* (n.p., 1600), 8–10, 11–18, 22, 26–31, 32, 37, 47; (Nicholas Fuller), *The Argument of Master Nicholas Fuller* (London, 1607), 7–13, 23, 28–29. Stowe MSS # 424, *folios* 158a–164b (British Museum) contains seventeen unreported cases of 1609–11 in most of which Coke invoked Magna Carta to rule on the illegality of the incriminatory oath ex officio; for reported decisions, see *Edwards's Case,* 13 Coke's Reports 9 (1609), *Huntley* v. *Cage,* 2 Brownlow & Goldesborough 14 (1611), and *Burrowes, Cox, Dyton et al.* v. *High Commission,* 3 Bulstrode 48 (1616). See also, "Of Oaths before an Ecclesiastical Judge *Ex Officio,*" 12 Coke's Reports 26 (1607). John H. Wigmore, *A Treatise on the Anglo-American System of Evidence in Trials at Common Law,* 3rd ed. (Boston, 1940), VIII (rev. 1961 by J. T. McNaughton), 280, gives a misleading account of Coke's opposition to the oath ex officio. For Parliament, see the bill passed by Commons against the oath ex officio on June 25, 1610, in Maurice F. Bond, ed., *Manuscripts of the House of Lords, Addenda 1514–1714,* Historical Manuscripts Commission, new series (London, 1962), XI, 125–126. During the reigns of Elizabeth and James I, the opposition to compulsory self-incrimination was, with rare exception, directed against the use of the oath ex officio by the ecclesiastical courts. In 1581, in the Star Chamber trial of Catholic laymen for their refusal to swear the oath ex officio before the Privy Council, the three leading common-law judges of England (Chief Baron Roger Manwood of the Exchequer, Chief Justice James Dyer of the Common Pleas, and Chief Justice Christopher Wray of the King's Bench) agreed, in the words of Wray, that "no man by lawe ought to sweare to accuse hymselfe when he might loose lyfe or lymme," in John Bruce, ed., "Narrative of the Proceedings in the Star-chamber against lord Vaux, sir Thomas Tresham, sir William Catesby, and others, for a contempt in refusing to swear that they had not harboured Campion the Jesuit," *Archaeologia: or, Miscellaneous Tracts Relating to Antiquity,* XXX (London, 1844), 103–104. In 1590 at the examination of John Udall by a special royal commission, *before* Udall was asked to take the oath, Chief Justice Edward Anderson of the Court of Common Pleas asked him whether he was the author of certain books, and Udall replied, "I think that by law I need not answer." Anderson said, "That is true if it concerned the loss of your life," in Trial of John Udall, comp. by T. B. Howell, *A Complete Collection of State Trials* (London, 1816), I, 1274. In a 1631 case involving seditious conspiracy, the two chief justices and the chief baron ruled that no defendant was obliged to answer questions that "do not concern himself," an oblique acknowledgment of the right against self-incrimination at common law, where the oath ex officio was unknown, in *ibid.,* III, 420. But these cases did not rely on Magna Carta. The claim that Magna Carta

vested a right against self-incrimination, wholly apart from the oath issue, originated with the Levellers. In 1645 John Lilburne, relying on chap. 29 of Magna Carta and the 1628 Petition of Right, claimed that "it is contrary to *Law*, to force a man to answer to Questions concerning himself . . ."; Lilburne, *Englands Birth-Right Justified Against all Arbitrary Usurpation, whether Regall or Parliamentary* (1645), in William Haller, ed., *Tracts on Liberty in the Puritan Revolution, 1638–1647* (New York, 1933), III, 263.

23 On the use of the incriminatory oath-procedure by Charles I, see "The Commission and Instructions for Raising the Forced Loan," September 23, 1626, in Samuel Rawson Gardiner, ed., *The Constitutional Documents of the Puritan Revolution, 1625–1660*, 3rd ed. (Oxford, 1906), p. 55; for the Petition of Right, see *ibid.*, p. 69.

24 *Twining v. New Jersey*, 108.

25 For the action of Congress in 1778, see below, note 98 and related text. For the Resolutions of the Stamp Act Congress and the Declaration and Resolves of the First Continental Congress, see Richard L. Perry, ed., *Sources of Our Liberties: Documentary Origins of Individual Liberties in the United States Constitution and Bill of Rights* (Chicago, 1959), pp. 270, 288.

26 Northwest Ordinance, Art. 2, in *ibid.*, p. 395.

27 Delaware Declaration of Rights, 1776, Sect. 15, in *ibid.*, *p.* 339; Constitution of Vermont, 1777, Sect. 10, in *ibid.*, p. 366. The six states named by Justice Moody were North Carolina, Pennsylvania, Virginia, Massachusetts, New Hampshire, and Maryland, in *Twining v. New Jersey*, 91.

28 For the amendments proposed by Virginia, New York, North Carolina, and Rhode Island, see Moody's summary, in *Twining*, 109.

29 *Ibid.*, p. 91. For a similar remark, see Wigmore, *Treatise on Evidence*, 2nd ed. (Boston, 1923), IV, 819. In *Miranda v. Arizona*, 384 U.S. 436, 458 (1966), Chief Justice Warren accurately observed that the roots of the principle "go back into ancient times," and in his note 27 Warren quoted Maimonides, *Mishneh Torah* (Code of Jewish Law), *Book of Judges*, Laws of the Sanhedrin, chap. 18, para. 6, in Abraham M. Hershman, ed., *The Code of Maimonides: Book Fourteen* (New Haven, 1949), pp. 52–53. Warren also cited Norman Lamm, "The Fifth Amendment and Its Equivalent in the Halakhah," *Judaism: A Quarterly Journal*, V (1956), 53–59. Rabbi Lamm's article is mainly a psychological analysis of Maimonides' statement. The same article, which praises Justice Douglas as "a great legal thinker," was quoted at length by Justice Douglas in *Garrity v. New Jersey*, 87 Sup. Ct. 616, 619, note 8. The article has its merits, but slights the Talmud which is much more to the point about "ancient times" than Maimonides, who completed his *Mishneh Torah* in 1180. For Talmudic references to the right against self-incrimination with appropriate cases or illustrations, see I. Epstein *et al.*, eds., *The Babylonian Talmud*, Soncino ed. (London, 1935ff.), *Nashim: Yebamoth* 25b, p. 154; *Nashim: Ketuboth* 18b, p. 102, and 41a, p. 228; *Nezikin: Sanhedrin* 9b, p. 39; *Nezikin: Baba Kamma* 64b, pp. 374–75, and 75b–75a, pp. 428–35; *Nezikin: Makkoth* 2b, pp. 5, 7. Among the various articles that the Court would have found useful are Haim J. Cohn, "The Privilege against Self-Incrimination: Israel," *Journal of Criminal Law, Criminology and Political Science*, LXI (1960), 175–78; Simcha Mendelbaum, "The Privilege against Self-Incrimination in Anglo-American and Jewish Law," *American Journal of Comparative Law*, V (1956), 115–19; and George Horowitz, "The Privilege against Self-Incrimination: How Did It Originate?" *Temple Law Quarterly*, XXXI (1958), 121–44. Lamm's article was a quixotic choice for the Court to honor in splendid isolation. For an excellent discussion in Hebrew of the Talmudic right, see the entry on "ein adam

meissim atamo rasha" (transliteration of the Hebrew maxim that "no one can incriminate himself") in the Hebrew *Entsiklopediyah Talmudit* (*Talmudic Encyclopedia: On Matters of Law*), Mayer Berlin and Solomon Joseph Zevin, eds., 3rd ed. (Tel Aviv, 1951), I, 355–356.

30 *Twining* v. *New Jersey*, 106. New York was the only state to recommend a due process of law clause; see Jonathan Elliot, ed., *The Debates in the Several State Conventions on the Adoption of the Federal Constitution*, 2nd rev. ed. (Philadelphia, 1941), I, 328. Although no state had a due process of law clause in its constitution before the Fifth Amendment, several states had a "law of the land" clause which was a historical equivalent.

31 The *Twining* decision was reaffirmed in *Palko* v. *Connecticut*, 302 U.S. 319, 324, 325 (1937); *Adamson* v. *California*, 332 U.S. 46 (1947); and *Cohen* v. *Hurley*, 366 U.S. 117, 128–29 note 7 (1961). For earlier cases, arising in the federal courts, in which the Supreme Court treated the right against self-incrimination as a fundamental right, see *Boyd* v. *United States*, 116 U.S. 616 (1886); *Counselman* v. *Hitchcock*, 142 U.S. 547 (1892); *Brown* v. *Walker*, 161 U.S. 596 (1896); and *Bram* v. *United States*, 168 U.S. 532 (1897). The Court first held the right to be fundamental in state cases, too, in *Malloy* v. *Hogan*, 378 U.S. 1 (1964). Franklin's remark is in his pamphlet, "Some Observations on the Proceedings against Mr. Hemphill" (1735), in Leonard W. Labaree *et al.*, eds., *Papers of Benjamin Franklin* (New Haven, 1959–), I, 44. For Gilbert, see *The Law of Evidence by a Late Learned Judge* (London, 1756), pp. 139–140.

32 350 U.S. 422 (1956).

33 *Ibid.*, 426, 427.

34 *Ibid.*, 438.

35 See below, notes 90–92 and related text.

36 See below, notes 83–86 and related text.

37 Douglas relied on Mitchell Franklin, "The *Encyclopédiste* Origin and Meaning of the Fifth Amendment," *Lawyers Guild Review*, xv (1955), 41–62, an article wholly without merit as an explanation of the historical origins of the Fifth Amendment. For Jefferson's proposed constitutions for Virginia, in 1776 and 1783, see *The Papers of Thomas Jefferson*, Julian Boyd *et al.*, eds. (Princeton, 1950–), I, 341, 348, 359; VI, 298. At the pages cited, Jefferson recommended a ban against torture. Jefferson made no reference to the right against self-incrimination in his letters of 1787–89, when he recommended provisions that should be included in a national bill of rights.

38 For the procedure of the Star Chamber, contrasting it with that of the High Commission, see Morice, *A briefe treatise of Oathes*, pp. 38–39. For a similar contrast by Robert Beale, see John Strype, *The Life and Acts of John Whitgift* (Oxford, 1822), II, 138. The best contemporary work on the Star Chamber is William Hudson, *A Treatise of the Court of Star Chamber* (ante 1635), in Francis Hargrave, ed., *Collectanea Juridica. Consisting of Tracts Relating to the Laws and Constitution of England* (London, 1791), I, 1–240.

39 Hudson, *Court of Star Chamber*, p. 169.

40 *Ibid.*, pp. 208–209; see also 64, 164.

41 On High Commission procedure and the practice of compulsory self-incrimination, see the book by a member of that court, Richard Cosin, *An Apologie for Sundrie Proceedings Ecclesiasticall* (London, 1593), Part II, 51–52, 57–58, 104; Part III, 43, 113–116. See also Strype, *John Whitgift*, I, 321–322.

42 For Beale and Morice, see note 38 above. For a similar distinction by Coke on the use of the oath by the Star Chamber and the High Commission, see 12 Coke's Reports 26 (1607). Wigmore, *Treatise on Evidence* (McNaugh-

ton rev.), VIII, 281, incorrectly traced the Star Chamber and its oath procedure to a statute of 1487, misstated that procedure, and charged Coke with inconsistency in opposing the use of the oath in the High Commission. The best study of the Star Chamber is the introduction by C. G. Bayne in Bayne and W. H. Dunham, eds., *Select Cases in the Council of Henry VII*, Selden Society Publications (London, 1958), LXXV, which corrects the common error concerning that statute of 1487.

 43 *Adamson* v. *California*, 88 novellae 14; *Miranda* v. *Arizona*, 384 U.S. 436, 459 (1966).

44 *Ibid.* for the remarks by Black and Warren; for Douglas, see *Ullmann* v. *United States*, 350 U.S. 422, 446–47 (1956).

45 Trial of Lilburne, Howell, comp., *State Trials*, III, 1315, 1318 (1637).

46 Lilburne, *The Christian Mans Triall*, 2nd ed. (London, 1641), 6.

47 Trial of Lilburne, *State Trials*, III, 1318.

48 The oath ex officio was abolished by Parliament in 1641, together with the High Commission and Star Chamber. But in 1648, preliminary to Pride's purge of the Presbyterian members of Parliament, a special committee of Parliament conducted an investigation into the loyalty of members whose opinions were offensive to the army leaders. The committee's inquisitional conduct and its requirement that witnesses take an oath to tell the truth provoked opponents to condemn what they regarded as a revival of Star Chamber tactics. As a result, Leveller protests, like Lilburne's, were matched by those of their Presbyterian enemies, the new victims of Parliament. See J. Howldin, *The Lawes Subversion* (London, 1648), pp. 6, 16; Theodorus Verax, *Anarchia Anglicana* (London, 1648), pp. 53–60.

49 Lilburne, *A Copy of a Letter from Lieutenant-Colonel John Lilburne to a friend* (London, 1645), pp. 2, 14; Lilburne, *Englands Birth-Right Justified Against all Arbitrary Usurpations* (London, 1645), in Haller, ed., *Tracts on Liberty*, III, 263. The Presbyterians made a similar claim. Thus, Clement Walker declared, ". . . and our accusation beginneth with the examination of our persons, to make us state a charge against ourselves, to betray ourselves, and cut our owne throats with our tongues, contrary to Magna Carta, the Petition of Right," in Verax, *Anarchia Anglicana*, p. 57.

50 Trial of Lilburne, *State Trials*, IV, 1269, 1292, 1340, 1341 (1649).

51 *Ibid.*, IV, 1292, 1340, 1341.

52 *Bradford's History*, p. 465.

53 Douglas said, "Partrich's answer is typical"; *Ullmann* v. *United States*, 448, and he cited the book by Bradford.

54 *Bradford's History*, pp. 472–473.

55 James Savage, ed., *The History of New England from 1630 to 1649. By John Winthrop* (Boston, 1853), II, 56.

56 Maverick's petition is quoted in George Lyman Kittredge, "Dr. Robert Child the Remonstrant," *Publications of the Colonial Society of Massachusetts*, XXI, Transactions, 1919, 58–59, note 5, citing Massachusetts Archives (MS) B xxviii, 228a, dated May 8, 1649.

57 Leonard W. Levy, *Origins of the Fifth Amendment: The Right against Self-Incrimination* (New York, 1968).

58 *Quinn* v. *United States*, 349 U.S. 155, 161 (1955).

59 *Ibid.*, 162; Wigmore, *Treatise on Evidence*, 2nd ed., IV, 819.

60 Philip B. Kurland, ed., *Of Law and Life and Other Things That Matter: Papers and Addresses of Felix Frankfurter, 1956–1963* (Cambridge, Mass., 1965), p. 256.

61 Mary Hume Maguire, "Attack of the Common Lawyers on the Oath

Ex Officio As Administered in the Ecclesiastical Courts of England," in *Essays in Honor of Charles H. McIlwain* (Cambridge, Mass., 1936), pp. 199–229.

⁶² Leonard W. Levy and Lawrence H. Leder, " 'Exotic Fruit': The Right Against Compulsory Self-Incrimination in Colonial New York," *William and Mary Quarterly*, 3d ser., xx (1963), 3–32, reprinted in this volume.

⁶³ R. Carter Pittman, "The Colonial and Constitutional History of the Privilege against Self-Incrimination in America," *Virginia Law Review*, xxi (1935), 763–789.

⁶⁴ Other studies treating the background of the Fifth Amendment are either derivative or repetitive. The best of these is Edmund M. Morgan, "The Privilege Against Self-Incrimination," *Minnesota Law Review*, xxxiv (1949), 1–45. See also John A. Kemp, "The Background of the Fifth Amendment in English Law," *William and Mary Law Review*, 1 (1958), 247–286; Charles H. Randall, "Sir Edward Coke and the Privilege against Self-Incrimination," *South Carolina Law Quarterly*, viii (1956), 417–453; Stephan A. Riesenfeld, "Law-Making and Legislative Precedent in American Legal History," *Minnesota Law Review*, xxxiii (1949), 103–144; Lewis Mayers, "The Federal Witness' Privilege against Self-Incrimination: Constitutional or Common Law?" *American Journal of Legal History*, iv (1960), 107–141; Edward S. Corwin, "The Supreme Court's Construction of the Self-Incrimination Clause," *Michigan Law Review*, xxix (1930), 1–27; Franklin, "*Encyclopédiste* Origin," *Lawyers Guild Review*, xv (1955), 41–62.

⁶⁵ "That in all capital or criminal prosecutions a man hath a right to demand the cause and nature of his accusation, to be confronted with the accusers and witnesses, to call for evidence in his favor, and to a speedy trial by an impartial jury of twelve men of his vicinage, without whose unanimous consent he cannot be found guilty; nor can he be compelled to give evidence against himself; that no man be deprived of his liberty, except by the law of the land or the judgment of his peers," Virginia Declaration of Rights, Sect. 8, 1776, in Perry, ed., *Sources of Our Liberties*, p. 312. Pennsylvania and North Carolina followed the same phraseology in 1776; Vermont did so in 1777. In 1780 Massachusetts also emulated Virginia, but referring to the criminal defendant said that no "subject" shall be compelled to "accuse, or furnish evidence against himself." New Hampshire copied Massachusetts in 1784. The constitutional provisions in Delaware and Maryland were significantly different from the Virginia model. In 1776 Delaware, instead of inserting the self-incrimination clause amidst the enumerated rights of the accused, gave it a separate section: "Sect. 15. That no man in the Courts of Common Law ought to be compelled to give evidence against himself." Maryland in 1776 did likewise, but provided for exceptions "in such cases as have been usually practised in this State, or may hereafter be directed by the Legislature." Perry, ed., *Sources of Our Liberties*, reprints all relevant documents.

⁶⁶ See Corwin, "The Supreme Court's Construction of the Self-Incrimination Clause," p. 2; Mayers, "The Federal Witness' Privilege against Self-Incrimination," p. 119; Charles T. McCormick, *Handbook of the Law of Evidence* (St. Paul, 1954), p. 258; and cases cited in notes 8–10.

⁶⁷ Corwin, Mayers, and McCormick, as cited in preceding note. See also Wigmore, *Treatise on Evidence* (McNaughton rev.), viii, 324; Claude R. Sowle, "The Privilege Against Self-Incrimination: Principles and Trends," *Journal of Criminal Law, Criminology, and Political Science*, li (1960), 132.

⁶⁸ 142 U.S. 547 (1892). The assault on the Counselman opinion in Mayers, "The Federal Witness' Privilege," p. 107, is historically unsound.

⁶⁹ *Counselman* v. *Hitchcock*, 562, emphasis added. Similarly, the Court said

in *Ullmann* v. *United States*, 438, that the clause "is not to be interpreted literally."

70 See *Ferguson* v. *Georgia*, 365 U.S. 570, 577 (1961), and Wigmore, *Treatise on Evidence* (McNaughton rev.), VIII, secs. 575–579.

71 *Counselman* v. *Hitchcock*, 562.

72 Pennsylvania provides the most striking example. The state constitution of 1776 had declared that "no man" should be compelled to give evidence against himself, but this clause appeared in the context of the rights of the accused. The state constitution of 1790 narrowed the clause by explicitly substituting "the accused" for "no man." Yet, in a case of 1802, counsel for defense argued that the clause in the 1790 constitution protected not only against answers tending to incriminate but also against those bringing the party into disgrace or infamy; and the state supreme court followed that argument, by dictum implying that such protection extended to witnesses as well as the accused. *Respublica* v. *Gibbs*, 3 Yeates (Pa.) 429, 437 (1802). In 1803, in a civil case, the same court held that no one could be forced to take the oath of a witness if his testimony tended to accuse him of an immoral act. *Galbreath* v. *Eichelberger*, 3 Yeates (Pa.) 515 (1803). For other cases, see below, notes 79, 81–82.

73 Madison's speech, June 8, 1789, in *Debates and Proceedings in the Congress of the United States (Annals of Congress)*, 1st Cong., 1st Sess., I, 434.

74 *Ibid.*, I, 753.

75 Charles Warren, "New Light on the History of the Federal Judiciary Act of 1789," *Harvard Law Review*, XXXVII (1923), 49, 111, 116, 118, 130 note, 177; E. S. Maclay, ed., *The Journal of William Maclay, United States Senator from Pennsylvania, 1789–1791* (New York, 1927), pp. 90–92; *Geyger's Lessee* v. *Geyger*, 2 Dallas (Circ. Ct. Pa.) 332, 333 (1795); "Applicability of Privilege against Self-Incrimination to Legislative Investigations," *Columbia Law Review*, XLIX (1949), 92–93.

76 John Somers, *The Security of Englishmens Lives, or the Trust, Power and Duty of Grand Juries of England* (London, 1681), reprinted in *A Guide to the Knowledge of the Rights and Privileges of Englishmen* (London, 1757), p. 170.

77 Ex parte Lindo, #8,364, 15 Fed. Cases 556 (Circ. Ct. D.C., 1807).

78 *State Trials*, IV, 989, 1101 (1649), and *ibid.*, VII, 296 (1679). For American manuals of practice, see (James Parker), *Conductor Generalis, Or the Office, Duty and Authority of Justices of the Peace* (New York, 1764), p. 167; (Richard Burn), *An Abridgment of Burns' Justice of the Peace* (Boston, 1773), p. 123; J. Davis, *The Office and Authority of a Justice of the Peace* (Newbern, N.C., 1774), p. 159; Richard Starke, *The Office and Authority of a Justice of the Peace* (Williamsburg, Va., 1774), p. 146; (John F. Grimké), *The South-Carolina Justice of the Peace* (Philadelphia, 1788), p. 191; William W. Hening, *The New Virginia Justice* (Richmond, Va., 1795), p. 177. For English law books, see William Hawkins, *A Treatise of the Pleas of the Crown* (London, 1716), II, 433; Matthew Bacon, *A New Abridgment of the Law* (Savoy, Eng., 1731), II, 288; Giles Jacob, *A New Law-Dictionary* (London, 1762), under title of "evidence"; William Blackstone, *Commentaries on the Laws of England* (London, 1768), III, 370.

79 For English authorities, see *Attorney General* v. *Mico*, 1 Hardres 123, 139–146 (1658); *Trevor* v. *Lesguire*, 1 Finch 72, 73 (1673); *Penrice* v. *Parker*, 1 Finch 75 (1673); *Bird* v. *Hardwicke*, 1 Vernon 109 (1682); *Att. Gen.* v. *Cresner*, 1 Parker 279 (1710); *Duncalf* v. *Blake*, 1 Atkyn 52, 53 (1737); *Smith* v. *Read*, 1 Atkyn 526, 529 (1737); *Earl of Suffolk* v. *Green*, 1 Atkyn 450

(1739); *Jones v. Meredith,* 2 Comyns 661, 672 (1739); *Baker v. Pritchard,* 2 Atkyn 387, 389 (1742); 634, 635; *Boteler v. Allington,* 3 Atkyn 453, 457 (1746); *East India Co. v. Campbell,* 1 Vesey Sr. 246, 247 (1749); *Harrison v. Southcote,* 2 Vesey Sr. 389, 394–395 (1751); *Brownsword v. Edwards,* 2 Vesey Sr. 244, 245–246 (1751). For American authorities, see *Trammell v. Hook,* 1 Harris & McHenry (Md.) 259 (1767); *Marbury v. Madison,* 1 Cranch (U.S.) 137, 144 (1803); *Grannis v. Branden,* 5 Day (Conn.) 260, 272–274 (1812); *Taney v. Kemp,* 4 Harris & Johnson (Md.) 348 (1818). See also cases cited below, note 81.

[80] *Marbury v. Madison,* 1 Cranch (U.S.) 137 (1803). See also *McCarthy v. Arndstein,* 266 U.S. 34 (1924).

[81] *Simons v. Payne,* 2 Root (Conn.) 406 (1796); *Starr v. Tracy,* 2 Root (Conn.) 528, 529 (1797); *Connor v. Bradey,* Anthon's Nisi Prius Rep. (N.Y.) 135, 136 (1809). In Tennessee the court acknowledged that the state constitutional provision referred only to criminal cases, neglecting to notice that it also referred only to the "accused"; nevertheless the court declared, "but we think the principle existed previous to the Constitution" and applied it to a witness in a civil case who refused to answer on ground that his answer would be prejudicial to his interest civilly; *Cook v. Corn,* 1 Overton (Tenn.) 340, 341 (1808). See also *Bell's Case,* 1 Browne (Pa.) 376 (1811), where the court said, "I have always overruled a question that would affect a witness civilly, or subject him to a criminal prosecution: I have gone farther; and where the answer to a question would cover the witness with infamy and shame, I have refused to compel him to answer it." But in *Baird v. Cochran,* 4 Sergeant & Rawle (Pa.) 397, 400 (1818), the preceding opinion was overruled, in effect, on the point that the witness need not answer against his interest civilly; otherwise, the opinion in *Bell's Case* was followed. For holdings, now the general rule, that the witness must answer questions against his interest though exposing himself to a civil suit, see *Taney v. Kemp,* 4 Harris & Johnson (Md.) 348 (1818), and *Planters' Bank v. Georgia,* 6 Martin O.S. (La.) 670 (1819). For a federal decision in accord with the earlier state decisions, see *Carne v. McLane,* #2,416, 5 Fed. Cases 89 (Circ. Ct. D.C., 1806).

[82] For Pennsylvania decisions, see the cases cited above, notes 72 and 81. See also *State v. Bailly,* 2 N.J. 396 (1807); *Vaughn v. Perrine,* 3 N.J. 299, 300 (1811); *Miller v. Crayon,* 2 Brevard (S. Car.) 108 (1806); *People v. Herrick,* 13 Johnson (N.Y.) 82 (1816). The English courts at this time were still applying the same rule; see *Rex v. Lewis,* 4 Espinasse 225, 226 (1802); *Macbride v. Macbride,* 4 Espinasse 242, 243 (1802).

[83] William Tyndale, *The Obedience of a Christen Man* (1528), reprinted in Henry Walter, ed., *Doctrinal Treatises and Introductions to Different Portions of the Holy Scriptures. By William Tyndale* (Cambridge, 1848), p. 355, where Tyndale said it was "a crule thing to break up into a man's heart, and to compel him to put either soul or body in jeopardy, or to shame himself." In 1584 Archbishop John Whitgift referred to a Puritan claim that *"nemo tenetur seipsum prodere, aut propriam turpitudinem revelare"* (no man is bound to accuse himself, or to reveal his own infamy); in Strype, *John Whitgift,* I, 319. See also the document of 1590 by Thomas Cartwright and others in Albert Peel and Leland H. Carlson, eds., *Cartwrightiana* (London, 1951), pp. 38ff., and a document of about the same date in Thomas Fuller, *The Church History of Britain,* J. S. Brewer, ed. (Oxford, 1845), V, 107–112.

[84] Morice, *A brief treatise,* p. 8; 1 Coke's Institutes 158b, and 4 *ibid.* 279.

[85] Hudson, *Court of Star Chamber,* pp. 208–09; Trial of Nathanael Reading, *State Trials,* VII, 259, 296–297 (1679); Trial of Peter Cook, *ibid.,* XIII, 311, 334–

335 (1696); Trial of Jonathan Freind, *ibid.*, XIII, 1, 17 (1696); *East India Co.* v. *Campbell*, 1 Vesey Sr. 246 (1749).

[86] Blackstone, *Commentaries*, III, 363, 370.

[87] See note 78 above for the references to Parker, Burn, Davis, Starke, Grimké, and Hening, at the pages cited, for a standardized quotation from Coke that "a witness alledging his own infamy or turpitude, is not to be heard."

[88] *Brown* v. *Walker*, 161 U.S. 591 (1896). There is little basis for the proposition in Wigmore, *Treatise on Evidence* (McNaughton rev.), VIII, 332, that a privilege against disclosing facts involving disgrace or infamy, irrespective of criminality, began later than and independent of the right against self-incrimination, nor for the companion proposition that in England the two were "never confused," that is, were unrelated. The three cases cited above in note 85 show the opposite, just as the evidence cited above in note 83 shows that the two "privileges"—against self-infamy and self-incrimination—were intimately allied in origin.

[89] *Ullmann* v. *United States*, 438, italics added.

[90] J. Hammond Trumbull and Charles J. Hoadly, eds., *The Public Records of the Colony of Connecticut* (Hartford, 1850–90), IV, 236.

[91] Gertrude MacKinney and Charles F. Hoban, eds., *Votes and Proceedings of the House of Representatives of the Province of Pennsylvania (1682–1776)*, in *Pennsylvania Archives* (n.p., 1931–35), 8th Series, VI, 4679.

[92] MS Minute Book of the Supreme Court of Judicature, October 19, 1762, to April 28, 1764, entries for October 28, 1763, pp. 273, 289, Engrossed Minutes, Hall of Records, New York County, N.Y.

[93] *Quinn* v. *United States*, 349 U.S. 155 (1955).

[94] See the pamphlets by Lilburne, in note 45 above, at pages cited. In 1742 Nicholas Paxton, the Solicitor of the Treasury, refused to answer incriminating questions before an investigating committee of Parliament. The Commons passed a bill of "indemnity" immunizing his testimony against prosecution, but the bill failed in the House of Lords. No one doubted at the time that the right against self-incrimination could lawfully be invoked before a legislative body. See "Debate on a Motion for Indemnifying Evidence," May 25, 1742, in *Gentleman's Magazine* (London), pp. 511–525, 555–573, 611–616.

[95] MacKinney and Hoban, eds., *Votes and Proceedings*, VI, 4445.

[96] Journal of the Votes and Proceedings of the General Assembly of the Colony of New York, 1769–1771, Public Records Office, Colonial Office Papers, Class 5, Vol. 1219, p. 8. Alexander McDougall, "To the Freeholders," *New-York Gazette: or, the Weekly Post-Boy*, December 24, 1770.

[97] *New-York Gazette: or, the Weekly Post-Boy*, March 25, 1771.

[98] Letter of Gouverneur Morris, in *The Freeman's Journal, or North-American Intelligencer* (Philadelphia), June 14, 1781; see also the statement by Henry Laurens, president of the Continental Congress, April 21, 1779, in Edmund C. Burnett, ed., *Letters of the Members of the Continental Congress* (Washington, 1928), IV, 166 note 12, 168.

[99] The "two sovereignties" rule was established in *United States* v. *Murdock*, 284 U.S. 141 (1931), following dicta in *Hale* v. *Henkel*, 201 U.S. 43, 69 (1906). See also *Fellman* v. *United States*, 322 U.S. 487 (1944), *Krapp* v. *Schweitzer*, 357 U.S. 371 (1958), and *Mills* v. *Louisiana*, 360 U.S. 230 (1959). In the Murdock case the Court declared: "The English rule of evidence against compulsory self-incrimination, on which historically that contained in the Fifth Amendment rests, does not protect witnesses against disclosing offenses in violation of the laws of another country. King of the Two Sicilies v. Willcox, 7 St. Tr. (N. S.) 1050, 1068; Queen v. Boyes, 1 B. & S. 311, 330." The Court did not know or

note that the Willcox decision had in effect been overruled or, at the least, distinguished away by the Court of Chancery Appeal in *United States of America* v. *McRae*, L.R. 3 Ch. 79 (1867). In the latter case, defendant pleaded the danger of incriminating himself under United States laws, citing a statute that would have subjected his lands to forfeiture. The other "precedent" cited in *Murdock*, the Boyes case of 1868, was not in point and was inappropriately cited. The historic precedent was *East India Co.* v. *Campbell*, 1 Vesey Sr. 246 (1749), where the English court ruled that Campbell did not have to disclose whether goods were illegally acquired in India, because he might be sent to Calcutta for punishment. This case was unknown to the Supreme Court when it misstated the English rule in the Murdock case. See J.A.C. Grant, "Federalism and Self-Incrimination," *University of California Los Angeles Law Review*, IV (1957), 549–582; V (1958), 1–25; and Grant, "Immunity from Compulsory Self-Incrimination in a Federal System of Government," *Temple Law Quarterly*, IX (1935), 57–78. In 1964 the Supreme Court bowed to scholarship and confessed its errors, saying that there was no historical justification for its "two sovereignties" rule; the Court completely repudiated that rule as contrary to history and to the policy of the Fifth Amendment, in *Murphy* v. *Waterfront Commission of New York*, 378 U.S. 79 (1964).

100 *Bram* v. *United States*, 168 U.S. 532 (1897); *Malloy* v. *Hogan*, 378 U.S. 1 (1964).

101 Wigmore, *Treatise on Evidence*, 3rd ed., III, 250 note 5, declared that the rule of *Bram* v. *United States* "must be specially repudiated" because the Court had confused the right against self-incrimination and the rule excluding coerced confessions; ". . . that history should be rashly tampered with by asserting any common origin is inexcusable." *Brown* v. *Mississippi*, 297 U.S. 278 (1936) was the first of a long line of cases in which state-coerced confessions were held to violate due process of law.

102 Wigmore, *Treatise on Evidence*, 3rd ed., III, 249–250. Wigmore was excessively technical, literal-minded, and sweeping in his generalizations when contrasting the rule against coerced confessions and the right against self-incrimination. From the fact that a separate rule against coerced confessions emerged in English decisions of the 18th century, nearly a century after the right against self-incrimination had become established, he concluded that the two rules had *no* connection. That the two operated differently in some respects and had differing rationales in other respects led him to the same conclusion. But he focused on their differences only and so exaggerated those differences that he fell into numerous errors and inconsistencies of statement. See Morgan, *Basic Problems of Evidence*, pp. 129–131, and John M. Maguire, *Evidence of Guilt: Restrictions upon Its Discovery or Compulsory Disclosure* (Boston, 1959), pp. 15–17. McCormick, under Wigmore's influence, declared that the language in *Bram* v. *United States*, to the effect that the Fifth Amendment privilege "was but a crystallization of the doctrine as to confessions," was "an historical blunder." Yet McCormick sensibly added, "Nevertheless, the kinship of the two rules is too apparent for denial. It is significant that the shadow of the rack and the thumbscrew was part of the background from which each rule emerged." *Handbook of the Law of Evidence*, p. 155. In support of the proposition that the disappearance of torture and the recognition of the right against compulsory self-incrimination were victories in the same political struggle, McCormick cited William Holdsworth, *A History of English Law* (London, 1903ff.), V, 184–187, and A. Lawrence Lowell, "The Judicial Use of Torture," *Harvard Law Review*, XI (1897), 220–233, 290–300. McCormick's point was well made. The relationship between torture, *compulsory* self-

incrimination, and *coerced* confessions was a historical fact as well as a physical and psychological one. In the 16th and 17th centuries, the argument against the three, resulting in the rules that Wigmore said had no connection, overlapped. Compulsory self-incrimination was always regarded by its opponents as a species of torture. An act of 1696 regulating treason trials required that confessions must be made willingly, without violence, and in open court; 7 & 8 Wm. III, chap 3, sect. 2, *Statutes of the Realm*, VII, 6. In 1730 the editor of the collected state trials observed that in other countries torture was used to coerce confessions, "but this is a practice which Englishmen are happily unacquainted with, enjoying the benefit of that just and reasonable Maxim, *Nemo tenetur accusare seipsum.*" *State Trials*, I, xxv. Similarly, Baron Gilbert, writing before 1726, declared that though the best evidence of guilt was a confession, "this Confession must be voluntary and without Compulsion; for our Law in this differs from the Civil Law, that it will not force any Man to accuse himself. . . ." *Law of Evidence*, pp. 139–140. When the rule against coerced confessions emerged its rationale was that a coerced confession is untrustworthy evidence. Trial of Matthew Mahoney, *State Trials*, XVII, 1003, 1053 (1741); *Rex v. Warickshall*, 1 Leach's Crown Cases 263 (1783). There remained, however, an indissoluble and crucial nexus with the right against self-incrimination, because both involved coercion or the involuntary acknowledgment of guilt. Significantly, the few references to the right against self-incrimination in the debates on the ratification of the Constitution identify the right with a protection against torture and inquisition, that is, against coerced confessions. See Elliot, ed., *Debates*, II, 111 and III, 447–448, 451–452; Maclay, ed., *Journal of William Maclay*, pp. 90–92. Wigmore fell into error by assuming that the right against self-incrimination had a single rationale and a static meaning. In fact it always had several rationales, was an expanding principle of law, and spun off into different directions. One offshoot was the development of a separate rule against coerced confessions. If there was "an historical blunder," it was made by the English courts of the 18th century when they divorced the confessions rule from the self-incrimination rule.

[103] On the preliminary examination conducted by justices of the peace, see James Fitzjames Stephen, *A History of the Criminal Law of England* (London, 1883), I, 219–226. See also Yale Kamisar, "Equal Justice in the Gatehouses and Mansions of American Criminal Procedure," in Kamisar *et al.*, *Criminal Justice in Our Time* (Charlottesville, Va., 1965), pp. 18–30.

[104] *Miranda* v. *Arizona*, 384 U.S. 436 (1966).

[105] Stephen, *A History of the Criminal Law*, I, 416, 424–425, 440.

[106] Felix Frankfurter and Thomas Corcoran, "Petty Federal Offenses and the Constitutional Guaranty of Trial by Jury," *Harvard Law Review*, XXXI (1926), 917, 982.

SIMS' CASE: THE
FUGITIVE SLAVE LAW
IN BOSTON IN 1851

WHEN hateful scenes of slavery were transferred from the South and enacted in the streets of Boston, the old city was confronted with a choice among cherished alternatives: liberty or union? freedom or property? The peculiar ingenuity of the Fugitive Slave Act of September 18, 1850, was that it brought the law of bondage home to a free state. It was a law of flint, and it produced a curious moral spectacle, for the question which distracted the minds of free men was whether to catch slaves or not to catch slaves.

To the antislavery hotspurs, zealously devoted to a "higher law" than the Constitution, the measure was diabolical; it violated the purest promptings of conscience and Christianity. Wendell Phillips resolved for "the Abolitionists of Massachusetts" that "CONSTITUTION OR NO CONSTITUTION, LAW OR NO LAW," they would fight the sins which black Daniel symbolized.[1] Those who praised Webster's patriotism and defended the law of 1850 denied that the Theodore Parkers and John Greenleaf Whittiers had a monopoly on moral justification. If the conservatives had retreated from the cause of individual freedom, it was in an anxious regard for even greater moral values: peace and Union. Or so they reasoned.[2] Charles Francis Adams wrote that while a shallow veneer of antislavery sentiment had been fashionable among them, it was "mere sentiment," without roots either in conviction or in material interests. "On the contrary," contended Adams, "so far as material interests were concerned, a great change had recently taken place. The manufacturing development of Massachusetts had been rapid, and a close affiliation had sprung up between the cotton spinners of the North and the cotton producers of the South—or as Charles Sumner put it, between 'the lords of the loom and the lords of the lash.' "[3]

By mid-century there was no longer any concealment by a great majority of Boston's "best people" of their warmness toward Southern interests. Their eagerness to keep on the best of terms with the South was later recalled by Edward L. Pierce, a student at Harvard Law School, 1850–1852. "A southern slave holder, or his son at Harvard," he wrote, "was more welcome in society than any guest except a foreigner. . . . The deference to rich southern planters was marked." [4] Almost all the wealth of the city was controlled by the "cotton Whigs," and as social and business Boston gradually became "almost avowedly a pro-slavery community," [5] its self-justification of loyalty to the Constitution and to national security approached hysteria. When the news came from Washington that the Fugitive Slave Act had been safely passed, one hundred guns roared a joyous salute across the Common.

A few weeks later, opponents of the law swelled Faneuil Hall to fire their invective against its supporters, to pledge their aid to colored fellow-citizens, and to demand "INSTANT REPEAL." A group of fifty— it soon grew to two hundred and ten—was appointed to act as a Committee of Vigilance and Safety which determined to render the abominable act a nullity. Then in the same hall, in November, defenders of the law swore their allegiance to it at a "Constitutional Meeting." [6]

Amidst the furious climate of irreconcilable loyalties and thunderous rallies engendered by the Fugitive Slave Act, men waited apprehensively to see whether a solemn act of Congress would be honored, or be superseded by the resolves of a Gideon's army of lawless agitators. Scarcely a month after the law was passed, the heroic Craft couple arrived in Boston, fugitives from a Georgia planter. Here was the first test—and the vigilance committee, led by the indomitable Parker, tracked down the slave-hunters and chased them out of town! [7] Then, on February 15, 1851, a score of colored men broke into the Court House in broad daylight, cowed the federal marshals on duty, and whisked away Shadrach, a captured fugitive.[8]

The amazing rescue threatened the success of "peace measures," and the nation protested. The Washington correspondent of the *New York Journal of Commerce* telegraphed from the capital: "Some sensation was produced here by the intelligence of the negro insurrection in Boston." [9] Secretary of State Webster thought the rescue was "a case of treason." [10] On February 17, President Fillmore called a special cabinet meeting to discuss measures to be taken, and, on the next day, issued a proclamation commanding all civil and military officers to assist in recapturing Shadrach and to prosecute all persons who took part in the "scandalous outrage" committed against the laws of the United States. On the Senate floor, Clay demanded to know whether a "government of white men was to be yielded to a government by blacks." [11] Boston's reputation had been "badly damaged" especially in the South. The *Savannah Republican* scourged the city as a "black speck on the map—disgraced by the lowest, the meanest, the BLACKEST kind of NULLIFICATION." [12]

In Boston, the press fulminated against the "mischief which mad Abolitionism will wantonly perpetrate." [13] On February 18, the Board of Mayor and Aldermen expressed regret that the Commonwealth's dignity had been criminally insulted, and it ordered the City Marshal to make "the whole police force" available to quell a similar breach of law should one be anticipated. Two days later, the Common Council approved unanimously of the Board's action and "cordially" endorsed the President's proclamation.[14]

The abolitionists, in their turn, ridiculed the furor which the rescue had occasioned. "Warrington" attacked as Tories the leading citizens who pretended outrage, writing: "State-street brokers and Milk-street jobbers who . . . hold mortgages on slave-property . . . dared not to disturb the good understanding between the planters and the manufacturers. . . ." [15] And was not the rescue for the greater glory of God and His children? Dr. Bowditch marked down the day in his calendar as "a holy day," and Parker thought the rescue was "the noblest deed done in Boston since the destruction of the tea in 1773." [16] Impishly, vigilance men recalled that Mr. Glasse, the celebrated cook, had prudently premised in his recipe for cooking a hare, "first, *catch* your hare!"

It was notorious that no fugitive slave had ever been returned from Boston. Webster Whigs were dismayed that the whole state of Massachusetts was known as the cradle of "mad Abolitionism." It had become a matter of pride, not alone in the South, that a fugitive should be seized in Boston and taken back to slavery. Then, on Thursday evening, April 3, 1851—before the excitement of the Shadrach case had subsided—the city government of Boston was presented with an opportunity to make good on its promises of loyally enforcing the Fugitive Slave Act: Thomas Sims was taken into custody as a fugitive slave belonging to Mr. James Potter, a rice planter of Chatham County, Georgia.

Sims was a slim, small, "very bright-looking mulatto" who appeared "considerably younger than his real age of 23." [17] For many years he had lived with his family in Savannah, where he worked as a bricklayer. Early in 1851, he took to frequenting the wharves and asking questions of seamen. On the night of February 21, he stealthily boarded the brig *M. & J. C. Gilmore* and hid away in the forecastle. Somehow, during that two-week wintry voyage, he managed to provide for himself, undiscovered by the crew; but on March 6, just when the lights of Boston signaled that refuge lay nearby, the stowaway was caught by the mate. Sims was cursed at, struck, and brought before the captain to whom he explained that he was a free man, not a slave. His story was that he had been born in Florida; that he had been purchased and freed when a child; and that he had fled from Georgia because someone threatened to inform authorities of his entrance into that state without paying the fine which was required of free Negroes at the risk of their being sold into slavery. He had had no choice except to escape. His story, however, was discounted. He was locked in a cabin while the brig lay anchored outside Boston Harbor. But his pocketknife had not been taken from him. That night, he escaped by jimmying the lock on the door of his prison. Stealing the small boat of the brig, he lowered it to the water and pulled for freedom.

Sims landed in South Boston. He took lodgings in a colored seamen's boarding house at 153 Ann Street, and, while in the city, made no effort to conceal himself.[18] Destitute, requiring funds to arrange for bringing his free wife and children, he wired home to Savannah for money. The telegram included his return address. Somehow the intelligence of Sims' whereabouts reached James Potter, the man who claimed him as chattel. Potter quickly executed the proper legal documents, and exactly one week later, on April 3, his agent, John B. Bacon, arrived in Boston seeking Thomas Sims as a fugitive slave.[19] Seth J. Thomas, whom the *Lowell American* lost no time in pillorying as "the legal pimp of the slave catchers," [20] was hired by Bacon to prosecute Potter's claim.

That same day, Thursday, Thomas appeared before George Ticknor Curtis,[21] Commissioner of the U. S. Circuit Court, and secured a warrant for Sims' arrest. At about nine in the evening, two police officers who had been on the prowl for Sims caught up with him in the street. The alleged fugitive resisted arrest. The officers sought to overpower him. He defended himself and stabbed at Asa O. Butman, one of his captors, wounding him in the thigh. The sounds of the struggle attracted some members of the city watch. Sims was no match for the posse. He was thrown into a carriage and driven to the Court House—but not before he uttered an anguished cry: "I'm in the hands of kidnappers!" [22]

The cry was heard by passersby who had gathered to watch the scene. The vigilance committee had its ways of learning about such things speedily; within the hour it was on the alert. At half-past ten, three grim, very determined members made their way to Court Square. They were the Reverend Theodore "Thunder and Lightning" Parker, Elizur Wright, the trenchant editor of *The Commonwealth*, and Samuel Eliot Sewall, the indefatigable lawyer-friend of fugitive slaves. The three spied U. S. Deputy Marshal Patrick Riley—he who had yelled "Shoot him! Shoot him!" from his place of safety behind the door while Shadrach was being rescued.[23] The abolitionists closed in around Riley and demanded information as to when Sims would be brought before Curtis. They feared that a certificate warranting the youth's return would be issued before they could offer him whatever help was in their power. Sewall was terribly earnest. He grabbed the officer, threatening: "Mr. Riley, I demand that you answer me. Is the prisoner to be examined tonight? Tell me at your peril." [24] Riley's answer was a summons to some nearby watchmen. Sewall was arrested and committed to the watch-house for some hours that he might reconsider his disrespectful attitude toward an officer of the law. Outnumbered, Parker and Wright left. Later they would be heard from the press, pulpit, and platform.

Sims spent that night, and the rest of his nights in Boston, confined to the jury room of the Court House which was reserved for use in federal cases. He was thus technically imprisoned in a federal jail. This expedient was resorted to, as in Shadrach's case, because there was no U. S. prison in Massachusetts, and because the 1843 "Latimer Law" [25] of the state prohibited the use of its prisons for detaining any person accused of being a fugitive slave. In the courtroom prison, Sims was kept under close guard by the men of Charles Devens, the U. S. Marshal.

On the next morning, Friday, Boston awoke to witness one of the most extraordinary spectacles in its existence. During the night, while the city slept, the Court House had been barricaded. Under the direction of City Marshal Francis Tukey, iron chains had been girded entirely around the building. Its approaches were cleared by a belt of ropes and chains along the sidewalks. Heavy links stretched across its doorways. The Court House was in fetters, "bound . . . to the Georgia cotton presses." [26] Here was a visible answer, thought Bronson Alcott, to the question, "What has the North to do with slavery?" [27] Tukey had concentrated his men on the scene. The entire regular police force, reinforced by great numbers of special police, patrolled the area and were stationed around and within the building.[28] Wendell Phillips estimated the total number of police at no less than five hundred! [29] Only authorized persons could get within ten feet of the Court House and pass the armed cordon.[30] In effect, this meant that the city government of Boston had temporarily suspended the right of an ordinary citizen of a free Commonwealth to attend public sessions of its courts. Nor even the British tyrants before '76 had gone that far!

News of the arrest and of the exceptional scenes at the Court House hurried about the city. Several hundred people, infected with curiosity, clogged Court Square from early morning till ten at night. There was no organized attempt at disturbance, although the police were jeered at and scolded by women; on the other hand, repeated cheers were given for the Union. Not till midnight was the square emptied of the crowds for that day.[31] Word of the whole affair reached Longfellow, who recorded in his journal: "April 4, 1851.

There is much excitement in Boston about the capture of an alleged fugitive slave. O city without soul! When and where will this end? Shame that the great Republic, the 'refuge of the oppressed,' should stoop so low as to become the Hunter of Slaves." [32]

Low indeed was the stooping, for the chains across the door of the temple of justice were neither low enough to step over nor high enough to walk under. Those who entered the Court House on special business, lawyers, city officers, members of the press—they could enter if their views on the slavery question were safe enough [33]—commissioners, and judges, even the judges, all had to bow their backs and creep beneath the chains. Tukey, the satrap in charge, had ordered it so. Chief Justice Lemuel Shaw of the Supreme Judicial Court, the great Shaw, venerated for his wisdom and for his advanced age, was among the first that morning to stoop beneath the chains.[34] Decades before, Shaw himself had commented that one of the many evils in legally sanctioning slavery was that it degraded ministers of the law and profaned the sanctuary of justice.[35] Senator Joseph T. Buckminster told the Massachusetts Senate that day about the Chief Justice's performance. "We are a law-and-order loving people," he declared. "With such an illustrious example of submission to law and order before them, I cannot believe that the citizens will commit any treason or violence." [36]

Chief Justice Wells of the Court of Common Pleas was evidently a man of more pride than Shaw, or was less willing to make of himself a symbol of submission to the Fugitive Slave Act. He demanded that the obstruction be removed immediately, and when his instructions were ignored, he sent the sheriff to the Board of Mayor and Aldermen to know the reason why. Their reply was that the chains were a precautionary measure to protect "public peace," and also that their power to erect a barrier derived from the fact that the Court House was the corporate property of the city. Wells accepted the explanation, but still refused to go under. At his insistence, the chains were lifted high so that he could pass erect with dignity.[37]

At nine that same Friday morning, Commissioner Curtis opened his court to hear the case of young Thomas Sims. The scene was the United States courtroom, up two high and narrow flights of stairs. Six guards were at the door. The prisoner sat with two policemen on each side of him and five more directly behind. Only his counsel could approach him from the front.[38] His counsel were men of first eminence—the vigilance committee had wasted no time in sounding out legal aid. Robert Rantoul was there, a volunteer in Sims' defense who was a U.S. Senator, and Webster's successor at that. In little more than a year Rantoul would be dead, and Whittier would write: "We saw him take the weaker side, And right the wronged, and free the thrall." [39] Charles G. Loring, a leader of the Boston bar, also appeared for the prisoner. Seth Thomas was present for the Southern claimants, such "despicable wretches," Dana had never beheld— "cruel, low-bred, dissolute, degraded beings!" [40]

Thomas produced documents to prove that Sims belonged not to himself, but to James Potter of Georgia. Bacon, the agent, and a witness he had brought from Savannah, took the stand to identify Sims as Potter's slave.[41] There was no testimony on behalf of the defendant. It would have taken weeks before witnesses might be found in Georgia and brought to Boston to speak in court for him. But the law of 1850 envisioned no such delays, only an informal hearing in which the fate of the alleged fugitive was to be decided in a "summary manner," as the law said. The claim of the slave-catcher, made by affidavit or testimony, was in effect sufficient proof to identify the prisoner as the person in fact owing service.[42]

Sims' attorneys moved to introduce as evidence for their client his sworn statement that he was born in Florida; that he had been free as long as he could remember; that his free papers were probably with Mr. Morris Potter of Savannah; and that he never knew nor heard of James Potter, the man who claimed him, until after his arrest. Curtis, however, rejected this affidavit by refusing to entertain the motion on ground that the law of 1850 stated: "In no trial or hearing under this Act shall the testimony of such alleged Fugitive be admitted as evidence." [43] Curtis then held the case over till the next day, Saturday.[44]

On Friday morning, when the hearing in the United States courtroom had just begun, Samuel E. Sewall appeared before the supreme court of the state. Years ago an enraged slaveholder had horsewhipped him in his own office because he had interferred with Southern "property rights" by defending two colored women, allegedly fugitives.[45] He knew the justice of his cause, and he appealed to Chief Justice Shaw for a writ of habeas corpus to bring Sims before the court on ground of illegal detention. After consulting with his associates a few moments, Shaw announced his decision to refuse the petition. He stated that if the writ were issued and the prisoner should be brought before the court, its duty would be to remand him to the custody from which he was taken, by reason of no jurisdiction to decide whether he was or was not a fugitive. Sewall then requested permission to argue on the unconstitutionality of the law of 1850. Again Shaw refused, informing him, somewhat crustily, that the court had already passed its judgment.[46] "When a Court of Justice sits in fetters . . . the ancient and prescriptive safeguards of personal liberty must of course give way," recorded the abolitionist society.[47]

Discouraged but resourceful, Sims' friends shifted to the familiar technique of agitation. Perhaps public opinion might pressure the courts to a more friendly view of the matter, or a crowd might even be incited to a rescue. The vigilance committee decided to hold a public meeting. Parker; Dr. Samuel Gridley Howe, the famous humanitarian; Robert Morris, the first colored member of the Boston bar; [48] Francis Jackson, the president of the state abolitionist society— vigilance men all—and twenty-three others petitioned the Massachusetts House of Representatives for use of the State House Yard.[49] Meanwhile, a notice was posted throughout the city: "PUBLIC MEETING—KIDNAPPERS IN BOSTON. Men of Boston, one of your fellow-citizens was last night seized by slave hunters. He is in most deadly peril. The citizens of Boston and its neighborhood are earnestly invited to assemble without arms in front of the State House, at four this (Friday) afternoon, to consult for the public good." [50] Then the legislature rejected the petition by a vote of 147 to 113; Faneuil Hall was also denied to the antislavery forces.[51]

Undaunted, they convened on the Common, and in the evening, adjourned to Tremont Temple, one thousand strong. Howe presided. Speeches of "the most extravagant character" were delivered. Wendell Phillips, the principal speaker was "treasonably violent"; he "maligned Chief Justice Shaw in terms that a gentleman would hardly apply to a pickpocket" for Shaw's refusal to grant the writ. Phillips advised resistance to the Fugitive Slave Act and declared that before a slave should be carried out of Massachusetts, its railroads and steamboats should be destroyed. He also counseled the colored men of the city to arm and defend themselves.[52]

The law-and-order element of the city was badly frightened. The *Daily Evening Transcript* stigmatized the abolitionists as an "imbecile faction" and promised that the overwhelming majority of citizens were resolved at all hazards "to uphold the laws, the Constitution, and the Union." [53] Because of the inflammatory appeals of the agitators, Mayor Bigelow and Marshal Tukey feared a repetition of the Shadrach affair. They doubtless considered the city police incompetent to deal with the poets, preachers, lawyers, and physicians who composed the vigilance committee. While the Tremont Temple meeting was in progress, Friday night, three companies of the military were ordered out by the mayor: the City Guards, the New England Guards, and the Boston Light Guards. In addition, 250 United States troops, with two pieces of ordnance, were kept on the alert at the Charlestown Navy Yard.[54] All that night, members of the vigilance committee, including the gentle Bronson Alcott, "beat the streets," in a gesture of supreme defiance, to protect other fugitives from being arrested.[55]

On Saturday, April 5, the Sims affair provoked sharp action in the state senate. Sims requested by petition that the legislature intervene in his favor by passing a special law requiring a writ of habeas corpus to be issued to him. His petition set forth that the writ had been refused by the supreme court, that he was a citizen of Massachusetts, and that he ought not to be "surrendered, exiled, or delivered to bondage, until proved to be a slave by a 'due process of law'." [56] Senator Keyes spoke at length in Sims' favor, declaring that as a result of Shaw's decision, the noble writ of habeas corpus lay a dead letter at the feet of the Fugitive Slave Act. Senator Robinson echoed these sentiments and claimed that the judiciary should be made responsible by popular election. He even hinted at Shaw's impeachment. However, the Chief Justice and his associates had many supporters who believed them to be "the purest and most incorruptible judiciary in the world." In the end, Sims' petition was laid on the table.[57]

In Court Square, the events of Saturday—and of the following week—resembled those of the preceding day. There was a repetition of the crowds, the armed cordon, and the judges passing under the chains. In the United States courtroom, Curtis listened to additional evidence that Sims was Potter's slave. That night, readers of the *Commercial Gazette* in New York learned that "The whole Union will probably know in a few days whether a fugitive slave can be arrested in the capital of Massachusetts, and in case the claim is made out, be delivered safely to his master in another State." [58] And a sensitive poet added another entry in his journals: "April 5. Troops under arms in Boston; the court house guarded; the Chief Justice of the Supreme Court forced to stoop under chains to enter the temple of Justice! This is the last point of degradation. Alas for the people who cannot feel an insult!" [59]

Over the weekend, a number of gentlemen of high standing, including Charles Loring, spoke privately to Shaw and his associates, persuading them to reconsider their refusal to hear an argument. Monday morning, Richard Henry Dana, he who had sailed before the mast, appeared with Rantoul before the Supreme Judicial Court.[60] They presented Sims' petition for a writ of habeas corpus. The petition set forth that Sims was imprisoned in the Court House by Marshal Devens on pretense of a warrant, issued by Curtis, describing him as a fugitive slave. Sims stated that he was free and prayed to the court to have him brought before it to be discharged. Shaw demanded that the court be satisfied of the unconstitutionality of the warrant before granting the writ, thereby rejecting Dana's plea that the writ should issue as of right.[61]

Rantoul delivered the main address, arguing two points: first, that Curtis, who was a federal officer but not a judge, exercised under the Act of 1850 a judicial power which Congress was empowered to confer only upon a judge appointed for good behavior and with a fixed compensation; [62] second, that the act itself was unconstitutional because Congress, which could exercise only powers expressly delegated, had no power to legislate at all on the subject of fugitive slaves, no such power being vested.[63] As Dana remarked, Rantoul made "a very striking and forcible argument, considered as a . . . piece of abstract reasoning, but not one calculated to meet the difficulties in the minds of the court." [64]

The unanimous judgment of the court, given at three on the afternoon of the same day, was a denial of the writ. Shaw's opinion was the first full dress sustention of the constitutionality of the Fugitive Slave Act of 1850 by any court. A decade later, Hurd, the historian of the law of bondage, wrote that the opinion was thereafter regarded as "the highest authority—to the degree that in opinions of judges in later cases who have maintained the action of commissioners in like circumstances, it has been taken to preclude all further juristical discussion." [65]

That the Chief Justice had reasoned through his stand on the controversial law before that Monday may be surmised from the length and maturity of an opinion written in only a few hours. As early as the Med case of 1836, he had indicated his intention, by *obiter dictum*, of giving effect to Congressional enactment should the duty of remanding a fugitive slave arise.[66] His conduct in the Shadrach case is also revealing. Dana had approached Shaw a few hours before the rescue and requested him to sign a writ of habeas corpus in Shadrach's behalf. Shaw's conduct in refusing to sign exposed an unfavorable attitude on his part toward the effort to save fugitives from rendition. With good reason, Dana recorded Shaw's "evident disinclination to act, the frivolous nature of his objections, and his insulting manner. . . ." His conduct, concluded Dana perspicaciously, "shows how deeply seated, so as to affect, unconsciously I doubt not, good men like him, is this selfish hunkerism of the property interest on the slave question." [67] Shaw's Whiggery was indeed robust, and he never lost his admiration for Webster's politics. Four months before the death of Webster, who had persuaded him to accept the Chief Justiceship, Shaw wrote that it would have been "a glorious thing to have so distinguished a man as Mr. Webster elected Prest [sic] of the U.S." [68] With the passing years, the intensification of the slavery controversy made the security and peace of the Union Shaw's passion; long ago these values had been elevated in his mind to a case of political and even "moral" necessity.[69] In December of 1860, at a time when his recent resignation from the bench allowed him to speak as a private citizen, he headed a group of prominent conciliationists who hoped to appease the South by recommending unconditional repeal of Massachusetts' Personal Liberty Laws.[70] It would have been contrary to the man had the direction of his opinion in the Sims case taken any other turn than it did.

In that opinion, Shaw first disposed of the petition for a writ of habeas corpus. He stated that the writ could not be awarded when there was insufficient ground for discharge and the prisoner would have to be remanded. He obviously implied by so stating the rule that if a cause bearing on Sims' right to a discharge were to be argued before the court—a procedure which would have followed the issuance of the writ—he would find against his freedom.[71]

Addressing himself to the argument on the alleged unconstitutionality of the law of 1850, Shaw defined two questions as being before the court. First, whether Congress was empowered to pass any law on the subject of fugitive slaves; and second, whether the law actually passed violated the provisions of the Constitution. He thought it necessary to the disposition of the first question to consider the historical circumstances under which the Constitution was framed and the objects of its adoption. He was obsessed with the fiction that it would never have come into being had it not provided for the return of runaways. It was an appalling picture he sketched of thirteen disunited states embroiled in "constant border wars" which resulted from hostile incursions of one sovereignty into another's territory for the purpose of recapturing escaped slaves. Before the thirteen states compacted to relinquish part of their independence and join in a union, their differences on slavery "must first be provided for." The clause in question must therefore be construed as a treaty entered into on the highest considerations of reciprocal benefit and to secure peace. Such was Shaw's view of the matter. The important observation to be made, of course, is not that his history was wrong but that it was considered essential to a decision of the case for reasons of high policy: the necessity for maintaining peace in the Union.[72]

In the light of his history, Shaw found that the fugitive slave clause was rock-bed upon which Congressional authority to legislate might be erected. He was satisfied that even if the Constitution did not direct in detail how the rights and benefits of the clause were to be secured, Article 1, Section 8, granted to Congress power to make all laws necessary and proper to carry into execution those powers specifically vested.[73]

It may be presumptuous to criticize such logic in view of its precedent in Story's opinion in Prigg's case.[74] Yet the provisions of the clause dealing with fugitives from service manifestly vest no power in Congress which that body under Article 1, Section 8, the "necessary and proper" clause, might give effect to by legislation. Rantoul had elaborated on this point which Shaw chose to ignore. Instead, the Chief Justice drew sweeping implications which permitted him to turn to the Fugitive Slave Act of 1793 with the assurance that its intent was to implement "the power and duty of Congress to secure and carry into effect a right confirmed by the Constitution. . . ."[75]

This first act he described as having authorized a summary and informal proceeding adapted to the exigency of the occasion. No regular suit at law was provided for. The fugitive was simply seized, brought before a United States judge or state magistrate, and on proof that he owed labor to the claimant, it was made the duty of the judge or magistrate to give a certificate which warranted the removal of the fugitive to the state from which he had fled.[76] But to *describe* the Act of 1793, as Shaw did, was not to join issue with the challenge that the Act of 1850 was unconstitutional because it made no provision for a trial by jury. As to the mode of trial contemplated, Shaw remarked: "The law of 1850 stands, in this respect, precisely on the same ground with that of 1793, and the same grounds of argument which tend to show the unconstitutionality of the one, apply with equal force to the other; and the same answer must be made to them." [77] That answer, to repeat, was that the laws had not described a suit, but a summary proceeding.

Shaw next rejected the contention that the Act of 1850 was unconstitutional because of Congressional inability to confer judicial authority upon Circuit Court Commissioners. The duties and powers of these commissioners he considered "very similar" to those delegated to justices of the peace by the Act of 1793. It was manifest to him that Congress had not deemed the functions of the justices of the peace, as they related to escaped slaves, to be judicial. And he pointed to the difficulty in marking "minute shades of difference" between judicial and nonjudicial powers, because under every government there were functions exercised which, requiring "skill and experience, judgment and even legal and judicial discrimination," resisted precise classification. They were "partly judicial and partly administrative." In consequence of this line of reason, he refused to distinguish between the powers authorized to justices of the peace and those to commissioners. He utterly avoided considering on its own merits the question whether the powers exercised by commissioners under the Act of 1850 were constitutionally delegated. This was not a "new question," he declared, "but one settled and determined by authorities which it would be a dereliction of official duty, and a disregard of judicial responsibility, to overlook." [78] With this last remark, Shaw launched into extensive quotations from the various authorities, state and especially federal, which had upheld the first fugitive slave law.[79]

The conclusion of the opinion is of interest because Shaw suggested some of the premises which underlay his logic. Not often do judges touch on the larger grounds of decision, their own views on public policy, which can sway their judgment in a case. Shaw did not, of course, crudely offer his personal endorsement of the Fugitive Slave Act of 1850 as a wise and necessary enactment. He did hint at his reluctance to decide Sims' case. He as much as informed counsel that he preferred them to bring their petition before United States judges; *they* would determine whether Sims was being illegally held.

As for himself, he recognized "no necessary occasion for drawing the authority of the State and United States Judiciary into conflict with each other." He had relied on Supreme Court precedent, in a case depending upon the Constitution, because such a procedure was "absolutely necessary to the peace, union, and harmonious action of the State and General Governments." [80] It would be a grave move to invalidate an act of Congress passed under a clause of the Constitution which was not only "the best adjustment" which could be made of conflicting interests in the Convention of 1787; this fugitive slave clause was also an "essential element" in the formation of the Union, "necessary to the peace, happiness and highest prosperity of all the states." Concluded Shaw: "In this spirit [of compromise], and with these views steadily in prospect, it seems to be the duty of all judges and magistrates to expound and apply these provisions in the constitution and laws of the United States. . . ." [81]

Many of the city's first merchants were present in the courtroom to hear Shaw's opinion—only a favored audience was permitted entry. George Bancroft, the historian, testified before a committee of the state senate that while a plain citizen of Massachusetts could not obtain admittance within her halls of justice, he could do so by saying to the officers at the door, "I am a gentleman from the South!" [82] When the opinion was read, the merchants in attendance, "who had swallowed their dinner in a hurry to get this as the dessert," muttered, "Good, good." [83] The anti-slavery men grieved over the decision; "most painful," reported Elizur Wright's paper.[84] "What a moment was lost when Judge Shaw declined to affirm the unconstitutionality of the Fugitive Slave Law!" exclaimed Emerson; "This filthy enactment was made in the nineteenth century by people who could read and write. I will not obey it, by God." [85] Parker wrote to Charles Sumner that he never had had any confidence in the supreme court anyway, adding with spiteful glee: "But think of old stiff-necked Lemuel visibly going under the chains! That was a spectacle!" [86] For public consumption, however, the abolitionists trumpeted the theme of the ermine having been dragged in the dust, and they libeled Shaw for having "spit in the face of Massachusetts. . . ." [87]

On Monday, the same day as his argument before the high court, Rantoul also argued for six hours before Curtis. Charles Loring concluded the next day for the anti-slavery side, followed by Thomas who relied on the law of 1850 to uphold the claimant.[88] Sewall requested a postponement for the reason that a telegraphic dispatch had been received stating that Sims was a free man. Delay was urgently needed to obtain proof of the fact, yet Curtis refused the request.[89] Higginson, the poet, plotted recklessly with another vigilance man to gain time by stealing certain essential court records, but gave up the idea as impracticable.[90]

The proceedings before Curtis and Shaw were only the first of a bewildering number of legal actions which the resourceful defense tried. To free Sims, his friends meant to exhaust every technicality, to use every legal device, and to argue before every court. So it was that on Monday, two more processes were begun by the legal battery of the vigilance committee. The first was a writ of personal replevin sued out against U.S. Marshal Devens, commanding him to produce Sims in court, there to submit to a trial by jury whatever claims he held upon him. Devens, however, refused to honor the writ when it was served by the sheriff, and warned that any attempt to take Sims would be resisted with force.[91] That process was temporarily dropped, but another had only begun, an expedient sired by desperation.

Since it was Devens who held Sims for eventual rendition, the abolitionist strategy was to get Sims out of his custody at any cost. Accordingly, two vigilance men conspired to secure Sims' freedom by sending him to prison! Better a few years safely spent in a Massachusetts jail than a lifetime spent in slavery. Had not brothers in the cause saved a fugitive in New York by sending him to Sing Sing? [92] Committeeman Charles List, a lawyer, drew up a criminal complaint against Sims for having stabbed police officer Asa O. Butman, and committeeman Richard Hildreth, the historian, who was justice of the peace for Suffolk County, issued a warrant for Sims' arrest for assault with intent to kill. The sheriff was then sent to demand Sims from Devens, being first advised that Curtis' warrant, by which the marshal held his prisoner, was only a civil process and must yield to the criminal process of the state. Come back in twenty-four hours, Devens told the sheriff; when he returned on Tuesday, he met with another refusal. Sims, said the marshal, was already being held for a crime against the United States, under a warrant issued by Commissioner Benjamin F. Hallett.[93] Charles Loring went to Hallett to find out what this warrant was for. Loring expressed his fear that it was a mere trick, only to be met with the candid reply that if it was a trick, it was to counteract another. And there the matter stood as of Tuesday, the eighth, with every legal action stymied. Dana grieved that there was not moral authority enough in Boston on Sims' side to sustain the state processes.[94]

Earlier on Tuesday, at ten in the morning, a rally was held in Tremont Temple of citizens opposed to the Fugitive Slave Act. Perhaps the moral indignation of Boston might be aroused, in spite of the penny papers. Hawthorne, Whittier, Bancroft, Charles Francis Adams, and many other distinguished men signed the call for the meeting. The hall was packed "almost to suffocation," reported *The Liberator*, and for seven hours an earnest, excited audience listened to angry protests, and after an adjournment for supper, reconvened in the evening for more of the same. There were speeches by the presiding officer, Horace Mann, and by Samuel Gridley Howe, John Gorham Palfrey, Anson Burlingame, Henry Wilson, Samuel Hoar, Elizur Wright, William Henry Channing, Thomas Wentworth Higginson, Wendell Phillips, and many others. Adams and William Seward of New York sent messages.[95] "Such vials of wrath as were poured and dashed indignantly on Webster and the abettors of the Fugitive Slave Law!" exclaimed Alcott. "There was no mercy. . . ." [96] A large number in the hall were for a rescue, including Higginson— in three years he would lead an attack on the Court House in a vain effort to save Anthony Burns. Howe, who had fought with the rebels in Greece, honored Higginson by telling him that his oratory "was bringing the community to the verge of revolution"; but moderate heads prevailed.[97] Resolves were adopted condemning the sinful law and the proceedings against Sims. It was clear that a few ultras would have to go it alone if Sims were to be rescued by lawless means.

Higginson gathered a half-dozen conspirators about him. Together they plotted a fantastic scheme which hinged upon the fact that the windows of the room where Sims was confined, three stories up, were without a grating. Mr. Grimes, the colored clergyman, went to visit the prisoner, ostensibly for religious purposes—it was probably the next day, Wednesday. Grimes told Sims that at a specified hour that evening, he should casually stroll over to a certain window, as if for a breath of air, and then jump to the street. Mattresses were to be laid a moment before, and a fast carriage would be waiting. Sims agreed. Preparations were made for the rescue. The carriage had been procured, and the mattresses were ready in a lawyer's office across the street—Dana's office was at 30 Court Street, directly opposite the Court House. Dusk came and the plan was about to go into effect. Higginson and a friend turned into Court Street. They raised their eyes toward the window out of which Sims would shortly come hurtling. All was lost! Workmen were busily fitting bars into that very window. Somehow Devens had gotten word of the plot, or he had been as clever as the vigilance men to take such extraordinary precautions.[98] Dana from his office could see Sims looking through the grates of his prison and lamented: "Our temple of justice is a slave pen!" [99]

Meanwhile, Sims' lawyers were still trying to save him by due process. On Wednesday, Sewall demanded and received from U.S. Marshal Devens a copy of the mysterious warrant which Hallett had issued. Ironically it turned out to be a warrant for Sims' arrest for the very assault upon Butman which the vigilance men themselves wanted to use as a pretext to send Sims to a Massachusetts jail, thereby saving him from rendition. The law-and-order men never, of course, intended to act upon Butman's complaint; instead Hallett's warrant was merely a clever device to forestall the scheme of the vigilance men. Devens, to whom the warrant was directed as arresting officer, had not even gone through the motions of answering it, that is, of making the formal return on it as directed by law.[100]

Thursday morning, Sewall obtained from Sims an affidavit to the effect that he had been held for three days under a criminal warrant without having been brought before a magistrate; that the warrant was "a trick against my freedom," [101] as Sims put it, because it was not issued for the purposes of trial; and finally that the warrant was void on ground of the defect of having no return to it. With this affidavit, an application was made to Judge Peleg Sprague of the U.S. District Court for a writ of habeas corpus. Sims was represented by Charles Sumner and Sewall.

Sprague, like Shaw, Curtis, and Hallett, was a Hunker. He had once made a speech in Faneuil Hall, the "Cradle of Liberty," apostrophizing Washington as a slaveholder. In the present case he refused to grant the writ for the reason that inasmuch as Sims was held in a civil process which was legal—Curtis' warrant under the Fugitive Slave Act—he suffered no illegal detention because he was also being held on another process—Hallett's warrant—the legality of which was contested. Dana observed that Sprague could not know judicially that Sims was held under a prior process until that fact should be disclosed by Devens' return, since the petition for the habeas corpus made no reference to it.[102] Sprague was bombarded with other petitions, all of which he rejected. One was for a writ of habeas corpus on grounds that the Act of 1850 was unconstitutional; another was for an injunction to stay the proceedings before Curtis; and still another was for a request to have Sprague appoint a person to serve on Devens the writ of personal replevin which he had refused to honor the Monday past.[103]

Thursday evening, Sumner, Sewall, and Dana appeared before Judge Woodbury of the U.S. Supreme Court, on circuit duty, and applied to him for a writ of habeas corpus on grounds that Hallett's warrant was fraudulent and defective. Benjamin R. Curtis, the Commissioner's brother, who had begun his career at the bar by arguing for the right of property in human flesh,[104] and Rufus Choate, next to Webster, Massachusetts' strongest advocate of the law of 1850, both hurried to Woodbury's court to defend Hallett's warrant and Devens' conduct. Woodbury granted the writ—a minor victory for Sims which would prove to be very short-lived—commanded Devens to make the return to Hallett's warrant in good faith, and held the hearing over till the next day, Friday, at three o'clock.[105]

It should be understood that Hunkerism had the advantage in the proceedings before Woodbury. Hallett's warrant had forced the abolitionists to waste crucial time in an effort to have it suspended. This was necessary so that they could then get Sims out of Devens' custody and prosecute Sims on Hildreth's warrant to save him from the certificate of rendition which everyone knew Curtis would grant to Potter's agent on Friday. Woodbury's writ of habeas corpus would bring Sims before him for a hearing which would be strictly confined to an inquiry whether the prisoner merited a release from Devens' custody only insofar as he was held under Hallett's warrant. The hearing would not, if favorable to Sims, discharge him absolutely. In Washington, the *National Intelligencer* expressed confidence that "the Constitution and Laws of the country will be faithfully sustained." [106]

Still the same day, Thursday, the Reverend Theodore Parker preached a scorching sermon on Sims' case at the Melodeon. He had had stimulus enough to provoke his terrible wrath, but with his own eyes he had seen the wretched Negro in jail in the courthouse. A policeman on guard, club in hand, had brazenly commanded him to get under the chains. Not Parker. He had pressed them down, stepped over, and mounted the stairs to the prison-room. As Parker recalled the incident: "Ruffians mounted guard at the entrance, armed with swords, fire-arms, and bludgeons. The door was locked and doubly barred. Inside the watch was kept by a horrid looking fellow, without a coat, a naked cutlass in his hand, and some twenty others, their mouths nauseous with tobacco and reeking also with half digested rum paid for by the city. In such company, I gave what consolation Religion could offer to the first man Boston ever kidnapped. . . . I could offer him no comfort this side the grave." [107]

In the Melodeon, Parker thunderingly inquired where he might find a parallel with the "brood of monsters" who would commit such a crime, commit it in Boston. "I will open the graves," he answered, "and bring up the most hideous tyrants from the dead!" And he invoked the specters of history's most hated men, Herod, Nero, Torquemada, and Bloody Jeffries, to compare them with Curtis, Thomas, Tukey, and company. And the specters from the fiery depths blenched and paled by the comparison.[108] Bronson Alcott commended Parker's discretion for having advised the women and children to bear with him and not scream as he called forth his monsters.[109]

But the abolitionists still hoped to depend on more than oratory, whether from the pulpit or at the bar, to save Sims. Parker met his fellow conspirators in his home. They discussed rescue plans. One was especially daring. Vigilance man Austin Bearse, a Cape Cod sea captain, was to be provided with a vessel. He was then to pursue the brig which would carry Sims back, capture it, and spirit its prisoner away. But the plan was laid aside as impracticable, not, however, because it involved piracy. There was no certainty that a vessel could be outfitted in time or that Sims would be carried south in the way expected.[110]

Friday was the day anticipated for rendition. Handbills had been extensively circulated asking the people of Massachusetts, in the name of the Committee of Vigilance and Safety, to be in Boston "by the thousands" to witness "the last sad scene of the State's disgrace. . . ." [111] If a great crowd might be stirred to its soul by the damnable scene, then perhaps. . . .[112] But Friday would pass quietly, without the rendition. That day would bring only judicial opinion sealing its inevitability.

In the morning, Commissioner Curtis delivered his opinion. As it became evident that he was leading up to an award of a certificate of ownership to Potter's agent, Sims gave way to hysteria. "I will not go back to Slavery," he exclaimed to his counsel. "Give me a knife, and when the Commissioner declares me a slave I will stab myself in the heart, and die before his eyes! I will not be a slave." [113] The finish of the opinion came as an anticlimax. The certificate identified Sims as "a chattel personal to all intents, uses, and purposes whatsoever." [114]

At three that afternoon, Sumner, Rantoul, and Sewall appeared before Judge Woodbury to argue the case of Sims' illegal detention under Hallett's warrant. Their efforts were in vain. Woodbury remanded Sims to the custody of Devens. One final appeal was made to Woodbury to force the marshal, on a writ of personal replevin, to submit his claim on Sims to a jury. At this point, Seth Thomas informed the judge that Curtis had closed the case. He read the certificate of rendition and asked to be admitted on the record as the lawyer of Sims' owner and, therefore, of Sims. Woodbury ruled that by virtue of the certificate Thomas had the better right to represent the slave than Sumner and the others. So ended the legal proceedings in the case of Thomas Sims.[115]

Friday had come and gone, and with it went Sims' last hope, and that of the Vigilance Committee, too. Some of the members met very late that night in Garrison's office at No. 21 Cornhill. They were still up, as though on a death watch, as the black hours of Saturday morning, April 12, arrived. At about 3 A.M., they noticed that the city police began to muster. The dreaded moment was at hand; the authorities meant to sneak Sims back into slavery while the city slept. It was not the bravest way to uphold the Constitution, but it was the safest. Word went out to some of the absent vigilance men, and they gathered together in Court Square to watch the grim event. In the darkness of the cool morning, a force of one hundred policemen, armed with straight, double-edged, pointed Roman swords, had assembled by the light of one gas-lamp. Commanded by the hoarse orders of their officers, they drilled for an hour with the efficiency of a military company. In addition to the police there were about a hundred armed volunteers. Bludgeons and horse pistols were carried. With few exceptions, the only spectators were the horrified abolitionists. In Faneuil Hall, the regular military, the "Sims Brigade," was being kept on the alert. Boston meant to redeem the reputation it had lost after Shadrach's rescue.[116]

At 4:15 A.M. the escort guard began its final maneuvers. The police, in double file and closely locked ranks, formed into a hollow square and marched to the east door of the Court House. A line was extended from the door to the square. City Marshal Tukey addressed his men, reminding them of their duties. In a few minutes, the City Watch, about a hundred strong, marched up with weapons and formed another double file around the hollow square. The volunteers, in closed platoons, took up their positions in a long line leading into Court Street. Then, the main doors of the Court House were swung open, and Sims appeared. Tears were streaming down his face, but he held his small dark frame erect. Under guard, he was escorted into the center of the square of armed men. Tukey took his place at the head of the column with Mayor Bigelow, Devens, and his U.S. Deputy Marshals. At the rough command "March!" the three hundred guards began a slow regular tramp.[117]

Instantly, from the group of men who owed their devotion to a "higher law," there arose cries of "Shame!" and "Infamy!" All along Court Street, Dr. Bowditch recalled, "we continually saluted their ears with our words of contempt. 'Where is Liberty?' says one. 'She is dead!' cried another. Still they tramped on . . . and the regular beat of feet on the pavement struck wildly on the ear." Preceded by the abolitionists, the troops turned down State Street. As they drew near the spot where Crispus Attucks, the colored patriot, was shot by the British during the Boston Massacre, Bowditch, Parker, Channing, and the others "pointed out to those minions of slavery the holy spot over which they were treading." [118]

The procession finally arrived at Long Wharf, by the spot where the "Indians" had dumped the taxed tea of the oppressor—none of the symbolism was lost on the abolitionists. Some of them who pressed too close to the scene were driven back by the drawn swords of a body of police who were waiting at the wharf. There the brig *Acorn*, owned by a Boston merchant, had been fitted out. All the square rigged sails lay unfurled and ready for sea. The hollow square then delivered up its prisoner. As he reached the deck, a voice called out, "Sims, preach Liberty to the Slaves!" The last words he uttered in answer were, "And is this Massachusetts liberty?" Immediately, the jib halyards rattled, the white flying jib went up, and the anchor was weighed. Within two minutes, the *Acorn*, with its two cannon and small arms, was moving, carrying a slave back to his master, guarded by six men of Devens' force. Morning was just dawning.[119]

The spectators on the wharf were terribly depressed. The Reverend David Foster of Concord got up on a box and proposed that all the friends of the departed slave should join with him in religious service. With uncovered heads, the little company kneeled in prayer. Someone begged that they sing, and together they took up Bishop Heber's "Missionary Hymn":

> From many a Southern river
> And field of sugar cane,
> They call us to deliver
> Their land from slavery's chain.

That day, the bells of Lynn, Plymouth, Newton, Waltham, and other towns tolled in mourning. One week later, at a total expense of about $20,000, Thomas Sims was returned to his master in Savannah, where he was publicly lashed thirty-nine times.[120]

In Boston, most of the respectable citizenry were relieved to be done with a disagreeable but necessary job.[121] To the benefit of peace and profits, the majesty of the law had prevailed. *The Commonwealth* accurately summed up the city's press: " 'Boston is redeemed!' shouts all hunkerdom, 'the Fugitive Slave Law has been enforced!' " [122] The *Boston Courier* praised the city authorities for having done their duty "in the handsomest manner during the whole of this exciting and harassing business. . . . Boston is sound to its heart's core in her attachment to the Union." [123] The *Boston Herald* was proud that the city had verified its mettle: "Our city has been redeemed from the opprobrious epithets which have been denounced against her, for her supposed inability and disinclination to yield to the laws of the Union, and the South will please accord us all the credit which is due therefore." [124] As if in reply, Sims' "home town" paper, the *Savannah Republican*, acknowledged its "pleasant duty to accord to the authorities and people of Boston great credit for the firm and energetic manner in which they have demeaned themselves." The paper was particularly pleased with the decision of the Massachusetts high court.[125] Another Savannah journal, however, was most crabbed about the manner in which Sims was returned. "If our people," it declared, "are obliged to *steal their property out of Boston in the night*, it would be more profitable to adopt a regular kidnapping system at once, without regard to law." [126] The nearby *Augusta Republic* responded in much the same way, adding that the slave could have been returned had it not been for "the countenance and support of a numerous, wealthy, and powerful body of citizens. It was in evidence that fifteen hundred of the most wealthy and respectable citizens—merchants, bankers and others—volunteered their services to aid the Marshal." [127]

Elsewhere in the nation there was much rejoicing in the vindication of the Act of 1850. Webster wrote the President that all that was needed now was to get rid of some of the "insane" abolitionists and free-soilers.[128] In the nation's capital, the *National Intelligencer* headlined its lead story, "SUPREMACY OF THE LAW SUSTAINED." [129] In Virginia, the *Richmond Whig* cried, "All honor to the brave old city!" The *New York Express* praised Shaw's opinion and waxed ecstatic over the way the Fugitive Slave Act had been "so beautifully" executed. It singled out City Marshal Tukey for special admiration: ". . . a prize in any city. He ought to be a field marshal before he dies." The *Louisville Journal* ridiculed the "cowardice" of the abolitionists because, at the crucial moment, their courage had oozed and they had taken to prayer rather than arms. And so it went in the press of other cities.[130]

Opinion was not, of course, unanimous. In New England, for example, little free-soiling dailies spoiled the festive occasion with words about "human freedom" and "conscience." The *Norfolk* (Mass.) *Democrat* cursed the affair as the "darkest and most disgraceful crime that has ever been perpetrated" in Boston's history. The *Massachusetts Spy* and the *Hartford Republican* recalled the "shame" of the rendition with anguish.[131] To the *Lowell American,* it was "a combination of the money and the Websterism of Boston" which was responsible for a "victory of cotton over the conscience of the people!" [132]

A Quaker poet memorialized the humiliating case and called his poem "Moloch in State Street." [133] And in his journals, the transcendental Alcott wrote: "I had fancied till now that certain beautiful properties were mine—by culture and the time and place I live in, if not by inheritance—namely a City, Civilization, Christianity, and a Country." [134]

NOTE: During the Civil War, Thomas Sims escaped again from slavery, crossed into Union lines, and returned to Boston a free man. In 1877, when former U.S. Marshal Charles Devens became U.S. Attorney General, he assuaged his conscience for having remanded Sims to slavery; the one-time slave became an employee in the Department of Justice.[135]

NOTES

[1] *Nineteenth Annual Report, Presented to the Massachusetts Anti-Slavery Society, by its Board of Managers, January 22, 1851* (Boston, 1851), p. 99.

[2] C. M. Fuess, *Rufus Choate, The Wizard of Law* (New York, 1928), p. 197; B. R. Curtis, Jr., ed., *A Memoir of Benjamin Robbins Curtis* (Boston, 1897), pp. 1, 131–136, 159.

[3] C. F. Adams, *Richard Henry Dana*, 3rd ed. (Boston, 1891), I, 127.

[4] E. L. Pierce, *Memoir and Letters of Charles Sumner* (Boston, 1893), III, 6.

[5] Adams, *Dana*, p. 127.

[6] *Nineteenth Annual Report*, pp. 31–32, 42–43. The complete membership list of the vigilance committee is in Austin Bearse's *Reminiscences of Fugitive-Slave Law Days in Boston* (Boston, 1880), pp. 3–5.

[7] H. S. Commager, *Theodore Parker* (Boston, 1936), pp. 214–216.

[8] *The Commonwealth*, Boston, February 17, 1851.

[9] Quoted in the *Daily Evening Transcript*, Boston, February 19, 1851.

[10] C. M. Fuess, *Daniel Webster* (Boston, 1930), II, 270.

[11] *The Liberator*, Boston, February 21 and February 28, 1851.

[12] Quoted in *The Liberator*, April 11, 1851. See the same issue for comment by the *New Orleans Picayune*.

[13] *Boston Courier*, April 12, 1851. See *The Liberator*, February 21, 1851, and *The Commonwealth*, February 17, 1851, for a characterization of the city's press comment.

[14] *The Liberator*, February 21, 1851.

[15] *Lowell American*, February 21, 1851, quoted in Mrs. W. S. Robinson, ed., *"Warrington" Pen-Portraits* (Boston, 1877), p. 191.

[16] V. I. Bowditch, *Life and Correspondence of Henry Ingersoll Bowditch* (Boston, 1902), I, 212; Commager, *Theodore Parker*, p. 219.

[17] *Daily Evening Transcript*, April 4, 1851. Other contemporary accounts give his age as seventeen or twenty-two.

[18] *National Intelligencer*, Washington, D.C., April 8, 1851; *Law Reporter*, 14 (Boston, 1852) 1–2; *The Liberator*, April 11, 1851.

[19] *Law Reporter*, 14 (1852), p. 2.

[20] Quoted in Robinson, *Pen Portraits*, note p. 192. Thomas was also the claimant's counsel in Shadrach's case.

[21] Curtis, a "cotton Whig," had also acted as commissioner during Shadrach's case. After the rescue he had wired Webster that "it was levying war." Theodore Parker, *The Trial of Theodore Parker for the "Misdemeanor" of a Speech in Faneuil Hall Against Kidnapping . . . April 3, 1855, with The Defense* (New York, 1864), p. 151.

[22] Bearse, *Reminiscences*, p. 22; *Daily Evening Transcript*, April 4, 1851; *The Liberator*, April 11, 1851.

[23] *Daily Evening Transcript*, February 15, 1851; *The Commonwealth*, February 17, 1851.

[24] *The Liberator*, April 11, 1851; *Daily Evening Transcript*, April 4, 1851.

[25] *Laws of the Commonwealth of Massachusetts* (Boston, 1843), ch. LXIX. So called after George Latimer, protagonist of the celebrated fugitive slave case of October 1842, whose abusive treatment by certain state officers, while he was confined in a state prison, had occasioned passage of a statute aimed at eliminating the state from any part in the capture or rendition of alleged runaways. The act was made possible by Story's opinion in *Prigg* v. *Pennsylvania*, 16 Peters 539, 611 (1842).

[26] *The Commonwealth*, April 14, 1851.

[27] Odell Shephard, ed., *The Journals of Bronson Alcott* (Boston, 1938), p. 234.

[28] *The Commonwealth*, April 5, 1851.

[29] Speech at Faneuil Hall, January 30, 1852, reported in the *Twentieth Annual Report, Presented to the Massachusetts Anti-Slavery Society, By Its Board of Managers* (Boston, 1852), p. 112. T. W. Higginson put the figure at "one or two hundred" in his *Cheerful Yesterdays* (Boston, 1899), p. 140.

[30] Higginson, *Cheerful Yesterdays*, p. 140; *Daily Evening Transcript*, April 5, 1851.

[31] *Daily Evening Transcript*, April 5, 1851; *National Intelligencer*, April 12, 1851.

[32] S. Longfellow, ed., *Life of Henry Wadsworth Longfellow, with Extracts from His Journals and Correspondence* (Boston, 1936), II, 192.

[33] *The Commonwealth*, April 5, 1851.

[34] *The Liberator*, April 11, 1851.

[35] Lemuel Shaw, "Slavery and the Missouri Question," *The North American Review and Miscellaneous Journal* (Boston), x (January 1820), 139.

[36] Quoted in the *Daily Evening Transcript*, April 7, 1851.

[37] *National Intelligencer*, April 12, 1851; *The Liberator*, April 11, 1851; *Twentieth Annual Report*, p. 20.

[38] Higginson, *Cheerful Yesterdays*, p. 141.

[39] H. E. Scudder, ed., "Rantoul," *The Complete Poetical Works of John Greenleaf Whittier* (Boston, 1894), p. 194.

[40] Adams, *Dana*, p. 185.

[41] *Daily Evening Transcript*, April 4, 1851; *The Liberator*, April 11, 1851.

[42] Section 6, Fugitive Slave Act, in H. S. Commager, ed., *Documents of American History*, 3rd ed. (New York, 1946), I, 322. Andrew C. McLaughlin states that if Webster himself had been haled before a commissioner by a slaveholder who produced "affidavits," he could not deny his obligation to serve as a slave. And, argues McLaughlin, if it be answered that the act was not directed against white men, does that mean that the Constitution presumed slavery to be the natural status of Negroes and all Negroes to be slaves? Indeed, was the presumption so conclusive that a Negro could not even deny his slavery; and did the Constitution establish a white man's government in which Negroes were not afforded protections of the law? ". . . On the face of the Constitution such does not appear to be the fact." *Constitutional History of the United States* (New York, 1935), pp. 536–537.

[43] Section 6, Fugitive Slave Act, Commager, ed., *Documents*. "But constitutional provisions and legal practices are in many respects directed to the protection of the innocent; an act making it quite legal and possible to deny a free man (indeed, white or black) ordinary protection, and forbidding him to deny his guilt, or his alleged status, can not be looked upon as wholly free from an unconstitutional stain." McLaughlin, *Constitutional History*, p. 537.

[44] *Law Reporter*, 14 (1852), 3–4; *The Liberator*, April 11, 1851.

[45] *Daily Evening Transcript*, August 29, 1836.

[46] *Ibid.*, April 4, 1851; *National Intelligencer*, April 8, 1851.

[47] *Twentieth Annual Report*, 21.

[48] Morris was under indictment for complicity in Shadrach's rescue, but like all the other defendants in the case was acquitted. The one man who prevented a conviction in one of the rescue cases later informed Dana, counsel for defense, that he himself was the man who drove Shadrach over the state line. Adams, *Dana*, pp. 210, 216–217.

[49] *National Intelligencer*, April 8, 1851.

[50] *Daily Evening Transcript*, April 5, 1851.

[51] *National Intelligencer*, April 8, 1851; *The Liberator*, April 11, 1851.

[52] *Daily Evening Transcript*, April 5, 1851.

[53] *Ibid.*

[54] *Ibid.* Every night while Sims was in Boston, a few companies of the Boston Brigade, thereafter styled the "Sims Brigade," were detailed to prevent a forcible rescue. *National Intelligencer*, April 8 and 10, 1851; *Twentieth Annual Report*, p. 22.

[55] *The Journals of Bronson Alcott*, p. 244.

[56] *The Commonwealth*, April 8, 1851; *Law Reporter*, 14 (1852), 14.

[57] *Ibid.*

[58] Quoted in the *National Intelligencer*, April 8, 1851.

[59] Longfellow, *Life*, p. 193.

[60] Dana proudly recorded in his diary that he had never been under the chains: "I either jump over it," he wrote near the close of the case, "or go round to the end, and have the rope removed, which they have at last graciously substituted for the last few links of the chain." Adams, *Dana*, p. 192.

[61] *Ibid.*, p. 185. "Thomas Sims's Case," 61 Mass. 285, 287 (1851).

[62] Curtis held office at the pleasure of a U.S. Circuit Court and was compensated by a fee which varied according to his decision: $5 if he found against the claimant and double if against the fugitive. This provision of the act, Section 8, was assailed by Anson Burlingame for having fixed the price of a slave at $1000 and the price of a Yankee's soul at $5. Henry Wilson, *History of the Rise and Fall of the Slave Power in America* (Boston, 1872), II, 309.

[63] 61 Mass. 285, 287–291. Article 4, Section 2, paragraph 3 of the Constitution states: "No Person held to Service or Labour in one State, under the laws thereof, escaping into another, shall, in Consequence of any Law or Regulation therein, be discharged from such Service or Labour, but shall be delivered up on Claim of the Party to whom such Service or Labour may be due."

[64] Adams, *Dana*, p. 185.

[65] J. C. Hurd, *The Law of Freedom and Bondage in the United States* (Boston, 1862), II, 653.

[66] *Commonwealth* v. *Aves*, 35 Mass. 193, 219–221 (1836).

[67] Adams, *Dana*, p. 183. "Now, hunkerism," wrote Dana, "making material *prosperity and ease* its pole star, will do nothing and risk nothing for a moral principle." *Ibid.*, p. 125.

[68] Letter of June 15, 1852, to Lemuel Shaw, Jr., Massachusetts Historical Society, *Shaw Papers*, Box 1851–54.

[69] Shaw, "Slavery and the Missouri Question," p. 143.

[70] F. H. Chase, *Lemuel Shaw* (Boston, 1918), pp. 177–179.

[71] 61 Mass. 285, 292–293.

[72] *Ibid.*, 295–297.

[73] *Ibid.*, 299.

[74] 16 Peters 539, 620 (1842).

[75] 61 Mass. 285, 300.

[76] *Ibid.*, 301.

[77] *Ibid.*, 310.

[78] *Ibid.*, 303–304.

[79] *Ibid.*, 304–308.

[80] *Ibid.*, 310.

[81] *Ibid.*, 318–319.

[82] *Newburyport Union*, quoted in *The Liberator*, May 2, 1851.

[83] *The Commonwealth*, April 8, 1851.

[84] *Ibid.*

[85] E. W. Emerson and W. E. Forbes, eds., *Journals of Ralph Waldo Emerson* (Boston, 1912), VIII, 201, 236.

[86] O. B. Frothingham, *Theodore Parker* (New York, 1880), p. 416.

[87] Parker, *Trial of Theodore Parker*, pp. 214–215; *The Commonwealth*, April 8, 1851.

[88] *The Trial of Thomas Sims* (Boston, 1851), 47pp., has the arguments of Sims' counsel.

[89] *Law Reporter*, 14 (1852), 2, 9.

[90] Higginson, *Cheerful Yesterdays*, p. 141.

[91] Adams, *Dana*, p. 187; *Laws of the Commonwealth of Massachusetts* (Boston, 1837), "An Act to restore the Trial by Jury on questions of personal freedom," 1837, chap. CCXXI.

[92] *The Commonwealth*, April 8, 1851.

[93] Hallett was a political opportunist who had once posed as an anti-slavery man but ended as a "Doughface."

[94] Adams, *Dana*, p. 188.

[95] *Ibid.*, p. 193; *The Commonwealth*, April 5, 1851; *The Liberator*, April 11, 1851; *Twentieth Annual Report*, p. 23.

[96] *The Journals of Bronson Alcott*, p. 245.

[97] Higginson, *Cheerful Yesterdays*, p. 142.

[98] *Ibid.*, p. 143.

[99] Adams, *Dana*, p. 191.

[100] *Ibid.*, p. 188; *Law Reporter*, 14 (1852), 15.

[101] *The Liberator*, April 18, 1851.

[102] Adams, *Dana*, pp. 188–190.

[103] *Law Reporter*, 14 (1852), 10–11. This writer is unable to understand the abolitionist effort to help Sims by means of a writ of personal replevin under the state statute of 1837, since Shaw had decided in the Latimer case, in 1842, that the writ was inapplicable to the case of a fugitive slave. *The Atlas*, Boston, November 1, 1842.

[104] *Commonwealth* v. *Aves*, 35 Mass. 193 (1836).

[105] *Law Reporter*, 14 (1852), 11–12; *The Commonwealth*, April 11, 1851; *The Liberator*, April 18, 1851.

[106] April 10, 1851.

[107] Parker, *Trial of Theodore Parker*, pp. 4–5.

[108] *The Liberator*, April 11, 1851.

[109] *The Journals of Bronson Alcott*, p. 245.

[110] Higginson, *Cheerful Yesterdays*, p. 144; Bearse, *Reminiscences*, pp. 24–25.

[111] *National Intelligencer*, April 10, 1851.

[112] The *Boston Courier* flayed the handbills as a "base and wicked" effort to collect a mob to effect a rescue, and the *Boston Post* promised that if "riot, rebellion, treachery, massacre, dare show their hideous features, they will be crushed to the earth never to rise again." *Ibid.*, April 12, excerpts.

[113] Parker, *Trial of Theodore Parker*, p. 151.

[114] *Ibid.* Curtis' opinion may be found in the *Trial of Thomas Sims, pp.* 39–47.

[115] *Law Reporter*, 14 (1852), 12–14; *The Liberator*, April 18, 1851.

[116] Bowditch, *Life*, pp. 216–217; *The Liberator*, April 18, 1851; *Twentieth Annual Report*, pp. 22–23; Parker, *Trial of Theodore Parker*, p. 151.

[117] Bowditch, *Life*, pp. 219–220; *Daily Evening Transcript*, April 12, 1851; *Twentieth Annual Report*, p. 22.

[118] Bowditch, *Life*, pp. 221–222.

[119] *Ibid.*, p. 222; *National Intelligencer*, April 17, 1851; Parker, *Trial of Theodore Parker*, p. 151; *Twentieth Annual Report*, p. 23.

[120] Bowditch, *Life*, p. 223; *The Liberator*, April 18 and 25, 1851; *The Commonwealth*, April 23, 1851; Samuel May, *The Fugitive Slave Law and its Victims* (New York, 1861), p. 17.

[121] *Daily Evening Transcript*, April 12, 1851.

[122] April 14, 1851.

[123] Quoted in *The Liberator*, April 25, 1851.

[124] *Ibid.*

[125] Quoted in the *Daily National Intelligencer*, April 25, 1851.

[126] Quoted in Bearse, *Reminiscences*, pp. 29–30.

[127] *Ibid.*

[128] April 13, 1851, *Writings, Letters and Speeches* (National Edition, 1903), XVI, 606.

[129] April 13.

[130] Quotations from *The Liberator*, May 2, 1851, which gives extensive excerpts from the press opinion of many cities, including Washington, Albany, Buffalo, Mobile, and Philadelphia.

[131] *Ibid.*

[132] Quoted in Robinson, *Pen Portraits*, pp. 193–194.

[133] *The Complete Poetical Works of John Greenleaf Whittier*, p. 314.

[134] *The Journals of Bronson Alcott*, p. 246.

[135] Adams, *Dana*, p. 194.

JIM CROW EDUCATION: ORIGINS OF THE "SEPARATE BUT EQUAL" DOCTRINE

with Douglas Jones

T HE "separate but equal" doctrine, the legal linchpin of Jim Crow in America, had its origins in the cradle of liberty, Boston, Massachusetts. In 1847, Sarah Roberts, a first-grade child, had to pass by five primary schools to reach the one on Belknap Street in the West End of Boston. Her father, Benjamin F. Roberts, had tried on no less than four separate occasions to enter Sarah in one of the other schools closer to her home, but each time her application for admission was rejected. On the fourth occasion, when she entered the school nearest her home, the teacher ejected her. Little Sarah was black. By the mandate of the Boston School Committee, all but two of the 161 primary schools were reserved exclusively for white children. Neither state law nor city ordinance required separate schools for Negroes, but the school committee, possessing the power to classify pupils, had segregated the public schools on the basis of race. Mr. Roberts, a militant opponent of racial segregation, brought suit against the City of Boston in Sarah's name to compel her admission to one of the white primary schools. He based his suit on a statute providing that any child illegally excluded from a city's public school might recover damages against the city.

Sarah Roberts lost her case, and the cause of compulsory racial segregation in public schools won an enormous legal victory. The 1850 opinion of Chief Justice Lemuel Shaw for the Supreme Judicial Court of Massachusetts was the genesis of the "separate but equal" doctrine, namely that Negroes are not denied equal protection of the laws when provided with separate facilities that are substantially the same as those for whites.[1] In 1896, when the Supreme Court of the

316

United States endorsed that doctrine, Justice Henry Billings Brown, the spokesman for the majority, relied on the Massachusetts opinion of 1849 as the leading precedent for the validity of state legislation requiring segregation of the white and colored races "in places where they are liable to be brought into contact." [2] The Roberts case, obviously, had a profound influence on the law of the land and on preventing black Americans from attaining their equal rights.

Boston's public schools had been segregated since 1798, when the first school for Negroes was established by the initiative of Negroes who were excluded "on account of the prejudice then existing against them." [3] At that time, the public school system of Boston did not expressly deny any Negro entrance to any school. Nevertheless, Negroes, intensely feeling the racial antipathy of the whites, refused to attend all-white schools.[4] Instead, Boston's Negroes created private schools for themselves, the first of which was located near the corner of George and May Streets in the home of Primus Hall, "a respectable colored man." Elisha Sylvester, a white man, taught the first few pupils. Although the school functioned only sporadically before 1806, Primus Hall's concern for educating black children persisted.[5]

In 1800, lacking the necessary funds to meet all of their expenses for a school for Negroes, sixty-six black citizens requested in a petition to the Boston School Committee that the city establish a school exclusively for Negroes. A subcommittee of the school committee, consisting of Josiah Quincy, Arnold Welles, the Reverend John I. Kirkland, Dr. Aaron Dexter, and the Reverend William Emerson, reported the petition favorably, but a special town meeting refused the request for a separate school for Negroes. Young blacks were left with the choice of attending public schools, where they encountered racial hatred, or the private school of Primus Hall. After the town meeting, Hall's school gained some financial support from several white citizens. Between 1798 and 1806, all of its teachers were white graduates of Harvard College; [6] thereafter black teachers were as common as white ones.

The cramped quarters of Primus Hall's home were partially alleviated in 1806, when the school moved to the newly erected African Meetinghouse, located on Belknap Street. The lower floor, or basement, was converted into a permanent schoolhouse for Negro children which operated until 1835. Although Boston had refused to provide a separate school for blacks, it did endorse the policy of separate schools for Negroes after 1806 by contributing $200 per year toward the support of the African Meetinghouse school. White benefactors and the parents of the schoolchildren contributed the remainder of the money.[7]

Of the school's first teachers, perhaps the best known was Prince Sanders, the son of a Negro lawyer from Vermont. A staunch believer in separatism in education, Sanders persuaded a wealthy Bostonian, Abiel Smith, of the need to establish a trust fund for the education of black children in Boston,[8] and when Smith, "the merchant prince," died in 1815, he left to the town of Boston an endowment whose income was to be used exclusively to maintain a school or schools "for the instruction of people of color,—meaning Africans and their descendants, either colored or mixed." This provision of Smith's will was later used by those favoring segregation to argue that the trust could not be broken to support integrated schools.[9]

The African Meetinghouse school existed privately until 1815, when Boston assumed control of the schools for local Negroes. Several other schools were organized at other sites but none survived. In 1835, the school committee honored the benefaction of Abiel Smith by naming a new school for Negroes—the Smith School. Built on the site of the African Meetinghouse, the Smith School became a focal point for the education of the black man in Boston.

One of the leading Negro reformers of the day, William C. Nell, an intimate of Wendell Phillips and William Lloyd Garrison, was educated in the African Meetinghouse. Nell was one of the first Negroes who sensed that a segregated education was inconsistent with a democracy. While reminiscing about his struggles for equal rights, he related that in 1829 he and two other students were judged to have been the three brightest pupils of the Negro school. Instead of receiving scholarship medals embossed with the picture of Benjamin Franklin, which was the customary award of the city schools, Mayor Harrison Gray Otis and Lieutenant Governor Samuel T. Armstrong gave the three students biographies of Benjamin Franklin. Moreover, the three were not invited to the awards dinner in Faneuil Hall. Nell, being curious and clever, offered to assist one of the waiters. During the dinner, Lieutenant Governor Armstrong said casually to Nell that he should have been there with the white boys and not waiting on their tables. Looking back on this incident some twenty-five years later, Nell declared that the discrimination struck his sensitivity acutely, provoking him to commit himself to the cause of equal school rights.[10] Indeed, Nell committed himself not only to equal school rights but to resistance to racial discrimination on all fronts.

In 1840, the first petition requesting equal school rights was presented to the "City Government" (presumably the Boston School Committee). Nell, William Lloyd Garrison, Wendell Phillips, Francis Jackson, and Henry W. Williams were the signatories to this earliest (and unsuccessful) attempt to persuade Boston to alter the segregated system of education which had existed formally for over twenty years.[11] The school issue soon slipped into the background, however, as Negro militants and the white abolitionists of the Massachusetts Anti-Slavery Society turned their attention to the railroad companies' policy of maintaining separate passenger cars for blacks and whites. Initially the militants challenged the policy by refusing to sit in separate cars unless forcibly removed by several white conductors. This early form of nonviolent civil disobedience was practiced by Frederick Douglass, among other well-known abolitionists, and Douglass suffered a severe beating at the hands of white men seeking to remove him from a train on which he was a passenger. As such isolated but persistent challenges to the Jim Crow cars continued to occur, militants opened a campaign to pressure the General Court of Massachusetts (the state legislature) to enact a bill outlawing the Jim Crow car. The General Court seriously considered such a bill in 1842 but failed to pass it. Nevertheless, the railroad companies acted on their own initiative in 1843 and eliminated their policy of separate cars for Negroes.[12] Boston's Negroes, politically and physically scarred but victorious in their battle over the Jim Crow car, again turned their attention to the segregated Boston public schools. Once a blessing but now an abomination, the Jim Crow school was a perfect target for the equalitarian-minded abolitionists of the Massachusetts Anti-Slavery Society and the militant Negroes, and a new petition was filed with the Boston Grammar School Committee in 1844. This petition was rejected, and another presented to the Primary School Committee a year later met the same fate.[13]

At the time of the presentation of these petitions, Boston had one Latin Grammar School, one English High School, 17 grammar and writing schools, and 117 primary schools. No more than three of these were reserved for Boston's black community of approximately 2,000 persons—only 2 percent of the city's total. The Smith School served as a grammar school for older Negro children, while at least two primary schools existed exclusively for blacks aged four to seven. Even in 1844 Abiel Smith's trust still paid part of the expenses of the schools for Negroes. Segregation of the races was accepted by the school committee as the norm for education: "The colored population in this city not being sufficiently numerous to require more than one [grammar] school, it has been thought proper to provide in this [the Smith School], the means of instruction in all the branches of learning which are taught in the several orders for white children." [14]

The textbooks used in the racially segregated schools were the same used in the other schools of the city, giving the illusion that the education of the blacks was the same as that of the whites. When, or if, a Negro child advanced enough in his studies to move into the Latin School or the English High School, the school committee did not insist upon separation of the races. It demanded only that the student was "well versed in the studies pursued in the Grammar and Writing Schools." [15] Over the years, a few Negroes were in fact admitted to the Boston Latin School. The City of Worcester had a similar provision for admitting black students into its high school. The success of the education of blacks in Worcester's high school was questionable, however, for only three Negroes, all girls, had entered the high school from the all-Negro primary school by 1849. [16]

Behind the political agitation for equal school rights for Negroes in Boston existed a source of discontent which was not itself strictly political: the acknowledged failure of the black educational system, a failure that, according to Negro militants and their allies, was the result of racial segregation in the school system. [17] The school committee of Boston which inspected the Smith School in 1845, observing that it was doing poorly, emphasized its failures without diagnosing its problems. The committee said that the school was "unsatisfactory" and "in a deplorable condition. The attainments of the scholars are of the lowest grade; a few can read aloud from the class reader, but cannot understand any other than the simplest passages." [18] The visiting committee members, Theophilus Parsons, Samuel Gridley Howe, and Rollin H. Neale, expected the Negro children to know certain parts of the geography of the world "most interesting to colored children, those relating to the West India Islands, the condition of the colored race in Cuba, Jamaica, Hayti [*sic*], &c; the colonies in Africa, the conditions of the natives, &c.; but the scholars of the Smith School seemed to know nothing about them. . . ." [19] Such expectations were schizophrenic: the American Negro was expected to be innately curious about his black past when still held largely in slavery, yet he was also expected to accept American ideals in the face of American realities. Not surprisingly, Negro children, especially the brighter ones, left school as soon as they were able to obtain employment. [20]

The "Report to the Primary School Committee, June 15, 1846, on the Petition of Sundry Colored Persons, for the Abolition of Schools for Colored Children" contains a detailed attempt by the school committee to justify its policy of racial segregation. A minority of the committee dissented from the findings and published their views in an unofficial report. The immediate reason for the majority report was yet another petition, this one submitted February 6, 1846, by Negro citizens of Boston who were parents, guardians, and friends of Negro children attending the primary schools. This petition labeled the separate schools "exclusive," asserting that they deprived the Negro children of the equal privileges and advantages in the public schools to which they were entitled as citizens. [21] Anticipating later sociological findings which verified their beliefs, the Negroes argued that "separate schools cost more and do less for the children than other schools, since all experience teaches that where a small and despised class are shut out from the common benefit of any public institutions of learning and confined to separate schools—neglect ensues, abuses creep in, the standard of scholarship degenerates, and the teachers and the scholars are soon considered and of course become an inferior class." [22]

The majority shrouded their answer to the petition of the Negroes in legalistic self-righteousness. The report acknowledged three possible grounds upon which the black schools could be said to be unlawful. First, the children could not go to any school which they or their parents had chosen; second, Negroes were not allowed to attend the school nearest their dwelling; third, "the separation, being made on the principle of a distinction in races or of color, does necessarily deprive the colored children of the full and equal benefits of the public schools." [23] The report then proceeded to reject each contention. No child had the right to attend any school he wanted—the power of pupil assignment rested solely with the school committee. Second, many students normally had to attend particular schools for special instruction. The school committee could not build a Latin School, for example, in every section of Boston. Finally, on the question of race, the report candidly stated that segregated education was best for the Negro population of Boston. Severely criticizing the Negroes for even asking for desegregated schools, since this implied that they could not "make their separate schools as good as those for the white children," the report urged that the two races be kept apart, and that the "African race" should cultivate "the genuine virtues, peculiar to that race." [24] "Let them not lean upon, nor look up to the whites; but trust, under God, to their own native energies, unmingled and uncorrupted. Let them cultivate a respect for themselves for their own race, their own blood, aye, and for their own *color*." [25]

The real question according to the report, was "one of *races*, not of colors, merely." Having been established by the "All-wise Creator," the difference between whites and blacks existed in "the physical, mental and moral natures of the two races. No legislation, no social customs, can efface this distinction." [26] Given such beliefs, the members of the school committee were incredulous when counsel for the Negro petitioners argued that black children had "the right to be mingled in and crumbled up with, the mass of society" through the process of education. The committee believed, rather, that public education should only "crumble up" those classes which were mutually agreeable, and that a "promiscuous intermingling in the public schools" was "disadvantageous" to both races.[27] The committee's attitude was not one of neglect, however. Because of "Christian benevolence," the school committee declared "the strong ought to bear the infirmities of the weak." [28]

A particular thorn in the school committee's side was the Constitution of Massachusetts, which contained clauses that courts of a later day would construe to mean the same as the equal-protection clause of the Fourteenth Amendment to the United States Constitution.[29] One judge of the Massachusetts Supreme Judicial Court, Richard Fletcher, had already presented to the school committee of Salem an advisory opinion holding unlawful the exclusion of Negroes from the public schools. Judge Fletcher's opinion was based on his initial discussion of the nature of the free, public school system of Massachusetts: "It is the principle of equality cherished in the free schools, on which our free government and free institutions rest. Destroy this principle in the schools and the people would soon cease to be a free people." Observing that a Negro was a free citizen with privileges and duties equal to those of any other citizen of the Commonwealth, Judge Fletcher doubted whether special schools could be created legally from public money for the children of particular classes, be they Negroes, mechanics, or laborers.[30] The subcommittee of the Primary School Committee of Boston, in its 1846 report, answered simply that Judge Fletcher's opinion was his own, that it did not apply to any other town except Salem, and that separation in Boston might be legal because of the larger number of Negroes involved.[31]

Ignoring the advisory opinion of Judge Fletcher was a bold act made easier by the city solicitor of Boston, Peleg W. Chandler. Chandler was an expert on municipal law and the founder of one of the earliest law journals in America, the *Law Reporter*. At the request of the school committee, he wrote an opinion on the lawfulness of separate schools for Negroes. That opinion, which was printed with the 1846 report, was the only authoritative one prior to the *Roberts* case which upheld segregation. In it, Chandler emphasized that, according to the statutory law, the Boston school committee had the legal power to classify students as it wanted.[32] The committee had adopted Chandler's position, and so too did Chief Justice Shaw three years later in his opinion in the *Roberts* case.

The "Report of the Minority of the Committee of the Primary School Board, on the Caste Schools of the City of Boston . . ." was not printed with the official report among the Boston city documents for the year 1846, because a motion to do so was defeated by the school committee.[33] The minority differed with the majority in its interpretation of segregation in relation to society. While the majority implied that blacks were inferior and argued that segregated schools were required for their own good as well as for that of the whites, the minority said that the existence of separate schools tended "to create in most [white children], and foster in all, feelings of repugnance and contempt for the colored race as degraded inferiors, whom they may, or must, treat as such." Because the minority did not believe the Negro was inferior, it contended that the school committee's power of discretion to classify pupils could not breach the constitutional guarantee of equality.[34] While the majority would have welcomed a court challenge to their power, the minority preferred to settle the issue without going to court.[35] With the Negro population only 2 percent, the minority argued, there seemed to be no reason for not permitting the schools to provide a fusion of all races or classes, at least educationally.[36] Salem, New Bedford, Nantucket, and Lowell provided the minority with examples of towns which were then operating desegregated public schools without incident.[37] The minority proposed a compromise that would have enabled those black children who preferred to attend a segregated school to attend one, while those who wished to go to the nearest school, regardless of race, could do that.[38]

Wendell Phillips, a leader of the Massachusetts Anti-Slavery Society, militant abolitionist, and forceful supporter of equal school rights, attacked Peleg Chandler's opinion in the minority report. Phillips portrayed Chandler as the Primary School Committee's "respectable" voice in sacrificing the rights of black children to "vulgar prejudice." [39] Chandler had proven that the school committee had wide discretionary powers in the assignment of pupils, choice of books, location of school houses—this Phillips acknowledged.[40] But the real point of controversy, he said, was whether segregation of children by races was "reasonable in the eye of the law." [41] Chandler had not pursued this point; he had asserted that it was reasonable, but he had not explained why. Phillips disavowed the reasonable basis for such a policy and warned Chandler: "Let me tell this young official that the moment the element of color mingles in any question, no confidence can be replaced in any American court." [42] In *The Liberator*, William Lloyd Garrison described the views of Chandler and the majority of the school committee as "flimsy yet venomous sophistries." [43]

For more than four years after the 1846 controversy, the issue of separate schools for Negroes was the occasion of discord among public officials and among the Negroes themselves. But 1849 was the highpoint of agitation for equal school rights in Boston, for in that year two developments rallied the anti-segregation forces and eventually caused the differing factions of Negroes to articulate their views more clearly. First, the school committee was again besieged with petitions from Negroes desiring the abolition of segregated schools. Second, Benjamin F. Roberts brought suit against the City of Boston in the name of his daughter, Sarah, under a statute which prohibited illegal exclusion of any child from the public schools. Fortified by abolitionist emotionalism, utopianian idealism, and the firm conviction that equality should be absolute in the public schools, Boston's Negroes and their white sympathizers girded for what they hoped would be a final victory over "exclusive," or racial, schools.[44]

In July 1849, the Boston Grammar School Board received a petition from the militant faction of Negroes who desired that the Smith School be abolished and that Negro children be admitted to all other schools of Boston. The Negroes behind this petition, and other petitions accompanying it, had consistently been in the forefront in the struggle for equal school rights: Benjamin F. Roberts, John T. Hilton, Lemuel Burr, and Jonas W. Clark.[45] The substance of the militants' petition did not differ in principle from the one presented to the Primary School Committee in 1846, except that in 1849, the petition was directed at the Smith Grammar School, and specific incidences of inequalities were cited to support the contention that separate schools were exclusive and therefore unequal.

The petition "signed by Jonas Clark and 201 others," cited the inconvenience caused by the existence of only one school for the Negroes, who were spread all over Boston; the fact that segregation in education was an obstacle to their "common rights"; that the child of an immigrant could attend a public school but a native-born black child could not; that separation because of color encouraged racism; and that Boston was the only city in Massachusetts which segregated blacks and whites in school.[46] The Clark petition made clear that the dissatisfaction of the militant Negroes was not with the white principal of the Smith School, Ambrose Wellington. The issue was not the color of the teacher; it was equality in education. A recommendation that a Negro should be principal of the school, said the petition, was "an attempt to quiet our efforts against its dissolution." [47]

Although the militants obtained the most signatures of any Negro group which presented a petition, two other Negro groups attempted to persuade the school committee not to abolish the Smith School, but rather to maintain segregation in education. Joseph Russell and the Reverend James Simmons, both Negroes, asked only for the appointment of a black teacher.[48] Others, who did not petition but testified before the school committee in its hearings, advocated that the Smith School remain segregated and keep a white teacher—but a new one.[49] Such Negroes feared integration because they considered segregated education better than the possibility of none at all under an all-white school system. Thomas P. Smith, for example, who professed to see "no baleful influences, no degradation, no oppression or prejudice, *caused* by colored schools," thought they might be unnecessary in Lowell, Cambridge, "and other places referred to by the gentlemen, where colored people are scarce as *hen teeth* [*sic*], yet they may be extremely politic, expedient, and useful in Boston." [50]

As in 1846, the school committee disagreed as to the wisest course of action, and two separate reports emerged. By 1849, however, the minority view had gained either sufficient prestige or enough votes to merit its report being printed in the official city documents. The school committee's majority, agreeing with Thomas P. Smith, recommended simply that the Smith School hire a black teacher with a college degree.[51] The majority's "Report of a Special Committee of the Grammar School Board, Presented August 29, 1849, on the Petition of Sundry Colored Persons Praying for the Abolition of the Smith School . . . ," covered many of the same arguments and historical facts which had been canvassed in 1846. The 1849 report, however, interpreted the motivations behind the petitions it reviewed and thus provided insight into the factional split within the Negro community. One also detects a note of impatience in the tone of the majority report, as if the issue had already been settled. The majority welcomed, for example, Benjamin Roberts' pending lawsuit against the city, saying that the "suit by the prosecuting party opens up . . . the whole question of the City's right to establish separate schools for complexional classes." [52] The majority added that they would bow to the wishes of the judicial process, implying that the Negroes should do likewise. Yet they thought it strange that Roberts would petition the committee to remove segregation when court action was pending. "To Caesar they have appealed," said the majority, "and to Caesar they should go." [53]

The militants did go to Caesar, in the form of Chief Justice Lemuel Shaw and his brethren, but not without an admonition from the majority for defaming those Bostonians, both black and white, who had organized the system of segregated education. Abiel Smith was portrayed with veneration as the initiator of a "golden age" of education for blacks with his generous gift. The petitioners, said the majority, would reverse progress, and gave the impression that they "thought that a white skin was really better than a dark one." [54] The majority, although disavowing any overt racial superiority, ambiguously exposed its own prejudices regarding race: "The colored man's skin,—the African's hue—is intrinsically, neither worse nor better than any different varieties. But it is a plain, ready mark of discrimination: It is a palpable sign manual, 'an epistle, known and read of all men.' " [55] The solution offered in 1849 was the same as that of 1846—racial segregation of school children. Moreover, the terms of the Abiel Smith Trust, which was the central financial prop for the Smith School, were held to require that an "exclusive" school for blacks be maintained.[56] Although the majority thus seemed to cover itself on all points, noticeably absent from its report was an attempt to defend racial segregation as consistent with the constitutional requirement of equality.

Charles Theodore Russell was the author of the "Report of the Minority of the Committee upon the Petition of John T. Hilton and others, Colored Citizens of Boston, Praying for the Abolition of the Smith School, and that Colored Children May be Permitted to Attend the Other Schools of the City." Russell saw two dominant questions, both of which centered on equality: first, did the school committee have a right to exclude colored children from the common schools; second, could the committee maintain exclusive schools for Negroes? His answer to both questions was an emphatic no.[57] Elaborating on the theme of equality, he contended that differences in social condition did not create any "ground of division, or exclusion in the school[s]," nor did religious and political distinctions.[58] The sole basis for segregation was color. Since complexion gave no rights, argued Russell, it should not give any disabilities.[59] He reached the problem of equal protection of the laws, which the majority never grasped, when he declared that although blacks were not totally excluded from schooling, confining them to separate schools because of color virtually excluded them from the common schools.[60] Russell was less concerned with the legal provisions of the Smith Trust; he suggested that it be converted into a fund for the education of adult Negroes.[61] In his conclusion, he offered the same freedom of choice plan found in the 1846 minority report: permit the Smith School to operate for those who wanted to attend a separate school, but open the other schools in Boston to all children regardless of race.[62]

Having failed to achieve integrated schools by petitioning the school committee, Boston Negroes focused their attention on the lawsuit of Benjamin F. Roberts. The suit was based on a Massachusetts statute passed in 1845, which permitted an action in tort against anyone who unlawfully excluded a child from a public school.[63] The statute provided for the recovery of damages but was silent as to any procedure, such as an injunction, which would permanently prevent exclusion. Charles Sumner represented Sarah Roberts, and one of the two black lawyers in Massachusetts, Robert Morris, acted as co-counsel. Sumner was a man of erudition and eloquence who devoted his enormous energies to the fight against slavery and to advocating reform causes. With a moralistic fervor characteristic of the times, he argued the Roberts case secure in the knowledge that he was right. He carried his drive and his devotion to abolitionism with him to the United States Senate, where he became slavery's most implacable foe and one of New England's greatest senators.

In an age of pamphlet literature and propaganda, the "Argument of Charles Sumner, Esq. Against the Constitutionality of Separate Colored Schools, in the Case of Sarah C. Roberts *v.* The City of Boston" received widespread dissemination. Conscious of his task to translate the social issue of racial segregation into a justiciable issue, Sumner nevertheless could not "forget that the principles of morals and of natural justice lie at the foundation of all jurisprudence. . . ." [64] "Precise equality" was his dominant theme, with his precedents coming from the concepts of equality expressed in the writings of Rousseau and of Condorcet, in the Declaration of Independence, and in the Massachusetts Constitution. The last was particularly important because it contained the equivalent of an equal-protection-of-the-laws clause.[65] Sumner asserted that a confluence of the ideas of equality underlying the French and American Revolutions had occurred in the American political tradition, and that his heritage of equality before the law, as embodied in the Massachusetts Constitution, denied that any man could be discriminated against because of his birth or his color. The separate schools for Negroes were unconstitutional, Sumner alleged, because of their "caste" nature.

Turning to the school committee, Sumner implied that the majority was motivated by racial prejudice. He argued that the power of the school committee, as delegated by the state, existed only to supervise the public schools and to determine "the number and qualifications of scholars." [66] The committee could not infer or assume the power to segregate blacks, because to do so would be to "brand a whole race with the stigma of inferiority and degradation." That power to segregate was arbitrary and usurped, and placed the committee "above the Constitution. It would enable them, in the exercise of a brief and local authority, to draw a fatal circle, within which the Constitution cannot enter;—nay, where the very Bill of Rights shall become a dead letter." [67] Sumner demanded that the committee's classifications of school children be reasonable, contending that the committee's *a priori* assumption that an entire race was inferior and therefore to be separated was an unreasonable exercise of the committee's discretion. Only such factors as age, sex, and moral and intellectual fitness were within the committee's judgment, said Sumner, not complexion.

Anticipating the "separate but equal" doctrine, Sumner rejected as unequal any facilities which were not integrated. A segregated school, stigmatized by caste or race, must be an illegal one and could not be an equivalent.[68] ". . . [A] school, exclusively devoted to one class, must differ essentially, in its spirit and character, from that public school known to the law, where all classes meet together in Equality. It is a mockery to call it an equivalent." [69]

Before closing his argument, Sumner made a stirring plea not strictly judicial, yet necessary to an understanding of his attack on segregated schools. His remarks have been validated by modern scholarship in the fields of sociology and psychology:

The whites themselves are injured by the separation. Who can doubt this? With the Law as their monitor, . . . they are taught practically to deny that grand revelation of Christianity, the Brotherhood of Man. Hearts, while yet tender with childhood, are hardened, and ever afterward testify to this legalized uncharitableness. Nursed in the sentiments of Caste, receiving it with the earliest food of knowledge, they are unable to eradicate it from their natures. . . .

The school is the little world where the child is trained for the larger world of life. . . . It . . . must cherish and develop the virtues and the sympathies needed in the larger world. [It should begin with] those relations of Equality which the Constitution and Laws promise to all.

Prejudice is the child of ignorance. It is sure to prevail, where people do not know each other. Society and intercourse are means established by Providence for human improvement. They remove antipathies, promote mutual adaptation and conciliation, and establish relations of reciprocal regard.[70]

Sumner's eloquence on behalf of Sarah Roberts and the cause of equal rights was met by a stern man of great legal knowledge and experience, Chief Justice Shaw of the Supreme Judicial Court. To him fell the task of expanding or further narrowing the legal concept of equality. Shaw was a formidable man of majestic reputation who gave the impression, it was said, of having "the absolute power of a crag vitalized by a human spirit." During his thirty years of service as Chief Justice of Massachusetts, he wrote a record number of opinions—over 2,200, only one of which was a dissent—imbuing hoary doctrines with such freshness, he once remarked, as "the advancement of civilization may require." No other state judge, through his opinions alone, had so great an influence on the course of American law. But no opinion by Shaw was more lacking in human spirit or more obstructive of the advancement of civilization than his opinion in the *Roberts* case.[71] Delivering the unanimous opinion of the Court, Shaw upheld fully the power of the Boston school committees to impose segregation in education. (No explanation is to be found for the absence from the Court in this case of Judge Richard Fletcher, who three years earlier, had given an opinion at bar holding unconstitutional segregated schools in Salem.)

The case required for its disposition no fine analysis of difficult legal points, and Shaw confined himself, as had the counsel before him, primarily to general principles—and to predilections. That his opinion has had an enduring influence may be attributed in part to the sweep and force with which the principles were announced, and to the articulation given the predilections.

In rejecting the contention of the plaintiff that she had been excluded unlawfully from the public schools, Shaw was quick to observe that her school was equal in all respects to any other school in Boston. Sarah Roberts "had access to a school set apart for colored children, as well conducted in all respects, and as well fitted, in point of capacity and qualifications of the instructors, to advance the education of children under seven years old, as the other primary schools." [72] Shaw's assertion is not contradicted by the evidence, but it applied to the Smith School (whose legality, Shaw acknowledged, would be affected by the Court's decision, although it was a grammar and not a primary school) only because, three months before the Roberts case was argued in the Supreme Judicial Court, an expensive face-lifting of the school was completed, "including an entire re-modeling of the building." [73] Three years earlier, however, its master had provided quite a different description: "The school rooms are too small, the paint is much defaced, and every part gives evidence of the most shameful negligence and abuse. There are no recitation rooms, or proper places for overclothes, caps, bonnets, etc. The yards, for each division, are but about fifteen feet square, and only accessible through a dark, damp cellar. The apparatus has been so shattered and neglected that it cannot be used until it has been thoroughly repaired." [74]

Physical facilities were not as important to Shaw as the issue of whether the school committee was empowered to classify the children as it pleased, "because, if they [the committee] have the legal authority, the expediency of exercising it in any particular way is exclusively with them." [75] This proposition was a reflection of the judicial self-restraint so characteristic of the Shaw Court. If government power was legitimately founded, the Chief Justice would not intervene simply because it established a policy that was unwise, illiberal, or inexpedient. In this instance, however, Shaw put the proposition without qualifications, as if the school committee possessed discretionary powers to classify children by race, religion, economic status, or national origin. In the course of his opinion he failed to provide any convincing reasons in support of such powers on the part of the school committee. He simply assumed that because the committee could segregate children for educational purposes by age, sex, and ability, it might with equal validity segregate them by race.

Shaw's other conclusions on the points at issue were characterized by a singular absence of considered judgment. He moved easily, for example, from his carte-blanche approval of the school committee's discretionary powers to an assumption—in itself sufficient to decide the case—that all individuals did not possess the same legal rights. Shaw's own words better describe the treatment the law provided to those individuals who did not possess equal rights—Negroes:

The great principle, advanced by the learned and eloquent advocate of the plaintiff, is, that by the constitution and laws of Massachusetts, all persons without distinction of age or sex, birth or color, origin or condition, are equal before the law. This, as a broad general principle, such as ought to appear in a declaration of rights, is perfectly sound; it is not only expressed in terms, but pervades and animates the whole spirit of our constitution of free government. But when this great principle comes to be applied to the actual and various conditions of persons in society, it will not warrant the assertion, that men and women are legally clothed with the same civil and political powers, and that children and adults are legally to have the same functions and be subject to the same treatment; but only that the rights of all, as they are settled and regulated by law, are equally entitled to the paternal consideration and protection of the law, for their maintenance and security. What these rights are, to which individuals, in the infinite variety of circumstances by which they are surrounded in society, are entitled, must depend on laws adapted to their respective relations and conditions.[76]

Shaw's words, stripped of their rhetoric, set forth two contradictory propositions later expressed more succinctly by the favored class, the pigs, in George Orwell's *Animal Farm:* "ALL ANIMALS ARE EQUAL BUT SOME ANIMALS ARE MORE EQUAL THAN OTHERS."

After asserting unreasoned grounds for the decision in the case, Shaw inverted the normal logic of a judicial opinion by next stating the question before the Court. He phrased that question in such a way as to make possible, by his answer, the "separate but equal" doctrine: "Conceding, therefore, in the fullest manner, that colored persons, the descendants of Africans, are entitled by law, in this commonwealth, to equal rights, constitutional and political, civil and social, the question then arises, whether the regulation in question, which provides separate schools for colored children, is a violation of any of these rights." [77]

Shaw proceeded to establish that legal rights depended upon provisions of law; that the Massachusetts Constitution declared only broad principles for the guidance of the state legislature; that, in turn, the legislature had defined only the general outlines and objectives of an educational system; and that the school committee had been vested with a discretionary power to make all reasonable rules for the classification of pupils. The Chief Justice was impressed by the fact that the committee, after long investigation, believed that the welfare of both races was best promoted by the separate education of their children. He demanded that the committee's power be "reasonably exercised, without being abused or perverted by colorable pretenses," and finding it to have been so exercised, he supported the committee's decision as conclusive. The Court, he ruled, had no basis for doubting that the committee had formed its decision "on just grounds of reason and experience, and in the results of a discriminating [sic] and honest judgment." [78]

In the face of an equality-of-rights clause in the Massachusetts Constitution, Shaw should have felt bound to establish that discrimination on the basis of race was reasonable. Instead, he relied on the reasonableness of the power delegated by the legislature to the school committee, a power he construed as allowing the committee to classify pupils according to any criteria whatsoever, and he contented himself with the predilection that the racial prejudice which existed "is not created by law, and probably cannot be changed by law." [79] He added that prejudice probably would be fostered "by compelling colored and white children to associate together in the same schools." [80] This was the court's answer to Sumner's contention that the maintenance of separate schools tended to perpetuate and deepen prejudice. Shaw did not attempt to test his and the school committee's views against the experience of the various towns of Massachusetts where children, without regard to race, attended the same schools with successful results. Sumner's presentation of the evidence concerning integrated school systems had fallen on deaf ears. Thus did the "separate-but-equal" doctrine as a constitutional justification for racial segregation first enter the mainstream of American jurisprudence, where it remained for more than one hundred years.

The decision of the Supreme Judicial Court provoked criticism even from the conservative white press, although public opinion, black as well as white, was divided. [81] Before Shaw announced the Court's opinion in April of 1850, black militants, meeting at the Belknap Street Church, described as "treacherous" the views of those in the Negro community who preferred racially separated schools. Benjamin F. Roberts, William C. Nell, John T. Hilton, Charles Slack, Robert Morris, and others at the meeting formed an Equal School Rights Committee that pledged itself to the abolition of segregated education. They resolved that should the Court "fail to award us justice," they would appeal to the people themselves for a mass petition to the legislature. [82] When the Court did fail them, Roberts, Nell, and the other members of the Equal School Rights Committee again assembled in the Belknap Street Church, expressed disappointment, resolved to continue "till the struggle results in victory," and sent a delegation to the New England Anti-Slavery Convention where allies might be found for the cause of integrated public schools. [83] With the support of the abolitionists, the Equal

331

School Rights Committee organized a campaign to secure from the state legislature a statute prohibiting separation of children within the school system on the basis of race or color. A bill to that effect was considered and rejected by the legislature in 1851.[84] Integrationist forces petitioned for reconsideration. Their petition, signed by more than nine hundred people, including members of the Massachusetts Anti-Slavery Society, asked "that we may receive what we have long sought for,—our rights in the public Schools of Boston. In all other places in the State, our opportunities are Equal." [85] The legislature, however, did not reconsider the bill, nor did a similar one come before it until 1855.

Despite the legislative setback in 1851, sentiment in favor of ending segregated schools grew in the Common Council of Boston, thanks to the lobbying activities of the Equal School Rights Committee and the Anti-Slavery Society. In April 1854, the Common Council ordered the Committee on Public Instruction to investigate whether any children were being excluded unjustly from the public schools of Boston.[86] Though disputing the Common Council's jurisdiction over the public schools, the Committee on Public Instruction complied. The investigation uncovered the case of a lad named Pindall whose parents were of African blood but who were very light-skinned. Pindall had been accepted into an all-white school but later was excluded when his true race was discovered.[87] George F. Williams, author of the subsequent "Report of Committee on Public Instruction, On Case of a Child Excluded from a Public School of this City" (1854), clearly did not share the views of the majority reports of 1846 and 1849, or those of Chief Justice Shaw. Although refusing to comment on the Pindall case because it was then in litigation, Williams established that while there was no rule or regulation which specifically excluded Negro children from the public schools, in practice almost all Negroes were excluded. Contradicting Shaw on every major point, he asserted for a number of reasons that Boston should experiment with integrated schools. First, the experience of other Massachusetts towns and of Boston itself (the primary schools had by then started to integrate), indicated that integration did not pose any problems; [88] second, the laws of the state opposed separate schools; third, Negro children living in the East End and in other parts of Boston were too distant from the Smith School to expect, realistically, that they would attend. Taking Shaw at his word when the Chief Justice had ruled that the school committee controlled the power of classification, Williams suggested that since, "by the decision of the Supreme Court, delivered by Chief Justice Shaw, in the case of Roberts *vs.* City of Boston, the right to establish, and consequently to abolish a separate school for colored children, is declared to be vested in the School Committee, and we feel that they ought to exercise that right in accordance with the progress of the age, humanity, and of Christianity." [89] Williams emphasized, finally, that those who favored "law and order" should be in favor of equal participation in the public schools, because the republican form of government "is founded upon the general intelligence of our citizens." [90]

Approximately one year after the Common Council of Boston reopened the question of school segregation, the Massachusetts House of Representatives undertook to reexamine the laws of the Commonwealth concerning separate schools for blacks. As always, the militants were on top of the situation, securing twelve petitions from all over Massachusetts for presentation to the House Committee on Education. The petitioners requested that the Committee alter the power of the school committees to segregate children according to race.

In response to the petitions, the Education Committee, in House Report Number 167, said that "so far as *race* and religious opinions are concerned, your committee cannot learn that any practical difficulty has been experienced by any portion of the people by the exclusion of their offspring from the public schools on these accounts . . . . they rejoice to believe that, generally speaking, the people of the State have appreciated the true intent of our inestimable school system, and been willing to have educated under its beneficent influences children of every race and every form of religious belief." The Committee noted, however, that there was one exception; Boston has refused to lower the racial barriers in its schools.[91] Praising the language, logic, and ideas of Charles Sumner's "Argument" in the *Roberts* case, the Education Committee rejected the opinion of Chief Justice Shaw and quoted from Judge Richard Fletcher: "*The children of colored parents are . . . entitled to the benefit of the free schools equally with others . . . . the school committee have no lawful power to exclude the colored children from the public free schools.*" [92] The committee concluded, "first, that *colored children make less progress in a separate school;* and, *second,* that *no practical inconvenience need follow their abolition.*" [93]

As a result, another bill abolishing segregation in the public schools was introduced in the House of Representatives. After the second reading of the bill, there was a motion to postpone it indefinitely on the ground that "matters were well enough now in relation to School privileges in Boston." During the debate on that motion one representative inquired whether Negro children did not already have every accommodation that they needed in the Boston schools. A representative from Boston replied that "if living in East Boston, and going to Belknap Street for instruction in all weather, and at the trouble of a ferry, while white children, the dirtiest Irish included,

333

could step into the nearest school-house to their homes, was accommodation, then they did have them." The House then rejected the motion to postpone by an overwhelming vote and ordered the bill to its final reading "with an affirmative shout, not more than half a dozen voting audibly in opposition." The bill easily passed the Senate and was signed into law on April 28, 1855.[94]

This historic measure provided, in part, that "in determining the qualifications of scholars to be admitted into any public school or any district school in this Commonwealth, no distinction shall be made on account of the race, color or religious opinions of the applicant or scholar." There was also a provision that if any child suffered from such a distinction, he might recover damages in an action of tort, with the school committee subject to examination by any party to the suit.[95] With the passage of this statute, the last *legal* refuge of racial discrimination in Massachusetts disappeared.

In recognition of their eleven-year struggle to attain equal school rights, the militant Negroes of Boston and their abolitionist compatriots celebrated the occasion with a banquet on December 7, 1855. The grand old man of equal rights for Negroes, William C. Nell, received a gold watch, and numerous speeches testified to his unending devotion to the cause of equality.[96] The history of the Boston Negro's movement for equal civil rights unfolded that evening with just enough pomp and emotion to make the occasion a success. Charles W. Slack told of the many victories the Negro had won: the end of the Jim Crow car; the opening of places of amusement to blacks; the abolition of the "negro pew"; and, most recently, the triumph of equal school rights.[97] Wendell Phillips excited the crowd by placing part of the responsibility for the victory of equal school rights in the hands of the anti-slavery agitators. He added that one should never think of Massachusetts as a fit place in which to live until there were Negro graduates of Harvard College.[98] A more cautious note was sounded by Charles Lenox Remond of Salem, a prominent Negro abolitionist, who warned that blacks should not relax, for they still were excluded from the jury box. He advocated that when a Negro was tried, "one-half of the jury should also be colored." [99] Many of the other shining lights of the abolitionist and equal rights movement attended the banquet or sent their personal messages and congratulations. But the future did not ride with Boston's advocates of equal rights, for the opinion of Chief Justice Shaw in the *Roberts* case had a continuing vitality in American law.

The irony and the tragedy of the desegregation struggle in Boston was that its most significant legal legacy was not the integration statute of 1855, but rather Shaw's opinion that separate schools for Negroes were lawful. The *Roberts* case became the touchstone for state and federal court decisions concerning separate public facilities for colored races. It first was cited with approval in 1872 by the Supreme Court of the Territory of Nevada. That court's twisted logic specifically followed Shaw's as it affirmed the power of the school committee to segregate children according to race, though the committee might "not deny to any resident person of proper age an equal participation in the benefits of the common schools." [100] Only two years later the Supreme Court of California, in a similar case, quoted Shaw at length, concluding, "we concur in these views, and they are decisive in the present controversy." [101] The courts of other jurisdictions, including New York, Arkansas, Missouri, Louisiana, West Virginia, Kansas, Oklahoma, South Carolina, and Oregon, also relied upon Shaw's opinion in the *Roberts* case as the leading precedent for upholding segregation.[102] The case even was mentioned in two lower federal court decisions in the 1940's, as well as in a number before then.[103]

The United States Supreme Court first referred to the *Roberts* case in 1877 in *Hall* v. *DeCuir*.[104] In a concurring opinion, Justice Nathan Clifford cited it as an authority for the principle that "equality does not mean identity." [105] *DeCuir* struck down as unconstitutional a Louisiana statute that barred separate accommodations on interstate common carriers, but Justice Clifford addressed himself more broadly to the subject of separate education to show that "questions of a kindred character have arisen in several of the States, which support [segregated education] in a course of reasoning entirely satisfactory and conclusive." [106] The *Roberts* case was shaping the law of the land.

Chief Justice Shaw's "separate but equal" doctrine became the constitutional rationalization of Jim Crow primarily through its acceptance by the Supreme Court in the historic case of *Plessy* v. *Ferguson*, decided in 1896.[107] *Plessy* involved the constitutionality of a Louisiana act compelling segregation of the races in transportation facilities. Justice Henry Billings Brown turned to Shaw's opinion as the leading precedent for the validity of Jim Crow legislation.[108] Lengthy quotations from Shaw's opinion satisfied Justice Brown that Shaw had decided correctly that Negroes are not denied the equal protection of the laws when a state requires separate facilities that are substantially equal to those provided for white people. The *Plessy* decision effectively emasculated the equal-protection clause of the Fourteenth Amendment.

With only Justice John Marshall Harlan dissenting, the Court stated: "A statute which implies merely a legal distinction between white and colored races—a distinction which is founded in the color of the two races . . . has no tendency to destroy the legal equality of the two races." [109] American constitutional law emerged from *Plessy* as a sanction for racism in the form of a segregation clothed

335

with the legal fiction of equalitarianism—the "separate but equal" doctrine. The fiction was necessary because, in contrast to Nazi Germany, which articulated in its law an ideology of unadulterated racism, the United States, through its Constitution, is committed to an ideology of democracy, the rhetoric of which declares the equality of all races. Thus the Court in *Plessy*, after acknowledging that although the object of the equal-protection clause "was undoubtedly to enforce the absolute equality of the two races before the law," added that "in the nature of things it could not have been intended to abolish distinctions based on color, or to enforce social, as distinguished from political equality, or a commingling of the two races." [110] The Confederacy thereby won a belated victory on the field of jurisprudence, as *Plessy* effected a shotgun marriage between equality and racial segregation.

When one considers that *Plessy* became the leading precedent for the "separate but equal" doctrine, the influence of the *Roberts* case is seen to be immeasurable. The Supreme Court again relied on *Roberts* in *Gong Lum* v. *Rice*,[111] decided in 1927, to support the proposition that segregation in education "has been many times" held to be constitutional. Chief Justice William Howard Taft, the spokesman for the unanimous Court in *Gong Lum*, added that Chief Justice Shaw had upheld "the separation of colored and white schools under a state constitutional injunction of equal protection, the same as the Fourteenth Amendment." [112]

Shaw's doctrine in the *Roberts* case remained the law of the land in both state and federal courts for more than a century. Not until the National Association for the Advancement of Colored People made a systematic assault on segregated facilities, beginning in the 1930's, did the legal structure of "separate but equal" begin to crumble. The legal process being so slow, "the absolute power of a crag"—Chief Justice Shaw and his noxious doctrine—was only gradually chipped away by the NAACP's Legal Defense and Education Fund under the brilliant leadership of Thurgood Marshall. A series of cases, *Sipuel* v. *Board of Education*,[113] *McLaurin* v. *Board of Regents*,[114] and *Sweatt* v. *Painter*,[115] challenged the "equality" of separate graduate and professional schools as well as the "separate but equal" doctrine itself. The Supreme Court preserved the doctrine in all three cases but began to enforce the requirement of equality in a way suggesting that the legal prop for segregation was weakening. In the *Sweatt* case, for example, the Court placed a practically impossible burden on those states which would maintain separate school systems; they must prove equality even with respect to such intangibles as reputation of the faculty, experience of administration, outstanding alumni, and prestige.[116]

Cracked but not toppled, Jim Crow education finally fell in the historic *Brown* v. *Board of Education of Topeka* decision.[117] Speaking for a unanimous bench, Chief Justice Earl Warren, on May 17, 1954, repudiated the doctrine and overruled *Plessy*. Relegating *Roberts* to a footnote, Warren acknowledged that the doctrine apparently had had its origin with Chief Justice Shaw. But Warren did not bother to untangle the tortured reasoning of those opinions which had upheld segregation for over one hundred years. He chose to declare outright that the doctrine was inconsistent with the Fourteenth Amendment: "Does segregation of children in public schools solely on the basis of race, even though the physical facilities and other 'tangible' factors may be equal, deprive the children of the minority group of equal educational opportunities? We believe that it does. . . . We conclude that in the field of public education the doctrine of "separate but equal" has no place. Separate educational facilities are inherently unequal." [118]

The law of the land was righted at last, but its promise has yet to be fulfilled. Though the *Roberts* case is dead law, its spirit, like the corpse of John Randolph's mackerel, shines and stinks in the moonlight. Warren has not yet prevailed over Shaw, neither in Mississippi nor even in Massachusetts.

NOTES

[1] *Roberts* v. *City of Boston*, 5 Cush. 198 (1849).

[2] *Plessy* v. *Ferguson*, 163 U.S. 537, 544 (1896).

[3] *Roberts* v. *City of Boston*, 5 Cush. 198, 200 (1849); see also *Report to the Primary School Committee, June 15, 1846, on the Petition of Sundry Colored Persons, for the Abolition of the Schools for Colored Children. With the City Solicitor's Opinion, Documents of the City of Boston for the year 1846* (Boston, 1846), p. 15, hereafter cited as *1846 Majority School Report*.

[4] *1846 Majority School Report*, p. 15.

[5] *Ibid.*, pp. 15–16; *Report of a Special Committee of the Grammar School Board, presented August 29, 1849, on the petition of sundry colored persons praying for the abolition of the Smith School: With an Appendix, Documents of the City of Boston for the Year 1849* (Boston, 1849), p. 18, hereafter cited as *1849 Majority School Report*.

[6] *1846 Majority School Report*, p. 16.

[7] *Ibid.*

[8] *Ibid.*, pp. 16–17.

[9] See the *1849 Majority School Report*, pp. 20–21, 43.

[10] "Address of Mr. Nell," *Triumph of Equal School Rights in Boston. Proceedings of the Presentation Meeting Held in Boston, Dec. 17, 1855 . . .* (Boston, 1856), p. 5.

[11] *Ibid.*, p. 5.

[12] Louis Ruchames, "Jim Crow Railroads in Massachusetts," reprinted in August Meier and Elliot Rudwick, eds., *The Making of Black America*, vol. 1, *The Origins of Black Americans* (New York, 1969), pp. 262–275.

[13] *1846 Majority School Report,* pp. 20–21.

[14] *Rules of the School Committee and Regulations of the Public Schools of the City of Boston, Documents of the City of Boston for the Year 1844* (Boston, 1844), pp. 3, 18; *1849 Majority School Report,* p. 10, and p. 28 for the case of a Negro child who was admitted to an all-white grammar school. The exact location and number of the primary schools for Negroes seems to have varied with time. In the 1820's there were two primaries for Negroes "in the same vicinity," apparently Belknap St., but one was discontinued because of a drop in attendance. Between 1831 and 1835 a second primary school for Negroes existed in the northern section of the city; it closed in 1835 and was reopened in 1843. *1846 Majority School Report,* p. 18. At the time of the *Roberts* case, Charles Sumner and Chief Justice Shaw both referred to the existence of two black primaries; Sumner located one on Belknap St. and the other on Sun Court. See *Sumner's Argument,* p. 74, cited in full in note 64, below. But the *1849 Majority School Report,* pp. 23, 28–29, referred to three black primaries, two of them on Belknap St. and a third in the neighborhood of North Square. A report entitled *The Organization of the Primary Schools. March, 1854, Documents of the City of Boston for the Year 1854,* vol. 1 (Boston, 1854), shows two primary schools for Negroes, both connected with Smith School on Belknap St., and shows a third located at Baldwin Place (pp. 142, 144). To compound the confusion, *The Liberator* (Boston), September 14, 1855, published a resolution of the school committee, adopted at a meeting on September 10, that abolished racially segregated schools; the resolution, however, referred to "the School now existing in Joy Street, and designated as the 'Smith School' together with the Primary School and the School for special instruction connected therewith, (and all other schools). . . ."

[15] *Rules of the School Committee and Regulations of the Public Schools of the City of Boston,* p. 18.

[16] *1849 Majority School Report,* p. 58.

[17] When the Smith Grammar School and its primary appendages were abolished in 1855, the *Boston Telegraph,* reporting the last graduation ceremony at Smith, observed that the annual display and award of medals had been omitted. "Indeed, it would be but a farce to present testimonials of scholarship to so inferiorly educated pupils. The position of this school in mental attainments is positively below mediocrity, and illustrates most forcibly the depressing results and the total lack of ambition and pride, which must ever follow a caste school, or any other caste institution. No competition, no rivalry, no enterprise, whatever, marked the pupils at the recent examination. Teachers and children alike seemed to be laboring under a load of bondage—as they were, to a most unjust and iniquitous prejudice. We rejoice that, by the recent State law, this whole establishment will be blotted from the face of our otherwise fair school system." Quoted in *The Liberator* (Boston), August 17, 1855.

[18] *Reports of the Annual Visiting Committees of the Public Schools of the City of Boston, Documents of the City of Boston for the Year 1846* (Boston, 1846), p. 22.

[19] *Ibid.*

[20] *Ibid.,* p. 159.

[21] *1846 Majority School Report,* p. [2].

[22] *Ibid.*

[23] *Ibid.,* p. 4.

[24] *Ibid.,* pp. 4–5, 7, 13–14.

[25] *Ibid.,* p. 13.

[26] *Ibid.,* p. 7.

[27] *Ibid.,* pp. 10, 11, 8.

[28] *Ibid.,* p. 7.

[29] Declaration of Rights, Article I: "All men are born free and equal, and have certain natural, essential and unalienable rights, among which may be reckoned the right of enjoying and defending their lives and liberties. . . ." Article IV: "No man, nor corporation, or association of men, have any other title to obtain advantages, or particular and exclusive privileges, distinct from those of the community, than what arises from the consideration of services rendered to the public. . . ." See *Lehew* v. *Brummell,* 103 Missouri 546, 553 (1890), and *Gong Lum* v. *Rice,* 275 U.S. 78, 85–87 (1927).

[30] "The Hon. R. Fletcher's Opinion." This is an undated newspaper clipping of the opinion, and can be found in "The Speeches of Charles Sumner," a personal collection of pamphlets by Sumner, in the Boston Public Library.

[31] *1846 Majority School Report,* pp. 8, 9.

[32] *Ibid.,* p. 34.

[33] *Report of the Minority of the Committee of the Primary School Board, on the Caste Schools of the City of Boston with some Remarks* [by Wendell Phillips] *on the City Solicitor's Opinion* (Boston, 1846), p. [1].

[34] *Ibid.,* quotation at p. 12, pp. 4–7.

[35] *Ibid.,* p. 10.

[36] *Ibid.,* p. 13.

[37] *Ibid.,* pp. 15, 21–27.

[38] *Ibid.,* p. 19.

[39] *Ibid.,* p. 28.

[40] *Ibid.*

[41] *Ibid.*

[42] *Ibid.,* p. 29.

[43] *The Liberator* (Boston), Aug. 21, 1846.

[44] *Eighteenth Annual Report Presented to the Massachusetts Anti-Slavery Society, by its Board of Managers* (Boston, 1850), pp. 46–47.

[45] *1849 Majority School Report,* p. [3].

[46] *Ibid.,* p. 4.

[47] *Ibid.,* p. 5.

[48] *Report of the Minority of the Committee upon the Petition of John T. Hilton and others, Colored Citizens of Boston, Praying for the Abolition of the Smith School, and that Colored Children May Be Permitted to Attend the Other Schools of the City, Documents of the City of Boston for the Year 1849* (Boston, 1849), p. [3], hereafter cited as *1849 Minority School Report.*

[49] *1849 Majority School Report,* p. 9.

[50] *Ibid.,* pp. 47–48.

[51] *Ibid.,* p. 49.

[52] *Ibid.,* p. 15.

[53] *Ibid.,* p. 16.

[54] *Ibid.,* pp. 23–24, 32–33.

[55] *Ibid.,* pp. 32–33.

[56] *Ibid.,* p. 43.

[57] *1849 Minority School Report,* p. 4.

[58] *Ibid.,* p. 6.

[59] *Ibid.,* p. 8.

[60] *Ibid.,* p. 9.

[61] *Ibid.,* p. 12.

[62] *Ibid.,* pp. 12–13.

63 Mass. St. 1845, chap. 214.

64 *Argument of Charles Sumner, Esq. Against the Constitutionality of Separate Colored Schools, in the Case of Sarah C. Roberts v. The City of Boston. Before the Supreme Court of Mass., Dec. 4, 1849* (Boston, 1849), p. 54. For Sumner's extensive references to a world tradition of equality and its relation to Massachusetts law, see pp. 54, 55–64, 64–66.

65 *Ibid.*, p. 83.

66 Rev. St. 1835, chap. 23, secs. 10 and 15, quoted in *Sumner's Argument*, p. 82.

67 *Sumner's Argument*, p. 83.

68 *Ibid.*, pp. 86–88.

69 *Ibid.*, p. 88.

70 *Ibid.*, pp. 93–94, 95, 96.

71 See Leonard W. Levy, *The Law of the Commonwealth and Chief Justice Shaw* (Cambridge, Massachusetts, 1957).

72 *Report of the Committee Appointed to Make the Annual Examination of the Writing Schools* (Boston, 1846), p. 29.

73 *Roberts v. City of Boston*, 5 Cush. 198, 205. The case was heard by the Court in December 1849 and decided on April 1, 1850.

74 *1849 Majority School Report*, p. 13.

75 *Ibid.*, p. 206.

76 *Ibid.*

77 *Ibid.*

78 *Ibid.*, pp. 209–210.

79 *Ibid.*, p. 209.

80 *Ibid.*

81 *The Liberator*, April 26 and May 3, 1850, gives excerpts of press opinion.

82 *Ibid.*, February 8, 1850.

83 *Ibid.*, April 26, 1850.

84 "Journal of the House of Representatives of the C. Wealth [sic.] of Massachusetts for the Session Commencing Jan. 1 and ending May 24," Vol. 73 (1851), p. 758, MS in Massachusetts State House Library.

85 "Equal Schools for all Without Regard to Color or Race, Boston, May 21, 1851," Broadside, Boston Public Library.

86 *Report of Committee on Public Instruction, On Case of a Child Excluded from a Public School of this City, Documents of the City of Boston for the Year 1854* (Boston, 1854), p. [3].

87 *Ibid.*, p. 4.

88 *Ibid.*, pp. 5–6, 8.

89 *Ibid.*, p. 7.

90 *Ibid.*, p. 8.

91 "Massachusetts House Report Number 167," p. 2.

92 *Ibid.*, p. 5.

93 *Ibid.*, p. 14.

94 *The Liberator*, April 6, 1855. See also *1849 Minority School Report*, p. 9.

95 Mass. St. 1855, chap. 254, sec. 1–3.

96 *Triumph of Equal School Rights in Boston: Proceedings of the Presentation Meeting held in Boston December 17, 1855, p. 3.*

97 "Speech of Charles W. Slack," *ibid.*, pp. 12–13.

98 "Speech of Wendell Phillips, Esq.," *ibid.*, pp. 14–15.

99 "Speech of Charles Lenox Remond," *ibid.*, p. 21.

100 *State ex rel. Stoutmeyer v. Duffy*, 7 Nev. 342, 347, 348 (1872).

[101] *Ward* v. *Flood*, 48 Cal. 36, 52–56 (1874).

[102] *People ex rel. King* v. *Gallagher*, 93 N.Y. 438, 441, 448, 453–454 (1883); *Maddox* v. *Neal*, 45 Ark. 121, 125 (1885); *Lehew* v. *Brummell*, 103 Mo. 546, 547, 553 (1890); Ex parte Plessy, 45 La. Ann 80, 85–86, 87–88 (1893); *Martin* v. *Board of Education*, 42 W. Va. 514, 516 (1896); *Reynolds* v. *Board of Education of the City of Topeka*, 66 Kan. 672, 684–686 (1903); *Board of Education of the City of Kingfisher* v. *Board of County Commissioners*, 14 Okla. 322, 332 (1904); *Tucker* v. *Blease*, 97 S. Car. 303, 330 (1913); *Crawford* v. *School District No. 7*, 68 Ore. 388, 396 (1913).

[103] *Claybrook* v. *City of Owensboro*, 16 Fed. 297, 302 (1883); *Wong Him* v. *Callahan*, 119 Fed. 381, 382 (1902); *Westminster School District of Orange County* v. *Mendez*, 161 Fed. 2d. 774, 779 (1947); *Corbin* v. *County School Board of Pulaski County, Va.*, 84 Fed. Supp. 253, 254–255 (1949).

[104] 95 U.S. 485 (1877).

[105] *Ibid.*, 503, 505.

[106] *Ibid.*, 504.

[107] 163 U.S. 537 (1896).

[108] *Ibid.*, 544–545.

[109] *Ibid.*, 543.

[110] *Ibid.*, 544.

[111] 275 U.S. 78 (1927).

[112] *Ibid.*, 86–87.

[113] 332 U.S. 631 (1948).

[114] 339 U.S. 637 (1950).

[115] 339 U.S. 629 (1950).

[116] *Ibid.*, 634. See also Douglas L. Jones, "The Sweatt Case and the Development of Legal Education for Negroes in Texas," *Texas Law Review*, 47 (March 1969), 677–693.

[117] 347 U.S. 483 (1954).

[118] *Ibid.*, 493, 495.

A Note on the Author

LEONARD W. LEVY was born in Toronto, Canada, in 1923. He studied at the University of Michigan and at Columbia University, where he received a Ph.D. Mr. Levy's books include *Legacy of Suppression, Jefferson and Civil Liberties, Freedom of the Press from Zenger to Jefferson,* and *Origins of the Fifth Amendment,* which won the Pulitzer Prize in history. Formerly Earl Warren Professor of American Constitutional History at Brandeis University, Mr. Levy is now William W. Clary Professor of History at the Claremont Graduate School.

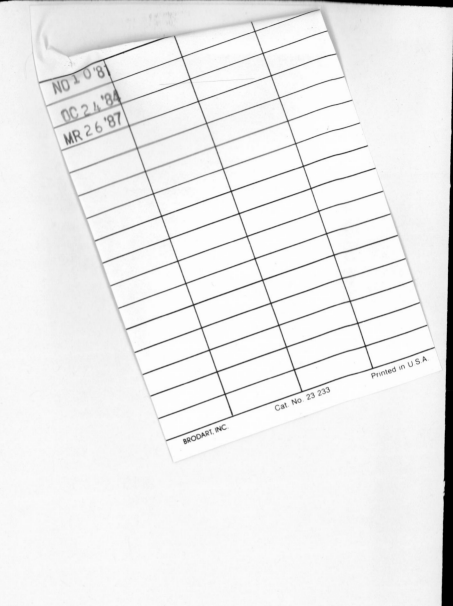